ANTHOLOGY OF JAPANESE LITERATURE

WORKS BY DONALD KEENE
PUBLISHED BY GROVE WEIDENFELD

Anthology of Chinese Literature, Vol. I: From Early Times to the 14th Century (with Cyril Birch, ed.)

Anthology of Japanese Literature from the Earliest Era to the Mid-Nineteenth Century

Modern Japanese Literature: An Anthology

World Within Walls: Japanese Literature of the Pre-Modern Era (1600–1867)

Anthology of

JAPANESE LITERATURE

from the earliest era to the mid-nineteenth century,

compiled and edited by Donald Keene

GROVE PRESS NEW YORK

UNESCO COLLECTION OF REPRESENTATIVE WORKS

Published simultaneously in Canada
Printed in the United States of America

This volume is published in accordance with an arrangement between UNESCO (United Nations Educational, Scientific and Cultural Organization) and the Japanese Government.

Library of Congress Catalog Card Number: 55-5110
ISBN 0-8021-5058-6 (pbk.)

Grove Press
841 Broadway
New York, NY 10003

98 99 00 01 50 49 48 47 46 45 44 43 42 41 40

TO ARTHUR WALEY

NOTE ON JAPANESE NAMES AND PRONUNCIATION

Japanese names are given in this book in the Japanese order: that is, the surname precedes the personal name. Thus, in the name Matsuo Bashō, Matsuo is the family name, Bashō the personal name. However, Japanese usually refer to famous writers by their personal names rather than by their family names and this practice has been observed in the anthology.

The pronunciation of Japanese in transcription is very simple. The consonants are pronounced as in English (with g *always hard), the vowels as in Italian. There are no silent letters. Thus, the name Ise is pronounced "ee-say."*

The Japanese words used in the text are those which have been taken into English and may be found in such works as the Concise Oxford Dictionary*.*

PREFACE

It can only be with diffidence that this first anthology of Japanese literature in English is offered to the reading public. I cannot recall ever having read a review of an anthology of European literature which did not point out glaring omissions and inexplicable inclusions—this in spite of the comparatively long tradition of such anthologies. How much less likely it is, then, that the present volume will escape such criticism!

A word must therefore be said as to what principles guided the compilation of this book. It is, first of all, an anthology of Japanese works which translate into interesting and enjoyable English. No matter how important a work may be in the original, if it defies artistic translation I could not include it. Secondly, the selection is as representative of all periods of Japanese literature as is consonant with the above caveat. Thirdly, the anthology is as representative as possible of the different genres of Japanese literature—poetry, novels, plays, diaries, etc.—although, again, it must be borne in mind that in Japan, as in every other country, these various genres have not progressed uniformly. There is, for example, much great dramatic literature from the Muromachi Period but very little quotable poetry.

The length of a selection is not necessarily an indication of the relative importance of the work from which it is taken. It is easier to make extracts from certain types of writing than from others.

One rather unusual feature of the anthology is the inclusion of a limited number of works written by Japanese in the classical Chinese language. Just as Englishmen at one time wrote poetry and prose in Latin, so Japanese wrote in Chinese, with the difference, of course, that while they were writing there was still a country called China where the classical language was constantly being developed.

As I have noted, the translations in this book are meant to be literary and not literal. For example, names of persons, titles, and places not essential to a story have sometimes been omitted in the interest of easy reading for Westerners not able to absorb large quantities of Japanese proper names. Puns, allusions, repetitions, and incommunicable stylistic fripperies have also been discarded whenever possible. Extracts have been made with the intent always of presenting the given work in as favorable a light as possible, even though it might at times be fairer if the book were presented as rather uneven.

There are many objections to the practices cited above, and I am aware of them. But I think it highly important that this first anthology of Japanese literature have as wide an appeal as possible. For those interested in more literal versions of Japanese works, there are at least two scholarly books of recent years designed to meet their needs: "Translations from Early Japanese Literature" by E. O. Reischauer and J. K. Yamagiwa and "The Love Suicide at Amijima" by D. H. Shively. Both of these books give translations of complete texts; all allusions, wordplays, etc., are explained; and words which have been supplied by the translator are enclosed in brackets.

In presenting the anthology I have, for the sake of convenience, divided the literature into political periods: Ancient, Heian, Kamakura, Muromachi, and Tokugawa. However, this division is to be considered as little more than a convenience; it is obvious that a change of regime did not instantly produce a new literature, and it is sometimes indeed difficult to decide to which period a given work belongs. But, just as "eighteenth-century literature" has a meaning for us in spite of the qualifications we may make about its appropriateness as a general term, so "Tokugawa literature" makes enough sense for such a division to be made.

It will be noted that a majority of the translations in this book have never before been printed. Some of them have been made especially at my request, and at some urgency when the translators were engaged on other projects. I wish therefore to take this opportunity of thanking them all for their collaboration.

As far as my own translations are concerned, I should like to thank first Professor Noma Kōshin of Kyoto University, under whom I have studied for two years; D. J. Enright and Carolyn Bullitt for help with the poetry; Hamada Keisuke and Matsuda Osamu for their useful suggestions on translations; and Edward Seidensticker for having read over my translations, pointing out the infelicities.

Acknowledgments are also due to: The Asiatic Society of Japan for the *"Kojiki"* and other works published in their Transactions; Professor Doi Kōchi and The Kenkyūsha Publishing Company for "The Diary of Lady Murasaki" and "The Sarashina Diary"; Nippon Gakujutsu Shinkōkai for the *"Man'yōshū";* Kenneth Rexroth for "100 Poems from the Japanese"; A. L. Sadler for "The Tale of the Heike"; Dr. Sakanishi Shio for "The Bird-Catcher of Hades" and poetry by Ishikawa Takuboku and Yosano Akiko; G. B. Sansom for "Essays in Idleness"; Thomas Satchell for *"Hizakurige";* Yukuo Uyehara and Marjorie Sinclair for "A Collection from a Grass Path" (University of Hawaii Press); Arthur Waley and George Allen and Unwin, Ltd., for "The Tale of Genji," "The Pillow Book," "The Lady who Loved Insects," *"Atsumori,"* "The Damask Drum," and "The *Uta*"; Columbia College Oriental Studies Program, Columbia University, for "Kūkai and His Master" and "Seami on the Art of the *Nō*"; and Meredith Weatherby and Bruce Rogers for "Birds of Sorrow."

Mr. Seidensticker, Mr. Watson, and I were in receipt of grants from the Ford Foundation during the period when the book was being prepared, and wish to express our thanks to the Foundation, which is not, however, responsible for the contents of the book.

Thanks are also due the Japan Society, Inc. for their cooperation in the production of the book.

Muhinju-an, Kyoto

CONTENTS

MUROMACHI PERIOD [1333-1600]

TOKUGAWA PERIOD [1600-1868]

INTRODUCTION

Japanese literature has about as long a history as English literature, and contains works in as wide a variety of genres as may be found in any country. It includes some of the world's longest novels and shortest poems, plays which are miracles of muted suggestion and others filled with the most extravagant bombast. It is, in short, a rich literature which deserves better understanding and recognition.

It is not the purpose of this brief introduction to give a history of Japanese literature[1]; I shall attempt instead to trace some of the developments linking the works included in this anthology. Most of the selections are prefaced by introductory remarks giving specific information on details of composition, etc., and it is hoped that the reader will consult them as the occasion requires.

The earliest surviving Japanese book is the *"Kojiki,"* or "Record of Ancient Matters," completed in 712 A.D. It is clear, however, that there were books before that date, as well as a considerable body of songs and legends such as are found in every country. Some of this oral literature is preserved in the *"Kojiki"* and elsewhere, but much of it must certainly have perished, in view of the failure of the Japanese to develop independently a means of recording their language. It is interesting, if essentially fruitless, to speculate what course Japanese literature might have taken if the Japanese had devised their own script or had first come in contact with a foreign nation which had an alphabet. It was in fact the widespread adoption of Chinese culture, including the wholly unsuitable Chinese method of writing, which was to determine the course of Japanese literature over the centuries.

In the Ancient Period, if so we may designate Japanese history up to the establishment of the capital at Kyoto in 794, the important

1 For a fuller introduction see Donald Keene, "Japanese Literature," and W. G. Aston, "A History of Japanese Literature."

works, such as the *"Kojiki"* and the *"Man'yōshū,"* or "Collection of Ten Thousand Leaves," still show comparatively little Chinese influence, and may with some justice be termed examples of "pure" Japanese literature. The *"Kojiki"* opens with the Creation and continues until the seventh century of our era, moving from a collection of sometimes engaging myths to an encomium of the Imperial family, particularly of the line of the ruling sovereign. In its early sections the *"Kojiki"* has something of the epic about it, but because it was a compilation of different sorts of material and not a single long story (however complex) known and recited by professional poets, it lacks the unity and artistic finish of a true epic and tends to break down into episodes of varying literary value.

The *"Man'yōshū,"* on the other hand, needs no apologies. It is one of the world's great collections of poetry. It can never cease to astonish us that Japanese literature produced within the same century the pre-Homeric pages of the *"Kojiki"* and the magnificent artistry of the *"Man'yōshū."* The latter owes its reputation mainly to the genius of a group of eighth-century poets, notably Hitomaro, Yakamochi, and Okura. The period when the majority of the poems were being written rather resembled the Meiji era, when the introduction of Western civilization led to a tremendous explosion of pent-up Japanese energies in every field. In the eighth century the gradual diffusion of Chinese civilization produced a similar result. Within the *"Man'yōshū"* itself there are traces of Chinese influence which become quite apparent in the later poems, but there can be no doubt of the book's essential Japaneseness: what inspired the poets were the mountains and the sea of the Japanese landscape, and their reactions were fresh, Japanese reactions, not echoes of Chinese example.[2] "Countless are the mountains in Yamato"; "In the sea of Iwami, By the cape of Kara, There amid the stones under sea"; "And lived secure in my trust As one riding a great ship"—these are truly Japanese lines in their imagery and evocation.

If Chinese influence is relatively small in the *"Man'yōshū"* there is another eighth-century collection which is almost purely Chinese

2 There are examples of direct Chinese influence on some of the poems, but their number is not very considerable.

in its inspiration. This is the *"Kaifūsō,"* or "Fond Recollections of Poetry," an anthology of poetry written in Chinese by members of the Japanese court. It was to be expected that Japanese poets writing in Chinese should have adhered closely to Chinese models, and some of the verses of the *"Kaifūsō"* are no more like original Chinese poems than Latin verses written by schoolboys today are like Horace. Why, it may be wondered, did Japanese choose to write poetry in a foreign language which few of them could actually speak? The answer is to be found partly in the prestige lent by an ability to write poetry in the difficult classical Chinese language, but partly also in the Japanese belief that there were things which could not be expressed within their own poetic forms. This was less true in the age of the *"Man'yōshū,"* when the poets enjoyed greater liberty than was to be known again in Japan for more than a thousand years, but even from the seventh century there are examples of parallel poems written in Japanese and Chinese which show what the poets thought to be the essential differences between the two mediums. The following were both written by Prince Ōtsu (662-687) shortly before his execution:

Today, taking my last sight of the mallards
Crying on the pond of Iware,
Must I vanish into the clouds! [3]

The golden crow lights on the western huts;
Evening drums beat out the shortness of life.
There are no inns on the road to the grave—
Whose is the house I go to tonight? [4]

The former poem, from the *"Man'yōshū,"* is purely Japanese in feeling; the latter, from the *"Kaifūsō,"* not only uses Chinese language and allusions but attempts to give philosophic overtones lacking in the simple Japanese verse. This distinction between the content of poetry written in Japanese and in Chinese became of increasingly great importance. In the Muromachi Period, for example, Zen priests

[3] Translated by Nippon Gakujutsu Shinkōkai.
[4] Translated by Burton Watson.

expressed their religious and philosophic doctrines in Chinese poetry. In the late Tokugawa Period many patriots who found that they could not adequately voice their burning thoughts within the tiny compass of a Japanese poem turned to poetry in Chinese. The function of Chinese poetry, from the time of the *"Kaifūsō"* almost until the present, has been principally to convey thoughts either too difficult or too extended for the standard Japanese verse forms—when, of course, it was not merely an instrument for the display of erudition.

Some of the early poetry in Chinese was devoted to Buddhist subjects[5]—which was less often true of poetry in Japanese. The Buddhism of the early period was an optimistic religion marked by pageantry and the lavish patronage of the great temples of Nara. With the Heian Period, particularly as a result of the activities of such men as Kūkai (774-835), Buddhism became the study of many of the best minds of the age. The Buddhism taught by Kūkai was essentially an aristocratic religion, or at least restricted to those people who had the intellectual capacity to understand its profundities and the taste to appreciate its aesthetic manifestations. Toward the end of the Heian Period, however, greater attention was given to spreading Buddhist teaching to all classes of the people, and it is in the light of this development that we should read such works as "Tales from the Uji Collection," which was designed to communicate in simple and interesting language some of the Buddhist doctrine. It was from about this time too that the invocation to Amida Buddha, a seven-syllabled prayer, came to be considered a certain means of gaining salvation.

Buddhism is to be found to a greater or lesser degree in most of the famous writings of the Heian Period. When in the novels—and indeed in real life—a situation was reached for which no other solution was immediately apparent, the person involved would usually "abandon the world," an act accompanied by the ritual gesture of shaving the head or at least trimming the hair, a moment accompanied by great lamentations. It was not, however, considered to be in very good taste for someone still "in the world" to show unusual piety. In the *"Kagerō Nikki,"* for example, the husband of the author

[5] See page 162.

bursts into the room to find her at her devotions: " 'Terrible,' he exclaimed, as he watched me burning incense and fingering my beads, the Sutras spread out in front of me. 'Worse even than I had expected. You really do seem to have run to an extreme.' "[6]

Japanese poetry, as I have noted, made amazing progress in the eighth century. In the tenth century Japanese prose evolved to its highest development. With respect to prose style itself, one of the most important contributors to this progress was Ki no Tsurayuki (died 946) whose preface to the *"Kokinshū,"* or "Collection of Ancient and Modern Poetry," is celebrated, and whose "Tosa Diary" was the first example of what was to become an important genre, the literary diary. One may note in Tsurayuki's prose some Chinese influence, such as the parallelism, but his is essentially a Japanese style both in vocabulary and construction.

The prose works of the early tenth century were of two main types: the fairy tales derived ultimately from the legends of Japan, China, and India; and the more realistic prose of the poem-tales.[7] It was not until these two streams united that the Japanese novel, in a true sense, could be born. The outstanding product of this convergence and, indeed, the supreme masterpiece of Japanese literature, was "The Tale of Genji." Although this novel contains many hundred poems, it is not, like "The Tales of Ise," merely a collection of poetry linked by prose descriptions, and if it benefited by the example of such earlier "novels" as "The Tale of the Bamboo-Cutter,"[8] it went immeasurably beyond them in depth and magnitude. It is a work of genius, which may justifiably be included among the great novels of the world. Thanks to the incomparable translation by Arthur Waley it is now available to Western readers.

One of the unusual features of Heian literature is that such works as the *"Kagerō Nikki,"* "The Pillow Book" of Sei Shōnagon, "The Tale of Genji," most of the diaries, and much of the poetry were written by women. The usual explanation for this curious fact is

[6] Translated by Edward Seidensticker.

[7] See page 67.

[8] There is a poor English translation by F. V. Dickins and a good French one by René Sieffert.

that the men considered writing in Japanese to be beneath them and devoted themselves to the composition of poetry and prose in Chinese, leaving the women to write masterpieces in the native language. This is not a complete explanation—some of the lesser novels and other prose works in Japanese were written by men—but it is close enough to the truth to warrant its acceptance. Of the literature written in Chinese during the period, the poems by Sugawara no Michizane (845-903) are especially fine. Michizane was an accomplished poet, and was so widely known for his learning that after his death he was enshrined as a god of literature and calligraphy.

The poetry of the Heian Period both in Japanese and Chinese is far more restricted in subject matter and manner than that of the earlier period. The Japanese poems are filled with falling cherry blossoms and maple leaves, the Chinese poems with the scent of plum blossoms and chrysanthemums. There is nothing wrong with these subjects, but it is hard to think of any fully developed poet devoting the major part of his attention to such themes. The aim of Heian poets was to perfect rather than to discover, to hit upon exactly the right adjective or image to be used in a familiar situation, rather than to invent a new one. This method may be most clearly illustrated by the following two tenth-century poems:

Aki kaze ni	The under leaves
Shitaha ya samuku	In the autumn wind
Narinuramu	Must have become cold:
Kohagi ga hara ni	In the moor of little lespedezas
Uzura naku nari	The quail are crying.

Fujiwara no Michimune

Tsuyu musubu	The under leaves of the lespedeza
Hagi ga shitaha ya	When the dew is gathering
Samukaramu	Must be cold:
Aki no nohara ni	In the autumn moor
Ojika naku nari	The young deer are crying.

Lady Sagami [9]

[9] Translated by Arthur Waley.

Both of these poems were honored by being included in Imperial collections, but it is obvious that they are in essence the same poem. To say this, however, would not detract from the value of either poem in the eyes of the authors or of traditional Japanese critics. It may be difficult for a modern Western reader to sympathize with such a point of view, but it might have seemed less strange to a seventeenth-century English poet who sang the beauties of Cynthia or who proclaimed the doctrine of *carpe diem*.

What draws most of us to Japanese poetry is not the polish of a perfectly turned verse on the red maple leaves floating on blue waves but the living voice of a poet talking about love, death, and the few other themes common to all men. The *"Man'yōshū"* is the easiest collection for us to appreciate because of its range of subjects and its powerful imagery. The *"Kokinshū"* also has poems which move us, but some of the most famous ones, masterpieces of diction and vowel harmonies, must unfortunately remain beyond communication to Western readers.

The court nobles, who wrote most of the poems in the *"Kokinshū,"* continued to be the chief contributors to the successive Imperial anthologies. The skill of some of these poets is quite remarkable, but the subjects to which they applied their skill were often inadequate.

The next major collection after the *"Kokinshū"* was the *"Shinkokinshū,"* or "New Collection of Ancient and Modern Poetry," compiled in the Kamakura Period, after the terrible warfare which ended the Heian Period. Much of the gloom and solitude of those times is discoverable in the poetry, particularly that of the outstanding contributor to the *"Shinkokinshū,"* the priest Saigyō (1118-1190). His *waka*—thirty-one-syllabled poems—are among the most beautiful and melancholy in the language.

The same melancholy may also be found in "The Tale of the Heike," the greatest of the war tales—which were among the characteristic literary products of the Kamakura Period. These tales contain many descriptions of military glory, of men in magnificent armor riding into battle, but what we remember most vividly are the scenes of loneliness and sorrow—the death of the boy Atsumori or the description of the life of the former Empress in the solitude of a mountain convent. The vanity of worldly things—often enough expressed by the Heian aristocrats but seldom very seriously—acquired meaning in the days of destruction and disaster; in Kamo no Chōmei's "Account of My Hut" we hear a cry from the heart of medieval darkness.

Separation is a contant theme in the writings of the Japanese medieval period—the Kamakura and Muromachi periods. Several emperors were driven into exile, and the account of their misfortunes is the chief theme of the *"Masukagami,"* or "The Clear Mirror," one of the important historical romances of the time. For sixty years after the beginning of the Muromachi Period sovereigns of the legitimate line were cut off from the capital (where there was a rival court) and forced to live in the mountains of Yoshino. In addition to those who were compelled by stronger adversaries to leave the capital, there were also many men who fled the world in disgust, voluntarily seeking refuge in one or another remote place. "Essays in Idleness" by Yoshida Kenkō (1283-1350) is one of the most cheerful examples of the writings of a medieval recluse, and indeed suggests at many places comparison with "The Pillow Book" of Sei Shōnagon, but a note of death is struck over and over, in a manner foreign to the Heian writer.

Death and the world of the dead figure prominently in the *Nō* play, one of the most beautiful of Japanese literary forms. In most of the plays there are ghosts or spirits, and in all of them is a sense of other-worldly mystery. The greatest master of the *Nō,* Seami Motokiyo (1363-1443), describing the three highest types of *Nō* performances, cited these verses: "In Silla at midnight the sun is bright"; "Snow covers the thousand mountains—why does one lonely peak remain unwhitened?"; "Snow piled in a silver bowl." With these three verses he attempted to suggest the essential qualities of the *Nō*—its other-worldliness, its profundity, and its stillness.

In contrast to the *Nō* are the *kyōgen* plays, brief comedies which came to be performed in conjunction with the *Nō*. Sometimes the *kyōgen* parody the tragic events of the *Nō* plays they follow, but more often they depend for humor on the situations in which such stock characters as the clever servant or the termagant wife find themselves. Unlike the *Nō,* with its innumerable allusions and complexities of diction, the *kyōgen* is very simple in its language, and must indeed have been quite close to the speech of the common people of its day.

One of the characteristic literary products of the Muromachi Period is linked-verse, of which the outstanding example is probably "Three Poets at Minase." [10] The mood of this poem changes from link to link, as the different poets take up each other's thoughts, but the prevailing impression is one of loneliness and grief, as was not surprising in a work composed shortly after the Ōnin Rebellion (1467-1477) which devastated Kyoto. From the period of the rebellion comes this curious allegorical poem found in a funeral register:

Mi hitotsu ni	Upon one body
Hashi wo narabete	Double heads opposing chop-
Motsu tori ya	Stick beaks in order,
Ware wo tsutsukite	Peck peck pecking off to death
Koroshihatsuramu	One bird: both heads and body.[11]

The image of the double-headed bird pecking itself to death is an apt one for the Japan of the period of wars. It was not until the end of the sixteenth century that Japan again knew peace.

The establishment of peace with the Tokugawa regime did not immediately bring about any flood of literature, for the country had still to recover from the wounds of a century of warfare. Humorous, or at least rather eccentric, verse began to be produced in large quantities, and a variety of frivolous tales also appeared. The first impor-

[10] See page 314 for an explanation of linked-verse.

[11] Translated by Sam Houston Brock. This is a very ambiguous poem and may be interpreted variously. The poet William Burford has rendered it:

> Carrion
> With your chop-
> stick beaks
> Pointed at me
>
> Have you come,
> at last,
> To peck me
> to death?

tant work of the new era was a novel by Ihara Saikaku (1642-1693) called "The Man Who Spent His Life at Love-Making." It is obvious that in writing this novel Saikaku looked back to "The Tale of Genji" for guidance, although two novels basically more different can hardly be imagined. The world that Saikaku described in this novel and most of his subsequent ones was that of the merchant class in the cities. Heian literature had dealt mainly with the aristocracy. With the Kamakura Period the warrior class came to figure prominently in literature, but in the new literature of the Tokugawa Period it was the merchant who was the most important. It was for him also that the novels and plays of the time were written, and it was the merchant class which supplied many of the leading writers. Saikaku's "Eternal Storehouse of Japan" is, in his own words, a "millionaire's gospel," a collection of anecdotes intended to help a man to make a fortune or prevent him from losing one. Saikaku was not, however, a dreary moralizer—his works are filled with a lively humor which sometimes borders on the indecent, and with a vigor that comes as a welcome relief after centuries of resigned melancholy.

Not all of the Tokugawa writers threw off the gloom of medieval Japan as readily as Saikaku did. The greatest of the poets of the age, Matsuo Bashō (1644-1694), was drawn in particular to Saigyō and the world of "Three Poets at Minase." But there is a great difference between Bashō's loneliness and that of the medieval poets. Bashō sought out loneliness in the midst of a very active life. There was no question of his taking refuge except from the attentions of his overly devoted pupils. The sorrows he experienced were those which any sensitive man might know, not those of a black-robed monk who sees the capital ravaged by plague or the depredations of a lawless soldiery. There is much humor in Bashō, and indeed in his last period he advocated "lightness" as the chief desideratum of the seventeen-syllabled *haiku.* He is the most popular of all Japanese poets and one of the chief men of Japanese literature.

The third of the great literary figures of the early Tokugawa Period was Chikamatsu Monzaemon (1653-1725). Chikamatsu wrote most of his plays for the puppet stage, and the care he devoted to making his plays successful in this medium has sometimes, we may feel, impaired their literary value. Nevertheless, Chikamatsu ranks with Seami as a dramatic genius, one of the rare ones Japan has produced. His plays are of two types—heroic dramas based on historical events (however loosely) and domestic dramas that often revolve around lovers' suicides. The former plays are usually more interesting to watch in performance at the puppet theatre, but the latter, dealing as they do with moving human experiences, have a greater attraction as literature. The poetry of Chikamatsu's plays is also remarkable, at times attaining heights seldom reached elsewhere in Japanese literature.

Saikaku, Bashō, and Chikamatsu were not only dominant figures in their own time but the objects of adulation and imitation for many years afterward. In the domain of the novel it was not until Ueda Akinari (1734-1809) that an important new voice was heard. Akinari was heavily indebted to Chinese novels and stories for the material of his own, but by the artistry at his command was able to produce several striking works. Takizawa Bakin (1767-1848) was also much influenced by Chinese novels, some of which he translated or adapted. In contrast to these writers of academic pretensions, we have also Jippensha Ikku (1766-1831) whose *"Hizakurige"* is a lively, purely Japanese work which now seems more likely to survive as literature than the towering bulk of Bakin's novels, so esteemed in their day.

There were several important *haiku* writers in the late Tokugawa Period, notably Yosa Buson (1716-1781) and Kobayashi Issa (1763-1828). Buson brought to the *haiku* a romantic quality lacking in Bashō's and was a poet of aristocratic distinction. Issa, on the other hand, lent to the *haiku* the genuine accents of the common people. *Haiku* poets had always prided themselves on using in their verses images drawn from daily life instead of the stereotyped cherry blossoms and maple leaves of the older poetry, but the mere fact that the word "snail" or "frog" appeared in a poem instead of "nightingale" did not automatically bring it much closer to the lives of the common people. Issa had a real love for the small and humble things of the world, and he makes us see them as no other Japanese poet did. Buson was a flawless technician, but Issa's verses, whatever their other qualities, often hardly seem like *haiku* at all.

The same desire to write of the common things of life may be found in the *waka* of Okuma Kotomichi (1798-1868) and, in particular, Tachibana Akemi (1812-1868). Almost any poem of Akemi's will reveal how great his break was with the traditional *waka* poets even of the Tokugawa Period:

The silver mine

Akahada no	Stark naked, the men
Danshi mureite	Stand together in clusters;
Aragane no	Swinging great hammers
Marogari kudaku	They smash into fragments
Tsuchi uchifurite	The lumps of unwrought metal.

Akemi was a violent supporter of the Emperor against the Tokugawa Shogunate, partly as the result of his studies of the classics (then under the domination of ultra-nationalist scholars) but partly also because he was a sharer in the growing discontent with the regime. The poets who wrote in Chinese were particularly outspoken. Rai Sanyō (1780-1832), the greatest master of Chinese poetry in the Tokugawa Period, if not all of Japanese literature, wrote bitter invective against the regime, usually only thinly disguised. When one reads the poetry of Issa, Akemi, or Sanyō one cannot help feeling that the Tokugawa regime was doomed in any case, even if its collapse had not been hastened by the arrival of the Westerners.

The literature produced in Japan after the Meiji Restoration is of so different a character that it has been felt advisable to devote a separate volume to it. It is hoped that with the publication of the two volumes of this anthology the Western reader will be able to obtain not only a picture of the literature produced in Japan over the centuries, but an understanding of the Japanese people as their lives and aspirations have been reflected in their writings.

ANCIENT PERIOD

TO 794 AD

MAN'YŌSHŪ

*The "Man'yōshū," or "Collection of Ten Thousand Leaves," is the oldest and greatest of the Japanese anthologies of poetry. It was compiled in the middle of the eighth century, but it includes material of a much earlier date—one cannot say with certainty just how early. There are about 4,500 poems in the "Man'yōshū," and they display a greater variety of form and subject than any other collection. In particular the long poems—*chōka *or* nagauta*—have a sustained power that could never be achieved in the* tanka *of thirty-one syllables which was to be the dominant verse form in Japan for centuries. Even in the shorter poems of the "Man'yōshū" there is a passion and a directness that later poets tended to polish away.*

The translations here given were made by the Japanese Classics Translation Committee under the auspices of the Nippon Gakujutsu Shinkōkai. The poet Ralph Hodgson was among those responsible for these excellent versions.

•

Your basket, with your pretty basket,
Your trowel, with your little trowel,
Maiden, picking herbs on this hillside,
I would ask you: Where is your home?
Will you not tell me your name?
Over the spacious Land of Yamato
It is I who reign so wide and far,
It is I who rule so wide and far.
I myself, as your lord, will tell you
Of my home, and my name.

Attributed to Emperor Yūryaku (418-479)

Climbing Kagu-yama and looking upon the land

Countless are the mountains in Yamato,
But perfect is the heavenly hill of Kagu;
When I climb it and survey my realm,
Over the wide plain the smoke-wreaths rise and rise,
Over the wide lake the gulls are on the wing;
A beautiful land it is, the Land of Yamato!

Emperor Jomei (593-641)

Upon the departure of Prince Ōtsu for the capital after his secret visit to the Shrine of Ise

To speed my brother
Parting for Yamato,
In the deep of night I stood
Till wet with the dew of dawn.

The lonely autumn mountains
Are hard to pass over
Even when two go together—
How does my brother cross them all alone!

Princess Ōku (661-701)

. .

In the sea of Iwami,
By the cape of Kara,
There amid the stones under sea
Grows the deep-sea *miru* weed;
There along the rocky strand
Grows the sleek sea tangle.

Like the swaying sea tangle,
Unresisting would she lie beside me—
My wife whom I love with a love
Deep as the *miru*-growing ocean.

But few are the nights
We two have lain together.

Away I have come, parting from her
Even as the creeping vines do part.
My heart aches within me;
I turn back to gaze—
But because of the yellow leaves
Of Watari Hill,
Flying and fluttering in the air,
I cannot see plainly
My wife waving her sleeve to me.
Now as the moon, sailing through the cloud-rift
Above the mountain of Yakami,
Disappears, leaving me full of regret,
So vanishes my love out of sight;
Now sinks at last the sun,
Coursing down the western sky.

I thought myself a strong man,
But the sleeves of my garment
Are wetted through with tears.

ENVOYS

My black steed
Galloping fast,
Away have I come,
Leaving under distant skies
The dwelling place of my love.

Oh, yellow leaves
Falling on the autumn hill,
Cease a while
To fly and flutter in the air,
That I may see my love's dwelling place!

Kakinomoto Hitomaro (Seventh Century)

On the occasion of the temporary enshrinement of Princess Asuka

Across the river of the bird-flying Asuka
Stepping-stones are laid in the upper shallows,
And a plank bridge over the lower shallows.
The water-frond waving along the stones,
Though dead, will reappear.
The river-tresses swaying by the bridge
Wither, but they sprout again.

How is it, O Princess, that you have
Forgotten the morning bower
And forsaken the evening bower
Of him, your good lord and husband—
You who did stand handsome like a water-frond,
And who would lie with him,
Entwined like tender river-tresses?

No more can he greet you.
You make your eternal abode
At the Palace of Kinohe whither oft in your lifetime
He and you made holiday together,
Bedecked with flowers in spring,
Or with golden leaves in autumntide,
Walking hand in hand, your eyes
Fondly fixed upon your lord as upon a mirror,
Admiring him ever like the glorious moon.

So it may well be that grieving beyond measure,
And moaning like a bird unmated,
He seeks your grave each morn.
I see him go, drooping like summer grass,
Wander here and there like the evening star,
And waver as a ship wavers in the sea.

No heart have I to comfort him,
Nor know I what to do.

Only your name and your deathless fame,
Let me remember to the end of time;
Let the Asuka River, your namesake,
Bear your memory for ages,
O Princess adored!

ENVOYS

Even the flowing water
Of the Asuka River—
If a weir were built,
Would it not stand still?

O Asuka, River of Tomorrow,
As if I thought that I should see
My Princess on the morrow,
Her name always lives in my mind.

After the death of his wife

Since in Karu lived my wife,
I wished to be with her to my heart's content;
But I could not visit her constantly
Because of the many watching eyes—
Men would know of our troth,
Had I sought her too often.
So our love remained secret like a rock-pent pool;
I cherished her in my heart,
Looking to aftertime when we should be together,
And lived secure in my trust
As one riding a great ship.
Suddenly there came a messenger
Who told me she was dead—
Was gone like a yellow leaf of autumn.
Dead as the day dies with the setting sun,
Lost as the bright moon is lost behind the cloud,

Alas, she is no more, whose soul
Was bent to mine like bending seaweed!

When the word was brought to me
I knew not what to do nor what to say;
But restless at the mere news,
And hoping to heal my grief
Even a thousandth part,
I journeyed to Karu and searched the market place
Where my wife was wont to go!

There I stood and listened,
But no voice of her I heard,
Though the birds sang in the Unebi Mountain;
None passed by who even looked like my wife.
I could only call her name and wave my sleeve.

ENVOYS

In the autumn mountains
The yellow leaves are so thick.
Alas, how shall I seek my love
Who has wandered away?
I know not the mountain track.

I see the messenger come
As the yellow leaves are falling.
Oh, well I remember
How on such a day we used to meet—
My wife and I!

• •

In the days when my wife lived,
We went out to the embankment near by—
We two, hand in hand—
To view the elm trees standing there
With their outspreading branches

Thick with spring leaves. Abundant as their greenery
Was my love. On her leaned my soul.
But who evades mortality?
One morning she was gone, flown like an early bird.
Clad in a heavenly scarf of white,
To the wide fields where the shimmering *kagerō* rises
She went and vanished like the setting sun.

The little babe—the keepsake
My wife has left me—
Cries and clamors.
I have nothing to give; I pick up the child
And clasp it in my arms.

In our chamber, where our two pillows lie,
Where we two used to sleep together,
Days I spend alone, broken-hearted:
Nights I pass, sighing till dawn.

Though I grieve, there is no help;
Vainly I long to see her.
Men tell me that my wife is
In the mountains of Hagai—
Thither I go,
Toiling along the stony path;
But it avails me not,
For of my wife, as she lived in this world,
I find not the faintest shadow.

ENVOYS

Tonight the autumn moon shines—
The moon that shone a year ago,
But my wife and I who watched it then together
Are divided by ever widening wastes of time.

When leaving my love behind
In the Hikite mountains—
Leaving her there in her grave,
I walk down the mountain path,
I feel not like one living.

Kakinomoto Hitomaro

Dialogue poems

If the thunder rolls for a while
And the sky is clouded, bringing rain,
Then you will stay beside me.

Even when no thunder sounds
And no rain falls, if you but ask me,
Then I will stay beside you.

From the Hitomaro Collection

• •

I thought there could be
No more love left anywhere.
Whence then is come this love,
That has caught me now
And holds me in its grasp?

Princess Hirokawa (Eighth Century)

An old threnody

The mallards call with evening from the reeds
And float with dawn midway on the water;
They sleep with their mates, it is said,
With white wings overlapping and tails asweep
Lest the frost should fall upon them.

As the stream that flows never returns,
And as the wind that blows is never seen,
My wife, of this world, has left me,
Gone I know not whither!
So here, on the sleeves of these clothes
She used to have me wear,
I sleep now all alone!

ENVOY

Cranes call flying to the reedy shore;
How desolate I remain
As I sleep alone!

Tajihi (Eighth Century)

. .

Oh how steadily I love you—
You who awe me
Like the thunderous waves
That lash the seacoast of Ise!

Lady Kasa (Eighth Century)

. .

More sad thoughts crowd into my mind
When evening comes; for then,
Appears your phantom shape—
Speaking as I have known you speak.

Lady Kasa

. .

If it were death to love,
I should have died—
And died again
One thousand times over.

Lady Kasa

Love's complaint

At wave-bright Naniwa
The sedges grow, firm-rooted—
Firm were the words you spoke,
And tender, pledging me your love,
That it would endure through all the vears;
And to you I yielded my heart,
Spotless as a polished mirror.
Never, from that day, like the seaweed
That sways to and fro with the waves,
Have I faltered in my fidelity,
But have trusted in you as in a great ship.
Is it the gods who have divided us?
Is it mortal men who intervene?
You come no more, who came so often,
Nor yet arrives a messenger with your letter.
There is—alas!—nothing I can do.
Though I sorrow the black night through
And all day till the red sun sinks,
It avails me nothing. Though I pine,
I know not how to soothe my heart's pain.
Truly men call us "weak women."
Crying like an infant,
And lingering around, I must still wait,
Wait impatiently for a message from you!

ENVOY

If from the beginning
You had not made me trust you,
Speaking of long, long years,
Should I have known now
Such sorrow as this?

Lady Ōtomo of Sakanoue (Eighth Century)

• •

Do you desire our love to endure?
Then, if only while I see you
After days of longing and yearning,
Pray, speak to me
Sweet words—all you can!

Lady Ōtomo

• •

Oh, the pain of my love that you know not—
A love like the maiden-lily
Blooming in the thicket of the summer moor!

Lady Ōtomo

Addressed to a young woman

Over the river ferry of Saho,
Where the sanderlings cry—
When can I come to you,
Crossing on horseback
The crystal-clear shallows?

Having seen your smile
In a dream by chance,
I keep now burning in my hear•
Love's inextinguishable flame.

How I waste and waste away
With love forlorn—
I who have thought myself
A strong man!

Ōtomo Yakamochi (718-785)

• •

Rather than that I should thus pine for you,
Would I had been transmuted
Into a tree or a stone,
Nevermore to feel the pangs of love.

Ōtomo Yakamochi

• •

In obedience to the Imperial command,
Though sad is the parting from my wife,
I summon up the courage of a man,
And dressed for journey, take my leave.
My mother strokes me gently;
My young wife clings to me, saying,
"I will pray to the gods for your safekeeping.
Go unharmed and come back soon!"
As she speaks, she wipes with her sleeves
The tears that choke her.
Hard as it is, I start on my way,
Pausing and looking back time after time;
Ever farther I travel from my home,
Ever higher the mountains I climb and cross,
Till at last I arrive at Naniwa of wind-blown reeds.
Here I stop and wait for good weather,
To launch the ship upon the evening tide,
To set the prow seawards,
And to row out in the calm of morning.
The spring mists rise round the isles,
And the cranes cry in a plaintive tone,
Then I think of my far-off home—
Sorely do I grieve that with my sobs
I shake the war arrows I carry
Till they rattle in my ears.

ENVOYS

On an evening when the spring mists
Trail over the wide sea,
And sad is the voice of the cranes
I think of my far-off home.

Thinking of home,
Sleepless I sit,
The cranes call amid the shore reeds,
Lost in the mists of spring.

Ōtomo Yakamochi

An elegy on the impermanence of human life

We are helpless before time
Which ever speeds away.
And pains of a hundred kinds
Pursue us one after another.
Maidens joy in girlish pleasures,
With ship-borne gems on their wrists,
And hand in hand with their friends;
But the bloom of maidenhood,
As it cannot be stopped,
Too swiftly steals away.
When do their ample tresses
Black as a mud-snail's bowels
Turn white with the frost of age?
Whence come those wrinkles
Which furrow their rosy cheeks?
The lusty young men, warrior-like,
Bearing their sword blades at their waists,
In their hands the hunting bows,
And mounting their bay horses,
With saddles dressed with twill,

Ride about in triumph;
But can their prime of youth
Favor them for ever?
Few are the nights they keep,
When, sliding back the plank doors,
They reach their beloved ones
And sleep, arms intertwined,
Before, with staffs at their waists,
They totter along the road,
Laughed at here, and hated there.
This is the way of the world;
And, cling as I may to life,
I know no help!

ENVOY

Although I wish I were thus,
Like the rocks that stay for ever,
In this world of humanity
I cannot keep old age away.

Yamanoue Okura (660-733)

A dialogue on poverty

On the night when the rain beats,
Driven by the wind,
On the night when the snowflakes mingle
With the sleety rain,
I feel so helplessly cold.
I nibble at a lump of salt,
Sip the hot, oft-diluted dregs of saké;
And coughing, snuffling,
And stroking my scanty beard,
I say in my pride,
"There's none worthy, save I!"

But I shiver still with cold.
I pull up my hempen bedclothes,
Wear what few sleeveless clothes I have,
But cold and bitter is the night!
As for those poorer than myself,
Their parents must be cold and hungry,
Their wives and children beg and cry.
Then, how do you struggle through life?

Wide as they call the heaven and earth,
For me they have shrunk quite small;
Bright though they call the sun and moon,
They never shine for me.
Is it the same with all men,
Or for me alone?
By rare chance I was born a man
And no meaner than my fellows,
But, wearing unwadded sleeveless clothes
In tatters, like weeds waving in the sea,
Hanging from my shoulders,
And under the sunken roof,
Within the leaning walls,
Here I lie on straw
Spread on bare earth,
With my parents at my pillow,
My wife and children at my feet,
All huddled in grief and tears.
No fire sends up smoke
At the cooking-place,
And in the cauldron
A spider spins its web.
With not a grain to cook,
We moan like the night thrush.
Then, "to cut," as the saying is,
"The ends of what is already too short,"
The village headman comes,

With rod in hand, to our sleeping place,
Growling for his dues.
Must it be so hopeless—
The way of this world?

ENVOY

Nothing but pain and shame in this world of men,
But I cannot fly away,
Wanting the wings of a bird.

Yamanoue Okura

Suffering from old age and prolonged illness, and thinking of his children

So long as lasts the span of life,
We wish for peace and comfort
With no evil and no mourning,
But life is hard and painful.
As the common saying has it,
Bitter salt is poured into the smarting wound,
Or the burdened horse is packed with an upper load,
Illness shakes my old body with pain.
All day long I breathe in grief
And sigh throughout the night.
For long years my illness lingers,
I grieve and groan month after month,
And though I would rather die,
I cannot, and leave my children
Noisy like the flies of May.
Whenever I watch them
My heart burns within.
And tossed this way and that,
I weep aloud.

ENVOYS

I find no solace in my heart;
Like the bird flying behind the clouds
I weep aloud.

Helpless and in pain,
I would run out and vanish,
But the thought of my children holds me.

No children to wear them in wealthy homes,
They are thrown away as waste,
Those silks and quilted clothes!

With no sackcloth for my children to wear,
Must I thus grieve,
For ever at a loss!

Though vanishing like a bubble,
I live, praying that my life be long
Like a rope of a thousand fathoms.

Humble as I am,
Like an armband of coarse twill,
How I crave a thousand years of life!

Yamanoue Okura

An elegy on the death of Furuhi

What worth to me the seven treasures,
So prized and desired by all the world?
Furuhi, born of us two,
Our love, our dear white pearl,
With dawn, with the morning star,
Frolicked about the bed with us, standing or sitting;

When dusk came with the evening star,
He pulled our hands, urged us to bed,
"Leave me not, father and mother,
Let me sleep between you,
Like *saki-kusa,* the three-stalked plant."
So spoke that lovely mouth.
Then we trusted, as one trusts in a great ship,
That he would grow up as time passed by,
And we should watch him, both in weal and woe.
But, as of a sudden sweeps the storm,
Illness caught our son.
Helpless and in grief,
I braced my sleeves with white cord,
Grasped my shining mirror,
And gazing up into the sky
I appealed to the gods of heaven;
Dropping my forehead to the ground
Madly I prayed to the gods of earth:
"It is yours to decide his fate,
To cure him or to let him die."
Nothing availed my prayers,
He languished day by day,
His voice failed each morning,
His mortal life ebbed out.
Wildly I leapt and kicked the floor,
Cried, stared up, stared down,
And beat my breast in grief.
But the child from my arms has flown;
So goes the world. . . .

ENVOYS

So young he will not know the way;
Here is a fee for you,
O courier from the Nether World,
Bear him on your back.

With offerings I beseech you,
Be true and lead him up
Straight along the road to heaven!

Attributed to Yamanoue Okura

On seeing a dead man while crossing the pass of Ashigara

He lies unloosened of his white clothes,
Perhaps of his wife's weaving
From hemp within her garden fence,
And girdled threefold round
Instead of once.
Perhaps after painful service done
He turned his footsteps home,
To see his parents and his wife;
And now, on this steep and sacred pass
In the eastern land of Azuma,
Chilled in his spare, thin clothes,
His black hair fallen loose—
Telling none his province,
Telling none his home,
Here on a journey he lies dead.

From the Tanabe Sakimaro Collection

• •

Love is a torment
Whenever we hide it.
Why not lay it bare
Like the moon that appears
From behind the mountain ledge?

Anonymous

• •

I will think of you, love,
On evenings when the gray mist

Rises above the rushes,
And chill sounds the voice
Of the wild ducks crying.

Poem of a Frontier Guard

Dialogue poems

Had I foreknown my sweet lord's coming,
My garden, now so rank with wild weeds,
I had strewn it with pearls!

What use to me a house strewn with pearls?
The cottage hidden in wild weeds
Is enough, if I am with you.

Since I had shut the gate
And locked the door,
Whence did you, dear one, enter
To appear in my dream?

Though you had shut the gate
And locked the door,
I must have come to you in your dream
Through the hole cut by a thief.

Anonymous

Lament for old age

When winter is gone and spring comes,
New is the year, and new the month;
But man grows old.

All things are best when new;
But perchance with man
He alone is good who is old.

Anonymous

Referring to flowers

That you like me not
It may well be—
Yet will you not come
Even to see the orange tree
Abloom in my dooryard?

Anonymous

Referring to snow

Having met you as in a dream,
I feel I would dissolve, body and soul,
Like the snow that falls,
Darkening the heavens.

Anonymous

• •

Tonight I am coming
To visit you in your dream,
And none will see and question me—
Be sure to leave your door unlocked!

Anonymous

THE LUCK OF THE SEA AND THE LUCK OF THE MOUNTAINS

[*Kojiki, XXXIX-XLII*]

The "Kojiki," or "Records of Ancient Matters," which was presented to the court in 712 A.D., is the oldest surviving Japanese book. The records begin with the creation of the world in the Age of the Gods and continue until the reign of the Empress Suiko (592-628), whose very name—it may be translated "Conjecture of the Past"—indicates perhaps that in this period history first came to be written in Japan.

The literary interest of the "Kojiki" lies mainly in the tales of the legendary period. Some of them, such as the one given here, have considerable charm, but often the intrinsic interest is destroyed by extraneous elements which creep into the story. Poems are interspersed in the tales of the "Kojiki." Their merits vary greatly, but some of them are of a quality that foreshadows the "Man'yōshū."

•

Fire-shine was a prince who got his luck on the sea, and caught things broad of fin and narrow of fin. Fire-fade was a prince who got his luck on the mountains and caught things rough of hair and soft of hair. One day Fire-fade said to his elder brother Fire-shine, "Let us make a change and use each other's luck." But though he made this request three times, his brother would not agree to it, and only with much difficulty could he persuade him to make the exchange. Then Fire-fade angled for fish with the sea-luck, but failed to get a single one, and moreover lost the fishhook in the sea. Thereupon his elder brother asked him for the hook, saying, "A mountain-luck is a luck of its own, and a sea-luck is a luck of its own. Let us now give each other back his own luck." To which the younger brother replied, "I did not get a single fish by angling with your fishhook, and I finally lost it in the sea." But the elder brother insisted all the more urgently that he return it. So the younger brother, breaking his ten-grasp saber that hung by his side, made five hundred fishhooks of the fragments to make up for the lost hook, but the elder brother would not accept them. He said, "I still want my old fishhook."

Hereupon, as the younger brother was weeping and lamenting by the seashore, the God of the Tide came and asked him, "Why are you weeping and lamenting?" The Prince replied, "I exchanged a fishhook with my elder brother, and then I lost it. Now he wants it back, and though I have given him many fishhooks in its place, he will not take them. He insists on having back his old fishhook. That is why I weep and lament." Then the God of the Tide said, "I will give you good counsel." He thereupon built him a stout little boat without seams and set him in it. He instructed the Prince, saying, "When I push the boat off, go on for some time. You will see a road, and if you steer your boat along that road, you will come to a palace with walls like fishes' scales. That is the palace of the God of the Sea. When you reach the gates of the palace you will see a cassia tree with many branches standing above a well at its side. If you sit on top of that tree, the daughter of the God of the Sea will notice you and give you counsel."

The Prince followed these instructions, and after he had gone a little way everything happened just as the God of the Tide had said. He climbed the cassia tree and sat there. When the handmaidens of the daughter of the God of the Sea, bearing jeweled vessels, went to draw water from the well, they saw a light in it. On looking up, they beheld a beautiful young man. They were much amazed. The Prince saw the handmaidens and begged them to give him some water. They at once drew some water, put it into a jeweled vessel, and respectfully offered it to him. Then, without drinking the water, he loosened the jewel at his neck, took it in his mouth, and spat it into the jeweled vessel. The jewel adhered to the vessel so fast that the handmaidens could not get it off. So they took it, with the jewel adhering to it, and presented it to the Princess.

When the Princess saw the jewel, she asked her handmaidens,

"Is there perhaps someone outside the gate?" They answered, "There is a very beautiful young man sitting on top of the cassia tree above our well. He is nobler in bearing even than our king. We offered him some water when he asked for it, but instead of drinking the water, he spat this jewel into the cup. We could not separate the jewel from the cup, so we have brought both to you."

The Princess, marveling at this, went out to look, and was delighted by what she saw. The Prince and the Princess exchanged glances, and then she went to speak to her father. She said, "There is a beautiful person at our gate," and the God of the Sea himself went out to look. "That is Prince Fire-fade," he said, and led him inside the palace. He spread out eight layers of rugs of sealskins, and then eight layers of rugs of silk above them, and then had the Prince sit down on top. A great banquet was arranged with a hundred guests, and the God of the Sea gave his daughter to the Prince in marriage.

Prince Fire-fade dwelt in that land for three years. One day, remembering the past, he heaved a great sigh. The Princess heard the sigh and told her father about it. The God of the Sea then questioned his son-in-law, "This morning my daughter told me that you who have never sighed before in all the three years that you have dwelt among us sighed last night. What was the reason for it? And why did you first come here?" The Prince told the God of the Sea all about how his brother had pressed him for the return of the lost fishhook. Thereupon the God of the Sea summoned together all the fishes of the sea, great and small, and asked them, "Has some fish perhaps taken this fishhook?" And all of the fish replied, "Lately the bream has complained of something sticking in his throat which prevents him from eating. No doubt it is the bream who has taken the hook." The throat of the bream was examined, and the fishhook found inside. It was removed, washed, and presented to the Prince.

The God of the Sea then said to him, "When you give this fishhook to your elder brother, you should say to him, 'This fishhook is a big hook, an eager hook, a poor hook, a silly hook.' When you have said this, give it to him with your hand behind your back.

Once you have done this, if your brother cultivates low fields, you should cultivate high fields. In this way your brother will certainly be impoverished in the space of three years, for I rule the water. If he should attack you out of anger, put forth the tide-flowing jewel to drown him. If he expresses grief, put forth the tide-ebbing jewel to save him. In this way you shall afflict him."

With these words the God of the Sea gave the Prince the two jewels. He thereupon summoned together all the crocodiles and said to them, "The Prince Fire-fade is now about to proceed to the Upper Land. Who will in how many days escort him there and bring back a report?" Each of the crocodiles answered in accordance with the length of his body. One of them, a crocodile one fathom long, answered, "I will escort him and return in one day." The God of the Sea said, "You shall be the one to escort him, but mind that you do not alarm him when crossing the middle of the sea." Forthwith he seated the Prince on the crocodile's head and saw him off. The crocodile escorted the Prince back to his home in one day, as he had promised. When the crocodile was about to return, the Prince untied the dirk that was by his side, and placing it on the crocodile's neck, sent him back.

Fire-fade gave the fishhook to his elder brother in exactly the manner that the God of the Sea had prescribed. Thenceforward the elder brother became poorer and poorer, and in his fury came to attack Fire-fade. When he was about to attack, Fire-fade put forth the tide-flowing jewel to drown him; when the brother repented, he put forth the tide-ebbing jewel to save him. After he had thus been afflicted, the elder brother bowed his head and said, "From now on I shall be your guard day and night, and respectfully serve you."

Hereupon the daughter of the God of the Sea came to Fire-fade and said, "I am with child, and the time for my delivery approaches. But I thought that the child of a heavenly deity should not be born in the sea plain, and I have come to you here." At the edge of the waves on the seashore she built a hall for her delivery, using cormorants' feathers for thatch. But before the thatch was completed, she could not restrain the urgency of her womb, and she entered the hall. When she was about to be delivered, she said to her husband, "Whenever a foreigner is about to give birth to a child, she takes the shape of her native land. I now will take my native shape. Pray look not upon me!" The Prince, thinking her words very strange, stealthily looked upon her at the moment of delivery, when she turned into a crocodile eight fathoms long, and crawled and writhed about. Terrified at the sight, he fled away.

The Princess knew then that he had looked upon her, and she felt ashamed. Straightway leaving the child she had borne, she said, "I had wished always to come and go across the paths of the sea to you. But now I feel ashamed because you have seen me in my real shape." So she closed the boundary of the sea and went down again. But though she remained angry that he had wished to look upon her, she could not restrain her loving heart, and she entrusted to her younger sister, when she was nursing the child, a song for the Prince, which said: "Even though the string on which the red jewels are strung shines, my lord who is like white jewels is yet more beautiful."

Her husband replied with a song which said: "My dear wife, whom I took to sleep with me on the island where light the wild duck, the birds of the offing, I shall not forget you till the end of my life."

Prince Fire-fade dwelt in his palace of Takachiho for five hundred and eighty years, and his tomb is likewise on the west of Mount Takachiho.

TRANSLATED BY B. H. CHAMBERLAIN (MODIFIED)

KAIFŪSŌ

The "Kaifūsō," or "Fond Recollections of Poetry," was the first anthology of poetry in Chinese written by Japanese. It was compiled in 751, and includes material written over a period of seventy-five years. The verses in the "Kaifūsō" sometimes give the effect rather of copy-book exercises than of true poetry—which is only natural considering that they were among the earliest attempts by Japanese writers, including emperors, to compose in Chinese. Even when the subject of a poem is Japanese—such as a visit to the Yoshino River—the main effort of the writer appears to be directed toward including as many allusions to Chinese literature and history as possible. Nevertheless, some of the poems reach a high level of competence, as is indicated in the following selection.

•

Approaching death
[*Written when the Prince faced execution for attempted rebellion*]

The golden crow [1] lights on the western huts;
Evening drums beat out the shortness of life.
There are no inns on the road to the grave—
Whose is the house I go to tonight?

Prince Ōtsu (662-687)

The border official

Last year service in the eastern hills,
This, the marches of the western sea.

[1] Conventional term for the sun.

How often in the span of an official's life
Must he weary himself with these border wars?

Fujiwara no Umakai (694-737)

Watching fish in the water

By the southern woods I have built my hut;
I drop my hook from the north lake banks.
Sporting birds dive when I draw near;
Green duckweed sinks before my gliding boat.
The quivering reeds reveal the fish below;
By the length of my line I know the bottom's depth.
With vain sighs I dangle the tempting bait
And watch the spectacle of avaricious hearts.

Ki no Suemochi (Early Eighth Century)

Composed at a party for the Korean envoy

Mountain windows scan the deep valley;
Groves of pine line the evening streams.
We have asked to our feast the distant envoy;
At this table of parting we try the pleasures of poetry.
The crickets are hushed, the cold night wind blows;
Geese fly beneath the clear autumn moon.
We offer this flower-spiced wine in hopes
To beguile the cares of your long return.

Abe no Hironiwa (Early Eighth Century)

TRANSLATED BY BURTON WATSON

HEIAN PERIOD

794–1185

KŪKAI AND HIS MASTER

[*from Shōrai Mokuroku*]

The outstanding religious leader of the Heian Period was Kūkai (774-835), who is also known by his title of Kōbō Daishi. He was enormously gifted in almost every art and science of his day, and was in particular distinguished as perhaps the first Japanese who could write literary Chinese which was not only accurate but elegant. He thus claims a place as a literary as well as a religious figure.

Kūkai sailed to China in 804 for study, returning in 806. The Buddhism which he learned and brought back to Japan was known as the True Words (Shingon *in Japanese). In Shingon Buddhism the mysteries of the faith are transmitted orally and not written down in books. The relationship between master and disciple is thus of the greatest importance. Often a master would divulge all of his knowledge of the secret teachings to only one pupil. This was the case with Hui-kuo (764-805), whose chosen disciple Kūkai became.*

In the text there is mention of the two Mandalas, representations of the indestructible potential aspect of the cosmos (the Diamond Mandala) and its dynamic aspect (the Womb Mandala). One important Shingon ritual requires the acolyte to throw a flower on both of the Mandalas. The Buddha on which his flower alights is the one he is particularly bound to worship and emulate. Kūkai's flower fell, in both cases, on Vairocana Buddha, the central and supreme Buddha.

•

During the sixth moon of 804 I sailed for China aboard the Number One Ship, in the party of Lord Fujiwara, ambassador to the

T'ang court. We reached the coast of Fukien by the eighth moon, and four months later arrived at Ch'ang-an, the capital, where we were lodged in the official guest residence. The ambassadorial delegation started home for Japan on the fifteenth of March, 805, but in obedience to an Imperial edict I alone remained behind in the Hsi-ming Temple.

One day, in the course of my calls on eminent Buddhist teachers of the capital, I happened by chance to meet the abbot of the East Pagoda Hall of the Green Dragon Temple. This great priest, whose Buddhist name was Hui-kuo, was the chosen disciple of the Indian master Amoghavajra. His virtue aroused the reverence of his age; his teachings were lofty enough to guide emperors. Three sovereigns revered him as their master and were ordained by him. The four classes of believers looked up to him for instruction in the esoteric teachings.

I called on the abbot in the company of five or six monks from the Hsi-ming Temple. As soon as he saw me he smiled with pleasure, and he joyfully said, "I knew that you would come! I have been waiting for such a long time. What pleasure it gives me to look on you today at last! My life is drawing to an end, and until you came there was no one to whom I could transmit the teachings. Go without delay to the ordination altar with incense and a flower." I returned to the temple where I had been staying and got the things which were necessary for the ceremony. It was early in the sixth moon, then, that I entered the ordination chamber. I stood in front of the Womb Mandala and cast my flower in the prescribed manner. By chance it fell on the body of the Buddha Vairocana in the center. The master exclaimed in delight, "How amazing! How perfectly amazing!" He repeated this three or four times in joy and wonder. I was then given the fivefold baptism and received the instruction in the Three Mysteries that bring divine intercession. Next I was taught the Sanskrit formulas for the Womb Mandala, and learned the yoga contemplation of all the Honored Ones.

Early in the seventh moon I entered the ordination chamber of the Diamond Mandala for a second baptism. When I cast my flower it fell on Vairocana again, and the abbot marveled as he had before.

On the day of my ordination I provided a feast for five hundred of the monks. The dignitaries of the Green Dragon Temple all attended, and everyone enjoyed himself.

I later studied the Diamond Crown Yoga and the five divisions of the True Words teachings, and spent some time learning Sanskrit and the Sanskrit hymns. The abbot told me that the esoteric scriptures are so abstruse that their meaning cannot be conveyed except through art. For this reason he ordered the court artist Li Chen and about a dozen other painters to execute ten scrolls of the Womb and Diamond Mandalas, and assembled more than twenty scribes to make copies of the Diamond and other important scriptures. He also ordered the bronzesmith Chao Wu to cast fifteen ritual implements.

One day the abbot said to me, "Long ago, when I was still young, I met the great master Amoghavajra. From the first moment he saw me he treated me like a son, and on his visit to the court and his return to the temple I was as inseparable from him as his shadow. He confided to me, 'You will be the receptacle of the esoteric teachings. Do your best! Do your best!' I was then initiated into the teachings of both the Womb and the Diamond, and into the secret gestures as well. The rest of his disciples, monks and laity alike, studied just one of the Mandalas, or one Honored One, or one ritual, but not all of them as I did. How deeply I am indebted to him I shall never be able to express.

"Now my existence on earth approaches its term, and I cannot long remain. I urge you, therefore, to take the two Mandalas and the hundred volumes of the teachings, together with the ritual implements and these gifts which were left to me by my master. Return to your country and propagate the teachings there.

"When you first arrived I feared that I did not have time enough left to teach you everything, but now my teaching is completed, and the work of copying the Sutras and making the images is also done. Hasten back to your country, offer these things to the court, and spread the teachings throughout your country to increase the happiness of the people. Then the land will know peace and everyone will be content. In that way you will return thanks to Buddha and to your teacher. That is also the way to show your devotion to your country and to your family. My disciple I-ming will carry on the teachings here. Your task is to transmit them to Japan. Do your best! Do your best!" These were his final instructions to me, and he was kindly and patient as always. On the night of the last full moon of the year he purified himself with a ritual bath and, lying on his right side with his hands making the gesture of Vairocana, breathed his last.

That night, while I sat in meditation in the hall, the abbot appeared to me in his usual form and said, "You and I have long been pledged to propagate the esoteric teachings. If I am reborn in Japan, this time I will be your disciple."

TRANSLATED BY DONALD KEENE

THE TALES OF ISE

[*Ise Monogatari*]

"The Tales of Ise" is basically a collection of verse, by the nobleman and poet Ariwara no Narihira (823-880), but each verse is preceded by a prose passage indicating the occasion of its composition. It contains 125 chapters, varying in length from a few lines to two or three pages, depending mainly on the number of poems included. Some of these poems are by other contemporaries—and even by "Man'yōshū" poets—but the majority are by Narihira, and the work was apparently edited and enlarged by an unknown compiler not long after his death. Although the hero of most of the episodes is identified in the original only as "a man," the work in large part is clearly autobiographical. The arrangement of the chapters is, however, haphazard, and in the excerpts given in the present translations an attempt has been made to restore a chronological order.

•

In former times there lived a young nobleman named Narihira. Upon receiving the ceremony of initiation into manhood, he set forth upon a ceremonial falconry excursion, to review his estates at the village of Kasuga, near the former capital of Nara.

In that village there dwelt alone two young sisters possessed of a disturbing beauty. The young nobleman gazed at the two secretly from the shade of the enclosure around their house. It filled his heart with longing that in this rustic village he should have found so unexpectedly such lovely maidens. Removing the wide sleeve from the silk cloak he was wearing, Narihira inscribed a verse upon it and sent it to the girls. The cloak he was wearing bore a bold pattern of passionflowers.

Kasugano no	Young maiden-flowers
Waka-murasaki no	Of Kasuga, you dye my cloak;
Surigoromo	And wildly like them grows
Shinobu no midare	This passion in my heart,
Kagiri shirarezu	Abundantly, without end.

The maidens must have thought this eminently suited to the occasion, for it was composed in the same mood as the well-known

Michinoku no	For whom has my heart
Shinobumojizuri	Like the passionflower patterns
Tare yue ni	Of Michinoku
Midaresomenishi	Been thrown into disarray?
Ware naranaku ni	All on account of you.

This is the kind of facile elegance in which the men of old excelled.

(1)

• •

In former times there was a girl who, beloved of the Emperor Seiwa, served him in the court, and was allowed even to wear the Imperial purple. She was cousin to the Empress Dowager. Narihira was a very young man at this time. He too was serving in direct attendance upon the Emperor, and he fell in love and became intimate with this girl.

Now Narihira was allowed free access to the palace where the ladies of the court dwelt,[1] and he would visit the chamber of this girl and sit directly beside her. But she entreated him, "If you come to see me thus, His Majesty will hear of it, and we shall perish. Please do not come this way again."

Narihira answered her:

Omou ni wa	In love with you
Shinoburu koto zo	I have lost all sense of

[1] Because of his youth he was permitted to frequent the ladies' palace.

Makenikeru	Hiding from men's eyes.
Au ni shi kaeba	If in exchange for meeting you,
Samo araba are	Is death so great a price to pay?

When she returned to her own chamber after serving in the court, he would follow after her, without trying to hide his destination. The girl, much upset, returned to her native village.

Once at home, she thought that he would no longer trouble her; but Narihira was delighted at this turn of events, thinking this a wonderful way of meeting far from the sight of men. His visits to the girl were frequent, causing much merriment among her ladies-in-waiting. When he returned to the court in the early morning from the girl's village, he would remove his shoes at the gate and place them among the footwear of those who had spent the night in the palace, taking care that the morning garden-sweepers did not observe him. Then he would go and wait attendance on the Emperor.

As thus he passed his days in stratagems, becoming more and more deeply involved in this dangerous love, his health began to fail. He wondered what escape there might be for him, and prayed to the gods and the Buddha that he be delivered from this fatal love. But the passion only grew upon him, and all his prayers served but to make him love her all the more.

Unable to drive her from his thoughts, he summoned exorcists and mediums, and had them set up by the Kamo River the divine symbols for deliverance from this love. However much he gave himself over to the chanting of the exorcists and dancers, he was never for an instant free from thoughts of her, and his passion instead became stronger even than before.

Koi seji to	"Love not!" they chanted,
Mitarashigawa ni	By the river's holy stream,
Seshi misogi	Purifying me.
Kami wa ukezu zo	But the gods listened not;
Narinikerashi mo	It was all, it seems, for nought.

Thus he recited, and left the riverside.

Now the Emperor was a person of beautiful countenance, and every morning when the girl heard him raise his fine voice fervently and reverently in prayers to the Buddha, she wept bitterly. "What a tragic stroke of Fate that I cannot truly serve this noble sovereign! Tied by the bonds of love to another man, only endless grief can be my lot."

It came to pass that His Majesty at last got word of the affair. He banished Narihira from the capital. As for the girl, her cousin the Empress Dowager had her expelled from the palace and locked up in a windowless tower in her village, and inflicted much torment on her.

Locked within the tower, the girl said in tears:

Ama no karu	Like the *warekara* [2]
Mo ni sumu mushi no	That lives among the seaweed
Warekara to	Fisherwomen gather,
Ne wo koso nakame	I cry none is to blame but me:
Yo wo ba uramiji	I have no hatred for the world.

Thus did she cry, and each night Narihira would journey from his place of banishment to her, and playing upon his flute with great feeling, sing a doleful plaint in his melodious voice. Though she was locked up in a windowless tower, she recognized her lover's voice, but bound and tormented as she was there was no way to catch a glimpse of him.

Saritomo to	My heart breaks that
Omouramu koso	He visits here each night
Kanashikere	In hopes of meeting me;
Aru ni mo aranu	Little does he realize
Mi wo shirazu shite	How hopeless is my plight.

Unable, despite all efforts, to meet his love, Narihira traveled back and forth between the tower and his place of exile.

[2] *Warekara* is at once the name of an insect that lives in seaweed and a word meaning "of itself" or "of its own will."

Itazura ni	All in vain, I know,
Yukite wa kinuru	Are my goings and comings;
Mono yue ni	So great, however,
Mimaku hoshisa ni	Is my desire to see her
Izanawaretsutsu	That I am ceaselessly drawn.

(LXV)

• •

In former times there lived a lady in East Gojō, in the Western Pavilion of the Empress Dowager's palace. Narihira visited her there, at first with no specific intentions but later in great infatuation. About the tenth day of the first month, however, she concealed herself elsewhere. Although he heard where her refuge was, it was impossible for him to go to her, and he became increasingly depressed. In the first month of the following year, when the plum blossoms were in their full glory, he went again to the Western Pavilion, remembering with longing the happenings of the previous year. He stood and looked, sat and looked, but nothing seemed the same. Bitterly weeping, he lay on the deserted bare wooden floor until the moon sank in the sky. Recalling the happiness of the year before, he composed the poem:

Tsuki ya aranu	Is not that the moon?
Haru ya mukashi no	And is not the spring the same
Haru naranu	Spring of the old days?
Wa ga mi hitotsu wa	My body is the same body—
Moto no mi ni shite	Yet everything seems different.

(IV)

• •

In former times a certain lascivious woman thought: "I wish I could somehow meet a man who would show me affection!" It was, however, impossible for her to express this desire openly. She therefore made up a most unlikely dream, called her three sons together, and related it to them. Two of them dismissed it with a curt reply, but the youngest son interpreted the dream as meaning that a fine man would certainly come along, and the old woman was delighted.

The son thought: "Other men are coldhearted—I wish that I could bring her together with Captain Narihira." One day he met the Captain while the latter was out hunting. He seized the bridle of the Captain's horse and told him of his request. The Captain took pity on the old woman, visited her house, and slept with her. He did not come again, and the woman went to his house, where she stealthily looked at him through an opening in the fence. The Captain, catching a glimpse of her, recited:

Momotose ni	Someone a year short
Hitotose taranu	Of a centenarian,
Tsukumogami	Hair disheveled and white,
Ware wo kourashi	Seems to be in love with me:
Omokage ni miyu	I saw her in a vision!

When the woman saw him saddle his horse and prepare to leave, she rushed off in such great confusion that she was not even aware how the thorny shrubs and plants scratched her. She returned home, lay down on her sleeping mat, and waited for him. While the Captain stood outside secretly watching her, as she had done at his house, she recited:

Samushiro ni	Shall I have to sleep
Koromo katashiki	All alone again tonight
Koyoi mo ya	On my narrow mat
Koishiki hito ni	Unable to meet again
Awade wa ga nemu	The man for whom I long?

It is a general rule in this world that men love some women but not others. Narihira did not make such distinctions.

(LXIII)

• •

In former times there was a nobleman named Narihira. He was once sent by the Emperor as Imperial envoy to the Great Shrine of Ise.

On this occasion the Imperial Princess who was serving as Vestal Virgin to the Shrine received from her mother in the capital the following message: "You are to treat the present envoy with greater consideration than is usual." Since this was her mother's command, the Princess went to great pains: in the morning she herself directed the preparations for the ceremonial falconry, and in the evening, when Narihira returned, she lodged him in her own palace. She treated him with the utmost solicitude.

On the evening of the second day Narihira suggested that they meet in greater intimacy than they had previously done. The Princess was not displeased with the idea, but as there were many people about, it was impossible for the moment. In his capacity of Imperial envoy, however, Narihira had been lodged in the Princess's own wing of the palace and, it being near to her own chamber, she came secretly to his quarters at midnight, after all were asleep.

Narihira likewise had been unable to sleep and, reclining in bed, had been gazing out the window. Just when the moon became subdued with clouds, the Princess appeared to him, with a little child in attendance on her. Narihira was filled with joy. He led the Princess to his bed, and she remained there with him until the third hour of the morning. Before they had time enough to reveal their feelings to each other, however, she was obliged to return to her own chamber.

Filled with melancholy, Narihira was unable to sleep. He longed to see her, but since it would be too apparent if he sent his own messenger, he could do nothing but await some word from her. A little after daybreak a messenger finally came from her. There was no letter, only the verse:

Kimi ya koshi	I know not whether
Ware ya yukikemu	It was I who journeyed there
Omohoezu	Or you who came to me:
Yume ka utsutsu ka	Was it dream or reality?
Nete ka samete ka	Was I sleeping or awake?

Narihira was greatly moved, and wept. He wrote in answer:

Kakikurasu	Last night I too
Kokoro no yami ni	Wandered lost in the darkness
Madoiniki	Of a disturbed heart;
Yume utsutsu to wa	Whether dream or reality
Koyoi sadame yo	Tonight let us decide!

After he sent this verse to her, he had to set forth on his official duties for the day. Yet even while he traveled through the moors, he could think of nothing but her, and he longed for the night to come swiftly, that they might meet again. Unfortunately, the governor of the province, who was also the guardian of the Vestal, learning that the Imperial envoy had arrived, insisted that the night be spent in festive celebration of his visit. Narihira, thus bound by enforced hospitality, could find no way to meet the Princess. Since he had the following morning to depart for Owari, unknown to anyone he shed bitter tears, but could in no wise meet her.

As dawn approached, a servant from the Princess's apartment brought a cup of parting. In it was written:

Kachibito no	Shallow the inlet
Wataredo nurenu	If the traveler wading it
Eni shi areba	Is not even wetted [3]

The poem was not completed.

Narihira took the wine cup in his hands, and with charcoal from a pinewood torch he added the last lines to the verse:

Mata Ausaka no	I shall cross again to you
Seki wa koenamu	Over Meeting Barrier.

When day dawned he set out for the Province of Owari.

(LXIX)

[3] A pun here between "inlet" and "connection" (*eni*). The reply has the usual play on the name Ausaka (Osaka), the name of a mountain and barrier east of Kyoto in which is imbedded the word *au*, "to meet."

• •

In former times when Narihira, having fallen ill, felt that he was going to die, he wrote this poem:

Tsui ni yuku	That it is a road
Michi to wa kanete	Which some day we all travel
Kikishikado	I had heard before,
Kinō kyō to wa	Yet I never expected
Omowazarishi wo	To take it so soon myself.

(CXXV)

TRANSLATED BY RICHARD LANE (I, LXV, LXIX)
AND F. VOS (IV, LXIII, CXXV)

KOKINSHŪ

The "Kokinshū," or "Collection of Ancient and Modern Poems," was the first of the anthologies of Japanese poetry compiled by Imperial order. It was completed in 905, and contains 1,111 poems, almost all of them waka. *The preface to the work by Ki no Tsurayuki (died 946) indicates the tone of the poetry included; and he lists some of the circumstances under which the "Kokinshū" poets expressed themselves: "when they looked at the scattered blossoms of a spring morning; when they listened of an autumn evening to the falling of the leaves; when they sighed over the snow and waves reflected with each passing year by their looking glasses; when they were startled into thoughts on the brevity of life by seeing the dew on the grass or the foam on the water; when, yesterday all proud and splendid, they have fallen from fortune into loneliness; or when, having been dearly loved, are neglected." These subjects were all capable of inspiring beautiful poetry, but the gentle melancholy they imply imposed severe limitations on the range of expression, certainly when compared with the "Man'yōshū. The "Kokinshū," however, was the model of* waka *composition for a thousand years (particularly until the eighteenth century) and as such is of the greatest importance. One curious feature is that many of the best poems are anonymous.*

•

Tagitsu se no	They say there is
Naka ni mo yodo wa	A still pool even in the middle of
Ari chō wo	The rushing whirlpool—
Nado waga koi no	Why is there none in the whirlpool
Fuchise to mo naki	of my love?

Anonymous

• •

Haru tateba
Kiyuru kōri no
Nokori naku
Kimi ga kokoro mo
Ware ni tokenamu

Like the ice which melts
When spring begins
Not leaving a trace behind,
May your heart melt toward me!

Anonymous

• •

Oiraku no
Komu to shiriseba
Kado sashite
Nashi to kotaete
Awazaramashi wo

If only, when one heard
That Old Age was coming
One could bolt the door
Answer "not at home"
And refuse to meet him!

Anonymous

• •

Yo no naka wa
Mukashi yori ya wa
Ukarikemu
Waga mi hitotsu no
Tame ni nareru ka

Can this world
From of old
Always have been so sad,
Or did it become so for the sake
Of me alone?

Anonymous

• •

Waga koi wa
Yukue mo shirazu
Hate mo nashi
Au wo kagiri to
Omou bakari zo

My love
Knows no destination
And has no goal;
I think only
Of meeting as its limit.

Ōshikōchi no Mitsune (859-907)

• •

Iro miede
Utsurou mono wa
Yo no naka no
Hito no kokoro no
Hana ni zo arikeru

A thing which fades
With no outward sign—
Is the flower
Of the heart of man
In this world!

Ono no Komachi[1] *(Ninth Century)*
TRANSLATED BY ARTHUR WALEY

• •

Ariake no
Tsurenaku mieshi
Wakare yori
Akatsuki bakari
Uki mono wa nashi

Since I left her,
Frigid as the setting moon,
There is nothing I loathe
As much as the light
Of dawn on the clouds.

Mibu no Tadamine (Ninth Century)
TRANSLATED BY KENNETH REXROTH

• •

Hito ni awamu
Tsuki no naki yo wa
Omoiokite
Mune hashiri hi ni
Kokoro yakeori

This night of no moon
There is no way to meet him.
I rise in longing—
My breast pounds, a leaping flame,
My heart is consumed in fire.

Ono no Komachi

• •

Omoitsutsu
Nureba ya hito no
Mietsuramu
Yume to shiriseba
Samezaramashi wo

Thinking about him
I slept, only to have him
Appear before me—
Had I known it was a dream,
I should never have wakened.

Ono no Komachi

[1] A famous poetess and subject of the *Nō* play *"Sotoba Komachi"* which appears on page 264.

• •

Wabinureba	So lonely am I
Mi wo ukigusa no	My body is a floating weed
Ne wo taete	Severed at the roots.
Sasou mizu araba	Were there water to entice me,
Inamu to zo omou	I would follow it, I think.

Ono no Komachi

• •

Yume ni da mo	Not even in dreams
Miyu to wa mieji	Can I meet him any more—
Asa na asa na	My glass each morning
Wa ga omokage ni	Reveals a face so wasted
Hazuru mi nareba	I turn away in shame.

Ise [2]

• •

Fuyugare no	If I consider
Nobe to waga mi wo	My body like the fields
Omoiseba	Withered by winter,
Moede mo haru wo	Can I hope, though I am burnt,
Matashimono wo	That spring will come again? [3]

Ise

• •

Wa ga yado wa	The weeds grow so thick
Michi mo naki made	You cannot even see the path
Arenikeri	That leads to my house:
Tsurenaki hito wo	It happened while I waited
Matsu to seshi ma ni	For someone who would not come.

Sōjō Henjō (815-890)

[2] Poetess and consort of the Emperor Uda.

[3] The fields were burnt before the new crop was planted.

• •

Hisakata no
Hikari nodokeki
Haru no hi ni
Shizu kokoro naku
Hana no chiruramu[4]

This perfectly still
Spring day bathed in the soft light
From the spread-out sky,
Why do the cherry blossoms
So restlessly scatter down?

Ki no Tomonori

• •

Ōzora wa
Koishiki hito no
Katami ka wa
Mono omou goto ni
Nagameraruramu

Are the vast heavens
Some keepsake of her I love?
No, that is absurd.
What then makes me stare skyward
Whenever I think of her?

Sakai no Hitozane (died 931)

• •

Tane shi areba
Iwa ni mo matsu wa
Hainikeri
Koi wo shi koiba
Awarazarame ya wa

Because there was a seed
A pine has grown even here
On these barren rocks:
If we really love our love
What can keep us from meeting?

Anonymous

• •

Kome ya to
Omou mono kara
Higurashi no
Naku yūgure wa
Tachimataretsutsu

Although I am sure
That he will not be coming,
In the evening light
When the locusts shrilly call
I go to the door and wait.

Anonymous

[4] Note how the use of words beginning in *h* intensifies the meaning of the poem.

• •

Yūgure wa	At the sunset hour
Kumo no hatate ni	The clouds are ranged like banners
Mono zo omou	And I think of things:
Amatsu sora naru	That is what it means to love
Hito wo kou to te	One who lives beyond my world.[5]

Anonymous

• •

Hana no iro wa	The flowers withered,
Utsurinikeri na	Their color faded away,
Itazura ni	While meaninglessly
Wa ga mi yo ni furu	I spent my days in the world
Nagame seshi ma ni	And the long rains were falling.

Ono no Komachi

TRANSLATED BY DONALD KEENE

[5] Meaning either a person in a distant place beyond the clouds, or someone in a hopelessly superior social position.

THE TOSA DIARY

[*Tosa Nikki*] *by Ki no Tsurayuki*

The "Tosa Diary," describing the return to Kyoto of a governor of Tosa Province, was probably written in the year 936, from notes taken on the voyage. Although the fiction is maintained throughout that the diary is being written by one of the ladies in the party, it is reasonably certain that the author is the governor himself, the celebrated poet Ki no Tsurayuki.

Tosa Province is the ancient name for the present Kōchi Prefecture, in the south of Shikoku Island.

•

Diaries are things written by men, I am told. Nevertheless I am writing one, to see what a woman can do.

Twenty-first day, twelfth moon (the year does not matter): Late at night we made our departure from the house. But I must set things down in a little more detail. A certain gentleman, after four or five years in the province, had finished his term of office as governor, and now, with all the usual round of business concluded and papers of release duly received, he set out from the official residence and moved to a place near the point of embarkation. Before he went, however, various people, acquaintances and strangers alike, came to take their leave. The farewells were particularly distressing for those who had been closely associated with him over these years. There was an endless coming and going all day long, and the commotion lasted well into the night.

Twenty-second day: We offered up prayers for a calm and peaceful voyage—"all the way to Izumi Province." Fujiwara no Tokizane arranged a farewell celebration "for the road" (not very appropriate for a ship, perhaps) at which everv one, from master to servant, became disgustingly drunk.

Twenty-third day: A man called Yagi no Yasunori is here. He appears to have not the remotest connection with the provincial government service, but he nevertheless arranged a farewell celebration for us on a magnificent scale. Perhaps the fault lies in the governor himself, but the general attitude of the people of Tosa is that an ex-governor no longer concerns them and is not worth the trouble of a visit. Still, there are some of the kinder sort who have not allowed this to deter them from paying their respects. In their case it cannot be said that they come in the hope of future advantages, or for the sake of prestige.

Twenty-fourth day: The provincial overseer of religion arrived to give us a farewell party. Every one, high and low, old and young, was fuddled with drink. Even people who have never learned to write the figure one were merrily dancing figures of eight.

Twenty-fifth day: A messenger arrived from the official residence, it seems, with an invitation for the ex-governor. The ex-governor accepted. The various entertainments lasted all day and night, and well into the next morning.

Twenty-sixth day: Today they were still at the new governor's residence, feasting and making merry. Even the servants have received presents, I am told. Chinese verses were declaimed, and the new governor, his guest, and others joined in an exchange of extempore Japanese poems. I cannot write Chinese verse in this diary, but one of the Japanese poems, composed by the new governor, went like this:

> For your sake I left Kyoto, and journeyed here to meet you—
> I journeyed in vain if I came but to lose you.

Before taking his leave the former governor replied:

> Over the white-crested waves I came, and following came another.

Where I return, he shall return—and who is that other but you?

There were more poems, by others, but apparently none of them was particularly well constructed. After exchanging a few more words the former governor and the present governor descended together into the garden. Present and former masters of the house grasped hands, wished each other good fortune—in accents unsteadied by wine—and went their respective ways.

Twenty-seventh day: Our boats left Ōtsu, rowing a course for Urado. As they cast off, I thought sadly of my master's young daughter—born in Kyoto, and suddenly taken from us in this remote province. While recording, in these last days, the busy preparations for our departure, I have said nothing on this matter; but now that we are at last under way on the return voyage to Kyoto, my only sensations are of grief and longing for a young girl who is not coming with us. There are others, too, who could not bear the sadness of it. Some one wrote this poem:

Kyoto bound, our thoughts are heavy yet
With grief for one who never shall return.

Later another poem was composed:

Forgetful, "Wherever is that child?" I cry
—And, oh, the sadness of the truth!

Meanwhile we reached a place called Kako Point, where we were overtaken by the brothers of the new governor and other friends, who brought us presents of saké and food. The whole company disembarked onto the beach, and we talked to each other of the sorrows of parting. Of all the people at the governor's residence, these who have now come are said to have shown themselves the most kind and considerate on that occasion. . . . While we were exchanging poems the chief pilot—a man of no sensibility—having taken his fill of saké and thinking it high time to be off, announced: "The tide is full. There should be a wind soon"; and we made ready to re-embark. . . . This evening we anchored at Urado, where we were later overtaken by Fujiwara no Tokizane, Tachibana no Suehira, and others.

Proceeding eastward from Urado along the Pacific coast of Shikoku, they reach a harbor called Ōminato the following night. Here they are detained for nine days, waiting for clear weather. After a disappointing New Year's Day, which only serves to increase their general yearning for Kyoto, they occupy themselves in receiving visitors and composing poems.

Ninth day, second moon: Early in the morning we left Ōminato, and made for the anchorage of Naha. A large number of people gathered to see us off, determined not to leave us so long as we remain within the confines of the provincial government district. . . .

From now on we row farther and farther out to sea. It is for this reason that all these people gathered here to see us off. Little by little, at every stroke of the oars, the watchers standing by the shore slip away into the distance, just as we on the boats, too, grow more and more indistinct to them. On the shore, perhaps, there are things they would like to say to us. On the boats there are thoughts we wish to convey to them—but to no avail. Even so, though we can expect no reply, we compose this last poem:

> No courier have we, and though with heavy hearts
> We leave—perhaps they'll never know we grieved.

Soon we pass the pine-covered beaches of Uta. Pines beyond number! How many tens of centuries have they stood there? Waves wash the roots of each tree, and from each topmost branch a crane soars into the air. We watched in tireless fascination. Someone on the boat recited this poem:

> As far as the eye can see, on each pine top there rests a crane—
> Each crane to each pine, perhaps, a faithful companion these
> thousand years!

The poem, however, cannot compare with the sight itself. As we proceed in this manner, absorbed in the scenery, night gradually draws on. The mountains and sea grow dark. Soon it becomes impossible to distinguish east from west, and for warning of a change in the weather we must rely completely on the pilot's judgment. Even the men, unaccustomed to such a situation, show signs of anxiety. With the women it is much worse—we hide our heads in the bottom of the boat and sob. But while we are in this sad condition, the pilot and the boatmen sing songs, completely unconcerned:

> In the spring fields lonely I cry.
> My hands I have cut, I have cut,
> Gathering herbs in the sharp pampas grass.
> And will my parents eat these herbs,
> Or are they for my husband's mother?
> Oh, I wish I had never got married!

or:

> Where is that lad who came last night?
> I'll ask him for the money.
> "I'll pay tomorrow," he said—but he lied.
> He's brought no money, of course, but worse—
> He hasn't come himself!

There are many others besides, but I shall not write them down. The sea grows rougher, but listening to these songs and to the boatmen's laughter we feel more easy at heart, and at last, after a long day's voyage, we reach harbor. An old gentleman and an old lady have meanwhile fallen sick, and they retire to bed without supper.

Tenth day: Today we remain at this harbor of Naha.

The following day they proceed to Murotsu, their last stopping place within the province of Tosa. Here they are detained by bad weather for five days.

Seventeenth day: The clouds have cleared, and in the early hours before dawn there is a fine clear moon. We set out in our boats. A perfect image of the clouds above is reflected in the bottom of the sea—it must have been on a night like this that the ancient poet wrote of "oars piercing the moon on the waves, the boat traversing skies in the sea's depths." At least, those are his words so far as I remember. Someone composed this poem on a similar theme:

As we row over the moon in the sea bottom,
Will our oars be entangled in a Katsura tree?

Hearing this, another said:

Gazing down, we row across a firmament
Beneath the water—how small we feel!

As we proceed it grows gradually lighter. "Dark clouds have suddenly appeared!" shouts the pilot. "It will blow, I think. I'm turning the boat back!" We return to the harbor amid rain, feeling miserable.

They wait for several more days at Murotsu, for a chance to round Muroto Cape.

Twenty-first day: At about the hour of the Hare we set out once more. All the other boats move out at the same time, so that, as we look around us, it seems as if the early spring seas are already dotted with fallen autumn leaves. Perhaps in answer to our constant prayers, the wind no longer blows, and we row along in bright sunshine. . . . As we continue on our way, talking of this and that, the master of the boat anxiously scans the seas. It seems that, now that we are leaving the bounds of the province, there is a danger that pirates may seek vengeance on the ex-governor. As we think of this, the sea once more becomes a place of terror. All of us have grown white-haired in these last weeks. Truly, an age of seventy or eighty years is soon reached on the sea!

Tell us, Lord of the Islands, which is the whitest—
The surf on the rocks or the snow on our heads?

Ask him, pilot!

Twenty-second day: We set out from last night's harbor. Mountains are visible in the far distance. A boy of eight—looking even less than his years—was amazed to discover that, as our boat moves, the mountains appear to move with us. He composed this poem:

> Viewed from a moving boat, even mountains move—
> But do the mountain pines know this?

It is a fitting poem for a child. Today the sea is rough. Around the rocks the foam is like driving snow, and the waves themselves are flowers in bloom:

> A wave is but a single thing, we're told; but from its hue
> You'd think it was a mixture—flowers and snow!

Twenty-third day: The sun appears, but is soon obscured by cloud. Since we have been told that this particular area is infested by pirates, we pray for the protection of the gods and Buddhas. . . .

Twenty-sixth day: Being told again (with what truth, I do not know) that pirates are on our tracks, we started out at about midnight, and on our way made offerings to the gods. The pilot cast our paper charms into the sea, and as they drifted off to the east he cried: "In the same direction in which these offerings drift, vouchsafe that this vessel may speed!" Hearing this, a young girl made the poem:

> Blow steadily, wind, behind our boat, even as you blow
> These charms offered to the ocean gods.

At about this time the wind was good, and the pilot—with an air of self-importance, and with evident relief—ordered the sails to be raised. Hearing his words of command we women, young and old alike, were overjoyed, feeling that Kyoto is not far off now. . . .

The next two days are stormy, and the boats remain in harbor—the place is not specified, but it is presumably somewhere in the region of the present city of Tokushima. On the twenty-ninth day of the second moon they move on to Naruto, and the following day they make for Awaji Island and the mainland.

Thirtieth day: The wind and rain have stopped. Having heard that pirates operate only by day, we started at about midnight, rowing past the Awa whirlpool. It was pitch dark and we could see to neither right nor left. As we passed the whirlpool men and women alike prayed fervently to the gods and Buddhas. Near dawn we passed a place called Nushima, and then Tanagawa. Pressing on in great haste, we arrived at Nada in Izumi Province. Today there has been nothing approaching a wave on the sea—it seems as if the gods and Buddhas have granted us their protection. It is now the thirty-ninth day from when we first embarked. Now that we have reached Izumi Province, there is no need to worry about pirates.

High seas detain them for three days at Nada.

Fourth day, third moon: "Today, judging by the wind and the clouds, we shall have very bad weather," said the pilot, and we did not venture from this harbor. But all day long there has been not a sign of wind or waves. Even as a judge of the weather, this pilot is useless. Along the beach of the harbor were innumerable shells and pebbles of great beauty, and someone in the boat, still unable to think of anything except the child who is no longer with us, composed this poem:

> Wash your shells to my ship, o waves!
> I'll gather forgetting-shells for one I loved.

Another, equally unable to bear his grief, and sick in spirit after the trials of the voyage, replies:

> I'll gather no forgetting-shells, but jewels,
> Mementos of the jewel-like one I loved.

In grief even a father grows childlike. It might be said, I suppose, that this particular child could hardly be likened to a jewel—but "a departed child has a beautiful face," goes the proverb. . .

Fifth day: Today we made haste out of Nada, and steered for the harbor of Ozu. Pines stretch endlessly along the beaches. . . . As we were rowed along, admiring the view and talking of this and that, a sudden wind rose, and no matter how desperately the boatmen rowed, we were driven slowly backwards. The boat was in danger of foundering in the waves. "This God of Sumiyoshi is the same as other gods. There is something on board the ship he wants," said the pilot. "Make an offering of paper symbols," he urged. The master complied, but the wind did not abate—it blew all the harder, and the waves rose higher. "Paper symbols are not to the god's taste. The ship makes no headway!" shouted the pilot. "Have you nothing which will please him better?" "There's nothing but this," said the master. "I have two eyes, but only one mirror. I shall give this mirror to the god." He threw it into the waves, and as it sank (a loss indeed!) the sea suddenly became as smooth as the face of a mirror. Someone composed this poem:

> Seeking to fathom the mind of the raging god, we cast
> A mirror into the stormy sea. In that his image is revealed.

An amazing experience! Surely this cannot be the god whom we commonly associate with such gentle things as "Limpid Waters," "The Balm of Forgetfulness," and "Pines along the Shore"? We have all seen with our own eyes—and with the help of a mirror—what sort of a god he is.

On the following day, to the great joy of all the passengers, Naniwa (Osaka) is reached, and the ship commences its voyage up the river Yodo towards Kyoto. Progress is slow, owing to the shallowness of the channel, but after five days the bridge at Yamazaki—the terminus for river traffic—is sighted.

Eleventh day: After a little rain the skies cleared. Continuing upriver, we noticed a line of hills converging on the eastern bank. When we learned that this is the Yawata Hachiman Shrine, there was great rejoicing and we humbly abased ourselves in thanks. The bridge of Yamazaki came in sight at last, and our feelings of joy could no longer be restrained. Here, close by the Ōōji Temple, our boat came to anchor; and here we waited, while various matters were negotiated for the remainder of our journey. By the riverside, near the temple, there were many willow trees, and one of our company, admiring their reflection in the water, made the poem:

A pattern of wave ripples, woven—it seems—
On a loom of green willows reflected in the stream.

They wait several days at Yamazaki for carriages to arrive from Kyoto. Kyoto is reached late at night, on the sixteenth day of the second moon.

Sixteenth day: As we reached the house and passed through the gate, everything stood out brightly under the clear moon. Things were even worse than we had heard—there was a wilderness of decay and dilapidation. The heart of the neighbor to whose care we entrusted the house has proved a wilderness, too. Seeing that his house and ours were like one, divided only by a fence, we left everything to his care with good hopes. Whenever we sent him news or instructions, we sent small presents as well. However, tonight we have no intention of showing any displeasure. Wretched though the place looks, we shall thank him for his trouble.

In a marshy spot in the garden we had excavated a pit, forming a pond, around which stood a grove of pine trees. It looks as if, in five or six years, a thousand years have left their mark here—one bank of the pond has collapsed, new trees have sprung up among the old, and such is the general air of neglect that all who look are afflicted with a sense of sadness. Old memories come flooding back, and the saddest of all are those of the child who was born in this house and who has not returned. To see others from the ship surrounded by excited, happy children, only makes our grief more difficult to bear. One who shares our inmost thoughts composed this poem:

When one, whose home is here, has not returned,
How sad to see these new young pines!

Still unconsoled, perhaps, he wrote another:

The one I knew—if only she had been an ageless pine!
What need then of these grievous farewells?

There are many things which we cannot forget, and which give us pain, but I cannot write them all down. Whatever they may be, let us say no more.

TRANSLATED BY G. W. SARGENT

POETRY FROM THE SIX COLLECTIONS

[*from the Gosenshū, 951 A.D.*]

Mizu no omo ni
Aya fukimidaru
Haru kaze ya
Ike no kōri wo
Kyō wa tokuramu

The breezes of spring
Are blowing the ripples astray
Along the water—
Today they will surely melt
The sheet of ice on the pond.

Ki no Tomonori

• •

Kore ya kono
Yuku mo kaeru mo
Wakaretsutsu
Shiru mo shiranu mo
Ausaka no seki

This is the Barrier
Where people come and people go
Exchanging farewells;
For friends and strangers alike
This is Meeting Barrier.[1]

Semimaru

TRANSLATED BY DONALD KEENE

[*from the Shūishū, 997*]

Kuraki yori
Kuraki michi ni zo
Irinubeki
Haruka ni terase
Yama no ha no tsuki

Out of the dark,
Into a dark path
I now must enter:
Shine on me from afar,
Moon of the mountain fringe![2]

Izumi Shikibu

1 The beauty of this poem is in its rhythm, created by the repetition of the word *mo* and the *k* sounds. It is the most famous of the poems about the Barrier of Ausaka (or Ōsaka), a place on the road near Kyoto where travelers to and from the east were stopped and questioned. The name contains the word *au,* "to meet," and occasioned endless *jeux d'esprit.*

2 Said to be her death-verse; the moon may refer to Buddha's teachings.

• •

Omoikane
Imo gari yukeba
Fuyu no yo no
Kawakaze samumi
Chidori naku nari

The time I went to see my sister [3]
Whom I loved unendurably,
The winter night's
River wind was so cold that
The sanderlings were crying.

Ki no Tsurayuki

• •

Yo no naka wo
Nani ni tatoemu
Asaborake
Kogiyuku fune no
Ato no shiranami

To what shall I compare
This world?
To the white wake behind
A ship that has rowed away
At dawn!

The Priest Mansei (c. 720)

TRANSLATED BY ARTHUR WALEY

• •

Wasuraruru
Mi wo ba omowazu
Chikaiteshi
Hito no inochi no
Oshiku mo aru kana

It does not matter
That I am forgotten,
But I pity
His forsworn life.

Lady Ukon

TRANSLATED BY KENNETH REXROTH

• •

Yaemugura
Shigereru yado no
Sabishiki ni
Hito koso mienu
Aki wa kinikeri

In the loneliness
Of a hut where rankly grows
The prickly goose-grass,
There is not a soul in sight:
Autumn has already come.

The Priest Egyō

[3] A word for a sweetheart commonly found in the *"Man'yōshū,"* but rather archaic by this time, when the usual word was "person," *hito*.

• •

Yume yo yume Dreams, listen, my dreams!
Koishiki hito ni Do not bring me together
Aimisu na With the man I love—
Samete no nochi wa When once I have awakened
Wabishikarikeri It makes me feel so lonely.

Anonymous

• •

Koi su chō They say I'm in love—
Wa ga na wa madaki The rumor is already
Tachinikeri In circulation;
Hito shirezu koso Yet when I began to love
Omoisomeshika There was not a soul who knew.

Mibu no Tadami

TRANSLATED BY DONALD KEENE

[*from the Goshūishū, 1086*]

Yasurawade I should not have waited.
Nenamashi mono wo It would have been better
Sayo fukete To have slept and dreamed,
Katabuku made no Than to have watched night pass,
Tsuki wo mishi kana And this slow moon sink.

Lady Akazome Emon

TRANSLATED BY KENNETH REXROTH

Sent when ill to someone

Arazaramu Soon I shall be dead.
Kono yo no hoka no As a final remembrance
Omoide ni To take from this world,
Ima hito tabi no Come to me now once again—
Au koto mo gana[4] That is what I long for most.

Izumi Shikibu

[4] The use of *o* and *a* sounds contributes to the effect of this poem.

• •

Hi mo kurenu	The day has ended
Hito mo kaerinu	And the visitors have left—
Yamazato wa	In the mountain village
Mine no arashi no	All that remains is the howl
Oto bakari shite	Of the storm winds from the peak.

Minamoto no Yorizane

• •

Yo wo komete	The night is still dark—
Tori no sorane wa	Even though you counterfeit
Hakaru to mo	The morning cockcrows,
Yo ni Ausaka no	They will never let you through
Seki wa yurusaji	Ausaka Barrier.[5]

Sei Shōnagon

TRANSLATED BY DONALD KEENE

[*from the Kinyōshū, 1128*]

Awaji shima	Guardian of the gate
Kayou chidori no	Of Suma, how many nights
Naku koe ni	Have you awakened
Iku yo nezamenu	At the crying of the shore bird
Suma no sekimori	Of the Isle of Awaji?

Minamoto no Kanemasa

TRANSLATED BY KENNETH REXROTH

• •

Murakumo ya	The clustering clouds—
Tsuki no kuma wo ba	Can it be they wipe away
Nogofuramu	The lunar shadows?
Hareyuku tabi ni	Every time they clear a bit
Terimasaru kana	The moonlight shines the brighter.

Minamoto no Toshiyori

5 Refers to a Chinese story of a man who got through a barrier by imitating a cock's crowing and thus making the keeper of the barrier think that dawn had come—when the barrier was opened.

[*from the Shikashū, c. 1151*]

Kaze wo itami
Iwa utsu nami no
Onore no mi
Kudakete mono wo
Omou koro kana

Whipped by a fierce wind
And dashed like the ocean waves
Against the rocks—
I alone am broken to bits
And now am lost in longing.

Minamoto no Shigeyuki (d. 1000)

[*from the Senzaishū, 1188*]

Mushi no ne wa
Asaji ga moto ni
Uzumorete
Aki wa sue ha no
Iro ni zo arikeru

The cries of the insects
Are buried at the roots of
The sparse pampas grass—
The end of autumn is in
The color of the last leaves.

The Priest Jakuren (d. 1202)

TRANSLATED BY DONALD KEENE

KAGERŌ NIKKI

The "Kagerō Nikki" is the journal of a noblewoman known only as "the mother of Michitsuna." Beyond what she herself tells us, almost nothing is known of her life except that she probably died in 995. Her journal covers the years 954 to 974 and deals principally with her unhappy marriage to a distant kinsman, Fujiwara Kaneie (the "Prince" in the excerpts given here), who later became civil dictator. In this selection an attempt has been made to trace the main aspects of her relations with her husband by giving excerpts from the first two of the three volumes of the journal. It should be remembered that at this period husbands and wives of the nobility lived in separate establishments.

•

The years of my youth have passed, and I can see little in them that suggests greatness. It is, I suppose, natural that I should have fallen into such mediocrity. I am less handsome than most, and my character is hardly remarkable. But as the days and nights have gone by in monotonous succession, I have had occasion to read most of the old romances, and I have found them masses of the rankest fabrication. Perhaps, I think to myself, the events of my own life, if I were to put them down in a journal, might attract attention, and indeed those who have been misled by the romancers might find in it a description of what the life of a well-placed lady is really like. But I must begin at the beginning, and I see that my memories of those first years have blurred. I shall not be surprised then if one finds traces of fiction here too. . . .

It had become clear that I was to have a child. I passed a most unpleasant spring and summer, and toward the end of the eighth moon gave birth to a boy. The Prince showed every sign of affection.

But the following month I received a shock. Toying with my writing box one morning just after he had left, I came upon a note obviously intended for another woman. My chagrin was infinite, and I felt that I must at least send something to let him know I had seen the thing. "Might this be a bill of divorcement," I wrote, "this note that I see for another?"

As the weeks went by my anxiety increased. Toward the end of the tenth moon he stayed away three nights running, and when he finally appeared he explained nonchalantly that he had hoped by ignoring me for a few days to find out what my feelings really were. But he could not stay the night: he had an appointment, he said, which could not very well be broken. I was of course suspicious, and I had him trailed. I found that he spent the night in a house off a certain narrow side street. It was so, then, I thought. My worst suspicions were confirmed.

Two or three days later I was awakened toward dawn by a pounding on the gate. It was he, I knew, but I could not bring myself to let him in, and presently he went off, no doubt to the alley that interested him so. . . .

His visits became still more infrequent. I began to feel listless and absent-minded as I had never been before, and I fell into the habit of forgetting things I had left lying around the house. "Perhaps he has given me up completely," I would say to myself; "and has he left behind nothing to remember him by?" And then, after an interval of about ten days, I got a letter asking me to send him an arrow he had left attached to the bed pillar. He had indeed left that behind—I remembered now.

I returned it with a verse: "I am aroused by this call for an arrow, even as I wonder what is to bring memories."

My house was directly on his way to and from the palace, and in the night or early in the morning I would hear him pass. He would cough to attract my attention. I wanted not to hear, but, tense and unable to sleep, I would listen through the long nights for his approach. If only I could live where I would not be subjected to this, I thought over and over. I would hear my women talking among themselves of his current indifference—"He used to be so fond of her," they would say—and my wretchedness would increase as the dawn came on. . . .

Summer came, and a child was born to his paramour. Loading the lady into his carriage and raising a commotion that could be heard through the whole city, he came hurrying past my gate—in the worst of taste, I thought. And why, my women loudly asked one another, had he so pointedly passed our gate when he had all the streets in the city to choose from? I myself was quite speechless, and thought only that I should like to die on the spot. I knew that I would be capable of nothing as drastic as suicide, but I resolved not to see him again.

Three or four days later I had a most astonishing letter: "I have not been able to see you because we have been having rather a bad time of it here. Yesterday the child was born, however, and everything seems to have gone off well. I know that you will not want to see me until the defilement has worn off."

I dismissed the messenger without a reply. The child, I heard, was a boy, and that of course made things worse.

He came calling three or four days later, quite as though nothing unusual had happened. I did my best to make him uncomfortable, and shortly he left. . . .

It began to appear that the lady in the alley had fallen from favor since the birth of her child. I had prayed, at the height of my unhappiness, that she would live to know what I was then suffering, and it seemed that my prayers were being answered. She was alone, and now her child was dead, the child that had been the cause of that unseemly racket. The lady was of frightfully bad birth—the unrecognized child of a rather odd prince, it was said. For a moment she was able to use a noble gentleman who was unaware of her shortcomings, and now she was abandoned. The pain must be even sharper than mine had been. I was satisfied. . . .

It had become painful even to get his rare letters, little flashes into the past, and I was sure, moreover, that there would be more insults like the recent one as long as he could pass my gate. I determined therefore to go away, as I had planned earlier, to that temple in the western mountains, and to do so before he emerged from his penance.

The mountain road was crowded with associations. We had traveled it together a number of times, and then there had been that time, just at this season, when he had played truant from court and we had spent several days together in this same temple. I had only three attendants with me this time.

I hurried up to the main hall. It was warm, and I left the door open and looked out. The hall was situated on an eminence in a sort of mountain basin. It was heavily wooded and the view was most effective, although it was already growing dark and there was no moon. The priests made preparations for the early watch, and I began my prayers, still with the door open.

Just as the conch shells blew ten there was a clamor at the main gate. I knew that the Prince had arrived. I quickly lowered the blinds, and, looking out, saw two or three torches among the trees.

"I have come to take your mother back," he said to the boy, who went down to meet him. "I have suffered a defilement, though, and cannot get out. Where shall we have them pick her up?"

The boy told me what he had said, and I was quite at a loss to know how to handle such madness. "What can you be thinking of," I sent back, "to come off on such a weird expedition? Really, I intend to stay here only the night. And it would not be wise for you to defile the temple. Please go back immediately—it must be getting late."

Those were the first of a great number of messages the boy had to deliver that night, up and down a flight of stairs that must have been more than a hundred yards long. My attendants, sentimental things, found him most pathetic.

Finally the boy came up in tears: "He says it is all my fault—that I am a poor one not to make a better case for him. He is really in a rage." But I was firm— I could not possibly go down yet, I said.

"All right, all right," the Prince stormed. "I can't stay here all night. There is no help for it—hitch the oxen."

I was greatly relieved. But the boy said that he would like to go back to the city with his father, and that he would probably not come again. He went off weeping. I was quite desolate: how could he, whom of all in the world I had come most to rely on, leave me like this? But I said nothing, and presently, after everyone had left, he came back alone.

He was choked with tears. "He says I am to stay until I am sent for."

I felt extremely sorry for the boy, but I tried to distract him by ridiculing his weakness. Surely he did not think his father would abandon him, too, I said. . . .

I spent the days in the usual observances and the nights praying before the main Buddha. Since the place was surrounded by hills and there seemed no danger of my being seen, I kept the blinds up; but once, so great still was my lack of self-possession, I hastily started to lower them when an unseasonal thrush burst into song in a dead tree nearby.

Then the expected defilement approached, and I knew I should have to leave. But in the city a rumor had spread that I had become a nun, and I felt sure I could not be comfortable there. I decided therefore to withdraw to a house some distance below the temple. My aunt visited me there, but she found it a strange and unsettling place.

Five or six days after my removal came the night of the full moon. The scene was a lovely one. The moon flooded through the trees, while over in the shadow of the mountain great swarms of fireflies wheeled about. An uninhibited cuckoo made me think ironically of how once, long ago and back in the city, I had waited with some annoyance for a cuckoo that refused to repeat his call. And then suddenly, so near at hand that it seemed almost to be knocking on the door, came the drumming of a moor hen. All in all it was a spot that stirred in one the deepest emotions.

There was no word from the Prince. But I had come here by my own choice, and I was content.

In the evenings came the booming of the great sunset bells and the hum of the cicadas, and the choruses of small bells from the temples in the hills around us, chiming in one after another as though afraid to be left out, and the chanting of Sutras from the shrine on the hill in front of us.

Five days or so later the defilement passed and I returned to the temple. . . .

Then, after a time, I got several letters from the city. They all said the same thing: it appeared that the Prince was starting out to see me again, and that if I did not go back with him this time public opinion would label my behavior completely outrageous; that this was surely the last time he would come after me, and that if, after he had thus done everything possible to move me, I should come weakly back to the city by myself, I would be publicly laughed at.

My father had just that day come back from the provinces, and he hurried up to see me. "I had thought it would not be unwise for you to go away for a little while by yourself," he said, "but now that I see how the boy has wasted away I think it would be best for you to return. I can take you back today or tomorrow, whichever would be better. I shall come for you whenever you say."

It was clear that he was ordering me home. I felt quite drained of strength.

"Well, tomorrow then," he said, and started for the city.

My mind jumped about like the fisherman's bob in the poem—what could I do? And then came the usual shouting, and I knew the Prince had arrived. This time there was no hesitation. He marched straight in. I pulled up a screen to hide behind, but it was no use.

"Terrible," he exclaimed, as he watched me burning incense and fingering my beads, the Sutras spread out in front of me. "Worse even than I had expected. You really do seem to have run to an extreme. I thought you might be ready to leave by this time, but I now suspect that it would be a sin and a crime to take you back." And, turning to my son, "How about it? Do you feel like staying on?"

"I don't like the idea at all," the boy answered, his eyes on the floor, "but what can we do?"

"Well, I leave it to you. If you think she should go back, have the carriage brought up."

And almost before he had finished speaking, the boy began dashing about, picking things up, poking them into bags, loading the carts, tearing the curtains down and rolling them into bundles. I was taken quite by surprise, and could only watch helplessly. The Prince was most pleased with himself. Now and then he would exchange an amused wink with the boy.

"Well, we have everything cleaned up," he finally said. "There is not much for you to do but come with us. Tell your Buddha politely that you are leaving—that is the thing to do, I hear." He seemed to think it all a great joke.

I was too numb to answer, but somehow I managed to keep the tears back, and still I held out. The carriage was brought up at about four, and at dark, when I still showed no sign of getting in, the Prince turned to my son in great annoyance.

"All right, all right, I am going back," he exclaimed. "I leave everything to you."

The boy, almost in tears, took my hand and pleaded with me to get in, and finally, since nothing else seemed possible, I allowed myself to be taken away, quite in a daze. Outside the main gate we divided up for the trip back, and the Prince got in with me. He was in a fine humor, but I was unable to appreciate his witty remarks. My sister was riding with us, however—she felt it would be all right since it was already dark [1]—and now and then she took up the conversation.

We reached the city at about ten in the evening. My people had of course known of his trip and my probable return, and had cleaned the place thoroughly and left the gates open for us. Barely conscious, I lay down behind a curtain. Immediately one of my women came bustling up. "I thought of gathering seeds from the pinks," she said, "but the plants died. And then one of your bamboos fell over, but I had it put back up again." I thought it would be better to discuss these problems some other time, and did not answer. . . .

The New Year lists were published on the twenty-fifth, and the Prince, I heard, was made a senior councilor. I knew that his promotion probably would keep him from me more than ever, and when people came around to congratulate me it was as if they were joking.

[1] It was improper for women to reveal their faces to men other than their husbands.

My son, however, appeared more delighted than he could say.

The following day the Prince sent a note: "Does this happy event mean nothing to you? Is that why you have sent no congratulations?" And toward the end of the month, "Has something happened to you? We have been very busy here, but it is not kind of you to ignore me." And thus my silence had the effect of making him the petitioner, a position that had to then been exclusively mine. "It is sad that your duties keep you so busy," I answered. I was sure that he had no intention of visiting me.

The days went by, and it became clear that I was right. But I had finally learned not to let his silence bother me. I slept very well at night.

Then one evening after I had gone to bed I was startled by a most unusual pounding outside. Someone opened the gate. I waited rather nervously, and presently the Prince was at the end door demanding to be let in. My people, all in night dress, scurried about for shelter. I was no better dressed than they, but I crawled to the door and let him in.

"You so seldom come any more even to pass the time of day," I said, "that the door seems to have gotten a little stiff."

"It is because you are always locking me out that I do not come," he retorted pleasantly. And how would one answer that? . . .

My house was meanwhile going to ruin. My father suggested that it would be best to let it out, since my retinue was a small one, and move into his place on the Nakagawa. I had spoken to the Prince many times of the possibility that I might move, but now that the time approached I felt I should let him know I was finally leaving. I sent to tell him that I wanted to talk to him, but he replied coldly that he was in retreat. "If that is how he feels," I said to myself. I went ahead with the move.

The new place fronted on the river, near the mountains. I found it rather satisfying to think that I was there by my own choice.

The Prince apparently did not hear for two or three days that I had moved. Then, on the twenty-fifth or twenty-sixth, I had a letter complaining that I had not informed him.

"I did think of telling you," I answered, "but this is such a poor place that I assumed you would not want to visit it. I had hoped to see you once more where we used to meet."

I spoke as though I considered our separation final, and he seemed to agree. "You are perhaps right. It might not be easy for me to visit you there." And I heard no more for some weeks.

The ninth moon came. Looking out early one morning after the shutters were raised, I saw that a mist had come in over the garden from the river, so that only the summits of the mountains to the east were visible. Somehow it seemed to shut me in from the world, alone. . . .

The New Year came, and on the fifteenth the boy's men lit ceremonial fires to chase out the devils. They made rather a party of it, well on into the night. "Quiet down a bit," someone shouted, and I went to the edge of the room for a look. The moon was bright, and the mountains to the east shone dim and icy through the mist. Leaning quietly against a pillar, I thought about myself and my loneliness, how I should like to go off to a mountain temple somewhere if only I could, and how I had not seen him for five months, not since the end of the summer. I could not keep back my tears. "I would join my song with the song thrush," I whispered to myself, "but the thrush has forgotten the New Year."

TRANSLATED BY EDWARD SEIDENSTICKER

YŪGAO

[from Genji Monogatari] *by Murasaki Shikibu*

"The Tale of Genji," probably written during the first decade of the eleventh century, is the great masterpiece of Japanese literature. It is a novel of complexity and magnitude, which deals mainly with the loves of Prince Genji, the son of an emperor by a consort of inferior rank. The episode of Yūgao, given here, occurs early in the book, when Genji is seventeen. Shortly before, he and some other young nobles had been classifying women according to their qualities, and had decided that the "lowest class" was quite unworthy of consideration. But it is in Yūgao, a woman of that class, that Genji finds his first great love, and her memory returns frequently to haunt him even when he has won women of far greater attractions.

The translation by Arthur Waley is a marvelous re-creation of the original, capturing its beauty and its unique evocative power.

•

It was at the time when he was secretly visiting the lady of the Sixth Ward.[1] One day on his way back from the palace he thought that he would call upon his foster mother who, having for a long while been very ill, had become a nun. She lived in the Fifth Ward. After many inquiries he managed to find the house; but the front gate was locked and he could not drive in. He sent one of his servants for Koremitsu, his foster nurse's son, and while he was waiting began to examine the rather wretched-looking by-street. The house next door was fenced with a new paling, above which at one place were four or five panels of open trelliswork, screened by blinds which were very white and bare. Through chinks in these blinds a

[1] Lady Rokujō. Who she was gradually becomes apparent in the course of the story.

number of foreheads could be seen. They seemed to belong to a group of ladies who must be peeping with interest into the street below.

At first he thought they had merely peeped out as they passed; but he soon realized that if they were standing on the floor they must be giants. No, evidently they had taken the trouble to climb onto some table or bed; which was surely rather odd!

He had come in a plain coach with no outriders. No one could possibly guess who he was, and feeling quite at his ease he leant forward and deliberately examined the house. The gate, also made of a kind of trelliswork, stood ajar, and he could see enough of the interior to realize that it was a very humble and poorly furnished dwelling. For a moment he pitied those who lived in such a place, but then he remembered the song "Seek not in the wide world to find a home; but where you chance to rest, call that your house"; and again, "Monarchs may keep their palaces of jade, for in a leafy cottage two can sleep."

There was a wattled fence over which some ivy-like creeper spread its cool green leaves, and among the leaves were white flowers with petals half-unfolded like the lips of people smiling at their own thoughts. "They are called *Yūgao,* 'evening faces,'" one of his servants told him; "how strange to find so lovely a crowd clustering on this deserted wall!" And indeed it was a most strange and delightful thing to see how on the narrow tenement in a poor quarter of the town they had clambered over rickety eaves and gables and spread wherever there was room for them to grow. He sent one of his servants to pick some. The man entered at the half-opened door, and had begun to pluck the flowers, when a little girl in a long yellow tunic came through a quite genteel sliding door, and holding out toward Genji's servant a white fan heavily perfumed with incense, she said to him, "Would you like something to put them on? I am afraid you have chosen a wretched-looking bunch," and she handed him the fan. Just as he was opening the gate on his way back, the old nurse's son Koremitsu came out of the other house full of apologies for having kept Genji waiting so long—"I could not find the key of the gate," he said. "Fortunately the people of this humble quarter were not likely to recognize you and press or stare; but I am afraid you must have been very much bored waiting in this hugger-mugger back street," and he conducted Genji into the house. Koremitsu's brother, the deacon, his brother-in-law Mikawa no Kami and his sister all assembled to greet the Prince, delighted by a visit with which they had not thought he was ever likely to honour them again.

The nun too rose from her couch: "For a long time I had been waiting to give up the world, but one thing held me back: I wanted you to see your old nurse just once again as you used to know her. You never came to see me, and at last I gave up waiting and took my vows. Now, in reward for the penances which my Order enjoins, I have got back a little of my health, and having seen my dear young master again, I can wait with a quiet mind for the Lord Amida's Light," and in her weakness she shed a few tears.

"I heard some days ago," said Genji, "that you were very dangerously ill, and was in great anxiety. It is sad now to find you in this penitential garb. You must live longer yet, and see me rise in the world, that you may be born again high in the ninth sphere of Amida's Paradise. For they say that those who died with longings unfulfilled are burdened with an evil karma in their life to come."

People such as old nurses regard even the most blackguardly and ill-favored foster children as prodigies of beauty and virtue. Small wonder then if Genji's nurse, who had played so great a part in his early life, always regarded her office as immensely honorable and important, and tears of pride came into her eyes while he spoke to her.

The old lady's children thought it very improper that their mother, having taken holy orders, should show so lively an interest in a human career. Certain that Genji himself would be very much shocked, they exchanged uneasy glances. He was on the contrary deeply touched. "When I was a child," he said, "those who were dearest to me were early taken away, and although there were many who gave a hand to my upbringing, it was to you only, dear nurse, that I was deeply and tenderly attached. When I grew up I could not any longer be often in your company. I have not even been able to come here and see you as often as I wanted to. But in all the long time which has passed since I was last here, I have thought a great deal about you and wished that life did not force so many bitter partings upon us."

So he spoke tenderly. The princely scent of the sleeve which he had raised to brush away his tears filled the low and narrow room, and even the young people, who had till now been irritated by their mother's obvious pride at having been the nurse of so splendid a prince, found themselves in tears.

Having arranged for continual masses to be said on the sick woman's behalf, he took his leave, ordering Koremitsu to light him with a candle. As they left the house he looked at the fan upon which the white flowers had been laid. He now saw that there was writing on it, a poem carelessly but elegantly scribbled: "The flower that puzzled you was but the *yūgao,* strange beyond knowing in its dress of shining dew." It was written with a deliberate negligence which seemed to aim at concealing the writer's status and identity. But for all that the hand showed a breeding and distinction which agreeably surprised him. "Who lives in the house on the left?" he asked. Koremitsu, who did not at all want to act as a go-between, replied that he had only been at his mother's for five or six days and had been so much occupied by her illness that he had not asked any questions about the neighbors. "I want to know for a quite harmless reason," said Genji. "There is something about this fan which raises a rather important point. I positively must settle it. You would oblige me by making inquiries from someone who knows the neighborhood." Koremitsu went at once to the house next door and sent for the steward. "This house," the man said, "belongs to a certain Titular Prefect. He is living in the country, but my lady is still here; and as she is young and loves company, her brothers who are in service at the court often come here to visit her." "And that is about all one can expect a servant to know," said Koremitsu when he repeated this information. It occurred at once to Genji that it was one of these courtiers who had written the poem. Yes, there was certainly a self-confident air in the writing. It was by someone whose rank entitled him to have a good opinion of himself. But he was romantically disposed; it was too painful to dismiss altogether the idea that, after all, the verses might really have been meant for him, and on a folded paper he wrote: "Could I but get a closer view, no longer would they puzzle me—the flowers that all too dimly in the gathering dusk I saw." This he wrote in a disguised hand and gave to his servant. The man reflected that though the senders of the fan had never seen Genji before, yet so well known were his features, that even the glimpse they had got from the window might easily have revealed to them his identity. He could imagine the excitement with which the fan had been dispatched and the disappointment when for so long a time no answer came. His somewhat rudely belated arrival would seem to them to have been purposely contrived. They would all be agog to know what was in the reply, and he felt very nervous as he approached the house.

Meanwhile, lighted only by a dim torch, Genji quietly left his nurse's home. The blinds of the other house were now drawn and only the firefly glimmer of a candle shone through the gap between them.

When he reached his destination [2] a very different scene met his eyes. A handsome park, a well-kept garden; how spacious and comfortable it all was! And soon the magnificent owner of these splendors had driven from his head all thought of the wooden paling, the shutters and the flowers.

He stayed longer than he intended, and the sun was already up when he set out for home. Again he passed the house with the shutters. He had driven through the quarter countless times without taking the slightest interest in it; but that one small episode of the fan had suddenly made his daily passage through these streets an event of great importance. He looked about him eagerly, and would have liked to know who lived in all the houses.

For several days Koremitsu did not present himself at Genji's palace. When at last he came, he explained that his mother was growing much weaker and it was very difficult for him to get away. Then drawing nearer, he said in a low voice, "I made some further inquiries, but could not find out much. It seems that someone came

[2] Lady Rokujō's house.

very secretly in June and has been living there ever since; but who she really is not even her own servants know. I have once or twice peeped through a hole in the hedge and caught a glimpse of some young women; but their skirts were rolled back and tucked in at their belts, so I think they must have been waiting maids. Yesterday some while after sunset I saw a lady writing a letter. Her face was calm, but she looked very unhappy, and I noticed that some of her women were secretly weeping." Genji was more curious than ever.

Though his master was of a rank which brought with it great responsibilities, Koremitsu knew that in view of his youth and popularity the young prince would be thought to be positively neglecting his duty if he did not indulge in a few escapades, and that everyone would regard his conduct as perfectly natural and proper even when it was such as they would not have dreamed of permitting to ordinary people.

"Hoping to get a little further information," he said, "I found an excuse for communicating with her, and received in reply a very well-worded answer in a cultivated hand. She must be a girl of quite good position." "You must find out more," said Genji; "I shall not be happy till I know all about her."

Here perhaps was just such a case as they had imagined on that rainy night: a lady whose outward circumstances seemed to place her in that "lowest class" which they had agreed to dismiss as of no interest; but who in her own person showed qualities by no means despicable. . . .

It was autumn. Genji had brought so many complications into his life that he had for some while been very irregular in his visits to the Great Hall, and was in great disgrace there. The lady [3] in the grand mansion was very difficult to get on with; but he had surmounted so many obstacles in his courtship of her that to give her up the moment he had won her seemed absurd. Yet he could not deny that the blind intoxicating passion which possessed him while she was still unattainable, had almost disappeared. To begin with, she was far too

[3] Rokujō.

sensitive; then there was the disparity of their ages,[4] and the constant dread of discovery which haunted him during those painful partings at small hours of the morning. In fact, there were too many disadvantages.

It was a morning when mist lay heavy over the garden. After being many times roused Genji at last came out of Rokujō's room, looking very cross and sleepy. One of the maids lifted part of the folding-shutter, seeming to invite her mistress to watch the Prince's departure. Rokujō pulled aside the bed-curtains and tossing her hair back over her shoulders looked out into the garden. So many lovely flowers were growing in the borders that Genji halted for a while to enjoy them. How beautiful he looked standing there, she thought. As he was nearing the portico the maid who had opened the shutters came and walked by his side. She wore a light green skirt exquisitely matched to the season and place; it was so hung as to show to great advantage the grace and suppleness of her stride. Genji looked round at her. "Let us sit down for a minute on the railing here in the corner," he said. "She seems very shy," he thought, "but how charmingly her hair falls about her shoulders," and he recited the poem: "Though I would not be thought to wander heedlessly from flower to flower, yet this morning's pale convolvulus I fain would pluck!" As he said the lines he took her hand and she answered with practiced ease: "You hasten, I observe, to admire the morning flowers while the mist still lies about them," thus parrying the compliment by a verse which might be understood either in a personal or general sense. At this moment a very elegant page wearing the most bewitching baggy trousers came among the flowers brushing the dew as he walked, and began to pick a bunch of the convolvuli. Genji longed to paint the scene.

No one could see him without pleasure. He was like the flowering tree under whose shade even the rude mountain peasant delights to rest. And so great was the fascination he exercised that those who knew him longed to offer him whatever was dearest to them. One who had a favorite daughter would ask for nothing better than to make her Genji's handmaiden. Another who had an exquisite sister

[4] Genji was now seventeen; Rokujō twenty-four.

was ready for her to serve in his household, though it were at the most menial tasks. Still less could these ladies who on such occasions as this were privileged to converse with him and stare at him as much as they pleased, and were moreover young people of much sensibility—how could they fail to delight in his company and note with much uneasiness that his visits were becoming far less frequent than before?

But where have I got to? Ah, yes. Koremitsu had patiently continued the inquiry with which Genji entrusted him. "Who the mistress is," he said, "I have not been able to discover; and for the most part she is at great pains not to show herself. But more than once in the general confusion, when there was the sound of a carriage coming along past that great row of tenement houses, and all the maidservants were peering out into the road, the young lady whom I suppose to be the mistress of the house slipped out along with them. I could not see her clearly, but she seemed to be very pretty.

"One day, seeing a carriage with outriders coming toward the house, one of the maids rushed off calling out 'Ukon, Ukon, come quickly and look. The Captain's carriage is coming this way.' At once a pleasant-faced lady no longer young, came bustling out. 'Quietly, quietly,' she said holding up a warning finger; 'how do you know it is the Captain? I shall have to go and look,' and she slipped out. A sort of rough drawbridge leads from the garden into the lane. In her excitement the good lady caught her skirt in it and falling flat on her face almost tumbled into the ditch: 'A bad piece of work His Holiness of Katsuragi [5] made here!' she grumbled; but her curiosity did not seem to be at all damped and she stared harder than ever at the approaching carriage. The visitor was dressed in a plain, wide cloak. He had attendants with him, whose names the excited servant girls called out as one after another they came near enough to be recognized; and the odd thing is that the names were certainly those of Tō no Chūjō's [6] grooms and pages."

"I must see that carriage for myself," said Genji. What if this

[5] The god of bridges. He built in a single night the stone causeway which joins Mount Katsuragi and Mount Kombu.

[6] Genji's brother-in-law.

should be the very lady whom Chūjō, at the time of that rainy night's conversation, despaired of rediscovering? Koremitsu, noting that Genji was listening with particular attention, continued: "I must tell you that I too have reason to be interested in this house, and while making inquiries on my own account I discovered that the young lady always addresses the other girls in the house as though they were her equals. But when, pretending to be taken in by this comedy, I began visiting there, I noticed that though the older ladies played their part very well, the young girls would every now and then curtsey or slip in a 'My Lady' without thinking; whereupon the others would hasten to cover up the mistake as best they might, saying anything they could think of to make it appear that there was no mistress among them," and Koremitsu laughed as he recollected it.

"Next time I come to visit your mother," said Genji, "you must let me have a chance of peeping at them." He pictured to himself the queer, tumbled-down house. She was only living there for the time being; but all the same she must surely belong to that "bottom class" which they had dismissed as having no possible bearing on the discussion. How amusing it would be to show that they were wrong and that after all something of interest might be discovered in such a place!

Koremitsu, anxious to carry out his master's every wish and intent also on his own intrigue, contrived at last by a series of ingenious stratagems to effect a secret meeting between Genji and the mysterious lady. The details of the plan by which he brought this about would make a tedious story, and as is my rule in such cases I have thought it better to omit them.

Genji never asked her by what name he was to call her, nor did he reveal his own identity. He came very poorly dressed and—what was most unusual for him—on foot. But Koremitsu regarded this as too great a tribute to so unimportant a lady, and insisted upon Genji riding his horse, while he walked by his side. In doing so he sacrificed his own feelings; for he too had reasons for wishing to create a good impression in the house, and he knew that by arriving in this rather undignified way he would sink in the estimation of the inhabitants. Fortunately his discomfiture was almost unwitnessed, for Genji took with him only the one attendant who had on the first occasion plucked the flowers—a boy whom no one was likely to recognize; and lest suspicions should be aroused, he did not even take advantage of his presence in the neighborhood to call at his foster nurse's house.

The lady was very much mystified by all these precautions and made great efforts to discover something more about him. She even sent someone after him to see where he went to when he left her at daybreak; but he succeeded in throwing his pursuer off the scent and she was no wiser than before. He was now growing far too fond of her. He was miserable if anything interfered with his visits; and though he utterly disapproved of his own conduct and worried a great deal about it, he soon found that he was spending most of his time at her house.

He knew that at some time or another in their lives even the soberest people lose their heads in this way; but hitherto he had never really lost his, or done anything which could possibly have been considered very wrong. Now to his astonishment and dismay he discovered that even the few morning hours during which he was separated from her were becoming unendurable. "What is it in her that makes me behave like a madman?" he kept on asking himself. She was astonishingly gentle and unassuming, to the point even of seeming rather apathetic, rather deficient perhaps in depth of character and emotion; and though she had a certain air of girlish inexperience, it was clear that he was not by any means her first lover; and certainly she was rather plebeian. What was it exactly that so fascinated him? He asked himself the question again and again, but found no answer.

She for her part was very uneasy to see him come to her thus in shabby old hunting clothes, trying always to hide his face, leaving while it was still dark and everyone was asleep. He seemed like some demon-lover in an old ghost tale, and she was half-afraid. But his smallest gesture showed that he was someone out of the ordinary, and she began to suspect that he was a person of high rank, who had used Koremitsu as his go-between. But Koremitsu obstinately pretended to know nothing at all about his companion, and continued to amuse himself by frequenting the house on his own account.

What could it mean? She was dismayed at this strange love-making with—she knew not whom. But about her too there was something fugitive, insubstantial. Genji was obsessed by the idea that, just as she had hidden herself in this place, so one day she would once more vanish and hide, and he would never be able to find her again. There was every sign that her residence here was quite temporary. He was sure that when the time came to move she would not tell him where she was going. Of course her running away would be proof that she was not worth bothering about any more, and he ought, thankful for the pleasure they had had together, simply to leave the matter at that. But he knew that this was the last thing he would be likely to do.

People were already beginning to be suspicious, and often for several nights running he was unable to visit her. This became so intolerable that in his impatience he determined to bring her secretly to the Nijō-in.[7] There would be an appalling outcry if she were discovered; but that must be risked.

"I am going to take you somewhere very nice where no one will disturb us," he said at last. "No, no," she cried; "your ways are so strange, I should be frightened to go with you." She spoke in a tone of childish terror, and Genji answered smiling: "One or the other of us must be a fox-in-disguise.[8] Here is a chance to find out which it is!" He spoke very kindly, and suddenly, in a tone of absolute submission, she consented to do whatever he thought best. He could not but be touched at her willingness to follow him in what must appear to her to be the most hazardous and bizarre adventure. Again he thought of Tō no Chūjō's story on that rainy night, and could not doubt that this must indeed be Chūjō's fugitive lady. But he saw that she had some reason for wishing to avoid all questions about her past, and he restrained his curiosity. So far as he could see she showed no signs of running away; nor did he believe that she would

[7] His own palace.

[8] Foxes, dressed up as men, were believed to be in the habit of seducing and bewitching human beings.

do so as long as he was faithful. Tō no Chūjō, after all, had for months on end left her to her own devices. But he felt that if for an instant she suspected him of the slightest leaning in any other direction it would be a bad business.

It was the fifteenth night of the eighth month. The light of an unclouded full moon shone between the ill-fitting planks of the roof and flooded the room. What a queer place to be lying in! thought Genji, as he gazed round the garret, so different from any room he had ever known before. It must be almost day. In the neighboring houses people were beginning to stir, and there was an uncouth sound of peasant voices: "Eh! how cold it is! I can't believe we shall do much with the crops this year." "I don't know what's going to happen about my carrying trade," said another; "things look very bad." Then (banging on the wall of another house), "Wake up, neighbor. Time to start. Did he hear, d'you think?" and they rose and went off each to the wretched task by which he earned his bread.

All this clatter and bustle going on so near her made the lady very uncomfortable, and indeed so dainty and fastidious a person must often in this miserable lodging have suffered things which would make her long to sink through the floor. But however painful, disagreeable, or provoking were the things that happened, she gave no sign of noticing them. That, being herself so shrinking and delicate in her ways, she could yet endure without a murmur the exasperating banging and bumping that was going on in every direction, aroused his admiration, and he felt that this was much nicer of her than if she had shuddered with horror at each sound. But now, louder than thunder, came the noise of the threshing mills, seeming so near that they could hardly believe it did not come from out of the pillow itself. Genji thought that his ears would burst. What many of the noises were he could not at all make out; but they were very peculiar and startling. The whole air seemed to be full of crashings and bangings. Now from one side, now from another, came too the faint thud of the bleacher's mallet, and the scream of wild geese passing overhead. It was all too distracting.

Their room was in the front of the house. Genji got up and

opened the long, sliding shutters. They stood together looking out. In the courtyard near them was a clump of fine Chinese bamboos; dew lay thick on the borders, glittering here no less brightly than in the great gardens to which Genji was better accustomed. There was a confused buzzing of insects. Crickets were chirping in the wall. He had often listened to them, but always at a distance; now, singing so close to him, they made a music which was unfamiliar and indeed seemed far lovelier than that with which he was acquainted. But then, everything in this place where one thing was so much to his liking seemed despite all drawbacks to take on a new tinge of interest and beauty. She was wearing a white bodice with a soft, gray cloak over it. It was a poor dress, but she looked charming and almost distinguished; even so, there was nothing very striking in her appearance—only a certain fragile grace and elegance. It was when she was speaking that she looked really beautiful, there was such pathos, such earnestness in her manner. If only she had a little more spirit! But even as she was he found her irresistible and longed to take her to some place where no one could disturb them: "I am going to take you somewhere not at all far away where we shall be able to pass the rest of the night in peace. We cannot go on like this, parting always at break of day." "Why have you suddenly come to that conclusion?" she asked, but she spoke submissively. He vowed to her that she should be his love in this and in all future lives and she answered so passionately that she seemed utterly transformed from the listless creature he had known, and it was hard to believe that such vows were no novelty to her.

Discarding all prudence he sent for the maid Ukon and bade her order his servants to fetch a coach. The affair was soon known to all the household, and the ladies were at first somewhat uneasy at seeing their mistress carried off in this fashion; but on the whole they did not think he looked the sort of person who would do her any harm. It was now almost daylight. The cocks had stopped crowing. The voice of an old man (a pilgrim preparing for the ascent of the Holy Mountain) sounded somewhere not far away; and, as at each prayer he bent forward to touch the ground with his head, they could hear with what pain and difficulty he moved.

What could he be asking for in his prayers, this old man whose life seemed fragile as the morning dew? *"Namu tōrai no Dōshi,"* "Glory be to the Saviour that shall come": now they could hear the words. "Listen," said Genji tenderly, "is not that an omen that our love shall last through many lives to come?" And he recited the poem: "Do not prove false this omen of the pilgrim's chant: that even in lives to come our love shall last unchanged."

Then, unlike the lovers in the "Everlasting Wrong" who prayed that they might be as the "twin birds that share a wing" (for they remembered that this story had ended very sadly), they prayed, "May our love last till Maitreya comes as a Buddha into the World." But she, still distrustful, answered his poem with the verse: "Such sorrow have I known in this world that I have small hope of worlds to come." Her versification was still a little tentative.[9]

She was thinking with pleasure that the setting moon would light them on their way, and Genji was just saying so when suddenly the moon disappeared behind a bank of clouds. But there was still great beauty in the dawning sky. Anxious to be gone before it was quite light, he hurried her away to the coach and put Ukon by her side.

They drove to an untenanted mansion which was not far off. While he waited for the steward to come out Genji noticed that the gates were crumbling away; dense shinobu-grass grew around them. So somber an entrance he had never seen. There was a thick mist and the dew was so heavy that when he raised the carriage blind his sleeve was drenched. "Never yet has such an adventure as this befallen me," said Genji; "so I am, as you may imagine, rather excited," and he made a poem in which he said that though love's folly had existed since the beginning of the world, never could man have set out more rashly at the break of day into a land unknown. "But to you this is no great novelty?" She blushed and in her turn made a poem: "I am as the moon that walks the sky not knowing what menace the cruel hills may hold in store; high though she sweeps, her light may suddenly be blotted out."

She seemed very depressed and nervous. But this he attributed to

[9] We gather later that she was only nineteen.

the fact that she had probably always lived in small houses where everything was huddled together, and he was amused at the idea that this large mansion should overawe her. They drove in, and while a room was being got ready, they remained in the carriage which had been drawn up alongside of the balustrade. Ukon, looking very innocent all the while, was inwardly comparing this excursion with her mistress's previous adventures. She had noticed the tone of extreme deference with which this latest lover had been received by the steward, and had begun to draw her own conclusions.

The mist was gradually clearing away. They left the coach and went into the room which had been prepared for them. Though so quickly improvised, their quarters were admirably clean and well-provided, for the steward's son had previously been a trusted house servant of Genji's and had also worked at the Great Hall. Coming now to their room he offered to send for some of Genji's gentlemen, "For," he said, "I cannot bear to see you going unattended." "Do nothing of the kind," said Genji; "I have come here because I do not wish to be disturbed. No one but yourself is to know that I have used this house," and he exacted a promise of absolute secrecy. No regular meal had been prepared, but the steward brought them a little rice porridge. Then they lay down again to sleep together for the first time in this unfamiliar and so strangely different place.

The sun was high when they woke. Genji went and opened the shutters himself. How deserted the garden looked! Certainly here there was no one to spy upon them. He looked out into the distance: dense woods fast turning to jungle. And nearer the house not a flower or bush, but only unkept, autumn grasslands, and a pond choked with weeds. It was a wild and desolate place. It seemed that the steward and his men must live in some outbuilding or lodge at a distance from the house; for here there was no sign or sound of life. "It is, I must own, a strange and forsaken place to which we have come. But no ghost or evil fairy will dare molest you while *I* am here."

It pained her very much that he still was masked; [10] and indeed

[10] I.e. covered part of his face with a scarf or the like, a practice usual with illicit lovers in medieval Japan.

such a precaution was quite out of keeping with the stage at which they had now arrived. So at last, reciting a poem in which he reminded her that all their love down to this moment when "the flower opened its petals to the evening dew" had come from a chance vision seen casually from the street, half-turning his face away, for a moment he let her see him unmasked. "What of the 'shining dew?'" he asked, using the words that she had written on the fan. "How little knew I of its beauty who had but in the twilight doubted and guessed . . ."—so she answered his poem in a low and halting voice. She need not have feared, for to him, poor as the verses were, they seemed delightful. And indeed the beauty of his uncovered face, suddenly revealed to her in this black wilderness of dereliction and decay, surpassed all loveliness that she had ever dreamed of or imagined. "I cannot wonder that while I still set this barrier between us, you did not choose to tell me all that I longed to know. But now it would be very unkind of you not to tell me your name." "I am like the fisherman's daughter in the song,"[11] she said, "'I have no name or home.'" But for all that she would not tell him who she was, she seemed much comforted that he had let her see him. "Do as you please about it," said Genji at last; but for a while he was out of temper. Soon they had made it up again; and so the day passed. Presently Koremitsu came to their quarters, bringing fruit and other viands. He would not come in, for he was frightened that Ukon would rate him mercilessly for the part he had played in arranging the abduction of her mistress. He had now come to the conclusion that the lady must possess charms which he had wholly overlooked, or Genji would certainly never have taken all this trouble about her, and he was touched at his own magnanimity in surrendering to his master a prize which he might well have kept for himself. It was an evening of marvelous stillness. Genji sat watching the sky. The lady found the inner room where she was sitting depressingly dark and gloomy. He raised the blinds of the front room, and came to sit with her. They watched the light of the sunset glowing in each other's eyes, and in her wonder at his adorable beauty and tenderness she forgot all her fears. At last she

11 *"Shinkokinshū."*

was shy with him no longer, and he thought that the new-found boldness and merriment became her very well. She lay by his side till night. He saw that she was again wearing the plaintive expression of a frightened child; so quickly closing the partition-door he brought in the great lamp, saying: "Outwardly you are no longer shy with me; but I can see that deep down in your heart there is still some sediment of rancor and distrust. It is not kind to use me so," and again he was cross with her.

What were the people at the palace thinking? Would he have been sent for? How far would the messengers pursue their search? He became quite agitated. Then there was the great lady in the Sixth Ward.[12] What a frenzy she must be in! This time, however, she really had good cause to be jealous. These and other unpleasant considerations were crowding into his head, when looking at the girl who lay beside him so trustfully, unconscious of all that was going on in his mind, he was suddenly filled with an overwhelming tenderness toward her. How tiresome the other was, with her eternal susceptibilities, jealousies, and suspicions! For a while at any rate he would stop seeing her. As the night wore on they began sometimes to doze. Suddenly Genji saw standing over him the figure of a woman, tall and majestic: "You who think yourself so fine, how comes it that you have brought to toy with you here this worthless common creature, picked up at random in the streets? I am astonished and displeased," and with this she made as though to drag the lady from his side. Thinking that this was some nightmare or hallucination, he roused himself and sat up. The lamp had gone out. Somewhat agitated he drew his sword and laid it beside him, calling as he did so for Ukon. She came at once, looking a good deal scared herself. "Please wake the watchman in the cross-wing," he said, "and tell him to bring a candle." "All in the dark like this? How can I?" she answered. "Don't be childish," said Genji, laughing, and clapped his hands.[13] The sound echoed desolately through the empty house. He could not make anyone hear; and meanwhile he noticed that his mistress was trembling from

[12] Lady Rokujō.

[13] To summon a servant.

head to foot. What should he do? He was still undecided, when suddenly she burst out into a cold sweat. She seemed to be losing consciousness. "Do not fear, Sir," said Ukon, "all her life she has been subject to these nightmare fits." He remembered now how tired she had seemed in the morning and how she had lain with her eyes turned upwards as though in pain. "I will go myself and wake someone," he said; "I am tired of clapping with only echoes to answer me. Do not leave her!" and drawing Ukon toward the bed he went in the direction of the main western door. But when he opened it, he found that the lamp in the cross-wing had also gone out. A wind had risen. The few attendants he had brought with him were already in bed. There was indeed only the steward's son (the young man who had once been Genji's bodyservant), and the one young courtier who had attended him on all his visits. They answered when he called and sprang to their feet. "Come with a candle," he said to the steward's son, "and tell my man to get his bow and keep on twanging the string as loud as he can. I wonder anyone should sleep so soundly in such a deserted place. What has happened to Koremitsu?" "He waited for some time, but as you seemed to have no need of him, he went home, saying he would be back at daybreak."

Genji's man had been an Imperial Bowman, and making a tremendous din with his bow he strode toward the steward's lodge crying "Fire, fire" at the top of his voice. The twanging of the bow reminded Genji of the palace. The roll call of night courtiers must be over; the Bowman's roll call must be actually going on. It was not so very late.

He groped his way back into the room. She was lying just as he had left her, with Ukon face downward beside her. "What are you doing there?" he cried. "Have you gone mad with fright? You have heard no doubt that in such lonely places as this fox-spirits sometimes try to cast a spell upon men. But, dear people, you need not fear. I have come back, and will not let such creatures harm you." And so saying he dragged Ukon from the bed. "Oh, Sir," she said, "I felt so queer and frightened that I fell flat down upon my face; and what my poor lady must be going through I dare not think."

"Then try not to add to her fright," said Genji, and pushing her aside, bent over the prostrate form. The girl was scarcely breathing. He touched her; she was quite limp. She did not know him.

Perhaps some accursed thing, some demon had tried to snatch her spirit away; she was so timid, so childishly helpless. The man came with the candle. Ukon was still too frightened to move. Genji placed a screen so as to hide the bed and called the man to him. It was of course contrary to etiquette that he should serve Genji himself and he hesitated in embarrassment, not venturing even to ascend the dais. "Come here," said Genji impatiently; "use your common sense." Reluctantly the man gave him the light, and as he held it toward the bed, he saw for a moment the figure which had stood there in his dream still hovering beside the pillow; suddenly it vanished He had read in old tales of such apparitions and of their power, and was in great alarm. But for the moment he was so full of concern for the lady who now lay motionless on the bed that he gave no thought to that menacing vision, and lying down beside her, began gently to move her limbs. Already they were growing cold. Her breathing had quite stopped. What could he do? To whom could he turn for help? He ought to send for a priest. He tried to control himself, but he was very young, and seeing her lying there all still and pale, he could contain himself no longer and crying "Come back to me, my own darling, come back to life. Do not look at me so strangely!" he flung his arms about her. But now she was quite cold. Her face was set in a dull, senseless stare.

Suddenly Ukon, who had been so busy with her own fears, came to herself again, and set up the most dismal weeping. He disregarded her. Something had occurred to him. There was a story of how a certain minister was waylaid by a demon as he passed through the Southern Hall. The man, Genji remembered, had been prostrate with fear; but in the end he revived and escaped. No, she could not really be dead, and turning to Ukon he said firmly: "Come now, we cannot have you making such a hideous noise in the middle of the night." But he himself was stunned with grief, and though he gave Ukon distracted orders, scarce knew what he was doing. Presently he sent for the steward's son and said to him: "Someone here has had a fright and is in a very bad way. I want you to go to Koremitsu's house and tell him to come as quickly as he can. If his brother the priest is there too, take him aside and tell him quietly that I should like to see him at once. But do not speak loud enough for the nun their mother to hear; for I would not have her know of this excursion." But though he managed to say the words, his brain was all the while in a hideous turmoil. For added to the ghastly thought that he himself had caused her death there was the dread and horror with which the whole place now inspired him.

It was past midnight. A violent storm began to rise, sighing dismally as it swept the pine trees that clustered round the house. And all the while some strange bird—an owl, he supposed—kept screeching hoarsely. Utter desolation on all sides. No human voice; no friendly sound. Why, why had he chosen this hideous place?

Ukon had fainted and was lying by her mistress's side. Was she too going to die of fright? No, no. He must not give way to such thoughts. He was now the only person left who was capable of action. Was there nothing he could do? The candle was burning badly. He lit it again. Over by the screen in the corner of the main room something was moving. There it was again, but in another corner now. There was a sound of footsteps treading cautiously. It still went on. Now they were coming up behind him. . . .

If only Koremitsu would return! But Koremitsu was a rover and a long time was wasted in looking for him. Would it never be day? It seemed to him that this night was lasting a thousand years. But now, somewhere a long way off, a cock crowed.

Why had fate seen fit to treat him thus? He felt that it must be as a punishment for all the strange and forbidden amours into which in these last years he had despite himself been drawn, that now this unheard-of horror had befallen him. And such things, though one may keep them secret for a time, always come out in the end. He minded most that the Emperor would be certain to discover sooner or later about this and all his other affairs. Then there was the general scandal. Everyone would know. The very gutter boys would make merry over him. Never, never must he do such things again, or his reputation would utterly collapse. . . .

At last Koremitsu arrived. He prided himself on being always ready to carry out his master's wishes immediately at whatever hour of the night or day, and he thought it very provoking of Genji to have sent for him just on the one occasion when he was not to hand. And now that he had come, his master did not seem able to give him any orders, but stood speechless in front of him.

Ukon, hearing Koremitsu's voice, suddenly came to herself and remembering what had happened, burst into tears. And now Genji, who while he alone was there had supported and encouraged the weeping maidservant, relieved at last by Koremitsu, could contain himself no longer, and suddenly realizing again the terrible thing that had befallen him, he burst into uncontrollable weeping. "Something horrible has happened here," he managed to say at last, "too dreadful to explain. I have heard that when such things as this suddenly befall, certain scriptures should be read. I would have this done, and prayers said. That is why I asked you to bring your brother. . . ."

"He went up to the mountain yesterday," said Koremitsu. "But I see that there has been terrible work here afoot. Was it in some sudden fit of madness that you did this thing?" Genji shook his head. So moved was Koremitsu at the sight of his master weeping that he too began to sob. Had he been an older man, versed in the ways of the world, he might have been of some use in such a crisis, but both of them were young and both were equally perplexed. At last Koremitsu said: "One thing at least is clear. The steward's son must not know. For though he himself can be depended upon, he is the sort of person who is sure to tell all his relatives, and they might meddle disastrously in the affair. We had best get clear of this house as quietly as we can." "Perhaps," said Genji; "but it would be hard to find a less frequented place than this." "At any rate," Koremitsu continued, "we cannot take her to her own house; for there her gentlewomen, who loved her dearly, would raise such a weeping and wailing as would soon bring a pack of neighbors swarming around, and all would quickly be known. If only I knew of some mountain temple—for there such things are customary [14] and pass

[14] The bringing of a corpse. Temples were used as mortuaries.

almost unnoticed." He paused and reflected. "There is a lady I once knew who has become a nun and now lives on the Higashi yama. She was my father's wet nurse and is now very old and bent. She does not of course live alone; but no outside people come there." A faint light was already showing in the sky when Koremitsu brought the carriage in. Thinking that Genji would not wish to move the body himself, he wrapped it in a rush-mat and carried it toward the carriage. How small she was to hold! Her face was calm and beautiful. He felt no repulsion. He could find no way to secure her hair, and when he began to carry her it overflowed and hung toward the ground. Genji saw, and his eyes darkened. A hideous anguish possessed him.

He tried to follow the body, but Koremitsu dissuaded him, saying, "You must ride back to your palace as quickly as you can; you have just time to get there before the stir begins," and putting Ukon into the carriage, he gave Genji his horse. Then pulling up his silk trousers to the knee, he accompanied the carriage on foot. It was a very singular procession; but Koremitsu, seeing his master's terrible distress, forgot for the moment his own dignity and walked stolidly on. Genji, hardly conscious of what went on around him, arrived at last in ghostly pallor at his house. "Where do you come from, my Lord?" "How ill you look. . . ." Questions assailed him, but he hurried to his room and lay behind his curtain. He tried to calm himself, but hideous thoughts tormented him. Why had he not insisted upon going with her? What if after all she were not dead and waking up should find that he had thus abandoned her? While these wild thoughts chased through his brain, a terrible sensation of choking began to torment him. His head ached, his body seemed to be on fire. Indeed he felt so strange that he thought he too was about to die suddenly and inexplicably as she had done. The sun was now high, but he did not get up. His gentlemen, with murmurs of astonishment, tried every means to rouse him. He sent away the dainties they brought, and lay hour after hour plunged in the darkest thoughts. A messenger arrived from the Emperor: "His Majesty has been uneasy since yesterday when his envoys sought everywhere for Your Highness in vain."

The young lords too came from the Great Hall. He would see none of them but Tō no Chūjō, and even him he made stand outside his curtain while he spoke to him: "My foster mother has been very ill since the fifth month. She shaved her head and performed other penances, in consequence of which (or so it seems) she recovered a little and got up, but is very much enfeebled. She sent word that she desired to see me once more before she died, and as I was very fond of her when I was a child, I could not refuse. While I was there a servant in the house fell ill and died quite suddenly. Out of consideration for me they removed the body at nightfall. But as soon as I was told of what had happened, I remembered that the Fast of the Ninth Month was at hand and for this reason I have not thought it right to present myself to the Emperor my father. Moreover, since early morning I have had a cough and very bad headache, so you will forgive me for treating you in this way."

"I will give the Emperor your message. But I must tell you that last night when you were out he sent messengers to look for you and seemed, if I may venture to say so, to be in a very ill humor." Tō no Chūjō turned to go, but pausing a moment came back to Genji's couch and said quietly: "What really happened to you last night? What you told me just now cannot possibly be true." "You need not go into details," answered Genji impatiently. "Simply tell him that unintentionally I became exposed to a pollution, and apologize to him for me as best you can." He spoke sharply, but in his heart there was only an unspeakable sadness; and he was very tired.

All day he lay hidden from sight. Once he sent for Tō no Chūjō's brother Kurodo no Ben and gave him a formal message for the Emperor. The same excuse would serve for the Great Hall, and he sent a similar message there and to other houses where he might be expected.

At dusk Koremitsu came. The story of Genji's pollution had turned all visitors from the door, and Koremitsu found his palace utterly deserted. "What happened?" said Genji, summoning him; "you are sure that she is dead?" and holding his sleeve before his face he wept. "All is over; of that there is no doubt," said Koremitsu, also in tears; "and since it is not possible for them to keep the body long, I have arranged with a very respectable aged priest who is my friend that the ceremony shall take place tomorrow, since tomorrow chances to be a good calendar day." "And what of her gentlewoman?" asked Genji. "I fear she will not live," said Koremitsu. "She cries out that she must follow her mistress and this morning, had I not held her, she would have cast herself from a high rock. She threatened to tell the servants at my lady's house, but I prevailed upon her to think the matter over quietly before she did this." "Poor thing," said Genji, "small wonder that she should be thus distracted. I too am feeling strangely disordered and do not know what will become of me." "Torment yourself no more," said Koremitsu. "All things happen as they must. Here is one who will handle this matter very prudently for you, and none shall be the wiser." "Happen as they must. You are right," said Genji, "and so I try to persuade myself. But in the pursuit of one's own wanton pleasures to have done harm and to have caused someone's death—that is a hideous crime; a terrible load of sin to bear with me through the world. Do not tell even your sister; much less your mother the nun, for I am ashamed that she should even know I have ever done that kind of thing." [15] "Do not fear," answered Koremitsu. "Even to the priests, who must to a certain extent be let into the secret, I have told a long made-up tale," and Genji felt a little easier in his mind.

The waiting-women of his palace were sorely puzzled: "First he says he has been defiled and cannot go to court, and now he sits whispering and sighing." What could it all mean? "Again I beg you," said Genji at last, "to see that everything is done as it should be." He was thinking all the time of the elaborate court funerals which he had witnessed (he had, indeed, seen no others) and imagined Koremitsu directing a complicated succession of rituals. "I will do what I can; it will be no such great matter," he answered and turned to go. Suddenly Genji could bear no longer the thought that he should never see her again. "You will think it very foolish of me," he said, "but I am coming with you. I shall ride on horseback." "If your

[15] I.e. pursued illicit amours.

heart is set upon it," said Koremitsu, "it is not for me to reason with you. Let us start soon, so that we may be back before the night is over." So putting on the hunting dress and other garments in which he had disguised himself before, he left his room.

Already the most hideous anguish possessed him, and now, as he set out upon this strange journey, to the dark thoughts that filled his mind was added a dread lest his visit might rouse to some fresh fury the mysterious power which had destroyed her. Should he go? He hesitated; but though he knew that this way lay no cure for his sadness, yet if he did not see her now, never again perhaps in any life to come would he meet the face and form that he had loved so well. So with Koremitsu and the one same groom to bear him company he set out upon the road.

The way seemed endless. The moon of the seventeenth night had risen and lit up the whole space of the Kamo plain, and in the light of the outrunners' torches the countryside toward Toribeno now came dimly into sight. But Genji in his sickness and despair saw none of this, and suddenly waking from the stupor into which he had fallen found that they had arrived.

The nun's cell was in a chapel built against the wall of a wooden house. It was a desolate spot, but the chapel itself was very beautiful. The light of the visitors' torches flickered through the open door. In the inner room there was no sound but that of a woman weeping by herself; in the outer room were several priests talking together (or was it praying?) in hushed voices. In the neighboring temples vespers were over and there was absolute stillness; only toward the Kiyomizu were lights visible and many figures seemed to throng the hillside.[16]

A senior priest, son of the aged nun, now began to recite the Scriptures in an impressive voice, and Genji as he listened felt the tears come into his eyes. He went in. Ukon was lying behind a screen; when she heard him enter, she turned the lamp to the wall. What terrible thing was she trying to hide from him? But when he came nearer he saw to his joy that the dead lady was not changed in any way whatsoever, but lay there very calm and beautiful; and

16 Pilgrimages to Kiyomizu Temple are made on the seventeenth day.

feeling no horror or fear at all he took her hand and said, "Speak to me once again; tell me why for so short a while you came to me and filled my heart with gladness, and then so soon forsook me, who loved you so well?" and he wept long and bitterly by her side.

The priests did not know who he was, but they were touched by his evident misery and themselves shed tears. He asked Ukon to come back with him, but she answered: "I have served this lady since she was a little child and never once for so much as an hour have I left her. How can I suddenly part from one who was so dear to me and serve in another's house? And I must now go and tell her people what has become of her; for (such is the manner of her death) if I do not speak soon, there will be an outcry that it was I who was to blame, and that would be a terrible thing for me, Sir," and she burst into tears, wailing, "I will lie with her upon the pyre; my smoke shall mingle with hers!"

"Poor soul," said Genji, "I do not wonder at your despair. But this is the way of the world. Late or soon we must all go where she has gone. Take comfort and trust in me." So he sought to console her, but in a moment he added: "Those, I know, are but hollow words. I too care no longer for life and would gladly follow her." So he spoke, giving her in the end but little comfort.

"The night is far spent," said Koremitsu; "we must now be on our way." And so with many backward looks and a heart full to bursting he left the house. A heavy dew had fallen and the mist was so thick that it was hard to see the road. On the way it occurred to him that she was still wearing his scarlet cloak, which he had lent her when they lay down together on the last evening. How closely their lives had been entwined!

Noting that he sat very unsteadily in his saddle, Koremitsu walked beside him and gave him a hand. But when they came to a dike, he lost hold and his master fell to the ground. Here he lay in great pain and bewilderment. "I shall not live to finish the journey," he said; "I have not strength to go so far." Koremitsu too was sorely troubled, for he felt that despite all Genji's insistence, he ought never to have allowed him, fever-stricken as he was, to embark upon this disastrous journey. In great agitation he plunged his hands in the river and prayed to Our Lady Kwannon of Kiyomizu. Genji too roused himself at last and forced himself to pray inwardly to the Buddha. And so they managed to start upon their journey again and in the end with Koremitsu's help he reached his palace.

This sudden journey undertaken so late at night had seemed to all his household the height of imprudence. They had noted for some while past his nightly wanderings grow more and more frequent; but though often agitated and preoccupied, never had he returned so haggard as that morning. What could be the object of these continual excursions? And they shook their heads in great concern. Genji flung himself upon his bed and lay there in fever and pain for several days. He was growing very weak. The news was brought to the Emperor who was greatly distressed and ordered continual prayers to be said for him in all the great temples; and indeed there were more special services and purification ceremonies and incantations than I have room to rehearse. When it became known that this prince, so famous for his great charm and beauty, was likely soon to die, there was a great stir in all the kingdom.

Sick though he was he did not forget to send for Ukon and have her enrolled among his gentlewomen. Koremitsu, who was beside himself with anxiety concerning his master, yet managed on her arrival to calm himself and give to Ukon friendly instruction in her new duties; for he was touched by the helpless plight in which she had been left. And Genji, whenever he felt a little better, would use her to carry messages and letters, so that she soon grew used to waiting upon him. She was dressed in deep black and though not at all handsome was a pleasant enough looking woman.

"It seems that the same fate which so early stayed your lady's course has willed that I too should be but little longer for this world. I know in what sore distress you are left by the loss of one who was for so many years your mistress and friend; and it was my purpose to have comforted you in your bereavement by every care and kindness I could devise. For this reason, indeed, it grieves me that I shall survive her for so short a time." So, somewhat stiltedly, he whispered to Ukon, and being now very weak he could not refrain from tears. Apart from the fact that his death would leave her utterly without resource, she had now quite taken to him and would have been very sorry indeed if he had died.

His gentlemen ran hither and thither, distracted; the Emperor's envoys thronged thick as the feet of the raindrops. Hearing of his father's distress and anxiety, Genji strove hard to reassure him by pretending to some slight respite or improvement. His father-in-law too showed great concern, calling every day for news and ordering the performance of various rites and potent liturgies; and it was perhaps as a result of this, that having been dangerously ill for more than twenty days, he took a turn for the better, and soon all his symptoms began to disappear. On the night of his recovery the term of his defilement also ended and hearing that the Emperor was still extremely uneasy about him, he determined to reassure the court by returning to his official residence at the palace. His father-in-law came to fetch him in his own carriage and rather irritatingly urged upon him all sorts of remedies and precautions.

For some while everything in the world to which he had now returned seemed strange to him and he indeed scarce knew himself; but by the twentieth day of the ninth month his recovery was complete, nor did the pallor and thinness of his face become him by any means ill.

At times he would stare vacantly before him and burst into loud weeping, and seeing this there were not wanting those who said that he was surely possessed.

Often he would send for Ukon, and once when they had been talking in the still of the evening he said to her, "There is one thing which still puzzles me. Why would she never tell me who she was? For even if she was indeed, as she once said, 'a fisherman's child,' it was a strange perversity to use such reticence with one who loved her so well."

"You ask why she hid her name from you?" said Ukon. "Can you wonder at it? When could she have been expected to tell you her name (not that it would have meant much to you if you had heard it)? For from the beginning you treated her with a strange mistrust, coming with such secrecy and mystery as might well make her doubt whether you were indeed a creature of the waking world.

But though you never told her she knew well enough who you were, and the thought that you would not be thus secret had you regarded her as more than a mere plaything or idle distraction was very painful to her."

"What a wretched series of misunderstandings," said Genji. "For my part I had no mind to put a distance between us. But I had no experience in such affairs as this. There are many difficulties in the path of such people as I. First and foremost I feared the anger of my father the Emperor; and then, the foolish jesting of the world. I felt myself hedged in by courtly rules and restrictions. But for all the tiresome concealments that my rank forced upon me, from that first evening I had so strangely set my heart upon her that though reason counseled me I could not hold back; and indeed it seems sometimes to me that an irresistible fate drove me to do the thing of which I now so bitterly and continually repent. But tell me more about her. For there can now be no reason for concealment. When on each seventh day I cause the names of the Buddhas to be written for her comfort and salvation, whom am I to name in my inward prayer?"

"There can be no harm in my telling you that," said Ukon, "and I should have done so before, did I not somehow feel it a shame to be prating to you now about things she would not have me speak of while she was alive. Her parents died when she was quite small. Her father, Sammi Chūjō, loved her very dearly, but felt always that he could not give her all the advantages to which her great beauty entitled her; and still perplexed about her future and how best to do his duty by her, he died. Soon afterwards some accident brought her into the company of Tō no Chūjō [17] who was at that time still a lieutenant and for three years he made her very happy. But in the autumn of last year disquieting letters began to arrive from the Great Hall of the Right,[18] and being by nature prone to fits of unreasoning fear she now fell into a wild panic and fled to the western part of the town where she hid herself in the house of her old wet nurse. Here she was very uncomfortable, and had planned to move

[17] Chūjō means "Captain."

[18] From Tō no Chūjō's wife, who was the daughter of the Minister of the Right.

to a certain village in the hills, when she discovered that it would be unlucky, owing to the position of the stars since the beginning of the year, to make a journey in that direction; and (though she never told me so) I think, Sir, it troubled her sorely that you should have come upon her when she was living in so wretched a place. But there was never anyone in the world like my lady for keeping things to herself; she could never bear that other people should know what was on her mind. I have no doubt, Sir, that she sometimes behaved very oddly to you and that you have seen all this for yourself."

Yes, this was all just as Tō no Chūjō had described. "I think there was some mention of a child that Chūjō was vexed to have lost sight of," said Genji more interested than ever; "am I right?" "Yes, indeed," she answered; "it was born in the spring of last year, a girl, and a fine child it was." "Where is it now?" asked Genji. "Could you get hold of it and bring it to me here without letting anyone know where you were taking it? It would be a great comfort to me in my present misery to have some remembrance of her near me"; and he added, "I ought of course to tell Chūjō, but that would lead to useless and painful discussions about what has happened. Somehow or other I will manage to bring her up here in my palace. I think there can be no harm in that. And you will easily enough find some story to tell to whatever people are now looking after her." "I am very glad that this has entered your head," said Ukon, "it would be a poor lookout for her to grow up in the quarter where she is now living. With no one properly belonging to her and in such a part of the town. . . ."

In the stillness of the evening, under a sky of exquisite beauty, here and there along the borders in front of his palace some insect croaked its song; the leaves were just beginning to turn. And as he looked upon this pleasant picture he felt ashamed at the contrast between his surroundings and the little house where Yūgao had lived. Suddenly somewhere among the bamboo groves the bird called iyebato uttered its sharp note. He remembered just how she had looked when in the gardens of that fatal house the same bird had startled her by its cry, and turning to Ukon, "How old was she?" he suddenly asked; "for though she seemed childlike in her diffidence and helplessness, that may only have been a sign that she was not long for this world." "She must have been nineteen," said Ukon. "When my mother, who was her first wet nurse, died and left me an orphan, my lady's father was pleased to notice me and reared me at my lady's side. Ah, Sir, when I think of it, I do not know how I shall live without her; for kind as people here may be I do not seem to get used to them. I suppose it is that I knew her ways, poor lady, she having been my mistress for so many years."

To Genji even the din of the cloth-beaters' mallets had become dear through recollection, and as he lay in bed he repeated those verses of Po Chü-i.

> In the eighth month and ninth month when the nights are
>   growing long
> A thousand times, ten thousand times the fuller's stick beats.

TRANSLATED BY ARTHUR WALEY

THE PILLOW BOOK OF SEI SHŌNAGON

[*Makura no Sōshi*]

"The Pillow Book" of Sei Shōnagon, written about 1002, is one of the most delightful works of Japanese literature. The author, a near contemporary of Murasaki Shikibu, was a woman of remarkable talent and wit, and her book is perhaps the closest approach to high comedy in Japanese literature. It is a work without precedent, filled with flashing impressions and delicate touches, if lacking in great depth. In this translation by Arthur Waley some of the most engaging episodes are given.

•

STRAY NOTES

One writes a letter, taking particular trouble to get it up as prettily as possible; then waits for the answer, making sure every moment that it cannot be much longer before something comes. At last, frightfully late, is brought in—one's own note, still folded or tied exactly as one sent it, but so finger-marked and smudged that even the address is barely legible. "The family is not in residence," the messenger says, giving one back the note. Or "It is his day of observance and they said they could not take any letters in." Such experiences are dismally depressing.

One has been expecting someone, and rather late at night there is a stealthy tapping at the door. One sends a maid to see who it is, and lies waiting, with some slight flutter of the breast. But the name one hears when she returns is that of someone completely different, who does not concern one at all. Of all depressing experiences, this is by far the worst.

Someone comes, with whom one has decided not to have further dealings. One pretends to be fast asleep, but some servant or person connected with one comes to wake one up, and pulls one about, with a face as much as to say "What a sleep-hog!" This is always exceedingly irritating.

If someone with whom one is having an affair keeps on mentioning some woman whom he knew in the past, however long ago it is since they separated, one is always irritated.

It is very tiresome when a lover who is leaving one at dawn says that he must look for a fan or pocket-book that he left somewhere about the room last night. As it is still too dark to see anything, he goes fumbling about all over the place, knocking into everything and muttering to himself, "How very odd!" When at last he finds the pocket-book he crams it into his dress with a great rustling of the pages; or if it is a fan he has lost, he swishes it open and begins flapping it about, so that when he finally takes his departure, instead of experiencing the feelings of regret proper to such an occasion, one merely feels irritated at his clumsiness. . . .

It is important that a lover should know how to make his departure. To begin with, he ought not to be too ready to get up, but should require a little coaxing: "Come, it is past daybreak. You don't want to be found here . . ." and so on. One likes him, too, to behave in such a way that one is sure he is unhappy at going and would stay longer if he possibly could. He should not pull on his trousers the moment he is up, but should first of all come close to one's ear and in a whisper finish off whatever was left half-said in the course of the night. But though he may in reality at these moments be doing nothing at all, it will not be amiss that he should appear to be buckling his belt. Then he should raise the shutters, and both lovers should go out together at the double doors, while he tells her how much he dreads the day that is before him and longs for the approach of night. Then, after he has slipped away, she can stand gazing after him, with charming recollections of those last moments. Indeed, the success of a lover depends greatly on his method of departure. If he springs to his feet with a jerk and at once begins fussing round, tightening in the waistband of his breeches, or adjusting the sleeves of his court robe, hunting jacket, or what not, collecting a thousand odds and ends, and thrusting them into the folds of his dress, or pulling in his overbelt—one begins to hate him.

I like to think of a bachelor—an adventurous disposition has left him single—returning at dawn from some amorous excursion. He looks a trifle sleepy; but, as soon as he is home, draws his writing case toward him, carefully grinds himself some ink and begins to write his next-morning letter—not simply dashing off whatever comes into his head, but spreading himself to the task and taking trouble to write the characters beautifully. He should be clad in an azalea-yellow or vermilion cloak worn over a white robe. Glancing from time to time at the dewdrops that still cling to the thin white fabric of his dress, he finishes his letter, but instead of giving it to one of the ladies who are in attendance upon him at the moment, he gets up and, choosing from among his page-boys one who seems to him exactly appropriate to such a mission, calls the lad to him, and whispering something in his ear puts the letter in his hand; then sits gazing after him as he disappears into the distance. While waiting for the answer he will perhaps quietly murmur to himself this or that passage from the Sutras. Presently he is told that his washing water and porridge are ready, and goes into the back room, where, seated at the reading table, he glances at some Chinese poems, now and then reciting out loud some passage that strikes his fancy. When he has washed and got into his court cloak, which he wears as a dressing gown (without trousers), he takes the sixth chapter of the Lotus Scripture and reads it silently. Precisely at the most solemn moment of his reading—the place being not far away—the messenger returns, and by his posture it is evident that he expects an instant reply. With an amusing if blasphemous rapidity the lover transfers his attention from the book he is reading to the business of framing his answer.

• •

From the beginning of the fifth month,[1] it had been dark, rainy weather all the time. I became so bored that at last I suggested we

[1] Of the year 995.

had better go out and see if we couldn't somewhere hear the cuckoo singing. This idea was very well received, and one of the girls suggested we should try that bridge behind the Kamo Shrine (it isn't called Magpie Bridge, but something rather like it). She said that there was a cuckoo there every day. Someone else said it was not a cuckoo at all, but a cricket. However, on the morning of the fifth day, off we went. When we ordered the carriage, the men said they didn't suppose that in such weather as this anyone would mind if we were picked up outside our own quarters and taken out by the Northern Gate.[2] There was only room for four. Some of the other ladies asked whether we should mind their getting another carriage and coming too. But the Empress said "No," and though they were very much disappointed we drove off rather hardheartedly without attempting to console them or indeed worrying about them at all. Something seemed to be happening at the riding ground, where there was a great press of people. When we asked what was going on, we were told that the competitions were being held, and that the archers were just going to shoot on horseback. It was said, too, that the officers of the Bodyguard of the Left were there; but all we could see, when we had pulled up, was a few gentlemen of the Sixth Rank wandering vaguely about. "Oh, do let us get on," someone said; "there's no one of any interest here." So we drove on toward Kamo, the familiar road making us feel quite as though we were on our way to the festival.[3] Presently we came to my lord Akinobu's[4] house, and someone suggested we should get out and have a look at it. Everything was very simple and countrified—pictures of horses on the panels, screens of wattled bamboo, curtains of plaited grass —all in a style that seemed to be intentionally behind the times. The house itself was a poor affair and very cramped, but quite pretty in its way. As for cuckoos, we were nearly deafened! It is really a great pity Her Majesty never hears them. And when we thought of the

[2] Instead of walking to the Eastern Gate, the only one which the palace staff was supposed to use.

[3] The Kamo festival, in the fourth month.

[4] The Empress's maternal uncle. The Empress's mother came of a comparatively humble family.

ladies who had wanted so badly to come with us, we felt quite guilty. "It's always interesting to see things done on the spot," said Akinobu, and sending for some stuff which I suppose was husked rice, he made some girls—very clean and respectable—along with others who seemed to come from neighboring farms, show us how the rice was thrashed. Five or six of them did this, and then the grain was put into a sort of machine that went round, two girls turning it and at the same time singing so strange a song that we could not help laughing, and had soon forgotten all about the cuckoos. Then refreshments were brought on a queer old tray-stand such as one sees in Chinese pictures. As no one seemed much interested in its contents, our host said: "This is rough country fare. If you don't like it, the only thing to do in a place like this is to go on bothering your host or his servants till you get something you can eat. We don't expect you people from the capital to be shy. These fern-shoots, now. I gathered them with my own hand." "You don't want us to arrange ourselves round the tray-stand like a lot of maid-servants sitting down to their supper?" I protested.

"Hand the things round," he said . . . and while this was going on, in the midst of the clatter, one of the men came in and said that it was going to rain, and we hurried back to our carriage. I wanted to make my cuckoo-poem before we started; but the others said I could do it in the carriage. Before going we picked a huge branch of white-flower and decorated our carriage with it, great trails of blossom hanging over the windows and sides, till one would have thought a huge canopy of white brocade had been flung across the roof of the coach. Our grooms, throwing themselves into the thing, began with shouts of laughter squeezing fresh boughs of blossom into every cranny that would hold them. We longed to be seen by someone on our way back, but not a soul did we meet, save one or two wretched priests or other such uninteresting people. When we were nearly home we made up our minds it would be too dull to finish the day without anyone having seen us in our splendor, so we stopped at the palace in the First Ward and asked for the Captain,[5] saying we were just back from hearing the cuckoo. We were told he

[5] Fujiwara no Kiminobu, aged eighteen; cousin of the Empress.

had been off duty for some time and had got into easy clothes; but was now being helped into his court trousers. Wouldn't we wait? We said we couldn't do that, and were driving on to the Eastern Gate, when he suddenly appeared running after us down the road. He had certainly changed in a marvelously short space of time, but was still buckling his belt as he ran. Behind him, barefooted in their haste, panted several dressers and grooms. We called to the coachman to drive on and had already reached the gate when, hopelessly out of breath, he staggered up to us. It was only then that he saw how we were decorated. "This is a fairy chariot," he laughed. "I do not believe there are real people in it. If there are, let them get down and show themselves."

"But, Shōnagon, what poems did you make today? That's what I should like to hear." "We're keeping them for Her Majesty," I replied. Just then it once more began to rain in earnest. "I have always wondered," he said, "why when all the other gates have arches, this Eastern Gate should have none. Today, for example, one badly needs it." "What am I to do now?" he asked presently. "I was so determined to catch up with you that I rushed out without thinking what was to become of me afterward." "Don't be so ridiculous," I said. "You can come with us to the palace." "In an *eboshi*?" [6] he asked. "What can you be thinking of?" "Send someone to fetch your hat," I suggested. But it was now raining badly and our men, who had no raincoats with them, were pulling in the carriage as quickly as they could.[7] One of his men presently arrived from his palace with an umbrella, and under its shelter he now, with a slow reluctance that contrasted oddly with his previous haste, made his way home, continually stopping to look back at us over his shoulder. With his umbrella in one hand and a bunch of white-flower in the other, he was an amusing sight.

When we were back in the palace, Her Majesty asked for an account of our adventures. The girls who had been left behind were at first inclined to be rather sulky; but when we described how the Captain had run after us down the Great Highway of the First

[6] A soft, high-crowned cap.

[7] The bulls that drew it had to be unyoked at the palace gate.

Ward, they could not help laughing. Presently the Empress asked about our poems, and we were obliged to explain that we had not made any. "That is very unfortunate," she said. "Some of the gentlemen at court are bound to hear of your excursion, and they will certainly expect something to have come of it. I can quite understand that on the spot it was not very easy to write anything. When people make too solemn an affair of such things, one is apt suddenly to feel completely uninterested. But it is not too late. Write something now. You're good for that much, surely." This was all true enough; but it turned out to be a painful business. We were still trying to produce something when a messenger arrived, with a note from the Captain. It was written on thin paper stamped with the white-flower pattern, and was attached to the spray that he had taken from our carriage. His poem said: "Would that of this journey I had heard. So had my heart been with you when you sought the cuckoo's song." Fearing that we were keeping the messenger waiting, her Majesty sent round her own writing case to our room, with paper slipped into the lid. "You write something, Saishō," I said. But Saishō was determined that I should write, and while we argued about it the sky suddenly grew dark, rain began to pour, and there were such deafening peals of thunder, that we forgot all about our poem, and frightened out of our wits ran wildly from place to place, closing shutters and doors. The storm lasted a long time, and when at last the thunder became less frequent, it was already dark. We were just saying we really must get on with our answer, when crowds of visitors began to arrive, all anxious to talk about the storm, and we were obliged to go out and look after them. One of the courtiers said that a poem only needs an answer when it is addressed to someone in particular, and we decided to do no more about it. I said to the Empress that poetry seemed to have a bad karma today, and added that the best thing we could do was to keep as quiet as possible about our excursion. "I still don't see why some of you who went should not be able to produce a few poems," she replied, pretending to be cross. "It isn't that you can't; of that I am sure. You have made up your minds not to." "The time has passed," I said. "One must do those things when one is in the right mood." "Right mood? What nonsense!" she exclaimed indignantly. But all the same, she did not worry me any more about it.

Two days afterward Saishō was talking about our excursion, and mentioned the fern-shoots that Akinobu had "plucked with his own hand." The Empress was amused that Saishō seemed to have retained a much clearer memory of the refreshments than of anything else that happened during the expedition, and picking up a stray piece of paper she wrote: "The memory of a salad lingers in her head," and bade me make a beginning for the poem. I wrote: "More than the cuckoo's song that she went out to hear." "Well, Shōnagon," she said, laughing, "how you of all people can have the face to mention cuckoos, I cannot imagine." I felt very crestfallen, but answered boldly: "I don't see anything to be ashamed of. I have made up my mind only to make poems when I feel inclined to. If, whenever there is a question of poetry, you turn upon me and ask me to compose, I shall stay in your service no longer. When I am called upon like that, I can't even count the syllables, still less think whether I am writing a winter song in spring, or a spring song in autumn. . . . I know there have been a lot of poets in my family; and it would certainly be very nice if, after one of these occasions, people said: 'Of course, hers was much the best; but that is not surprising, considering what her father was.' As it is, not having the slightest degree of special talent in that direction, I object strongly to being perpetually thrust forward and made to behave as though I thought myself a genius. I feel I am disgracing my father's memory!" I said this quite seriously; but the Empress laughed. However, she said I might do as I pleased, and promised that for her part she would never call upon me again. I felt immensely relieved. . . .

TRANSLATED BY ARTHUR WALEY

THE DIARY OF MURASAKI SHIKIBU

[*Murasaki Shikibu Nikki*]

The diary of Murasaki Shikibu (978?-1015?) is the chief source of information we have about the author of "The Tale of Genji." However, it is not merely for its autobiographical data that the work is prized; it is a vivid and delightful portrayal of life at the court when Heian culture was at its height. If this life falls far short of that described by Murasaki in "The Tale of Genji," it is nevertheless one of great charm, and it is fortunate that Murasaki recorded it in her inimitable style.

•

Tenth day of the long-moon month:
When day began to dawn the decorations [1] of the Queen's chamber were changed and she removed to a white bed. The Prime Minister, his sons, and other noblemen made haste to change the curtains of the screens, the bedcover, and other things. All day long she lay ill at ease. Men cried at the top of their voices to scare away evil spirits. There assembled not only the priests who had been summoned here for these months, but also itinerant monks who were brought from every mountain and temple. Their prayers would reach to the Buddhas of the Three Worlds. All the soothsayers in the world were summoned. Eight million gods seemed to be listening with ears erect for their Shinto prayers. Messengers ran off to order Sutra-reciting at various temples; thus the night was passed. On the east side of the screen [placed around the Queen's bed] there assembled the ladies of the court. On the west side there were lying the Queen's substitutes possessed with [or who were enticing] the evil spirits.[2] Each was ly-

[1] Hangings, screens, and clothes of attendants were all white at the time of a birth.

[2] Which would otherwise have attacked the Queen. Some of the ladies-in-waiting undertook this duty.

ing surrounded by a pair of folding screens. The joints of the screens were curtained and the priests were appointed to cry Sutras there. On the south side there sat in many rows abbots and other dignitaries of the priesthood, who prayed and swore till their voices grew hoarse, as if they were bringing down the living form of Fudō.[3] The space between the north room and the dais [on which was the Queen's bed] was very narrow, yet when I thought of it afterward I counted more than forty persons who were standing there. They could not move at all, and grew so dizzy that they could remember nothing. The people [i.e. the ladies-in-waiting and the maids of honor] now coming from home could not enter the main apartment at all. There was no place for their flowing robes and long sleeves. Certain older women wept secretly.

Eleventh day: At dawn the north sliding doors were taken away to throw the two rooms together. The Queen was moved toward the veranda. As there was no time to hang *misu,*[4] she was surrounded by *kichō*. The Reverend Gyōchō and the other priests performed incantations. The Reverend Ingen recited the prayer written by the Lord Prime Minister on the previous day adding some grave vows of his own. His words were infinitely august and hopeful. The Prime Minister joining in the prayer, we felt more assured of a fortunate delivery. Yet there was still lingering anxiety which made us very sad, and many eyes were filled with tears. We said, "Tears are not suitable to this occasion," but we could not help crying. They said that Her Majesty suffered more because the rooms were too crowded, so the people were ordered to the south and east rooms. After this there remained in the royal apartment only the more important personages. . . . The Prime Minister's son, Lieutenant General Saishō, Major General Masamichi of the Fourth Rank, not to speak of Lieutenant General Tsunefusa, of the Left Bodyguard, and Miya no Tayu, who had not known Her Majesty familiarly, all looked over her screen for some time. They showed eyes swollen up with weeping [over her

[3] Fudō: a terrible-looking Guardian King who was thought to have the power to subdue all evil spirits.

[4] *Misu:* bamboo screens. *Kichō:* curtains.

sufferings], forgetting the shame of it. On their heads rice [5] was scattered white as snow. Their rumpled clothes must have been unseemly, but we could only think of those things afterward. A part of the Queen's head was shaved.[6] I was greatly astonished and very sorry to see this, but she was delivered peacefully. The afterbirth was delayed, and all priests crowded to the south balcony, under the eaves of the magnificent main building, while those on the bridge recited Sutras more passionately, often kneeling.

Among the ladies-in-waiting on the east side were seen some of the courtiers.[7] Lady Kochūjō's eye met that of the Lieutenant General. People afterwards laughed over her astonished expression. She is a very fascinating and elegant person, and is always very careful to adorn her face. This morning she had done so, but her eyes were red, and her rouge was spoiled by tears. She was disfigured, and hardly seemed the same person. The imperfectly made-up face of Lady Saishō was a rare sight, but what about my own? It is lucky for me that people cannot notice such things at such a time. . . .

For seven nights every ceremony was performed cloudlessly. Before the Queen in white the styles and colors of other people's dresses appeared in sharp contrast. I felt much dazzled and abashed, and did not present myself in the daytime, so I passed my days in tranquillity and watched persons going up from the eastern side building across the bridge. Those who were permitted to wear the honorable colors [8] put on brocaded *karaginu,* and also brocaded *uchigi.*[9] This was the conventionally beautiful dress, not showing individual taste. The elderly ladies who could not wear the honorable colors avoided anything dazzling, but took only exquisite *uchigi* trimmed with three or five folds, and for *karaginu* brocade either of one color or of

[5] For good luck.

[6] So that she might be ordained as a priestess and insured a good reception in the next world, only done when the sick person is in great danger.

[7] This was contrary to etiquette and shows the extreme excitement of the moment. Ladies and gentlemen of the court remained in separate rooms on social occasions.

[8] Purple and scarlet.

[9] A long unconfined flowing robe put on over the dress.

a simple design. For their inner kimonos they used figured stuffs or gauzes. Their fans, though not at first glance brilliant or attractive, had some written phrases or sentiments in good taste, but almost exactly alike, as if they had compared notes beforehand. In point of fact the resemblance came from their similarity of age, and they were individual efforts. Even in those fans were revealed their minds which are in jealous rivalry. The younger ladies wore much-embroidered clothes; even their sleeve openings were embroidered. The pleats of their trains were ornamented with thick silver thread and they put gold foil on the brocaded figures of the silk. Their fans were like a snow-covered mountain in bright moonlight; they sparkled and could not be looked at steadily. They were like hanging mirrors.

On the third night Her Majesty's major-domo gave an entertainment. He served the Queen himself. The dining table of aloe wood, the silver dishes, and other things I saw hurriedly. Minamoto Chūnagon and Saishō presented the Queen with some baby clothes and diapers, a stand for a clothes chest, and cloth for wrapping up clothes and furniture. They were white in color, and all of the same shape, yet they were carefully chosen, showing the artist mind. The Governor of Ōmi Province was busy with the general management of the banquet. On the western balcony of the East building there sat court nobles in two rows, the north being the more honorable place. On the southern balcony were court officials, the west being the most honorable seat. Outside the doors of the principal building [where the Queen was] white figured-silk screens were put.

On the fifth night the Lord Prime Minister celebrated the birth. The full moon on the fifteenth day was clear and beautiful. Torches were lighted under the trees and tables were put there with rice-balls on them. Even the uncouth humble servants who were walking about chattering seemed to enhance the joyful scene. All minor officials were there burning torches, making it as bright as day. Even the attendants of the nobles, who gathered behind the rocks and under the trees, talked of nothing but the new light which had come into the world, and were smiling and seemed happy as if their own private wishes had been fulfilled. Happier still seemed those in the audience chamber, from the highest nobles even to men of the fifth rank, who, scarcely to be counted among the nobility, met the joyful time going about idly, and bending their bodies obsequiously.

To serve at the Queen's dinner eight ladies tied their hair with white cords, and in that dress brought in Her Majesty's dining table. The chief lady-in-waiting for that night was Miya no Naishi. She was brilliantly dressed with great formality, and her hair was made more charming by the white cords which enhanced her beauty. I got a side glance of her when her face was not screened by her fan. She wore a look of extreme purity. . . .

. .

The following are portraits of prominent ladies of the court.

Lady Dainagon is very small and refined, white, beautiful, and round, though in demeanor very lofty. Her hair is three inches longer than her height. She uses exquisitely carved hairpins. Her face is lovely, her manners delicate and charming.

Lady Senji is also a little person, and haughty. Her hair is fine and glossy and one foot longer than the ordinary. She puts us to shame, her carriage is so noble. When she walks before us we feel so much in the shade that we are uncomfortable. Her mind and speech make us feel that a really noble person ought to be like her.

—If I go on describing ladies' manners I shall be called an old gossip, so I must refrain from talking about those around me. I will be silent about the questionable and imperfect.

Lady Koshōshō, all noble and charming. She is like a weeping willow tree at budding time. Her style is very elegant and we all envy her her manners. She is so shy and retiring that she seems to hide her heart even from herself. She is of childlike purity even to a painful degree—should there be a low-minded person who would treat her ill or slander her, her spirit would be overwhelmed and she would die. Such delicacy and helplessness make us anxious about her. . . .

Among the younger ladies I think Kodayu and Genshikibu are beautiful. The former is a little person quite modern in type. Her pretty hair is abundant at the roots, but gets too thin at the end, which is one foot longer than she is. Her face is full of wit. People will think her very pretty, and indeed there is no feature one would wish to improve. The latter is tall and rather superior. Her features are fine; she is smile-giving and lovable. She is very refined and seems to be a favorite daughter of some person of dignity.

Lady Kohyōe no Jō is also refined. These ladies cannot be looked down upon by court nobles. With every one some fault is to be found, but only those who are ever mindful to conceal it *even when alone,* can completely succeed. . . .

A Lady Koma had very long hair, an agreeable lady in those days; now she has become like the bridge of a lute which has been immovably fastened with glue. She has gone home.

So much for their appearance and now for their dispositions. Here few can be selected, though each has some good points and few are entirely bad. It is very difficult to possess such qualities as prudence, wit, charm, right-mindedness, all at once. As to many ladies, the question is whether they excel most in charms of mind or person. It is hard to decide! Wicked, indeed, to write so much of others!

There is Lady Chūjō who waits upon the Princess dedicated to the service of the Kamo Shrine. I had heard of her and secretly managed to see her letters addressed to other persons. They were very beautifully written but with such an exalted opinion of herself; in the whole world she is the person of profoundest knowledge! None to compare with her, it seems she is thinking. On reading them my heart beat faster, I was furiously indignant for every one here [the ladies of her own Queen's court], although it may be it is wrong to feel so. "Be it in composition or poetry, who can judge save our Princess-Abbess, who will have bright futures but the ladies attending our Princess?" ! ! It may be reasonable, yet I have never seen, compared to ours, any good poems by the lady attendants of that Princess-Abbess. They seem to be living an idle poetic life, but if they were to compete with us, it is not necessarily certain they would be superior, though no one knows them well. On a beautiful moonlight night or morning, at the time of flowers or of cuckoo, courtiers might visit their residence. Other-worldly and sacred it is, and made to the taste of their Princess. There they remain undisturbed, admiring her. On the other hand, with us many things occur. The Queen has to go up to His Majesty's apartment, the Lord Prime Minister comes, and we have to keep watch at night. But there is nothing of all this in that world all their own where they may indulge in elegance and avoid blunders. If I could live there like an old piece of buried wood thrown in among them, I might succeed in freeing myself from the reproach of shallowness—would that I might indulge in elegance there, relaxing myself! Forward young ladies there can devote themselves to dress, making themselves inferior to none and pleasing to courtiers. On the other hand, in our Queen's court we rather neglect to adorn ourselves, for our Queen has no rivals now. Moreover, she thinks unfavorably of frivolous women, so those who wish to serve her and remain in favor keep from association with men. Of course everywhere there are lighthearted, unashamed, thoughtless women, and men who visit our court to find them say we are awkward and unversed in social usage. Our ladies of the higher ranks are, indeed, much too reserved and haughty; it is not in this way that they can bring honor to our Queen. It is painful to see them. The attendants of the Princess-Abbess seem to have been alluding to these ladies, but both defects and merits are found in every one, so we may not be inferior to them after all. Even our young ladies nowadays have heard of self-respect. It would be embarrassing if they were too frivolous, but one would not wish them to be heartless either.

Our Queen of perfect mind, enviably lovely, is reserved and never obtrusive, for she believes that few who are forward can avoid blunders. In fact, imperfect wit is worse than reserve. Our Queen when she was very young was much annoyed to hear persons of shallow culture saying vulgar, narrow things with conceit, so she favored ladies who made no mistakes, and childlike persons pleased her very well. This is why our ladies have become so retiring. As Her Majesty grows older, she begins to see the world as it is, the bad and good qualities of the human heart. Reserve or boldness—she knows neither is good. The court nobles rather look down on us—"Nothing interesting here!" they seem to say. The Queen knows this, but she knows we cannot please everybody. If we stumble, hideous things may happen. Yet we must not be faint-hearted and bashful either, so Her Majesty says, but our old habits are not so easily shaken off, and all the young nobles of the present day are, on their side, only indulgent pleasure-seekers. . . .

Lady Izumi Shikibu [10] corresponds charmingly, but her behavior is improper indeed. She writes with grace and ease and with a flashing wit. There is fragrance even in her smallest words. Her poems are attractive, but they are only improvisations which drop from her mouth spontaneously. Every one of them has some interesting point, and she is acquainted with ancient literature also, but she is not like a true artist who is filled with the genuine spirit of poetry. Yet I think even she cannot presume to pass judgment on the poems of others. . . .

Lady Sei Shōnagon. A very proud person. She values herself highly, and scatters her Chinese writings all about. Yet should we study her closely, we should find that she is still imperfect. She tries to be exceptional, but naturally persons of that sort give offence. She is piling up trouble for her future. One who is too richly gifted, who indulges too much in emotion, even when she ought to be reserved, and cannot turn aside from anything she is interested in, in spite of herself will lose self-control. How can such a vain and reckless person end her days happily!

Here there is a sudden change from the court to her own home.

Having no excellence within myself, I have passed my days without making any special impression on any one. Especially the fact that

[10] See above, pp. 92, 94.

I have no man who will look out for my future makes me comfortless. I do not wish to bury myself in dreariness. Is it because of my worldly mind that I feel lonely? On moonlight nights in autumn, when I am hopelessly sad, I often go out on the balcony and gaze dreamily at the moon. It makes me think of days gone by. People say that it is dangerous to look at the moon in solitude, but something impels me, and sitting a little withdrawn I muse there. In the wind-cooled evening I play on the koto, though others may not care to hear it. I fear that my playing betrays the sorrow which becomes more intense, and I become disgusted with myself—so foolish and miserable am I.

My room is ugly, blackened by smoke. I play on a thirteen or six-stringed koto, but I neglect to take away the bridges even in rainy weather, and I lean it up against the wall between the cabinet and the door jamb. On either side of the koto stands a lute [Japanese *biwa*]. A pair of big bookcases have in them all the books they can hold. In one of them are placed old poems and romances. They are the homes of worms which come frightening us when we turn the pages, so none ever wish to read them. As to the other cabinet, since the person [11] who placed his own books there no hand has touched it. When I am bored to death I take out one or two of them; then my maids gather around me and say: "Your life will not be favored with old age if you do such a thing! Why do you read Chinese? Formerly even the reading of Sutras was not encouraged for women." They rebuke me in the shade [i.e. behind my back]. I have heard of it and have wished to say, "It is far from certain that he who does no forbidden thing enjoys a long life," but it would be a lack of reserve to say it to the maids. Our deeds vary with our age and deeds vary with the individual. Some are proud to read books, others look over old cast-away writings because they are bored with having nothing to do. It would not be becoming for such a one to chatter away about religious thoughts, noisily shaking a rosary. I feel this, and before my women keep myself from doing what otherwise I could do easily. But after all, when I was among the ladies of the court I did

[11] Her husband who was a scholar in Chinese literature. He died in 1001. It is now 1008.

not say what I wanted to say either, for it is useless to talk with those who do not understand one and troublesome to talk with those who criticize from a feeling of superiority. Especially one-sided persons are troublesome. Few are accomplished in many arts and most cling narrowly to their own opinion.

Pretty and coy, shrinking from sight, unsociable, proud, fond of romance, vain and poetic, looking down upon others with a jealous eye—such is the opinion of those who do not know me, but after seeing me they say, "You are wonderfully gentle to meet with; I cannot identify you with that imagined one."

I see that I have been slighted, hated, and looked down upon as an old gossip, and I must bear it, for it is my destiny to be solitary. The Queen said once, "You were ever mindful not to show your soul, but I have become more intimate with you than others." I hope that I may not be looked at obliquely even by those who are ill-natured, affected, and unsociable. As a rule one is easy at the back [i.e. not afraid of gossip] who is modest, gentle, and of tranquil disposition. Even a coquettish and frivolous person is not rebuked if she is good-natured and of a disposition not embarrassing to others. A person who is self-exalted and eccentric with scornful mouth and demeanor can be unmistakably perceived, and one can be on one's guard; by observing closely one may discover faults of speech and behavior. Those whose words and deeds are not in harmony, or who are always trying to outdo one another, attract notice. One seldom wishes to criticize those who have defects, but are good-natured. One cannot but sympathize with them. Those who habitually do evil with intention deserve to be freely talked about and laughed at even though sometimes they do it without intention. We ought to love even those who hate us, but it is very difficult to do it. Even the Buddha of Profound Mercy does not say that the sins against Buddha, the laws of religion, and priests, are slight. Moreover, in this muddy world it is best to let alone the persons who hate us. If we compare one who tries to excel in hatred saying extraordinary words and watching their effect ill-humoredly face to face, with one who coldly hides her heart with a tranquil manner, we can see which is superior.

There is a lady, Saémon no Naishi, who unreasonably cherished hatred of me. I was not at first aware of it, but later heard of much criticism of me in my absence. Once the King was listening to a reading of my *"Genji Monogatari,"* and said, "She is gifted, she must have read the Chronicle of Japan." This lady heard of it, and unreflectingly spread abroad among the courtiers the idea that I am very proud of my learning, giving me the name of "The Japanese Chronicle lady"—it is laughable, indeed! I am reserved even before the maids of my own house; how then should I show my learning in court? When my elder brother Shikibu no Jō was a boy he was taught to read the Chinese classics. I listened, sitting beside him, and learned wonderfully fast, though he was sometimes slow and forgot. Father, who was devoted to study, regretted that I had not been a son, but I heard people saying that it is not beautiful even for a man to be proud of his learning, and after that I did not write so much as the figure one in Chinese. I grew clumsy with my writing brush. For a long time I did not care for the books I had already read. Thus I was ashamed to think how others would hate me on hearing what Lady Saémon said, and I assumed an air of not being able to read the characters written on the royal screen. But the Queen made me read to her the poetical works of Li T'ai Po, and as she wished to learn them I have been teaching her since the summer of two years ago the second and third volumes of that collection very secretly when none were present. Her Majesty and I tried to conceal it, but His Majesty the King and the Lord Prime Minister finding it out, the latter presented to the Queen many poetical books which he had had copied. I think that bitter Saémon does not know it yet. If she did, how she would criticize me! . . .

TRANSLATED BY ANNIE SHEPLEY OMORI AND KŌCHI DOI

THE SARASHINA DIARY

[Sarashina Nikki] by the Daughter of Takasue

•

1037: In the tenth month we changed our abode to the capital. Mother had become a nun and although she lived in the same house, shut herself up in a separate chamber. Father rather treated me as an independent woman than as his child. I felt helpless to see him shunning all society and living hidden in the shade.

A person [the Princess Yūshi, daughter of the Emperor Gosuzaku] who had heard about me through a distant relative called me to her saying it would be better to be with her than passing idle lonely days.

My old-fashioned parents thought the court life would be very unpleasant, and wanted me to pass my time at home, but others said: "People nowadays go out as ladies-in-waiting at the court, and then fortunate opportunities for marriage are naturally numerous; why not try it?" So at the age of twenty-six I was sent to the court against my will.

I went for one night the first time. I was dressed in an eight-fold *uchigi* of deep and pale chrysanthemum colors, and over it I wore the outer flowing robe of deep red silk.

As I have said before, my mind was absorbed in romances, and I had no well-placed relatives from whom I could learn distinguished manners or court customs. Apart from the romances I could not know them. I had always been in the shadow of my antiquated parents, and had been accustomed not to go out except to see the moon and flowers. So when I left home I felt as if I were not I nor was it the real world to which I was going. I started in the early morning. I had often fancied in my countrified mind that I should hear more interesting things for my heart's consolation than were to be found living fixed in my parents' house.

I felt awkward in court in everything I did, and I thought it sad, but there was no use in complaining. I remembered with grief my nieces who had lost their mother and had been cared for by me alone, even sleeping at night one on either side of me.

Days were spent in musing with a vacant mind. I felt as if some one were always spying on me, and I was embarrassed.[1] After ten days or so I got leave to go out. Father and mother were waiting for me with a comfortable fire in a brazier.

Seeing me getting out of my palanquin, my nieces said: "When you were with us people came to see us, but now no one's voice is heard, no one's shadow falls before the house. We are very low-spirited; what can you do for us who must pass days like this?" It was pitiful to see them cry when they said it. The next morning they sat before me, saying: "As you are here many persons are coming and going. It seems livelier."

Tears came to my eyes to think what virtue I could have that my little nieces made so much of me.

It would be very difficult even for a saint to dream of his prenatal life. Yet, when I was before the altar of the Kiyomizu Temple, in a faintly dreamy state of mind which was neither sleeping nor waking, I saw a man who seemed to be the head of the temple. He came out and said to me:

"You were once a priest of this temple and you were born into a better state by virtue of the many Buddhist images which you carved as a Buddhist artist. The Buddha seventeen feet high which is enthroned in the eastern side of the temple was your work. When you were in the act of covering it with gold foil you died."

"Oh, undeservedly blessed!" I said. "I will finish it, then."

The priest replied: "As you died, another man covered it and performed the ceremony of offerings."

I came to myself and thought: "If I serve with all my heart the Buddha of the Kiyomizu Temple . . . by virtue of my prayers in this temple in the previous life . . ."[2]

[1] The custom of the court obliged the court ladies to lead a life of almost no privacy—sleeping at night together in the presence of the Queen, and sharing their apartments with each other.

[2] Some words are lost from this sentence.

In the Finishing month I went again to the court. A room was assigned for my use.

I went to the Princess's apartment every night and lay down among unknown persons. I could not sleep at all. I was bashful and timid and wept in secret. In the morning I retired while it was still dark and passed the days in longing for home where my old and weak parents, making much of me, relied upon me as if I were worthy of it. I yearned for them and felt very lonely. Unfortunate, deplorable, and helpless mind!—That was graven into my thought and although I had to perform my duty faithfully I could not always wait upon the Princess. She seemed not to guess what was in my heart, and attributing it only to shyness favored me by summoning me often from among the other ladies. She used to say, "Call the younger ladies!" and I was dragged out in spite of myself.

Those who were familiar with the court life seemed to be at home there, but I, who was not very young, yet did not wish to be counted among the elderly, was rather neglected, and made to usher guests. However, I did not expect too much of court life, and had no envy for those who were more graceful than I. This, on the contrary, set me at ease, and I from time to time presented myself before the Princess; and talked only with congenial friends about lovely things. Even on amusing, interesting occasions I shrank from intruding and becoming too popular, and did not go far into most things. . . .

The ladies who were charged with the duty of entertaining the court nobles seemed to have been fixed upon, and nobody noticed whether simple-hearted countrywomen like me existed or not. On a very dark night in the beginning of the gods-absent month, when sweet-voiced reciters were to read Sutras throughout the night, another lady and I went out towards the entrance door of the audience room to listen to it, and after talking fell asleep, listening, leaning, . . . when I noticed a gentleman had come to be received in audience by the Princess.

"It is awkward to run away to our apartment to escape him. We will remain here. Let it be as it will." So said my companion and I sat beside her listening.

He spoke gently and quietly. There was nothing about him to be regretted. "Who is the other lady?" he asked of my friend. He said nothing rude or amorous like other men, but talked delicately of the sad, sweet things of the world, and many a phrase of his with a strange power enticed me into conversation. He wondered that there should have been in the court one who was a stranger to him, and did not seem inclined to go away soon.

There was no starlight, and a gentle shower fell in the darkness; how lovely was its sound on the leaves! "The more deeply beautiful is the night," he said; "the full moonlight would be too dazzling." Discoursing about the beauties of spring and autumn he continued: "Although every hour has its charm, pretty is the spring haze; then the sky being tranquil and overcast, the face of the moon is not too bright; it seems to be floating on a distant river. At such a time the calm spring melody of the lute is exquisite.

"In autumn, on the other hand, the moon is very bright; though there are mists trailing over the horizon we can see things as clearly as if they were at hand. The sound of wind, the voices of insects, all sweet things seem to melt together. When at such a time we listen to the autumnal music of the koto we forget the spring—we think that is best—

"But the winter sky frozen all over magnificently cold! The snow covering the earth and its light mingling with the moonshine! Then the notes of the *hichiriki*[3] vibrate on the air and we forget spring and autumn." And he asked us, "Which captivates your fancy? On which stays your mind?"

My companion answered in favor of autumn and I, not being willing to imitate her, said:

> Pale green night and flowers all melting into one
>   in the soft haze—
> Everywhere the moon, glimmering in the spring night.

So I replied. And he, after repeating my poem to himself over and over, said: "Then you give up autumn? After this, as long as I live, such a spring night shall be for me a memento of your personality."

[3] A pipe made of seven reeds having a very clear, piercing sound.

The person who favored autumn said, "Others seem to give their hearts to spring, and I shall be alone gazing at the autumn moon."

He was deeply interested, and being uncertain in thought said: "Even the poets of the T'ang Empire could not decide which to praise most, spring or autumn. Your decisions make me think that there must be some personal reasons when our inclination is touched or charmed. Our souls are imbued with the colors of the sky, moon, or flowers of that moment. I desire much to know how you came to know the charms of spring and autumn. The moon of a winter night is given as an instance of dreariness, and as it is very cold I had never seen it intentionally. When I went down to Ise to be present as the messenger of the Emperor at the ceremony of installing the virgin in charge of the shrine, I wanted to come back in the early dawn, so went to take leave of the Princess whose installation had just taken place in a moon-bright night after many days' snow, half-shrinking to think of my journey.

"Her residence was an other-worldly place awful even to the imagination, but she called me into a pleasant apartment. There were persons in that room who had come down from the reign of the Emperor Enyū.[4] Their aspect was very holy, ancient, and mystical. They told of the things of long ago with tears. They brought out a well-tuned four-stringed lute. The music did not seem to be anything happening in this world; I regretted that day should even dawn, and was touched so deeply that I had almost forgotten about returning to the capital. Ever since then the snowy nights of winter recall that scene, and I without fail gaze at the moon even though hugging the fire. You will surely understand me, and hereafter every dark night with gentle rain will touch my heart; I feel this has not been inferior to the snowy night at the palace of the Ise virgin."

With these words he departed and I thought he could not have known who I was.

In the eighth month of the next year [1043] we went again to the Imperial palace, and there was in the court an entertainment throughout the night. I did not know that he was present at it,

[4] He ruled from 970 to 984. It was now 1042.

and I passed that night in my own room. When I looked out in early morning, opening the sliding doors on the corridor, I saw the morning moon very faint and beautiful. I heard footsteps and people approached—some reciting Sutras. One of them came to the entrance, and addressed me. I replied, and he, suddenly remembering, exclaimed, "That night of softly falling rain I do not forget, even for a moment! I yearn for it." As chance did not permit me many words I said:

What intensity of memory clings to your heart?
That gentle shower fell on the leaves—
    Only for a moment our hearts touched.

I had scarcely said so when people came up and I stole back without his answer.

That evening, after I had gone to my room, my companion came in to tell me that he had replied to my poem: "If there be such a tranquil night as that of the rain, I should like in some way to make you listen to my lute, playing all the songs I can remember."

I wanted to hear it, and waited for the fit occasion, but there was none, ever.

In the next year one tranquil evening I heard that he had come into the Princess's palace, so I crept out of my chamber with my companion, but there were many people waiting within and without the palace, and I turned back. He must have been of the same mind with me. He had come because it was so still a night, and he returned because it was noisy.

I yearn for a tranquil moment
To be out upon the sea of harmony,
In that enchanted boat.
Oh, boatman, do you know my heart?

So I composed that poem—and there is nothing more to tell. His personality was very excellent and he was not an ordinary man, but time passed, and neither called to the other. . . .

TRANSLATED BY ANNIE SHEFLEY OMORI AND KŌCHI DOI

POETRY IN CHINESE

[The first two poems, although they were written in the Ancient Period, are preserved in a Heian collection, and are therefore given here.]

In praise of Buddha

The sun of his wisdom lights a thousand worlds;
His merciful clouds all creatures hide.
A myriad destinies are fulfilled in His love;
The voice of His law—how it strikes my heart!

Empress Shōtoku (718-770)

The small hills

How march the four seasons in succession
Unwaywardly, from the eons past!
Grasses that greet the spring in flowered tapestry;
The summer trees curtained in leaves;
In the sad breath of autumn, the falling fruit;
Bare branches before the shrill winter wind—
When I see these seasonal things, I know
How man too must flourish and die.
Of the hills of Paradise have I heard but never seen;
Toward the land of the gods I gaze, knowing not the way.
I know only that to make a mountain
You must pile the little clods one by one.
Where then should I seek nobility?
In what delights the heart there is nothing mean.
I roof the narrow grotto in the garden end;
Lead the thin streams to flow before my hall.

Hills beneath heaven;
On the broad earth, trees—
These things that the small man spurns
The wise shall nourish.
Though I want in the straits of distress,
How should I decline the defenses of virtue?
At my ease I draw off the lakes of the west;
My gaze governs the northern waters.
And these ragged hills
That shut not out the coursing sun;
This clear bright pond
Ruffled in the wind;
Pines that nod from their crags in greeting;
Rocks shining from the river bottom beneath drifting watery mirrors;
Scattered clouds that cloak the summits in shadows;
The half-risen moon which lights the vales,
When from tree to tree dart crying birds:
To these will I abandon, will I entrust my life.
The Great Creator, in the variety of his works,
Blesses as well the lowly and small.
When all philosophy I resolve in this one act,
I may stride the leviathan seas and they will not hold me!
Into the dark heart of all being I shall ride
And dwell in the spacious halls of the ant.
Truly need one seek not beyond his door for wisdom;
Must a man see all mountains and seas to love them?
In these lines have I entrusted
The writing of what my heart has learned.

Isonokami no Yakatsugu (729-781)

The banished official

Wine and feasts I followed with the host of officials;
Unworthy, yet I stood in the Court of the Emperor.
With reverence I received the rites of investiture—

Next day I was banished from the council chamber.
On that noble ground, no room for my anxious feet;
From high heaven came accusations, to whom could I cry?
I left the company of the virtuous, the ranks of the adorned;
To me alone the sea-encircling dew came not.[1]
I listened outside the palace to the sound of singing;
Below the stairs, apart, I watched the ladies on the terrace.
I returned in the dusk to face my wife in shame;
Through the night I lay talking with my children in bed.
Great faults and small merit were mine, I know.
For mercy and light penalty I am forever grateful.
Though I may never again enter the gate of my lord,
I shall speak from this far land and Heaven may hear me.

Nakao-ō (Early Ninth Century)

Composed when her father, the Emperor Saga, visited the Kamo Shrine, where she was a priestess

Silent was my lonely lodge among the mountain trees
When to this far lake your fairy carriage came.
The lone forest bird tasted the dew of spring;
Cold flowers of the dark valley saw the sun's brightness.
Springs sound close by like the echo of early thunder;
High hills shine clear and green above the evening rain.
Should I once more know the warmth of this fair face,
All my life will I give thanks to the azure skies.

Princess Uchiko (807-847)

Washing my hair

I look at the comb, I look at the water, I look at what has fallen.
Age and youth are far apart; I cannot have them both.

[1] That is, Imperial favor. In reading Chinese and Japanese poetry, one should keep in mind that since the Emperor is the Son of Heaven metaphors relating to the sky, dew, etc., often refer to the throne.

Do not tell me that my hair gets thinner by the day—
See, instead, how the beards of my grandsons grow out!

Shimada no Tadaomi (828-891)

To comfort my little son and daughter

Michizane, a high official, was forced into exile. All of his twenty-three children were detained or sent to different places except the two youngest, who were allowed to accompany their father to Kyushu.

Your sisters must all stay at home,
Your brothers are sent away.
Just we three together, my children,
Shall chat as we go along.
Each day we have our meals before us,
At night we sleep all together.
We have lamps and tapers to peer in the dark
And warm clothes for the cold.
Last year you saw how the Chancellor's son
Fell out of favor in the capital.
Now people say he is a ragged gambler,
And call him names on the street.
You have seen the barefooted wandering musician
The townspeople call the Justice's Miss—
Her father, too, was a great official;
They were all in their day exceedingly rich.
Once their gold was like sand in the sea;
Now they have hardly enough to eat.
When you look, my children, at other people,
You can see how gracious Heaven has been.

The spider

There is craft in this smallest insect,
With strands of web spinning out his thoughts;
In his tiny body finding rest,

And with the wind lightly turning.
Before the eaves he stakes out his broad earth;
For a moment on the fence top lives through his life.
When you know that all beings are even thus,
You will know what creation is made of.

Sugawara no Michizane (845-903)

The puppeteers

These were a gypsy-like people who wandered about Japan making a living by singing and dancing, operating puppets, and performing feats of magic.

Ceaseless wanderers from of old, the puppeteers,
Over all the earth searching ever a new home.
They pitch their tents and sing in the night to the mountain moon;
Restless they seek new paths; I see their smoke in the spring fields.
Youth in the bright capital, their women pampered favorites;
The years of age alone, watching over a hut of thatch.
The traveler passing far off casts suspicious eyes
At the white hair, the vacant, wrinkled face.

Fujiwara no Tadamichi (1097-1164)

TRANSLATED BY BURTON WATSON

RYŌJIN HISHŌ

During the middle and late Heian Period a new verse form came to be widely used, especially in connection with popular religious movements. This was the imayō *or "modern-style," which generally consisted of four lines, each containing 7, 5 syllables. Most of the poems in the "Ryōjin Hishō" are in this form, although there are many variations. The "Ryōjin Hishō" is an anthology, originally in twenty books, of which only a small part still survives. It was compiled over a period of many years by the Emperor Goshirakawa (1127-1192), being finally completed in 1179. The surviving poems are of three kinds: Buddhist hymns, songs about Shinto shrines and festivals, and folk songs. The folk songs are by far the most interesting; the following translations are all of this type.*

•

May he that bade me trust him, but did not come,
Turn into a demon with three horns on his head,
That all men fly from him!
May he become a bird of the waterfields
Where frost, snow, and hail fall,
That his feet may be frozen to ice!
Oh, may he become a weed afloat on the pond!
May he tremble as he walks with the trembling of the hare,
with the trembling of the doe!

• •

When I look at my lovely lady,
"Oh that I might become a clinging vine," I yearn,

"That from toe to tip I might be twined about her."
Then though they should cut, though they should carve—
Inseparable our lots!

. .

Things that bend in the wind—
The tall branches of pine-tree tops,
Or the little twigs of bamboos,
Boats that run with spread sails on the sea,
Floating clouds in the sky,
And in the fields the flowering *susuki.*

. .

For sport and play
I think that we are born.
For when I hear
The voice of children at their play,
My limbs, even my
Stiff limbs, are stirred.

Dance, dance, Mr. Snail!
If you won't I shall leave you
For the little horse,
For the little ox
To tread under his hoof,
To trample to bits.
But if quite prettily
You dance your dance,
To a garden of flowers
I will carry you to play.

. .

Oh gods almighty!
If gods indeed you are,
Take pity on me;
For even the gods were once
Such men as we.

TRANSLATED BY ARTHUR WALEY

THE LADY WHO LOVED INSECTS

[*from Tsutsumi Chūnagon Monogatari*]

Next door to the lady who loved butterflies was the house of a certain provincial inspector. He had an only daughter, to whose upbringing he and his wife devoted endless care. She was a strange girl, and used to say: "Why do people make so much fuss about butterflies and never give a thought to the creatures out of which butterflies grow? It is the natural form of things that is always the most important." She collected all kinds of reptiles and insects such as most people are frightened to touch, and watched them day by day to see what they would turn into, keeping them in various sorts of little boxes and cages. Among all these creatures her favorite was the common caterpillar. Hour after hour, her hair pushed back from her eyes, she would sit gazing at the furry black form that nestled in the palm of her hand. She found that other girls were frightened of these pets, and her only companions were a number of rather rough little boys, who were not in the least afraid. She got them to carry about the insect-boxes, find out the names of the insects or, if this could not be done, help her to give them new names. She hated anything that was not natural. Consequently she would not pluck a single hair from her eyebrows nor would she blacken her teeth, saying it was a dirty and disagreeable custom. So morning, noon, and night she tended her insects, bending over them with a strange, white gleaming smile.[1] People on the whole were frightened of her and kept away; the few who ventured to approach her came back with the strangest reports. If anyone showed the slightest distaste for her pets, she would ask him indignantly how he could give way to so silly and vulgar a prejudice, and as she said this she would stare at the visitor under her black, bushy eyebrows in a way that made him feel extremely uncomfortable.

Her parents thought all this very peculiar and would much rather

1 Because of her unblackened teeth.

she had been more like other children; but they saw it was no use arguing with her. She for her part took immense trouble in explaining her ideas, but this only resulted in making them feel that she was much cleverer than they. "No doubt," they would say, "all you tell us is quite true, and so far as we are concerned you may do as you please. But people as a rule only make pets of charming and pretty things. If it gets about that you keep hairy caterpillars you will be thought a disgusting girl and no one will want to know you." "I do not mind what they think," she answered. "I want to inquire into everything that exists and find out how it began. Nothing else interests me. And it is very silly of them to dislike caterpillars, all of which will soon turn into lovely butterflies." Then she again explained to them carefully how the cocoon, which is like the thick winter clothes that human beings wear, wraps up the caterpillar till its wings have grown and it is ready to be a butterfly. Then it suddenly waves its white sleeves and flits away. . . .

This was no doubt quite accurate, and they could think of nothing to say in reply; but all the same her views on such matters made them feel very uncomfortable. She would never sit in the same room with her elders, quoting in self-defense the proverb, "Ghosts and girls are best unseen"; and the above attempt to bring her parents to reason was made through a chink in the half-raised blinds of the living room. Hearing of such conversations as this, the young people of the district were amazed at the profundity of her researches. "But what things for a girl to play with!" they said. "She must be an oddity indeed. Let us go and call upon the girl who loves butterflies."

Hearing some of the unflattering comparisons that were being made between herself and the butterfly lady, she rejoined: "I do not see anything very admirable in making a fuss over butterflies. Even those young men must know by now that the prettiest butterflies are but the sheddings of creatures like my hairy caterpillars, who discard them as a snake drops its skin. And caterpillars are much friendlier playthings. For it you catch hold of a butterfly it frees itself as soon as it can, leaving its golden powder on your hand, and this powder is very dangerous, often causing fevers and agues. Fancy trying to make pets of butterflies! It is horrible to think of."

To the little boys who formed her retinue she would give pretty things such as she knew they wanted, and in return they would give her all kinds of terrifying insects. She said the caterpillars would be unhappy if there were no creatures with them to admire their glossy coats, and she therefore collected a number of snails, and also of grass-crickets whose ferocious and incessant cries seemed to suggest that they were at war with one another, thus recalling to her mind the line, "For the ground between a snail's horns what use to fight?"[2] She said she was tired of ordinary boys' names and called her servitors by insect-names, such as Kerao (mole-cricket boy), Inagomaro (locust-man), Amabiko (centipede), and the like. All this was thought very queer and stupid.

Among those who had heard gossip about the girl and her odd pets was a certain young man of good family who vowed that, fond of strange creatures though she might be, he would undertake to give her a fright. So saying he made a marvelously lifelike snake with joints that moved and putting it into a scaly bag sent it to her with the poem: "Creeping and crawling I shall sneak my way to your side, for my persistence[3] is tireless as my body is long." The servant who brought the bag had no idea what it contained. "I wonder what can be in it," he said, as he untied the string. "Certainly something remarkably heavy!" The bag was opened, and to the horror of everyone present a snake protruded its head. But the lady was not at all put out, and having repeated several times the prayer *Namu Amida Butsu* she said, "Do not be frightened! Remember that any one of you may have been a snake in his former existence. Look at the kindly expression of his face and how he is making himself tremble all down his back. Could anything be clearer than that he is signaling to you not to be afraid? I am amazed that anyone should not understand him." So she muttered to herself, and drew the bag toward her. But all the same it seemed as though even she were a little bit afraid, for now she hovered near the creature and now fluttered away again, like a moth at the candle, crooning to it all the while in a low insect voice.

[2] From one of five drinking songs written by the Chinese poet Po Chü-i about 829.

[3] "Persistence" is "length of heart" (*kokoro-nagasa*) in Japanese.

Seeing several of the servants rush out of her room tumbling over one another and screaming with laughter the lady's father asked them what had happened, and at the mention of a snake exclaimed in great consternation, "A nice trick to play upon a young woman! I cannot understand anyone doing such a dastardly thing. A fine pack of rascals you are, to run off like this and leave her with a dangerous viper in the room." So saying, he seized his sword and brandishing it over his head rushed to his daughter's side. But the moment he saw the snake a doubt crossed his mind and examining it attentively he discovered it was only an extremely well-made toy. Picking it up he said, "I remember now that I have heard people say how clever the fellow is at making things of this sort. You must be sure to write at once and thank him for his kindness." When it was known that the snake was only a toy the people who had run away from it declared the joke to be a very silly one. But the lady agreed that it would be rude not to reply and taking a stout, sensible-looking sheet of paper she wrote the following poem, not in *hiragana,* which she never used, but in *katakana*:[4] "If indeed we are fated to meet, not here will it be, but in Paradise, thou crafty image of a snake." And at the side was written: "In the Garden of Blessings you must plant your seed."[5]

It happened that a certain Captain of Horse saw this letter and being much struck with it he determined to obtain an interview with the writer. Choosing a time when he knew her father to be busy elsewhere, he posted himself at a wattled gate on the woman's side of the house and peeped in. Several little boys were poking about among some very dull-looking bushes and shrubs. Presently one of them called out, "Just look at these bushes! They're simply covered with creatures. It's the best place we have ever found." And going to the window he pulled the blind. "Do look at them," he said again. "You can see them from the window. Aren't they the loveliest caterpillars you ever saw?" "Yes, they're not at all bad," said a voice from within. "You may bring them in here if you like." "I've noth-

[4] A square, inelegant, but eminently "sensible" form of syllabary, now used for telegrams, etc.

[5] The snake must by good behavior get itself reborn in some more dignified incarnation.

ing to put them in," said the boy. "You must look at them where they are." Presently the blind was pulled right aside and a girl appeared at the window, craning out toward the nearest boughs of the shrubbery. She had pulled her mantle over her head, but her hair hung loose beneath it, and very lovely hair it was too, but rather untidy-looking, and the Captain thought it must be a long time since she had combed it. Her thick, very dark eyebrows gave her face a rather forbidding air. Her other features were by no means bad. But when she smiled her white teeth gleamed and flashed in a manner that rather disgusted him, for there was something wild and barbaric about it.

"What a sad case!" thought the Captain. "If only she took an ordinary amount of trouble with herself she really would not be bad-looking." Even as she was he did not find her altogether unattractive; for there was about her a strange kind of vehemence, a liveliness of expression, a brilliance of complexion and coloring that could not fail to make some impression on him. With her clothes in themselves there was nothing wrong. She wore a robe of soft, glossy silk, with a spinner's jacket, and white trousers. In order to get a good view of the caterpillars she leaned right out of the window, crying, "Aren't they clever! They've come here in order to be out of the sun. Boy, you might just bring me that one there. I should like to have a better look at him. Be sure not to let him fall." Upon which the boy at once bumped into something and the caterpillar fell with a thud upon the ground. She then handed him a white fan with some Chinese characters written upon it in black ink, saying, "Pick him up quickly and carry him in on this."

It was only now that she caught sight of the Captain, who was still loitering at the wicker gate. To see anyone there was a considerable surprise, for the young men of the neighborhood had long ago decided that she was what they called "a disastrous character," and it was seldom indeed that anyone came that way. The little boy, too, had become aware of the visitor's presence and cried out in astonishment, "Look, there's a gentleman standing at the wicker gate. I can't make out what he is doing. He seems to be staring at us." One of the maids now came along and began to scold her. "Fie upon you," she said, "I shall go straight to your father and tell him you're busy with your nasty insects again, and leaning right out of the window where anyone can see you." But the girl continued to fiddle about with the hairy caterpillars on the bushes near the window. The maid, who had a horror of such creatures, was far too frightened to come any closer, but called again, "Madam, go in this instant. You can be seen!" "Well, what if I can be seen? I am not doing anything to be ashamed of." "I'm not joking, I assure you," said the maid indignantly. "There's a fine gentleman standing right there at the gate. Go away from the window at once!" "Kerao," said the girl at last, "just go to the gate and see if there is still someone there." He ran a little distance toward the gate and presently called out, "It's quite true, there is somebody." Upon which she gathered several caterpillars in her sleeve and stepped back into the interior of the house.

For a moment he saw her at full length. She was rather tall. Her hair floated out behind her as she moved. It was very thick, but the ends were somewhat wispy, no doubt through lack of trimming. But with a little more looking after it would have made (he thought) a fine crop of hair. Certainly she was no great beauty, but if she dressed and behaved like other people she would, he was sure, be capable of cutting quite a decent figure in society. What a pity it was! Where had she picked up the distressing opinions that forced her to make such a melancholy spectacle of herself?

He felt that he must at any rate let her know that he had seen her; and using the juice of a flower stem as ink he wrote the following poem on a piece of thickly folded paper: "Forgive me that at your wicker gate so long I stand. But from the caterpillar's bushy brows I cannot take my eyes." He tapped with his fan, and at once one of the little boys ran out to ask what he wanted. "Take this to your mistress," he said. But it was intercepted by the maid, to whom the little boy explained that the poem came from the fine gentleman who had been standing about near the gate. "Woe upon us all," cried the maid, "this is the handwriting of Captain So-and-So, that is in the Horse Guard. And to think that he has been watching you mess about with your nauseous worms!" And she went on for some time lamenting over the girl's deplorable oddity. At last the insect-lover could bear it no longer and said, "If you looked a little more below the surface of things you would not mind so much what other people thought about you. The world in which we live has no reality, it is a mirage, a dream. Suppose someone is offended by what we do or, for the matter of that, is pleased by it, does his opinion make any difference to us in the end? Before long both he and we shall no longer even appear to exist."

Several of the younger servants had by now gathered round. They found her argument hard to answer, but secretly felt that this was a very dismal view of life. It was not thought likely that she would send an answer, but the Captain was still waiting at the gate and the little boys, who had now all been called back into the house, said the gentleman was looking very unhappy; upon which everyone urged her to write something, and very reluctantly she sent the poem, "By this you may know the strangeness of my mood. Had you not called me *kawamushi*,[6] I would not have replied." To which he answered, "In all the world, I fear, exists no man so delicate that to the hairtips of a caterpillar's brow he could attune his life." Then he went back laughing to his home.

What happened next will be found in the second chapter! [7]

Anonymous (Twelfth Century)

TRANSLATED BY ARTHUR WALEY

[6] Hairy caterpillar.

[7] No second chapter exists.

KAMAKURA PERIOD

1185–1333

THE TALE OF THE HEIKE

[*Heike Monogatari*]

"The Tale of the Heike" deals mainly with the struggle for power at the end of the twelfth century between the Taira family (Heike) and the Minamoto family (Genji). The Minamoto, under Yoritomo and his brother Yoshitsune, were successful, and the Taira completely crushed. Stories of the splendors and fall of the Taira, and of the acts of heroism and pathos which marked the wars, were soon being recited by ballad-singers. These stories were assembled, more or less in the present form, by the middle of the thirteenth century, although we do not know by whom or in what way.

The work has many beautiful and famous sections, but it tends to be episodic. The selections given here are all from the latter part of the book. "The Death of Atsumori" takes place after the disastrous defeat suffered by the Taira at Ichi no tani. "Dan no ura" tells of the final Taira catastrophe, when soldiers, courtiers, and court ladies alike are drowned in the sinking ships. The remaining section, taken from the end of the book, tells of Kenreimon'in, the daughter of Taira no Kiyomori, consort of the Emperor Takakura and mother of the infant Emperor Antoku (who perished at Dan no ura). "The Tale of the Heike," which opens with the bell of the Gion Temple in India, closes with the tolling of the bell of the Jakkō-in, a convent outside Kyoto.

•

THE DEATH OF ATSUMORI

When the Heike were routed at Ichi no tani, and their nobles and courtiers were fleeing to the shore to escape in their ships, Kumagai

Naozane came riding along a narrow path onto the beach, with the intention of intercepting one of their great captains. Just then his eye fell on a single horseman who was attempting to reach one of the ships in the offing. The horse he rode was dappled-gray, and its saddle glittered with gold mounting. Not doubting that he was one of the chief captains, Kumagai beckoned to him with his war fan, crying out: "Shameful! to show an enemy your back. Return! Return!"

The warrior turned his horse and rode back to the beach, where Kumagai at once engaged him in mortal combat. Quickly hurling him to the ground, he sprang upon him and tore off his helmet to cut off his head, when he beheld the face of a youth of sixteen or seventeen, delicately powdered and with blackened teeth, just about the age of his own son and with features of great beauty. "Who are you?" he asked. "Tell me your name, for I would spare your life."

"Nay, first say who you are," replied the young man.

"I am Kumagai Naozane of Musashi, a person of no particular importance."

"Then you have made a good capture," said the youth. "Take my head and show it to some of my side, and they will tell you who I am."

"Though he is one of their leaders," mused Kumagai, "if I slay him it will not turn victory into defeat, and if I spare him, it will not turn defeat into victory. When my son Kojirō was but slightly wounded at Ichi no tani this morning, did it not pain me? How this young man's father would grieve to hear that he had been killed! I will spare him."

Just then, looking behind him, he saw Doi and Kajiwara coming up with fifty horsemen. "Alas! look there," he exclaimed, the tears running down his face, "though I would spare your life, the whole countryside swarms with our men, and you cannot escape them. If you must die, let it be by my hand, and I will see that prayers are said for your rebirth in Paradise."

"Indeed it must be so," said the young warrior. "Cut off my head at once."

Kumagai was so overcome by compassion that he could scarcely wield his blade. His eyes swam and he hardlv knew what he did.

but there was no help for it; weeping bitterly he cut off the boy's head. "Alas!" he cried, "what life is so hard as that of a soldier? Only because I was born of a warrior family must I suffer this affliction! How lamentable it is to do such cruel deeds!" He pressed his face to the sleeve of his armor and wept bitterly. Then, wrapping up the head, he was stripping off the young man's armor when he discovered a flute in a brocade bag. "Ah," he exclaimed, "it was this youth and his friends who were amusing themselves with music within the walls this morning. Among all our men of the Eastern Provinces I doubt if there is any one of them who has brought a flute with him. How gentle the ways of these courtiers!"

When he brought the flute to the Commander, all who saw it were moved to tears; he discovered then that the youth was Atsumori, the youngest son of Tsunemori, aged sixteen years. From this time the mind of Kumagai was turned toward the religious life.[1]

THE FIGHT AT DAN NO URA[2]

Yoshitsune, after his victory at Yashima, crossed over to Suwo to join his brother. Just at this time the High Priest of Kumano, who was under great obligations to the Heike, suddenly had a change of heart and hesitated as to which side he should support. He went to the shrine of Imakumano at Tanabe and spent seven days in retirement there, having sacred dances performed and praying before the deity. He received as a result an oracle commanding him to adhere to the white banner,[3] but he was still doubtful. He then held a cockfight before the shrine, with seven white cocks and seven red ones; the red cocks were all beaten and ran away. He therefore made up his mind to join the Genji.

Assembling all his retainers, to the number of some two thousand men, and embarking them on two hundred ships of war, he put the emblem of the deity of the shrine on board his ship, and painted the name of the Guardian God on the top of his standard. When this

1 He became the priest Rensei, as is related in the *Nō* play *"Atsumori."*

2 This section has been considerably abbreviated.

3 White was the color of the Genji, and red of the Heike.

vessel with its divine burden approached the ships of the Genji and Heike at Dan no ura both parties saluted it reverently, but when it was seen to direct its course toward the fleet of the Genji the Heike could not conceal their chagrin. To the further consternation of the Heike, Michinobu of the province of Iyo also came rowing up with a hundred and fifty large ships and went over to the fleet of their enemies.

Thus the forces of the Genji went on increasing, while those of the Heike grew less. The Genji had some three thousand ships, and the Heike one thousand, among which were some of Chinese build. Thus, on the twenty-fourth day of the third month of 1185, at Ta no ura in the province of Bungo and at Dan no ura in the province of Nagato, began the final battle of the Genji and the Heike.

Both sides set their faces against each other and fought grimly without a thought for their lives, neither giving an inch. But as the Heike had on their side an emperor endowed with the Ten Virtues and the Three Sacred Treasures of the Realm,[4] things went hard with the Genji and their hearts were beginning to fail them, when suddenly something that they at first took for a cloud but soon made out to be a white banner floating in the breeze came drifting over the two fleets from the upper air, and finally settled on the stern of one of the Genji ships, hanging on by the rope.

When he saw this, Yoshitsune, regarding it as a sign from the Great Bodhisattva Hachiman,[5] removed his helmet and after washing his hands did obeisance; his men all followed his example. Just then a shoal of thousands of dolphins appeared and made straight for the ships of the Heike. One of the Heike generals called a diviner and said, "There are always many dolphins about here, but I have never seen so many before; what may it portend?" "If they turn back," replied the diviner, "the Genji will be destroyed, but if

[4] The "Ten Virtues" was an adjective used of the Emperor, and meant someone not guilty of any of the ten sins (killing living beings, lying, obscene language, theft, adultery, cursing, being double-tongued, covetousness, anger, and foolishness). The Imperial Regalia, by which an emperor could prove his right to the throne, were the Sword, the Mirror, and the Jewels.

[5] The Shinto god Hachiman (the god of war) was officially also considered a bodhisattva.

they go on our own side will be in danger." No sooner had he finished speaking than the dolphins dived under the Heike ships and passed on.

As things had come to this pass, Shigeyoshi, who for three years had been a loyal supporter of the Heike, made up his mind that all was lost, and suddenly forsook his allegiance and deserted to the enemy.

The strategy of the Heike had been to put the stoutest warriors on board the ordinary fighting ships and the inferior soldiers on the big ships of Chinese build; the Genji would be induced to attack the big ships, thinking that the commanders were on board them, and the Heike could then surround and destroy them. But when Shigeyoshi went over and joined the Genji he revealed this plan to them, with the result that they left the big ships alone and concentrated their attacks on the smaller ones, which bore the Heike champions. Later on the men of Shikoku and Kyushu all left the Heike in a body and went over to the Genji. Those who had so far been their faithful retainers now turned their bows against their lords and drew their swords against their own masters. On one shore the heavy seas beat on the cliff so as to forbid any landing, while on the other stood the serried ranks of the enemy waiting with leveled arrows to receive them. And so on this day the struggle for supremacy between the Genji and the Heike was at last decided.

Meanwhile the Genji warriors sprang from one Heike vessel to the other, shooting and cutting down the sailors and helmsmen,—who left their posts and flung themselves in panic to the bottom of the ships. Tomomori rowed in a small boat to the Imperial vessel and cried out, "You see what affairs have come to! Clean up the ship, and throw everything unsightly into the sea!" He ran about the ship from bow to stern, sweeping and cleaning and gathering up the dust with his own hands. "How goes the battle, Tomomori?" asked the court ladies. "Oh, you'll soon see some rare gallants from the east," he replied, bursting into loud laughter. "What? Is this a time for joking?" they answered, and they lifted up their voices and wept aloud.

Then the Lady Nii, who had already resolved what she would do, donned a double outer dress of dark gray mourning and tucking up her long skirts put the Sacred Jewel under her arm and the Sacred Sword in her sash. She took the Emperor in her arms and said, "Though I am but a woman, I will not fall into the hands of the enemy. I will accompany our Sovereign Lord. Let those of you who will, follow me." She moved softly to the gunwale of the vessel.

The Emperor was seven years old that year but looked much older than his age. He was so lovely that he seemed to shed a brilliant radiance about him, and his long black hair hung loose far down his back. With a look of surprise and anxiety on his face he asked the Lady Nii, "Where are you going to take me?"

She turned to the youthful sovereign, with tears streaming down her cheeks, and answered, "Perhaps Your Majesty does not know that he was reborn to the Imperial throne in this world as a result of the merit of the Ten Virtues practiced in former lives. Now, however, some evil karma claims you. Turn to the east and bid farewell to the deity of the Great Shrine of Ise and then to the west and say the *nembutsu,* that Amida Buddha and the Holy Ones may come to welcome you to the Pure Western Land.[6] Japan is small as a grain of millet, but now it is a vale of misery. There is a pure land of happiness beneath the waves, another capital where no sorrow is. It is there that I am taking my Sovereign."

She comforted him, and bound up his long hair in his dove-colored robe. Blinded with tears, the child sovereign put his beautiful little hands together. He turned first to the east to say farewell of the deity of Ise and then to the west to repeat the *nembutsu.* The Lady Nii took him tightly in her arms and with the words, "In the depths of the ocean is our capital," sank with him at last beneath the waves.

THE FORMER EMPRESS BECOMES A NUN

Kenreimon'in, the former Empress, went to Yoshida at the foot of Higashiyama and entered the cell of a monk called Keiei. It was old

[6] The *nembutsu* is an invocation to Amida Buddha practiced by members of the Jōdo (Pure Land) sect.

and dilapidated, its garden was overgrown with weeds, and hare's-foot fern clustered thickly on the roof. The curtains were gone and the bedchamber exposed, and there was nothing to keep out the wind and rain. There were many kinds of flowers, but none to care for them, and no one was there to gaze at the moon streaming in every night. She who had formerly spent her days in the jeweled palace, within the brocade curtains, now suffered the unspeakable hardships of dwelling in this moldering cell, bereft of all her old companions, like a fish on the dry land or a bird torn from its nest, and she yearned for the times she had spent tossing on the sea.

On the first day of the fifth month of 1185 the former Empress cut short her hair and was instructed in the Way by the abbot of the Chōraku Temple. For the customary offering she presented him with the robe of the Emperor Antoku, one he had worn up to the time of his death, so that the perfume still clung to it. She had brought it with her to the capital from the far off Western Provinces, intending to keep it as a memento of him never to leave her person, but now, as she had nothing else to offer, and thinking moreover that it might be an aid to the Emperor's salvation, she handed it to the priest, weeping bitterly. The priest was so affected that he could utter no word, but pressing the sleeve of his black robe to his face retired weeping from her presence. This robe was afterward woven into a banner and suspended in front of the Buddha of the Chōraku Temple.

The Empress was appointed Imperial Consort at the age of fourteen, and at fifteen was raised to the rank of Empress. She was ever by the Emperor's side, helping him in the government by day and the only sharer of his love by night. At the age of twenty-one she bore a prince who was named Heir to the Throne, and when he assumed the Imperial dignity she became Retired Empress and took the name of Kenreimon'in.[7] She was the daughter of the Chancellor Kiyomori and as mother of the Emperor she was held in great reverence by the people. She was twenty-eight this year, and the beauty of her fair face was not yet dimmed; neither was the elegance of her

[7] Kenreimon'in was born in 1155.

slender form impaired; but what now availed the loveliness of her hair? She renounced the world and became a nun, but even when she had entered the True Way her grief was not assuaged. She seemed ever to see before her the figures of the Emperor and the Lady Nii and the others as they sank in the waves, and never in this life could she forget those melancholy scenes. She wondered why she had remained alive to bear such sorrows, and her tears were never dried.

It was not easy to keep awake on even the short nights of June, but if she did not fall asleep she would not dream of those who had passed away. Faintly the shadow of her single light fell on the wall outside, and all night the dismal drumming of the rain sounded on the lattice of the windows. And how it reminded her of the beloved past—this orange tree in blossom by the eaves that a former tenant had brought and planted there. Its heavy perfume was wafted into her chamber, and the notes of the nightingale were borne once and again to her ears.

The rest of the court ladies, who had thrown themselves into the sea but not with the same determination as the Lady Nii, had been roughly dragged out by the Genji soldiers and brought back to the capital. Young and old alike, they had all become nuns and were living in concealment in faraway valleys and dells in the mountains, wretched and emaciated in appearance and quite unrecognizable as their former selves.

The places where they lived have gone up in smoke, and the empty site, turned into overgrown moorland, is all that remains. No former intimate ever comes nigh. All is as unfamiliar now as his home to one who is bewitched by fairies and returns after seven generations.

THE FORMER EMPRESS GOES TO OHARA

On the ninth day of the seventh month the Empress's abode was ruined in the great earthquake. Its outer wall fell down, and she had nowhere to live. How the days had altered from the time the green-clad palace guards stood continually before her gate, for now the tumble-down wall, more bedewed with moisture than the outside moorland, seemed as if it understood the change of times and resented the incessant shrilling of the insects. Though the nights grew longer, the Empress could not sleep. She brooded continually over her melancholy condition, and this, added to the natural sadness of autumn, became almost too much for her to bear. In the changed world there was none to feel sympathy for her, and all those of her affinity were gone, leaving none to cherish her in her need.

Only the wife of Takafusa and the wife of Nobutaka used to help her secretly. "Ah," she exclaimed, "in former days who would have ever dreamed that I should come to accept anything from such as these?" The Empress thought that she would like to go somewhere far away in the depths of the mountains to spend her days remote from all sound of unrest, for her present dwelling was too near the capital and attracted the eyes of curious passers-by. For some time she did not hear of any suitable spot, but a lady came to tell her of a place in the mountains of Ohara, north of the capital, called the Jakkō-in. "A mountain abode is very lonely, it is true," she answered, "but it would be good to live in a place remote from the troubles of this world." The matter was settled, and the wives of Nobutaka and Takafusa sent a palanquin to fetch her.

At the end of the ninth month she proceeded to the temple of the Jakkō-in. As they went along she gazed at the beauty of the autumn tints while the sun sank gradually behind the mountains. The dreary boom of the evening bell of a wayside temple, and the thick-lying dew on the grass as they went by drew tears from her eyes. A fierce gale was whirling the leaves from the trees in all directions. Suddenly the sky grew dark and the autumn drizzle began to fall; the cry of a deer sounded faintly, and the shrilling of the insects was incessant. Nothing was wanting to add to the sum of her afflictions, which seemed indeed such as few had been made to suffer. Even when she had been driven about from shore to shore and from island to island her melancholy was not to be compared to this.

The place she had chosen to dwell was ancient and surrounded by mossy rocks. The reeds in the garden were now covered with hoar-frost instead of dew, and when she gazed on the faded hue of the withered chrysanthemums by the wall she could hardly fail to be reminded of her own condition. Entering before the Buddha, she prayed for the sacred spirit of the Emperor, that it might attain perfect Buddhahood, and for the departed spirits of all the Heike, that they might quickly enter the Way of Salvation. But still the image of the late Emperor was impressed on her mind, and wherever she might be, and in what world soever, she thought she could never forget it. They built for her a small cell ten feet square beside the Jakkō-in, and in it were two rooms; in one she put her shrine of Buddha and in the other she slept. There she spent her time continually repeating the *nembutsu* and performing the Buddhist services, both by night and by day.

It happened that once, on the fifth day of the tenth month, she heard the sound as of someone treading on the oak leaves which had fallen and covered the garden. "Who can it be," she exclaimed, "that comes to disturb one who has thus renounced the world? Go and see; for I will conceal myself if it be anyone I do not wish to meet." One of the ladies went to look, and it was only a young stag that had passed that way.

THE PRIESTLY SOVEREIGN GOES TO OHARA[8]

In the spring of 1186 the Priestly Sovereign expressed a wish to go to Ohara and see the place where Kenreimon'in was living in retirement, but March and April were stormy and the cold still lingered. The snow did not melt on the mountains nor the icicles thaw in the valleys. Spring passed and summer came, and the festival of Kamo was already over when His Majesty proceeded to the recesses of Ohara. The summer grasses had grown up thickly, and as they parted them on the little-trodden road His Majesty, who had never

[8] A priestly sovereign (*hōō*) was an emperor who had abdicated and taken Buddhist orders. The sovereign in question was Goshirakawa (1127-1192).

been there before, was much affected by the lonely uninhabited look of the place.

At the foot of the western mountains they came to a small temple. This was the Jakkō-in. It might be described by the lines: "The roof tiles were broken, and the mist, entering, lit perpetual incense; the doors had fallen from their hinges and the moonbeams were its sanctuary lamps." [9] The pond and trees of its ancient garden were dignified; the young grass grew thick and the green shoots of the willow were tangled. The water plants on the pond, floating in the little waves, might have been mistaken for brocade. On the island the purple of the flowering wistaria mingled with the green of the pine; the late-blooming cherry among the young leaves was even more wonderful than the early blossoms. From the clouds of kerria roses that were flowering in profusion on the bank came the call of the cuckoo, a note of welcome in honor of His Majesty's visit.

The sound of the water was pleasant as it fell from the clefts of the timeworn rocks, and the ivied walls and beetling crags would have defied the brush of the painter. When His Majesty came to the cell of the former Empress, ivy was growing on the eaves and the morning-glory was climbing up them; the hare's-foot fern and the day lily mingled together, and here and there was a useless gourd-plant; here was the grass that grew thick in the path of Yen Yüan and the white goosefoot that keeps men at a distance, and here too was the rain that moistened the door of Yüan Hsien.[10] The cedar boards of the roof were gaping, so that the rain, the hoar-frost, and the dew of evening vied with the moonbeams in gaining entrance, and the place appeared almost uninhabitable. Behind was the mountain and in front was the moor, and the bamboo grasses rustled loudly in the wind. As is the way with those who have no friends in the world, she seldom heard any news from the capital, but instead the cry of the monkeys as they sprang from tree to tree and the sound of the wood-cutter's axe.

[9] A quotation from an unknown source.

[10] Yen Yüan and Yüan Hsien were disciples of Confucius. The allusions here to Chinese and Japanese literature would be tedious to unravel.

The Priestly Sovereign called to her, but there was no answer. After a while a withered-looking old nun appeared, and he asked her, "Where has the former Empress gone?" "Over to the mountain to pick some flowers," was the reply. "How hard it is," said His Majesty, "that since she renounced the world she has had no one to perform such services for her."

"This fate has come upon her in accordance with the Five Precepts and the Ten Virtues," said the nun. "Why then should she spare herself the austerities of mortifying her flesh?"

The Priestly Sovereign looked at this nun and noticed that she was clothed in pieces of silk and cotton roughly put together. He thought it strange that one of such appearance should speak thus, and asked who she was. For some time she could answer nothing, but only wept. After a while she controlled her feelings and replied, "I am Awa no Naiji, daughter of the late Shinzei. Once you loved me very deeply, and if now you have forgotten me it must be because I have become old and ugly." She pressed her sleeve to her face, unable to control herself any longer: a sight too pitiful to behold.

"Yes," said His Majesty, "it is you, Awa no Naiji. I had forgotten all about you. Everything now seems like a dream." He could not stop the tears, and the courtiers with him said with emotion, "She seemed to speak so strangely for a nun, but she had good cause."

Presently two nuns clad in dark robes were seen making their way slowly and painfully down through the rough rocks of the mountainside. The Priestly Sovereign asked who they were, and the nun replied, "The one carrying a basket of mountain azaleas on her arm is the former Empress, and the other, with a load of bracken for burning, is the daughter of Korezane."

The former Empress, since she was living apart from the world in this way, was so overwhelmed with shame at seeing the visitors that she would gladly have hidden herself somewhere to avoid them, but she could not retrace her steps to the mountains nor was she able to go into her cell. The old nun came to her as she stood dumbfounded, and took her basket from her hands.

"Since you have renounced the world," said Awa no Naiji, "what does it matter about your appearance? I pray you come and greet His Majesty, for he will soon be returning to the capital."[11]

THE PASSING AWAY OF THE FORMER EMPRESS

The boom of the bell of the Jakkō-in proclaimed the closing day as the evening sun began to sink in the west. His Majesty, full of regret at saying farewell, set out on his return journey with tears in his eyes. The former Empress, her mind occupied in spite of herself with thoughts of bygone days and shedding tears she could not restrain, stood watching the Imperial procession until she could see it no more. Again entering her cell, she prostrated herself before the Buddha. . . .

The former Empress continued to live on unhappily for some years, till at length she fell ill and took to her bed. She had been awaiting death for a long time, and now she took in her hand the cord of five colors that was fastened to the hand of the Buddha[12] and repeated the *nembutsu,* "Hail Amida Buddha, Lord who guidest us to the Paradise of the West; in remembrance of thy Great Vow, I beseech thee receive me into the Pure Land." As she thus prayed, the daughter of Korezane and the nun Awa no Naiji, standing on either side of her couch, lifted up their voices in lamentation at their sad parting. As the sound of her prayer grew weaker and weaker, a purple cloud of splendor unknown grew visible in the west, and an unknown perfume of wondrous incense filled the cell, while celestial strains of music were heard from above. Thus, in the middle of the second month of 1213, the former Empress Kenreimon'in breathed her last.

TRANSLATED BY A. L. SADLER

[11] The meeting between the former Empress and the Priestly Sovereign, here omitted, consists almost entirely of a recounting, by the Empress, of the events of the past few months.

[12] In Jōdo Buddhism, the believer on his deathbed grasps a cord attached to a picture of the Buddha, and is supposed thus to be drawn into Paradise.

SHINKOKINSHŪ

The "Shinkokinshū," or "New Collection of Ancient and Modern Poems," was the eighth of the anthologies of Japanese poetry compiled by Imperial order. It was completed in 1205 by a committee headed by the celebrated Fujiwara no Teika (1162-1241), the leading figure in the world of letters of his day. The Emperor Gotoba,[1] who ordered the compilation, took an active interest in the "Shinkokinshū" and worked on it while in exile on the island of Oki.

The "Shinkokinshū" is often considered to be the greatest Japanese collection after the "Man'yōshū." It is known particularly for the craftsmanship displayed by its poets, although this same quality has been denounced by some critics as "artificiality." The attempt of its poets was to fill the elegantly wrought framework of their verses with content as poignant and moving as possible. With such poets as Saigyō (1118-1190) new heights in Japanese poetry were thereby reached. Needless to say, however, the technical perfection of the "Shinkokinshū" poems is largely lost in translation.

•

Murasame no	The hanging raindrops
Tsuyu mo mada hinu	Have not dried from the needles
Maki no ha ni	Of the fir forest
Kiri tachinoboru	Before the evening mist
Aki no yūgure	Of autumn rises.

The Priest Jakuren (died 1202)

TRANSLATED BY KENNETH REXROTH

[1] See page 242.

• •

Sayo chidori
Koe koso chikaku
Narumi-gata
Katabuku tsuki ni
Shio ya mitsuramu

The cries of the night
Sanderlings draw closer
To Narumi Beach;
As the moon sinks in the sky
The tide rises to the full.

Shōsammi Sueyoshi

• •

Katami to te
Hono fumi wakeshi
Ato mo nashi
Kishi wa mukashi no
Niwa no ogiwara

Nothing whatsoever
Remains of you in this grass
We once used to tread;
How long ago it was we came—
The garden now is a wilderness.

Fujiwara no Yasusue

• •

Hana wa chiri
Sono iro to naku
Nagamureba
Munashiki sora ni
Harusame zo furu

The blossoms have fallen.
I stare blankly at a world
Bereft of color:
In the wide vacant sky
The spring rains are falling.

Princess Shikushi (died 1201)

• •

Hakanakute
Suginishi kata wo
Kazōreba
Hana ni mono omou
Haru zo henikeru

When I tell over
The years of a past spent in
Empty promises,
How many springs have gone by
Lamenting with the blossoms!

Princess Shikushi

• •

Omoiamari	When I stare off
Sonata no sora wo	At the far sky where you are,
Nagamureba	In excess of grief,
Kasumi wo wakete	Filtering through the mists
Harusame zo furu	The spring rains are falling.

Fujiwara no Shunzei (1114-1204)

• •

Uchishimeri	The irises,
Ayame zo kaoru	Their petals damp, are fragrant.
Hototogisu	Listen! The cuckoos
Naku ya satsuki no	Are calling now, this rainy
Ame no yūgure	Evening in May.

Fujiwara no Yoshitsune (1169-1206)

• •

Ima komu to	He promised me then
Chigirishi koto wa	He would come to me at once—
Yume nagara	That was in a dream:
Mishi yo ni nitaru	And yet the moon at daybreak
Ariake no tsuki	Looked as it did the night we met.

Minamoto no Michitomo (1171-1227)

• •

Haru no yo no	When the floating bridge
Yume no ukihashi	Of the dream of a spring night
Todae shite	Was snapped, I awoke:
Mine ni wakaruru	In the sky a bank of clouds
Yokogumo no sora	Was drawing away from the peak.

Fujiwara no Teika

. .

Wasureji no — It will be hard
Yukusue made wa — To keep forever the vow
Katakereba — Never to forget—
Kyō wo kagiri no — Would today could be the limit,
Inochi to mo gana — And with it see our lives expire!

The Mother of Gidō Sanji

. .

Wasureji to — You said you would not
Iishi bakari no — Forget me—those were but words;
Nagori to te — All that still remains
Sono yo no tsuki wa — Is the moon which shone that night
Meguru kinikeri — And now has come again.

Fujiwara no Ariie (1155-1216)

. .

Sabishisa wa — Loneliness does not
Sono iro to shi mo — Originate in any one
Nakarikeri — Particular thing:
Maki tatsu yama no — Evening in autumn over
Aki no yūgure — The black pines of the mountain.

The Priest Jakuren

. .

Kokoro naki — Even to someone
Mi ni mo aware wa — Free of passions[2] this sadness
Shirarekeri — Would be apparent:
Shigi tatsu sawa no — Evening in autumn over
Aki no yūgure — A marsh where a snipe rises.

Saigyō

[2] Meaning here a monk.

. .

Miwataseba	In this wide landscape
Hana mo momiji mo	I see no cherry blossoms
Nakarikeri	And no crimson leaves—[3]
Ura no tomaya no	Evening in autumn over
Aki no yūgure	A straw-thatched hut by the bay.

Fujiwara no Teika

. .

Furuhata no	In a tree standing
Soba no tatsu ki ni	Beside a desolate field,
Iru hato no	The voice of a dove
Tomo yobu koe no	Calling to its companions—
Sugoki yūgure	Lonely, terrible evening.

Saigyō

. .

Toshi takete	Did I ever dream
Mata koyubeshi to	I should pass this way again
Omoiki ya	As an old man?
Inochi narikeri	I have lived such a long time—
Sayo no Nakayama	Nakayama of the Night.[4]

Saigyō

. .

Haruka naru	Living all alone
Iwa no hazama ni	In this space between the rocks
Hitori ite	Far from the city,
Hito me omowade	Here, where no one can see me,
Mono omowabaya	I shall give myself to grief.

Saigyō

TRANSLATED BY DONALD KEENE

[3] Cherry blossoms and crimson leaves were the conventionally admired natural objects of spring and autumn respectively.

[4] A place name famous in poetry; such common place names as Nakayama were often identified as here by some descriptive term. See also page 249.

AN ACCOUNT OF MY HUT

[*Hōjōki*] *by Kamo no Chōmei*

"An Account of My Hut" was written in 1212, the same year as the death of Hōnen, the great leader of Japanese popular Buddhism. There is a deeply Buddhist tinge to the work, a Buddhism quite unlike the intellectual, aesthetic religion which Kūkai had taught. The new Buddhism—and this work—was pessimistic, as was not surprising in view of the disasters which befell Japanese society in the late Heian Period. The author, Kamo no Chōmei (1153-1216), describes in this work some of the calamities which he personally witnessed; he does not allude, however, to the fighting between the Taira and the Minamoto which also ravaged the country. In such terrible times men often turn to religion as he did, and his account of the life he led before and after "abandoning the world" is still very moving.

•

The flow of the river is ceaseless and its water is never the same. The bubbles that float in the pools, now vanishing, now forming, are not of long duration: so in the world are man and his dwellings. It might be imagined that the houses, great and small, which vie roof against proud roof in the capital remain unchanged from one generation to the next, but when we examine whether this is true, how few are the houses that were there of old. Some were burnt last year and only since rebuilt; great houses have crumbled into hovels and those who dwell in them have fallen no less. The city is the same, the people are as numerous as ever, but of those I used to know, a bare one or two in twenty remain. They die in the morning, they are born in the evening, like foam on the water.

Whence does he come, where does he go, man that is born and

dies? We know not. For whose benefit does he torment himself in building houses that last but a moment, for what reason is his eye delighted by them? This too we do not know. Which will be first to go, the master or his dwelling? One might just as well ask this of the dew on the morning-glory. The dew may fall and the flower remain—remain, only to be withered by the morning sun. The flower may fade before the dew evaporates, but though it does not evaporate, it waits not the evening.

THE GREAT FIRE

In the forty and more years that have passed since first I became aware of the meaning of things, I have witnessed many terrible sights. It was, I believe, the twenty-eighth day of the fourth month of 1177, on a night when the wind blew fiercely without a moment of calm, that a fire broke out toward nine o'clock in the southeast of the capital and spread northwest. It finally reached the gates and buildings of the palace, and within the space of a single night all was reduced to ashes. The fire originated in a little hut where a sick man lodged.

The fire fanned out as the shifting wind spread it, first in one direction and then another. Houses far away from the conflagration were enveloped in the smoke, while the area nearby was a sea of flames. The ashes were blown up into the sky, which turned into a sheet of crimson from the reflected glare of the fire, and the flames, relentlessly whipped by the wind, seemed to fly over two or three streets at a time. Those who were caught in the midst could not believe it was actually happening: some collapsed, suffocated by the smoke, others surrounded by flames died on the spot. Still others barely managed to escape with their lives, but could not rescue any of their property: all their treasures were turned into ashes. How much had been wasted on them!

Sixteen mansions belonging to the nobility were burnt, not to speak of innumerable other houses. In all, about a third of the capital was destroyed. Several thousand men and women lost their lives, as well as countless horses and oxen. Of all the follies of human endeavor, none is more pointless than expending treasures and spirit to build houses in so dangerous a place as the capital.

THE WHIRLWIND

Again, on the twenty-ninth day of the fourth moon of 1180, a great whirlwind sprang up in the northeast of the capital and violently raged as far south as the Sixth Ward. Every house, great or small, was destroyed within the area engulfed by the wind. Some were knocked completely flat, others were left with their bare framework standing. The tops of the gates were blown off and dropped four or five hundred yards away, and fences were swept down, making neighboring properties one. Innumerable treasures from within the houses were tossed into the sky; roofs of bark or thatch were driven like winter leaves in the wind. A smoke-like dust rose, blindingly thick, and so deafening was the roar that the sound of voices was lost in it. Even so must be the blasts of Hell, I thought.

Not only were many houses damaged or destroyed, but countless people were hurt or crippled while repairing them. The whirlwind moved off in a southwesterly direction, leaving behind many to bewail its passage. People said in wonder, "We have whirlwinds all the time, but never one like this. It is no common case—it must be a presage of terrible things to come."

THE MOVING OF THE CAPITAL

In the sixth month of the same year the capital was suddenly moved, a most unexpected occurrence. It had been hundreds of years since the reign of the Emperor Saga when the capital was fixed in Kyoto.[1] The site of the capital was not a thing lightly to be changed without sufficient reason, and the people were excessively agitated and worried by the news.

However, complaints served no purpose and everyone moved, from the Emperor, his ministers, and the nobility on downward. Of

1 The capital was actually established at Kyoto by Saga's father, the Emperor Kammu, in 794.

all those who served the court, not a soul was left in the old capital. Those who had ambitions of office or favors to ask of the Emperor vied to be the first to make the move. Only those who, having lost their chances of success, were superfluous in the world and had nothing to hope for, remained behind, although with sorrow. The mansions whose roofs had rivaled one another fell with the passing days to rack and ruin. Houses were dismantled and floated down the Yodo River, and the capital turned into empty fields before one's eyes. People's ways changed completely—now horses were prized and oxcarts fell into disuse. Estates by the sea in the south or west were highly desired, and no one showed any liking for manors in the east or the north.[2]

About this time I happened to have business which took me to the new capital. The site was so cramped that there was not even enough space to divide the city into the proper number of streets.[3] To the north the land rose up high along a ridge of hills and to the south sloped down to the sea. The roar of the waves made a constant din, and the salt winds were of a terrible severity. The palace was in the mountains and, suggesting as it did the log construction of the ancient palaces, was not without its charms.

I wondered where they could have erected the houses that were daily dismantled and sent down the river so thick as to clog it. There were still many empty fields, and few houses standing. The old capital was now desolate but the new one had yet to be finished. Men all felt uncertain as drifting clouds. Those people who were natives of the place lamented the loss of their land, and those who now moved there complained over the difficulties of putting up houses. I could see on the roads men on horseback who should have been riding in carriages; instead of wearing court robes they were

[2] Oxcarts were the traditional vehicles of the court nobility, who now were changing to military ways. Estates near the new capital of Fukuhara (by the Inland Sea) were desirable, but those near the center of Minamoto power in the east and north were dangerous.

[3] According to the *yin-yang* system of Chinese divination, a capital should have nine streets running east-west and eight streets running north-south, as was observed in the building of Kyoto.

in simple service dress. The manners of the capital had suddenly changed and were now exactly like those of rustic soldiers.

Everywhere people could be heard wondering if future disorders were portended, and indeed, with the passage of the days, the country came to be torn by disturbances and unrest. The sufferings of the people were not, however, entirely in vain—in the winter of the same year the capital was returned to Kyoto. But what had happened to the dismantled houses? They could not all have been re-erected in their former grandeur.

Some faint reports have reached my ears that in the wise reigns of former days the country was ruled with clemency. Then the Imperial palace was thatched with straw, and not even the eaves were aligned.[4] When the Emperor saw that the smoke rising from the kitchen fires was thin, he went so far as to remit the taxes, although they were not excessive. That was because he loved his people and sought to help them. If we compare present conditions with those of ancient times, we may see how great is the difference.

THE FAMINE

Again, about 1181—it is so long ago that I cannot remember for certain—there was a famine in the country which lasted two years, a most terrible thing. A drought persisted through the spring and summer, while the autumn and winter brought storms and floods. One disaster followed another, and the grains failed to ripen. All in vain was the labor of tilling the soil in spring or planting in summer, for there was none of the joy of the autumn reaping or winter harvest. Some of the people as a result abandoned their lands and crossed into other provinces; some forgot their homes and went to live in the mountains. All manner of prayers were begun and extraordinary devotions performed, but without the slightest effect.

The capital had always depended on the countryside for its needs, and when supplies ceased to come it became quite impossible for

[4] A description combining the virtues of the legendary Chinese Emperor Yao with the Japanese Emperor Nintoku.

people to maintain their composure. They tried in their desperation to barter for food one after another of their possessions, however cheaply, but no one desired them. The rare person who was willing to trade had contempt for money and set a high value on his grain. Many beggars lined the roads, and their doleful cries filled the air.

Thus the first year of the famine at last drew to a close. It was thought that the new year would see an improvement, but it brought instead the additional affliction of epidemics, and there was no sign of any amelioration. The people were starving, and with the passage of days approached the extremity, like fish gasping in insufficient water. Finally, people of quality, wearing hats and with their legs covered,[5] were reduced to going from house to house desperately begging. Overwhelmed by misery, they would walk in a stupor, only presently to collapse. The number of those who died of starvation outside the gates or along the roads may not be reckoned. There being no one even to dispose of the bodies, a stench filled the whole world, and there were many sights of decomposing bodies too horrible to behold. Along the banks of the Kamo River there was not even room for horses and cattle to pass.

The lower classes and the wood-cutters were also at the end of their strength, and as even firewood grew scarce those without other resources broke up their own houses and took the wood to sell in the market. The amount obtainable for all that a man could carry, however, was not enough to sustain life a single day. Strange to relate, among the sticks of firewood were some to which bits of vermilion or gold and silver leaf still adhered. This, I discovered, came about because people with no other means of living were robbing the old temples of their holy images or breaking up the furnishings of the sacred halls for firewood. It was because I was born in a world of foulness and evil that I was forced to witness such heartbreaking sights.

There were other exceedingly unhappy occurrences. In the case of husbands and wives who refused to separate, the ones whose affections were the stronger were certain to die first. This was because, whether man or woman, they thought of themselves second and

[5] Ordinary beggars would have been bareheaded and barelegged.

gave to their beloved whatever food they occasionally managed to get. With parents and children it inevitably happened that the parents died first. Sometimes an infant, not realizing that its mother was dead, would lie beside her, sucking at her breast.

The Abbot Ryūgyō of the Ninnaji, grieving for the countless people who were dying, gathered together a number of priests who went about writing the letter A on the forehead of every corpse they saw, thus establishing communion with Buddha.[6] In an attempt to determine how many people had died, they made a count during the fourth and fifth months, and found within the boundaries of the capital over 42,300 corpses lying in the streets. What would the total have been had it included all who died before or after that period, both within the city and in the suburbs? And what if all the provinces of Japan had been included?

I have heard that a similar disaster occurred in 1134, during the reign of the Emperor Sutoku, but I did not myself experience what happened then. Of all that has passed before my eyes, this famine was the strangest and saddest of all disasters.

THE EARTHQUAKE

Then there was the great earthquake of 1185, of an intensity not known before. Mountains crumbled and rivers were buried, the sea tilted over and immersed the land. The earth split and water gushed up; boulders were sundered and rolled into the valleys. Boats that rowed along the shores were swept out to sea. Horses walking along the roads lost their footing. It is needless to speak of the damage throughout the capital—not a single mansion, pagoda, or shrine was left whole. As some collapsed and others tumbled over, dust and ashes rose like voluminous smoke. The rumble of the earth shaking and the houses crashing was exactly like that of thunder. Those who were in their houses, fearing that they would presently be crushed to death, ran outside, only to meet with a new cracking of the earth.

[6] In Shingon Buddhism, of which the Ninnaji was a center, great significance is given to *A,* the first letter of the Sanskrit alphabet, the beginning of things, and it is believed that all afflictions can be ended by contemplating this letter.

They could not soar into the sky, not having wings. They could not climb into the clouds, not being dragons. Of all the frightening things of the world, none is so frightful as an earthquake.

Among those who perished was the only child of a samurai family, a boy of five or six, who had made a little house under the overhanging part of a wall and was playing there innocently when the wall suddenly collapsed, burying him under it. His body was crushed flat, with only his two eyes protruding. His parents took him in their arms and wailed uncontrollably, so great was the sorrow they experienced. I realized that grief over a child can make even the bravest warrior forget shame—a pitiable but understandable fact.

The intense quaking stopped after a time, but the after-tremors continued for some while. Not a day passed without twenty or thirty tremors of a severity which would ordinarily have frightened people. After a week or two their frequency diminished, and there would be four or five, then two or three a day; then a day might be skipped, or there be only one tremor in two or three days. After-tremors continued for three months.

Of the four great elements, water, fire, and wind are continually causing disasters, but the earth does not normally afflict man. Long ago, during the great earthquake of the year 855, the head of the Buddha of the Tōdaiji fell off, a terrible misfortune, indeed, but not the equal of the present disaster. At the time everyone spoke of the vanity and meaninglessness of the world, and it seemed that the impurities in men's hearts had somewhat lessened, but with the passage of the months and the days and the coming of the new year people no longer even spoke in that vein.

HARDSHIPS OF LIFE IN THE WORLD

All is as I have described it—the things in the world which make life difficult to endure, our own helplessness and the undependability of our dwellings. And if to these were added the griefs that come from place or particular circumstances, their sum would be unreckonable.

When a man of no great standing happens to live next door to a powerful lord, however happy he may be he cannot celebrate too loudly; however grief-stricken, he cannot raise his voice in lamentations. He is uneasy no matter what he does; in his every action he trembles like a swallow approaching a falcon's nest. The poor man who is the neighbor of a wealthy family is always ashamed of his wretched appearance, and makes his entrances and exits in bursts of flattery. And when he sees how envious his wife and children and his servants are, or hears how the rich family despises him, his mind is incessantly torn by an agitation that leaves not a moment's peace. If a man's house stands in a crowded place and a fire breaks out in the neighborhood, he cannot escape the danger. If it stands in a remote situation, he must put up with the nuisance of going back and forth to the city, and there is always a danger of robbers.

Those who are powerful are filled with greed; and those who have no protectors are despised. Possessions bring many worries; in poverty there is sorrow. He who asks another's help becomes his slave; he who nurtures others is fettered by affection. He who complies with the ways of the world may be impoverished thereby; he who does not, appears deranged. Wherever one may live, whatever work one may do, is it possible even for a moment to find a haven for the body or peace for the mind?

RENUNCIATION OF THE WORLD

I inherited the house of my father's grandmother and for a long time lived there. Afterward I lost my position and fell on hard times.[7] Many things led me to live in seclusion, and finally, unable longer to remain in my ancestral home, in my thirties I built after my own plans a little cottage. It was a bare tenth the size of the house in which I had lived, and being intended just as a place where I might stay it had no pretensions about it. An earthen wall was, it is true, raised around it, but I lacked the means to put up an ornamental gate. I also built a rough shed of bamboo posts for my carriage. I must confess that when the snow fell or gales blew, I could

[7] Kamo no Chōmei's family enjoyed a hereditary position as Shinto priests at the Kamo Shrine, but in his generation this privilege was rescinded.

not but feel alarmed; and since the house was near the Kamo River, there was considerable danger of flooding as well as the threat of bandits.

For over thirty years I had tormented myself by putting up with all the things of this unhappy world. During this time each stroke of misfortune had naturally made me realize the fragility of my life. In my fiftieth year, then, I became a priest and turned my back on the world. Not having any family, I had no ties that would make abandoning the world difficult. I had no rank or stipend—what was there for me to cling to? How many years had I vainly spent among the cloud-covered hills of Ohara? [8]

THE HUT TEN FEET SQUARE

Now that I have reached the age of sixty, and my life seems about to evaporate like the dew, I have fashioned a lodging for the last leaves of my years. It is a hut where, perhaps, a traveler might spend a single night; it is like the cocoon spun by an aged silkworm. This hut is not even a hundredth the size of the cottage where I spent my middle years.

Before I was aware, I had become heavy with years, and with each remove my dwelling grew smaller. The present hut is of no ordinary appearance. It is a bare ten feet square and less than seven feet high. I did not choose this particular spot rather than another, and I built my house without consulting any diviners.[9] I laid a foundation and roughly thatched a roof. I fastened hinges to the joints of the beams, the easier to move elsewhere should anything displease me. What difficulty would there be in changing my dwelling? A bare two carts would suffice to carry off the whole house, and except for the carter's fee there would be no expenses at all.

Since first I hid my traces here in the heart of Mount Hino, I have added a lean-to on the south and a porch of bamboo. On the west I have built a shelf for holy water, and inside the hut, along the

[8] Chōmei felt that even the simplicity of his cottage was still not a suitable life; he had to become a true hermit.

[9] Normally the site of a house was selected after consulting *yin-yang* diviners, but for a Buddhist priest one place was as good as another.

west wall, I have installed an image of Amida. The light of the setting sun shines between its eyebrows.[10] On the doors of the reliquary I have hung pictures of Fugen and Fudō.[11] Above the sliding door that faces north I have built a little shelf on which I keep three or four black leather baskets that contain books of poetry and music and extracts from the sacred writings. Beside them stand a folding koto and a lute.

Along the east wall I have spread long fern fronds and mats of straw which serve as my bed for the night. I have cut open a window in the eastern wall, and beneath it have made a desk. Near my pillow is a square brazier in which I burn brushwood. To the north of the hut I have staked out a small plot of land which I have enclosed with a rough fence and made into a garden. I grow many species of herbs there.

This is what my temporary hut is like. I shall now attempt to describe its surroundings. To the south there is a bamboo pipe which empties water into the rock pool I have laid. The woods come close to my house, and it is thus a simple matter for me to gather brushwood. The mountain is named Toyama. Creeping vines block the trails and the valleys are overgrown, but to the west is a clearing, and my surroundings thus do not leave me without spiritual comfort.[12] In the spring I see waves of wistaria like purple clouds, bright in the west. In the summer I hear the cuckoo call, promising to guide me on the road of death. In the autumn the voice of the evening insects fills my ears with a sound of lamentation for this cracked husk of a world. In winter I look with deep emotion on the snow, piling up and melting away like sins and hindrances to salvation.

When I do not feel like reciting the *nembutsu* [13] and cannot put

[10] The Buddha was said to have emitted light between his eyebrows.

[11] Fugen (Sanskrit, Samantabhadra) is the highest of the bodhisattvas. Fudō Myōō (Sanskrit, Acalanātha) is the chief of the Guardian Kings.

[12] The west is the direction of Paradise and it was thus auspicious that it should have been clear in that direction. The purple cloud is the one on which Amida Buddha descends to guide the believer to the Western Paradise.

[13] The invocation to Amida Buddha practiced particularly by believers in Jōdo Buddhism.

my heart into reading the Sutras, no one will keep me from resting or being lazy, and there is no friend who will feel ashamed of me. Even though I make no special attempt to observe the discipline of silence, living alone automatically makes me refrain from the sins of speech; and though I do not necessarily try to obey the Commandments, here where there are no temptations what should induce me to break them?

On mornings when I feel myself short-lived as the white wake behind a boat,[14] I go to the banks of the river and, gazing at the boats plying to and fro, compose verses in the style of the Priest Mansei. Or if of an evening the wind in the maples rustles the leaves, I recall the river at Jinyō, and play the lute in the manner of Minamoto no Tsunenobu.[15] If still my mood does not desert me, I often tune my lute to the echoes in the pines, and play the "Song of the Autumn Wind," or pluck the notes of the "Melody of the Flowing Stream," modulating the pitch to the sound of the water. I am but an indifferent performer, but I do not play to please others. Alone I play, alone I sing, and this brings joy to my heart.

At the foot of this mountain is a rough-hewn cottage where the guardian of the mountain lives. He has a son who sometimes comes to visit me. When I am bored with whatever I am doing, I often go for a walk with him as my companion. He is sixteen and I sixty: though our ages greatly differ we take pleasure in each other's company.

Sometimes I pick flowering reeds or the wild pear, or fill my basket with berries and cress. Sometimes I go to the rice fields at the foot of the mountain and weave wreaths of the fallen ears. Or, when the weather is fine, I climb the peak and look out toward Kyoto, my old home, far, far away. The view has no owner and nothing can interfere with my enjoyment.

When I feel energetic and ready for an ambitious journey, I follow along the peaks to worship at the Iwama or Ishiyama Temple. Or I push through the fields of Awazu to pay my respects to the

[14] From a poem by the Priest Mansei. See page 93.

[15] Reference to the famous "Lute Song" (*P'i-p'a Chi*) by Po Chü-i. Minamoto no Tsunenobu (1016-1097) was a famous musician and poet.

remains of Semimaru's hut, and cross the Tanagami River to visit the tomb of Sarumaru.[16] On the way back, according to the season, I admire the cherry blossoms or the autumn leaves, pick fern-shoots or fruit, both to offer to the Buddha and to use in my house.

If the evening is still, in the moonlight that fills the window I long for old friends or wet my sleeve with tears at the cries of the monkeys.[17] Fireflies in the grass thickets might be mistaken for fishing-lights off the island of Maki; the dawn rains sound like autumn storms blowing through the leaves. And when I hear the pheasants' cries, I wonder if they call their father or their mother; when the wild deer of the mountain approach me unafraid, I realize how far I am from the world. And when sometimes, as is the wont of old age, I waken in the middle of the night, I stir up the buried embers and make them companions in solitude.

It is not an awesome mountain, but its scenery gives me endless pleasure regardless of the season, even when I listen in wonder to the hooting of the owls.[18] How much more even would the sights mean to someone of deeper thought and knowledge!

When I first began to live here I thought it would be for just a little while, but five years have already passed. My temporary retreat has become rather old as such houses go: withered leaves lie deep by the eaves and moss has spread over the floor. When, as chance has had it, news has come to me from the capital, I have learned how many of the great and mighty have died since I withdrew to this mountain. And how to reckon the numbers of lesser folk? How many houses have been destroyed by the numerous conflagrations? Only in a hut built for the moment can one live without fears. It is very small, but it holds a bed where I may lie at night and a seat for me in the day; it lacks nothing as a place for me to dwell. The hermit crab chooses to live in little shells because

16 Semimaru was a poet of the Heian Period who lived in a hut near the Barrier of Ausakayama. See page 92. Sarumaru-dayū was an early Heian poet, but nothing is known about him. For a later description of roughly the same area, see Bashō's "Unreal Dwelling," page 374.

17 This paragraph is full of allusions to old poems which it would be tedious to explain.

18 From a poem by Saigyō: "The mountain is remote; I do not hear the voices of the birds I love, but only the eerie cries of the owl."

it well knows the size of its body. The osprey stays on deserted shores because it fears human beings. I am like them. Knowing myself and the world, I have no ambitions and do not mix in the world. I seek only tranquillity; I rejoice in the absence of grief.

Most people do not build houses for their own sake. Some build for their families or their relatives; some for their friends and acquaintances. Some build for their masters or teachers, and some even to hold their possessions or beasts. I have built for myself and not for others. This is because in times like these, being in the position I am, I have no companion and no servant to help me. Supposing that I had built a spacious house, whom should I have lodged? Whom should I have had live there?

A man's friends esteem him for his wealth and show the greatest affection for those who do them favors. They do not necessarily have love for persons who bear them warm friendship or who are of an honest disposition. It is better to have as friends music and the sights of nature. A man's servants crave liberal presents and are deferential to those who treat them generously. But however great the care and affection bestowed on them, they do not care the slightest for their master's peace and happiness. It is best to be one's own servant.

If there is something which must be done, I naturally do it myself. I do sometimes weary of work, but I find it simpler to work than to employ a servant and look after him. If some errand requires walking, I do the walking myself. It is disagreeable at times, but it is preferable to worrying about horse-trappings or an oxcart. I divide my body and make two uses of it: my hands are my servants, my feet my vehicle, and they suit me well. When my mind or body is tired, I know it at once and I rest. I employ my servants when they are strong. I say "employ," but I do not often overwork them. If I do not feel like working, it does not upset me. And is it not true that to be thus always walking and working is good for the body? What would be the point in idly doing nothing? It is a sin to cause physical or mental pain: how can we borrow the labor of others?

My clothing and food are as simple as my lodgings. I cover my nakedness with whatever clothes woven of wistaria fiber and quilts of hempen cloth come to hand, and I eke out my life with berries of the fields and nuts from the trees on the peaks. I need not feel ashamed of my appearance, for I do not mix in society and the very scantiness of the food gives it additional savor, simple though it is.

I do not prescribe my way of life to men enjoying happiness and wealth, but have related my experiences merely to show the differences between my former and present life. Ever since I fled the world and became a priest, I have known neither hatred nor fear. I leave my span of days for Heaven to determine, neither clinging to life nor begrudging its end. My body is like a drifting cloud—I ask for nothing, I want nothing. My greatest joy is a quiet nap; my only desire for this life is to see the beauties of the seasons.

The Three Worlds are joined by one mind.[19] If the mind is not at peace, neither beasts of burden nor possessions are of service, neither palaces nor pavilions bring any cheer. This lonely house is but a tiny hut, but I somehow love it. I naturally feel ashamed when I go to the capital and must beg, but when I return and sit here I feel pity for those still attached to the world of dust. Should anyone doubt the truth of my words, let him look to the fishes and the birds. Fish do not weary of the water, but unless one is a fish one does not know why. Birds long for the woods, but unless one is a bird one does not know why. The joys of solitude are similar. Who could understand them without having lived here?

Now the moon of my life sinks in the sky and is close to the edge of the mountain. Soon I must head into the darkness of the Three Ways:[20] why should I thus drone on about myself? The essence of the Buddha's teaching to man is that we must not have attachment for any object. It is a sin for me now to love my little hut, and my attachment to its solitude may also be a hindrance to salvation. Why should I waste more precious time in relating such trifling pleasures?

19 From the Avatamska Sutra. The Three Worlds mav be interpreted as the past, the present, and the future.

20 The three paths in the afterworld leading to different types of hells.

One calm dawning, as I thought over the reasons for this weakness of mine, I told myself that I had fled the world to live in a mountain forest in order to discipline my mind and practice the Way. "And yet, in spite of your monk's appearance, your heart is stained with impurity. Your hut may take after Jōmyō's,[21] but you preserve the Law even worse than Handoku. If your low estate is a retribution for the sins of a previous existence, is it right that you afflict yourself over it? Or should you permit delusion to come and disturb you?" To these questions my mind could offer no reply. All I could do was to use my tongue to recite two or three times the *nembutsu,* however inacceptable from a defiled heart.

It is now the end of the third moon of 1212, and I am writing this at the hut on Toyama.

TRANSLATED BY DONALD KEENE

21 Jōmyō (Vimalakirti) was a priest of Sakyamuni's time who built himself a stone hut much like Chōmei's. Handoku (Panthaka) was the most foolish of Sakyamuni's disciples.

TALES FROM THE UJI COLLECTION

[*Uji Shūi Monogatari*]

This is a collection of 194 tales divided into fifteen books and including examples of every type of theme, ranging from the Buddhist moral tale to humorous anecdotes and traditional fairy stories. The date of the collection is unknown, but it is now generally accepted as probably early thirteenth century. *See also the Introduction, page 22.*

•

THE GRATEFUL SPARROW

In times now long ago, one bright sunny day in early spring an old woman of about sixty was sitting outside her house picking lice. In the courtyard a sparrow hopped about. Some children who were playing nearby started to throw stones at the bird, and one of them struck it, breaking its back. While it struggled about, helplessly flapping its wings, a crow came swooping down upon it. "Oh, what a pity! The crow will get it!" cried the old woman. She rushed over to the sparrow and picked it up. Then she blew on it with her warm breath and fed it. She put the bird into a little pail which she took indoors for the night. The next morning she fed it some rice and made it some medicine of copper dust. Her children and grandchildren said sneeringly, "What a dear old lady she is, to take care of a sparrow in her old age!"

Nevertheless, she tenderly looked after the bird for several months until at last it was hopping about again. Though a mere sparrow, it felt very happy and grateful that she had restored it to health. Whenever the old woman left the house, even on the briefest of errands, she would give instructions to her family. "Look after the sparrow and see that it gets something to eat." And her children and grandchildren laughed at her and teased her. "How touching! Why do you worry so much about a sparrow?" "Say what you please, it's a poor helpless creature," she would reply.

As a result of the good care she took of it, the bird finally was able to fly once more. "Now no crow will get it," said the old woman, and took it outdoors to see how well it could fly. When she placed it on the palm of her hand and held it out at arm's length, away the sparrow flew with a flutter of its wings. After that the old woman, in the loneliness and tedium of her life, longed for the bird. She would say, "How sad that it has flown away after so many months and days of taking it in for the night and feeding it in the morning!" As usual, everyone laughed at her.

Some twenty days later the woman heard the loud chirping of a sparrow outside her house. "Why, that's a sparrow! Perhaps the same one has come back," she thought, going out to look. Indeed, it was the very same sparrow. "Oh, how touching! How touching that it has not forgotten me and has come back," she said. The sparrow, peering at the old woman's face, dropped something very small that it held in its beak, apparently intending to leave whatever it was for her, and then flew away. "What can the sparrow have dropped?" wondered the woman. She went over and discovered that it had let fall a single gourd seed. "It must have had some reason for bringing this," she said, picking it up. Her children mocked her, "How wonderful! She gets a present from a sparrow and acts as if it were some great treasure!" "Say what you will, I'll plant it and see what happens," she replied, and this she did.

When autumn came the plant bore a great many gourds. They were not of the usual kind, but much larger and more numerous. The old woman was exceedingly pleased. No matter how many she picked or gave away to the neighbors, more still remained than she could possibly use. Her children and grandchildren who had laughed at her ate the gourds every day.

At last, when she had distributed the gourds to everyone in the village, she decided that she would cure seven or eight of the largest and finest to use as containers. These she hung indoors and left to dry. When several months had elapsed, she inspected them, thinking that by this time they would be about ready. The gourds had indeed turned out very well, but when she took one of them down, she was surprised to find how heavy it was. She cut open the gourd all the same, only to discover that it was stuffed with something. She poured it out to see what it might be—the gourd was full of white rice! Amazed at this prodigy, she emptied the gourd into a big container, but when she had finished it was full again, just as when she began. Astonished and overjoyed, she said, "This is most unusual. The sparrow must be back of this." She put the rice into containers and stored it away. When she examined the other gourds, she found that they were full of rice too. No matter how much she poured out or used, there was still more left than she knew what to do with, and she thus became a very wealthy person indeed. The other villagers were amazed and envious at her good fortune.

Now the children of the old woman who lived next door said to their mother, "Other people, though they're no different from you, manage to become rich, but you can't even do the simplest thing." As the result of such complaints, the old woman from next door went to visit the first old woman. "Now then, what's all this about? I've heard some rumors about a sparrow, but I really know nothing about it. Please tell me the whole story from the beginning, just as it happened."

"It all came about from planting a gourd seed that a sparrow dropped," replied the first old woman, and would not give any further details. But the second old woman kept pressing her. "I insist! Do tell me all about it!" And so, thinking that it would be wrong to be petty and keep the matter a secret, she said, "I took care of a sparrow that had a broken back, and nursed it back to health. It must have felt so grateful that it brought me a gourd seed which I planted, and this is what happened."

"Please give me just one of the seeds," said the second old woman, but she refused. "I will give you some of the rice that was inside the gourds, but I can't give you any seeds. Those I most certainly cannot give away."

Having been thus unsuccessful in getting a seed, the second old woman began to keep a sharp lookout in the hope that she too might find a sparrow with a broken back to take care of, but not a single sparrow of that description was to be seen. Every morning when she looked out of her house, there would be some sparrows hopping about outside the back door eating any grains of rice that had happened to fall. The old woman would pick up stones and throw them at the birds on the chance of hitting one. Since she threw a great many stones at a great many sparrows, she naturally succeeded at last in hitting one and wounding it so that it could not fly. Very pleased with herself, the old woman went over to the bird and, after making sure that its back was thoroughly broken, she picked it up, fed it, and gave it medicine with great solicitousness. Then she thought, "If the old lady next door gets so much in return for taking care of a single sparrow, how much richer I could be if there were several! I would be superior to her, and my children would praise me."

She spread some rice in a winnowing tray and kept watch. When some sparrows gathered to eat the rice, she threw stone after stone at them, and at last succeeded in striking down three. Deciding that would do for the time being, she put the three injured sparrows in a pail, powdered some copper and fed it to them. After several months of treatment they all recovered. She joyfully took them outdoors, and they flew away with fluttering wings. "How clever I am!" she thought. But the sparrows felt only the bitterest hatred toward her, even though she had nursed them, for she was the one who had broken their backs.

About ten days later the sparrows returned. The happy old woman looked first to see whether they had anything in their beaks, whereupon they each let fall a single gourd seed and flew away. "I thought so!" she said and, gleefully picking up the seeds, planted them in three places. The seedlings grew unusually fast and soon became very large. But they did not produce so many gourds—not more than seven or eight on a plant. Nevertheless, the old woman watched them with a broad grin on her face. She told her children, "You said that I was never good for anything, but I'll show you that I am better than the old lady next door." They were quite convinced now that things would indeed turn out as she said.

Since the gourds were few in number, the old woman, wishing to get the largest possible amount of rice out of them, neither gave any away to other people nor ate any herself. But her children said, "The old lady next door gave some gourds to her neighbors and ate some herself. All the more should you do so, since you had three seeds to start with. You ought to give some away, and we should eat some ourselves." Accordingly, she picked quite a number of gourds, both for the neighbors and her own family, but the gourds proved to be horribly bitter, and made everyone feel nauseous and giddy. Everyone who ate any fell violently ill, and the old woman's outraged neighbors went in a body to her house intending to scold her. "What on earth has she given us?" they asked one another. "How dreadful of her! Even those of us who no more than smelled one vomited, and we were so sick that we nearly died." When they arrived at her house, however, the old woman and her children were prostrate and vomiting all over the room. There was evidently no use in complaining, and the neighbors went home.

It was two or three days before they had all recovered. The old woman thought to herself, "I wanted to keep the gourds so that they would all produce rice, but we were in too much of a hurry to eat them. That is no doubt why this accident happened." She picked all the remaining gourds and put them away.

When several months had passed, and she thought that the gourds had reached the proper stage, she went into the storeroom with some tubs in which to hold the rice after she had poured it out. She was immensely pleased, and her toothless old mouth was grinning from ear to ear as she carried over one of the tubs and poured the contents of a gourd into it. But what came out was not rice, but hornets, bees, centipedes, scorpions, snakes, and other such creatures, and they fastened upon her and stung her eyes and nose and her whole body. Yet for the moment the old woman felt no pain at all. She thought that they were just grains of rice bouncing up out of the container and hitting her. She said, "Just wait a while, you sparrows! I'll see that you each get a little bit."

The many poisonous insects that emerged from the seven or eight gourds stung and bit her children too, and the old woman herself was stung to death. It seems that the sparrows, hating her for breaking their backs, had persuaded all the insects to hide inside the gourds and help them with their revenge. The sparrow next door had been grateful to the old woman who had cared for it and restored it to health when its back was already broken and it was in mortal danger of being seized by a crow. We must not be envious of others.

(III, 16)

THE HOLY MAN OF SHINANO PROVINCE

In times now long ago there lived in Shinano Province a priest who, having entered the priesthood in a remote country district, had never been properly ordained. He determined that he would somehow go up to the capital and receive ordination at the Tōdaiji.[1] At last he succeeded in making the journey and the ceremony was duly performed. He had intended to return to his native province afterward, but it really seemed a mistake to go back to so heathenish a place where no one even knew about the Buddha, and he therefore decided to remain in the neighborhood of the capital. He sat down in front of the Buddha of the Tōdaiji and looked all about him at the surrounding countryside to see whether he could detect any suitable place where he might live peacefully and perform his devotions. At last his eye hit upon a certain mountain which could be dimly seen off to the southwest. "That is where I will live and pray," he thought, and went there.

As a result of the many rigorous austerities which the priest performed, he was at length able, thanks to the magical powers he gained, to produce out of thin air a small image of Bishamon, of about the size that would fit into a miniature shrine. He built a small chapel in the mountains where he enshrined the image, and spent the years and months in practicing devotions of an unparalleled fervor.

[1] The Tōdaiji is a temple completed in 752 in Nara, and is known for the colossal statue of the Buddha Vairocana which is its principal object of worship.

Now at the foot of this mountain there lived a certain man who, though of humble birth, was exceedingly rich. It became a habit with the holy man to have his begging bowl fly down to this man's house, where it would be filled with food and then return. One day the rich man had opened up his stoutly built log storehouse, and was engaged in removing some wares when the bowl came flying down to beg for its usual portion of food. "What a very greedy bowl you are!" he said, and picking it up tossed it into a corner of the storehouse instead of filling it immediately.

The bowl waited there patiently, but when the rich man had finished putting his possessions in order he forgot all about the bowl, which he neither filled nor removed from the storehouse. Locking the door behind him, the rich man went home. After a short while, the storehouse began to shake and tremble in a strange and unaccountable fashion. Everyone looked on in great excitement, wondering what could be the matter, and as they watched, it swayed and moved all the more violently, until it had risen about a foot off the ground. The onlookers were astounded, and excitedly asked one another what could be the meaning of this prodigy. "That's right!" cried someone, "the master forgot the holy man's begging bowl and left it inside the storehouse. That must be what has caused it." Meanwhile the bowl could be seen protruding from under the storehouse; and the building itself, riding on the bowl, sailed up into the air until it had reached a height of ten or twenty feet and then flew off, while the people gazed on in astonishment, shouting and jabbering at one another.

The owner of the storehouse, powerless to stop its flight, could only follow along to see where it would go. All the people of the neighborhood went running after it too. The storehouse flew at a leisurely pace until it arrived at the mountain where the holy man had his retreat, and dropped down with a thud beside his hut. At this everyone marveled more than ever. The owner could scarcely permit such a situation to continue, however, and approached the holy man, saying, "What an astonishing thing to have happened! Whenever your bowl has come to my house I have always filled it with food, but today I was so busy that I forgot all about the bowl and locked my storehouse without removing it. Then the storehouse began to shake and sway, and now it has flown all the way here. Please return it to me."

"It is, to be sure, most remarkable, but since it came here of its own accord I cannot return the storehouse to you. I have never had anything of the kind, and it will be convenient for me to keep things in. However, you may take away whatever is inside as soon as you wish," replied the holy man.

"But how," asked the rich man, "can I carry these things home with me now? There are a thousand measures of rice inside the storehouse."

"That is a very simple matter. I will see to it that they are transported for you," said the holy man. He had someone load one of the bales of rice on his bowl, which he caused to fly into the sky. Thereupon all the other bales followed along after it, just like a flock of geese.

When the rich man saw the bales flying off, he was more than ever astonished and struck with awe, and he said to the holy man, "Wait! Don't send them all back! Please keep two or three hundred measures of rice for your own use."

"That may not be," said the holy man. "What would I do with them if they were left here?"

"Then let me give you as many as you can use—say, ten or twenty measures," suggested the rich man.

The holy man still would not accept. "If I had any need for so much rice, I would take your ten or twenty measures, but I have not." He made certain that every last bale landed at the rich man's house.

While the holy man went on living thus, performing miracles of every description, the Emperor Daigo [2] fell seriously ill. All manner of prayers, exorcisms, and recitations of the scriptures were performed on his behalf, but he showed no signs of recovery. Someone said, "There lives at Shigi a holy man who has been practicing austerities for many years, and has never once come down from his solitary retreat. He possesses supernatural powers and performs all man-

[2] Reigned 897-929.

ner of miracles. Without so much as budging from his seat, he can make his begging bowl fly through the air. If he is summoned to court and offers prayers for His Majesty, he cannot fail to effect a recovery."

It was decided to adopt this suggestion, and an archivist was sent as an Imperial messenger to summon the holy man. On his arrival, the messenger was greatly impressed by the hermit's noble and venerable bearing. He announced to the holy man that he was commanded by Imperial decree to appear at court, and that he must proceed to the capital in all haste. The holy man showed no sign whatever of stirring. "Why am I being summoned?" he asked.

"His Majesty is suffering from a serious complaint. Please come and pray for him," explained the messenger.

"Why," asked the holy man, "may I not pray for him here?"

"In that case," objected the messenger, "if His Majesty should recover, how would we know that it was due to the efficacy of your prayers?"

The holy man said, "So long as his health is restored, it hardly matters whose miraculous powers are responsible."

"Just the same," insisted the messenger, "it would be best to have some way of telling which of the many prayers and rituals performed is the one that has had the desired effect."

"Very well then," said the holy man, "when I perform my ritual, I shall send the Sword Guardian to His Majesty as a sign. If he should happen to see this guardian either in a dream or a vision, he may know that he comes from me. The Sword Guardian wears a cloak of swords woven together. Under no circumstances can I go up to the capital."

The Imperial messenger returned to the court and made his report. Toward noon of the third day following, the Emperor, while fully awake, caught sight of something glittering near him. When he looked at it closely, he saw that it was the Sword Guardian of which the holy man had spoken. From that moment on, His Majesty became cheerful, all symptoms of his illness disappeared, and he was his former self again. Everyone was delighted, and the holy man was honored and praised by all. His Majesty was also greatly impressed, and sent a man with the message, "You must let me make you an archbishop, or at least let me bestow a manor on your temple."

When the holy man received the message, he answered, "I cannot possibly become an archbishop or a bishop, and if a manor were made over to my temple, it would certainly entail having an intendant and other people to manage it. That would be as unwelcome to me as being tormented for my sins. Let me remain as I am." And so the matter was dropped.

Now this holy man had an elder sister. She had not laid eyes on him since he went to Nara to be ordained and, being worried over how he had fared during the long years of their separation, she went to look for him. She made inquiries all around the neighborhood of the Tōdaiji for a man named Mōren, but not a soul knew of him. Though she grew weary with searching, she told herself, "I will not go home until I have found out what has become of him." That evening she prayed all night long before the Great Buddha of the Tōdaiji, asking that she be shown where Mōren was. At last she fell into a doze, and in her dream Buddha said to her, "The priest whom you seek lives on a mountain southwest of here. Go there and look for him on the side of the mountain from which a cloud is trailing."

When she awoke it was already close to dawn, and she waited impatiently for the day to break. As soon as the first pale light appeared, she gazed off to the southwest, and could see the faint outlines of a mountain from which trailed a purple cloud. Overjoyed, she made her way in that direction. When she arrived, she found that there really was a temple at the very spot indicated, and going over to a building which looked as if it might be inhabited, she called out, "Is Mōren there?"

"Who is it?" asked the holy man, coming out of his hut. What was his surprise to discover his elder sister from Shinano! "How did you ever find me?" he asked. "I never expected to see you."

She told him all that had happened, adding, "You must be suffering terribly from the cold. Here is something for you to wear." She took out what she had brought, a kind of padded underjacket. It was by no means an ordinary one; it was carefully sewn with stout thread and fashioned exceptionally thick and strong. The holy man gladly accepted it, and put it on. Up to then he had had only a single paper garment to wear, and had therefore been very cold indeed; but when he put the jacket on underneath his paper robe, he felt warm and comfortable.

In this way he went on performing his devotions for many years. The nun, his sister, did not return to her native province, but remained with him and worshiped beside him. He wore the padded underjacket constantly for many years, until it fell into shreds. The storehouse which was carried to the mountain by his begging bowl is called the Flying Storehouse. The tattered remains of the jacket and other relics of the holy man are kept inside and are said still to be there. Those who happen, through some fortunate karma affinity, to obtain even so much as a scrap of that underjacket use it as a charm. The storehouse is now in a very dilapidated state, but is still there. People who manage to get hold of even a splinter of the wood from which it was built, make it into a charm, and those who obtain larger pieces and have them carved into images of Bishamon never fail to become rich and prosperous. It is no wonder that everyone who hears this story is anxious to buy a piece of wood from the storehouse. The name of the mountain where the holy man lived all those years is Shigi; it is a place so rich in wonderful miracles that even today it is crowded morning and night with pilgrims. The image of Bishamon enshrined there is said to be the very one that the holy man Mōren miraculously produced through his devotions.[3]

(VIII, 3)

TRANSLATED BY ROBERT H. BROWER

[3] The events described in this story are depicted in the *"Shigisan Engi,"* or "Illustrated History of Mount Shigi," a famous picture scroll of the late Heian Period.

THE CAPTAIN OF NARUTO

[*Naruto Chūjō Monogatari*]

This tale, which was probably written in the late thirteenth century, ostensibly relates an actual event at the court of the Emperor Gosaga, who reigned from 1242 to 1246. It was intended to edify, but the modern reader may find that it affords instead a rather sardonic insight into the court life of the time.

•

One year, in the spring, when the cherry blossoms were at their peak, there took place in a courtyard within the palace grounds a football match in which distinguished members of the court took part. Among the spectators were a number of ladies, one of whom attracted the Emperor's interest. His attention was diverted from the game, and he allowed his glance to wander repeatedly in the direction of this lady, who was so distressed by his gaze that she slipped away toward the Left Gate. The Emperor summoned a secretary, instructing him to follow and report the lady's destination. When the secretary had overtaken her, the lady who understood and meant to mislead him somehow, beckoned him to draw near, and with a smile said, "Tell His Majesty, 'Of the young bamboo.' I will wait here, I promise, until I receive his reply." The secretary, never dreaming that she might deceive him, assumed that she merely wished to arrange a rendezvous and hurried away. The Emperor, on receiving this report, felt certain that she had quoted a line from a poem and inquired what it might be. None of those in attendance, however, were familiar with it, and Lord Tameie [1] was sent for. "It is an old poem," he said without hesitation.

[1] Fujiwara no Tameie (1198-1275), famous as a poet and compiler of anthologies.

"Tall though it be, what can one do with the useless lengths of the young bamboo with its one or two joints?"[2]

On hearing this, the Emperor became more and more intrigued, and without composing a reply he ordered the secretary to find out where the lady lived. When the secretary returned to the Gate, however, he found that she had quite vanished. He reported this to the Emperor, who with a terrible look told him that unless he discovered her whereabouts he would be held guilty of a crime. The secretary paled and withdrew. The Emperor, as a result of this, lost all interest in the football match and retired.

For some time afterward he wore a bitter scowl and caused everyone concern. One day Lord Konoe and others were in attendance at an Imperial entertainment. The Emperor was not his usual self. He seemed preoccupied and gazed listlessly about him. Lord Konoe had the wine cup presented and remarked, "Is it true that Your Majesty was not long ago 'singed by a smudge-fire at a house in some unknown quarter?' If it were looked for it wouldn't remain hidden long, I daresay. In China the search was carried as far as Paradise.[3] Her house is within the capital; finding it should be a simple matter." He offered the cup to the Emperor who, though he smiled faintly, was not amused and, drawing himself up, retired.

Meanwhile, the secretary was searching in every imaginable quarter, hoping to encounter the lady, and even offered prayers to the gods and to Buddha, but without avail. He was in despair when he remembered a certain diviner, named Fumpira, who was famed for his effortless predictions and who would be able to divine her whereabouts. The secretary called upon this man and asked his aid. "Word has reached me privately about this. A very grave matter," said the diviner. "Now let us see what Fumpira's divining can do about it. We have come under Mars. Today's sign is the Serpent. From this I take it that she is in hiding only temporarily. You will find her

[2] Puns in the poem give it the additional meaning of "Exalted though you are, what would be the good of one or two nights of idle love-making with the 'young bamboo'?"
[3] Reference to the search for the soul of the Emperor Hsüan Tsung's favorite Yang Kuei-fei (718-756), discovered in the Taoist paradise.

in good time. Now, Mars in the summer term is very lucky, and being governed by the Serpent she will appear from the same hole she went into. You are sure to find her this summer at the spot where she disappeared." The secretary, though he did not put too much stock in the words of the diviner, who after all was but an ordinary mortal, was still sufficiently impressed by what he had heard, and from this time, instead of going about in a daze as before, stationed himself by the Left Gate.

It was on the thirteenth day of the fifth month, at the opening of the lectures on the *Suvarna-prabhāsa* Sutra, that he suddenly came upon the lady, this time in company with five others. He was so overjoyed that he scarcely knew whether to believe his eyes. In order to avoid arousing her suspicions, he mingled with the throng and saw her sitting among those in the west gallery of the Chamberlain's pavilion, listening to the sermon. Fearful lest he lose sight of her in the scramble at the end of the lecture, he asked Lord Tsunetoshi, who happened to be at the entrance to the Imperial loge, to report his discovery to the Emperor. "His Majesty is with the Empress listening to the sermon. It is out of the question," replied Tsunetoshi. He looked about for a herald who might deliver the message, but saw no one. Finally he approached a lady-in-waiting. "Forgive the interruption," he said apologetically, "but it is His Majesty's wish," and asked her to convey his message quickly to the Emperor. She had prior knowledge of the affair and promptly obeyed. The Emperor replied, through the lady-in-waiting, "Admirable. This time find out for certain where she goes, and tell me."

By the time the sermon was over it was dusk. The lady and her party seemed about to set off in a single coach. The secretary, fearing that she might be suspicious of him a second time, sent a certain resourceful woman to observe her in his stead. The lady's destination proved to be the house of a certain Junior Captain in Sanjō Shirakawa. No sooner had the Emperor been informed of this than he sent the following letter. "Was it an empty dream or did I really see the young bamboo, that morning and night I yearn for with a love that is torment? Tonight without fail."

This was all. The secretary went to her house with the letter.

The lady, being a married woman, was much upset, and lamented her lot. The messenger pressed her heartlessly for a reply, and, deciding that concealment was out of the question, she told her husband just what had happened. The Captain was understandably disturbed. "As a man I have an abhorrence of sending you," he said, "but there is no point in presuming to admonish the Emperor. Things are not the same for one man as for another in this world, and in a way it is an honor. Let tongues wag if they will. Hurry and go," he urged. She broke into tears, however, and protested repeatedly that it would never do. "These past three years," he went on, "we have spent in the deepest love, as though we were made for each other, but for you to have been summoned in this way shows his attachment is not superficial. If you fail to go, out of pride, it is sure to look very bad, and who can say what will become of me? People will not think the worse of us for it. Hurry and go," he insisted. Sobbing, the lady opened the letter, and beneath the words "Tonight without fail," wrote in thick black ink the single word *"wo,"* and refolding the letter sent it by the messenger.

The Emperor, seeing the letter returned, and no different in appearance than before, was about to conclude reluctantly that it had been without effect, when he noticed that the knot was carelessly tied. He undid it and beheld the word *"wo."* Ponder over it as he would, he could make nothing of it. He summoned several ladies-in-waiting who would be likely to know and asked them about the word. One of them said, "Long ago a certain prime minister wrote the word 'moon' and sent it to the daughter of Izumi Shikibu, a lady well versed in such matters. She may have spoken of it to her mother, for she readily understood and wrote beneath 'moon' the single word *'wo.'* That is the allusion, I imagine. 'Moon' meant that he would be waiting that night for her to come. And in answer to a summons from above, men should reply *'yo,'* while women say *'wo.'* The lady went to him, and he was more in love with her than ever. This lady too will surely come."

The Emperor was much pleased at this and was filled with anticipation. The night grew later and later, but still he delayed retiring to his bedchamber. Just as he heard the watchmen's cry—

could it be the hour of the Ox[4] already, he wondered in despair —the secretary announced the lady's secret arrival. Overjoyed, the Emperor had her conducted in immediately. Not even Han Wu's meeting with the Lady Li or Hsüan Tsung's winning of Yang Kuei-fei could surpass this moment, he felt. The night was far too short for him to tell her all that was in his heart. As daybreak neared she explained to him that her position, unkind as it was for her to say it, was distasteful to her, and so, for the while, he allowed her to be escorted home. His desire for her, however, was boundless, and he considered installing her among his consorts, with her own apartments inside the palace, but to this proposal she responded with unaffected sorrow that were he to do that, it would be to show her no mercy at all; that she would feel like someone unable to escape from a deep pool. As long as things remained as they were, and no one knew about her, she would always be at his command. At length he agreed that she might remain in her own home, and thence from time to time he would summon her secretly.

The Captain, her husband, who had been living in retirement, was summoned to court on some pretext and had conferred upon him untold marks of the Emperor's favor. He was included in the ranks of the Imperial retinue and shortly afterward was promoted to Middle Captain. The promotion was kept quiet, but news of it got about, and he came to be known on the vulgar tongues of the day as "the Captain of Naruto." He received this sobriquet, it is to be supposed, because Naruto is the place from which the seaweed called "maiden of Naruto" is sent up to the capital.

A prince is to his subjects as water is to fish. However high the prince, he should not be guilty of arrogance or contemptuousness; however low his subjects, they should not be disordered by envy. Emperor Gosaga's gracious feelings and the Captain's generous sacrifice in the present story deserve to be remembered as examples of truly noble conduct. It is indeed natural that from the earliest times it has ever been said that between the prince and his subjects there should be no estrangement, but bonds of deep sympathy.

TRANSLATED BY CHARLES E. HAMILTON

4 2 A.M. to 4 A.M.

MUROMACHI PERIOD

1333–1600

ESSAYS IN IDLENESS

[*Tsurezure-Gusa*] *by Yoshida Kenkō*

"Essays in Idleness" is a collection in 243 sections which range in length from a few lines to three or four pages. It was written about 1340. Yoshida Kenkō (1283-1350) was a celebrated poet and court official of his time, who became a Buddhist monk in 1324. In many ways "Essays in Idleness" seems to echo the delightful "Pillow Book" of Sei Shōnagon, but there is a melancholy tinge to its worldly wisdom which is perhaps due more to the tragic period in which the essays were composed than to Kenkō's religious convictions.

•

To while away the idle hours, seated the livelong day before the inkslab, by jotting down without order or purpose whatever trifling thoughts pass through my mind, verily this is a queer and crazy thing to do!

• •

It is desirable to have a knowledge of true literature, of composition and versifying, of wind and string instruments; and it is well, moreover, to be learned in precedent and court ceremonies, so as to be a model for others. One should write not unskilfully in the running hand, be able to sing in a pleasing voice and keep good time to music; and, lastly, a man should not refuse a little wine when it is pressed upon him.

• •

However gifted and accomplished a young man may be, if he has no fondness for women, one has a feeling of something lacking, as of a precious wine cup without a bottom. Admire the condition of a lover! Drenched with dews and frosts and aimlessly wandering; ever concerned to shun the world's reproof and escape his parents' reproaches; hither and thither pursued by doubt and distress; and spending his nights withal sleepless upon a solitary couch.

But it is well that a man do not become addicted to lewdness, a constant and familiar companion of women.

• •

Were we to live on for ever—were the dews of Adashino never to vanish, the smoke on Toribeyama [1] never to fade away—then indeed would men not feel the pity of things.

Truly the beauty of life is its uncertainty. Of all living things, none lives so long as man. Consider how the ephemera awaits the fall of evening, and the summer cicada knows neither spring nor autumn. Even a year of life lived peacefully seems long and happy beyond compare; but for such as never weary of this world and are loath to die, a thousand years would pass away like the dream of a single night.

What shall it avail a man to drag out till he becomes decrepit and unsightly a life which some day needs must end? Long life brings many shames. At most before his fortieth year is full, it is seemly for a man to die.

After that age it is pitiful to see how, unashamed of his looks, he loves to thrust himself into the society of others and, cherishing his offspring in the evening of his days, craves to live on and on that he may watch them grow and prosper. So he continues, his heart set on nought but worldliness, and hardening to the pity of things.

• •

Of all things that lead astray the heart of man there is nought like fleshly lust. What a weakly thing is this heart of ours. Though a perfume, for example, is but a transient thing, and though he knows

[1] Adashino and Toribeyama were places of cremation.

full well that incense is burned to give an odor to garments, yet a man's heart will always be stirred by a vague perfume.

The Magician of Kume, the legend runs, lost his magic power through looking at a maiden washing clothes. This may well have been, for here was no charm from without, but the real beauty of plump and glistening limbs.

• •

There is a charm about a neat and proper dwelling house, although this world, 'tis true, is but a temporary abode. Even the moonshine, when it strikes into the house where a good man lives in peaceful ease, seems to gain in friendly brilliancy.

The man is to be envied who lives in a house, not of the modern, garish kind, but set among venerable trees, with a garden where plants grow wild and yet seem to have been disposed with care, verandas and fences tastefully arranged, and all its furnishings simple but antique.

A house which multitudes of workmen have devoted all their ingenuity to decorate, where rare and strange things from home and abroad are set out in array, and where even the trees and shrubs are trained unnaturally—such is an unpleasant sight, depressing to look at, to say nothing of spending one's days therein. Nor, gazing on it, can one but reflect how easily it might vanish in a moment of time.

The appearance of a house is in some sort an index to the character of its occupant.

• •

Once in the month of September I passed over the plain of Kurusu and sought out a certain village among the hills beyond, when, threading my way far down a narrow moss-grown path, I came upon a lonely hut. There was never a sound to greet me, save the dripping of water from a pipe buried in fallen leaves, but I knew that someone lived there, for sprays of chrysanthemum and maple leaves bestrewed the shelf before the shrine, and "Ah!" thought I, "In such a place a man can spend his days." But as I stood and gazed in wonder, I perceived in the garden beyond a great orange tree, its branches weighted down with fruit. It was strongly closed in on all sides by a fence. This broke the spell, and I thought to myself, "If only that tree had not been there!"

• •

It is a joyful thing indeed to hold intimate converse with a man after one's own heart, chatting without reserve about things of interest or the fleeting topics of the world; but such, alas, are few and far between. Not that one desires a companion who will sit opposite and never utter a word in contradiction—one might as well be alone. Far better in hours of loneliness the company of one who, while he will listen with respect to your views, will disagree a little, and argue, saying "Yes, that is so, but . . . ," or "For this reason such and such is the case."

And yet, with those who are not of the same way of thinking or are contentious, a man can discuss only things of passing interest, for the truth is there must not be any wide gulf between bosom friends.

• •

To sit alone in the lamplight with a book spread out before you, and hold intimate converse with men of unseen generations—such is a pleasure beyond compare.

• •

It wakes one up to go away from home for a time, no matter whither. Exploring and rambling about the countryside you come upon a host of unwonted sights in rustic spots and mountain hamlets. You get a messenger to take letters to the capital, and you write and say "Do not forget to send me so-and-so at the next opportunity." All this is in its way amusing. Of course you have a thousand things to think of in such a place.

Pleasant also to slip away and go into retreat in some mountain temple.

• •

It is well for a man to be frugal, to abstain from luxury, to possess no treasure nor to covet this world's goods. Since olden times there has rarely been a sage who was wealthy.

In China there was once a man called Hsü Yu. He had not a single possession in the world. He even scooped up water with his hands, until a friend gave him a gourd. But one day, when he had hung it from a branch, it rattled in the wind; whereupon, disturbed by the noise, he threw it away and once more took to drinking from his clasped hands. How pure and free the heart of such a man.

• •

A certain recluse, I know not who, once said that no bonds attached him to this life, and the only thing he would regret leaving was the sky.

• •

Though the breeze blow not, the flower of the heart of man will change its hue. Now looking back on months and years of intimacy, to feel that your friend, while you still remember the moving words you exchanged, is yet growing distant and living in a world apart —all this is sadder far than partings brought by death.

• •

In hours of quiet thought one cannot but be overcome by longing for the past.

When, to while away the long nights after folk have gone to rest, we go through our odd belongings, sometimes, as we throw away such scraps of paper as we do not want to keep, the handwriting of one who is no more, or an idle sketch maybe, will catch the eye and vividly recall the moment it was made.

It is affecting, too, after the lapse of many years, to come across the letters even of one who is still living, and to call to mind the year and the occasion when they were written.

The things they were wont to use have no heart, yet remain unchanged throughout the long, long years. A melancholy reflection.

• •

There is no such mournful time as follows on a death. For the days of retirement a crowd of people go up together to some mountain village, into a cramped and incommodious house, and there they busily perform the offices for the dead. So the appointed time passes with unwonted quickness. The last day is pitiless indeed; for in silence they gather together their possessions, each for himself, and go their several ways. Only when they have returned to their own homes will they begin to feel exceeding sad.

Months and years pass by, and still they do not forget, though, as the saying goes, the departed grows more distant every day. However that may be, they seem not to feel so deeply as at the time of death, for now they chatter and laugh together. The body is laid to rest upon some lonely mountainside, whither the mourners come on rare appointed days, soon the tablet is overgrown with moss, buried in fallen leaves, and looks in time as if none came to visit there save even storms and the nocturnal moon.

There may be some who will recall the dead, and think of him with grief. But soon they themselves must pass away. Then how can later generations grieve, who know him only by repute? After a time they go no longer to his tomb, and people do not even know his name or who he was. True, some feeling folk may gaze with pity on what is now but the growth of grasses of succeeding springs; but at last there comes a day when even the pine trees that groaned in the storms, not lasting out their thousand years of life, are split for fuel, and the ancient grave, dug up and turned to rice field, leaves never a trace behind.

• •

Although some will say, "After all this time, why stand on ceremony?" I myself feel that it is a sign of genuine and proper feeling when even the most inseparable friends treat one another, if the occasion demands, with due reserve and decorum. On the other hand, it is sometimes well for people who are not intimate to speak freely.

• •

In the Province of Inaba there was a girl, the daughter of a certain lay priest of noble family, whose hand was asked in marriage by many that heard of her beauty. However, this girl ate nothing but chestnuts, never touching rice or other grain, and her parents therefore refused, saying that such an unusual thing ought not to be seen by others.

• •

This is a story of the priests of the Ninnaji. They had a feast to celebrate the farewell to the world of a young acolyte about to enter the priesthood. In their revels they became drunken, and the acolyte, beginning to feel merry, took a three-legged iron pot that lay nearby and put it on his head. Then, though it fitted very tight, he flattened out his nose, pulled the pot over his face, and began to dance. The whole company grew merry beyond measure, until after performing awhile, he at length tried to pull it off—but in vain! This sobered the feast, and they were thrown into confusion and doubt, wondering what they should do. While they were debating, the pot cut into his head, and blood began to flow and his face swelled up so that he could hardly breathe. They tried to break it, but it was not easily broken, and as the force of the blow went to his head, he could not bear it, and they were obliged to stop. They did not know what to do next, so, throwing a black gauze cloak over the three legs, which looked like horns, they led him, supported by a staff, to the house of a physician in Kyoto. People looked at them with amazement as they went along. It must have been a queer scene when they brought him face to face with the physician on entering his house. When he spoke, his voice was muffled, and resounded so that they could not hear what he said. The physician said that he had never seen such a case in the books, nor had he ever had any oral instruction on the point, so they were obliged to return to the temple.

There his friends and relatives, with his old mother, gathered at his bedside and wept and grieved—not that they thought he could hear! At last someone said, "Suppose he does lose his ears and nose, so far as living goes there is no reason why he should not survive. Let us then pull the thing off by main force." So they thrust rice straw all round between his head and the metal, and pulled as if to drag off his head. His ears and nose were torn away, and he escaped with his bare life, suffering afterward many a long day.

• •

A house should be built with the summer in view. In winter one can live anywhere, but a poor dwelling in summer is unbearable. Deep water does not give a cool sensation. Far cooler is a shallow running stream. A room with sliding doors is lighter than one with doors on hinges. When the ceiling is high the room is cold in winter and difficult to light. As for construction, people agree in admiring a place with plenty of spare room, as being pleasing to the eye and at the same time useful for all sorts of purposes.

• •

As soon as we hear a person's name we form in our minds a picture of his appearance; but when we come to see him, he is never the man whose face we had imagined.

I suppose we all feel, when we hear stories of ancient times, that the houses were more or less the same as people's houses nowadays, and think of the people as like people we see about us. And am I alone in having sometimes within me a feeling that words I have just heard, or things I have just seen, have happened once before—*when,* I cannot recollect, but none the less certainly have happened.

• •

When in the presence of a new acquaintance, to carry on a conversation in fragments, laughing and exchanging meaningful looks with a companion who knows the phrases and names of things you commonly use, makes the stranger feel as if he understood nothing—this is ignorant behavior, and a sure sign of ill breeding.

. .

One should never make a show of having a deep knowledge of any subject. Well-bred people do not talk in a superior way even about things they have a good knowledge of. It is people who come from the country who offer opinions unasked, as though versed in all manner of accomplishments. Of course some among them do have a really enviable knowledge, and it is their air of self-conceit which is so stupid.

It is a fine thing when a man who thoroughly understands a subject is unwilling to open his mouth, and only speaks when he is questioned.

. .

Are we only to look at flowers in full bloom, at the moon when it is clear?

Nay, to look out on the rain and long for the moon, to draw the blinds and not to be aware of the passing of the spring—these arouse even deeper feelings. There is much to be seen in young boughs about to flower, in gardens strewn with withered blossom.

Men are wont to regret that the moon has waned or that the blossoms have fallen, and this must be so; but they must be perverse indeed who will say, "This branch, that bough is withered, now there is nought to see."

In all things it is the Beginning and End that are interesting. The love of men and women—is it only when they meet face to face? To feel sorrow at an unaccomplished meeting, to grieve over empty vows, to spend the long night sleepless and alone, to yearn for distant skies, in a neglected house to think fondly of the past—this is what love is.

Rather than to see the moon shining over a thousand leagues, it sinks deeper into the heart to watch it when at last it appears toward the dawn. It never moves one so much as when seen in gaps between the trees, pale green over the tops of the cedars on distant hills, or behind the clustering clouds after showers of rain. When it shines bright on the leaves of oak and evergreen, and they look wet, the sight sinks deeply into one's being, and one feels "Oh! for a friend with whom to share this!" and longs for the capital.

And must we always look upon the moon and the blossoms with the eye alone? Nay, in the very thought thereof, in the spring though we do not go abroad, on moonlit nights though we keep our chamber, there is great comfort and delight.

A well-bred man does not show strong likings. His enjoyment appears careless. It is rustic boors who take all pleasures grossly. They squirm and struggle to get under the blossoms, they stare intently, they drink wine, they link verses, and at last they heartlessly break off great branches. They dip their hands and feet in springs; they get down and step on the snow, leaving footmarks; there is nothing they do not regard as their own.

• •

A man who would follow the world must first of all be a judge of moods, for untimely speeches will offend the ears and hurt the feelings of others, and so fail in their purpose. He has to beware of such occasions.

But falling sick and bearing children and dying—these things take no account of moods. They do not cease because they are untimely. The shifting changes of Birth, Life, Sickness, and Death, the real great matters—these are like the surging flow of a fierce torrent, which delays not for an instant but straightway pursues its course.

And so, for both priest and layman, there must be no talk of moods in things they must needs accomplish. They must be free from this care and that, they must not let their feet linger.

It does not turn to summer after spring has closed, nor does the fall come when the summer ends. The spring betimes puts on a summer air, already in the summer is the fall abroad, and anon the fall grows cold. In the tenth month comes a brief space of spring weather. Grass grows green, plum blossoms bud. So with the falling of leaves from the trees. It is not that the trees bud, once the leaves have fallen, but that because they are budding from beneath, the leaves, unable to withstand the strain, perforce must fall. An onward-urging influence is at work within, so that stage presses on stage with exceeding haste.

This again is exceeded by the changes of birth, age, sickness, and death. The four seasons have still an appointed order. The Hour of Death waits for no order. Death does not even come from the front. It is ever pressing on from behind. All men know of death, but they do not expect it of a sudden, and it comes upon them unawares. So, though the dry flats extend far out, anon the tide comes and floods the strand.

TRANSLATED BY G. B. SANSOM

THE EXILE OF GODAIGO

[*Masukagami, Book XVI*]

The "Masukagami"—variously translated as "Mirror of Increase" or "Mirror of Clarity"—is an historical romance based on events which took place between 1184 and 1333. It begins with the accession of the Emperor Gotoba (1180-1239) and ends with the return from exile of the Emperor Godaigo (1288-1339). These were two of the most energetic and literarily gifted of the Japanese emperors. Both attempted to assert themselves against the military class, and both were defeated and sent to exile on the remote island of Oki.

The selection given here covers Godaigo's journey from Kyoto to Oki, and the life he led in lonely exile. Godaigo was more fortunate than Gotoba (who is the "former emperor" of the translation) in that he was able to return from exile thanks to his supporters. Once back in power, however, he continued to make the mistakes that had caused his first exile, and it was not long before his forces were driven from Kyoto again, this time to the mountains of Yoshino where for some sixty years the "Southern Court" held sway.

Neither the date nor the author of the "Masukagami" is known, but it is believed to have been written about 1370, possibly by Nijō Yoshimoto (1320-1388) the famous poet of linked-verse.

•

The spring of 1332 had come. The beginning of the first year of the new reign was surprisingly festive. The new Emperor, being young and handsome, lent a special brilliance to everything, and the palace ceremonies were performed in exact observance of tradition. On the occasions of official functions, and even on quite ordinary days, there was so dense a press of carriages before the palace and the residences of the cloistered sovereigns,[1] which were situated within the same area, that it was scarcely possible to move, but among all those who thronged to the court, there was not a single familiar face.

The Emperor Godaigo was still held captive at Rokuhara. Along about the second moon, when the skies were serene and lightly veiled in mist, and the gently blowing spring breezes brought from the eaves the nostalgic fragrance of plum blossoms, so melancholy was his cast of mind that even the clear notes of the thrush sounded harshly in his ears. Their situations were different, of course, but one could not help thinking of some neglected court lady in the women's palace at the Chinese court. Perhaps it was with the intent of consoling him, now that the lengthening of the days made it all the harder for him to pass his time, that the Empress sent him his lute, together with this poem written on a scrap of paper:

omoiyare	Turn your thoughts to me,
chiri no mi tsumoru	And behold these, my tears,
yotsu no o ni	Too thick to brush away;
harai mo aezu	They fell on the strings of the lute
kakaru namida wo	When I saw how thick the dust lay.

The Emperor, understanding that these must have been her actual feelings, was deeply saddened, and the tears coursed down his face like raindrops. He wrote in reply:

kakitateshi	When I plucked the notes
ne wo tachihatete	After many months of silence,
kimi kouru	I yearned for you,
namida no tama no	And the notes became cords
o to zo narikeru	On which to thread my tears.

Just at this time there arrived in Kyoto an emissary from Kamakura named Nagai Takafuyu. His family had been important samurai in Kamakura since the days of General Yoshitomo, and al-

[1] At the time two emperors who had abdicated and taken Buddhist orders were living in the capital—Gofushimi (1288-1336) and Hanazono (1297-1348).

though he was still young he was chosen for the important mission of informing the Emperor that the time had at last come for him to remove to Oki; on the seventh day of the third moon he must depart from the capital. It may well be imagined how great was the Emperor's consternation when he learned that the dreaded moment was now at hand. Great were the lamentations also of the Empress and the princes, and those who were in attendance on him could not control their grief. He attempted to keep others from seeing how greatly distressed he was, but in spite of himself tears welled up, which he concealed as best he could. Whenever he recollected what had happened to that former emperor, he realized how unlikely it was that he himself would ever return to govern the country again. He lived in the conviction that everything had now come to an end, and he ceaselessly lamented that his sorrows were due not to the wickedness of others, but had all been imposed on him from a previous existence.

tsui ni kaku	If it is my fate
shizumihatsubeki	To terminate thus my days,
mukui araba	In the depths of ruin,
ue naki mi to wa	Why was I ever born
nani umarekemu	Sovereign supreme of men?

The Emperor set out about ten o'clock in the morning. He rode in the split-bamboo Imperial carriage. The outriders consisted of all those still alive who had served at the court since the reign of the late Emperor Go-uda.[2] The Middle Counselor Saionji served as carriage attendant. The Emperor wore the Imperial crown, an ordinary court robe and trousers, and an unlined cloak of white damask. He recalled with sorrow that on the same day a year before he had held a cherry-blossom party in the northern hills, and one after another of the happy events of that day came back to him. The robes which he then had presented to the different gentlemen to celebrate the occasion were today altered into traveling garments, and this thought made him lament all the more bitterly the fickle usages of

[2] Go-uda (1267-1324) reigned from 1275 to 1288.

the world. Just before he left his prison to enter the carriage, he wrote on the paper-door beside which he always used to sit:

isa shirazu	I do not know—
nao ukikata no	If I go from here to some
mata mo araba	Yet more hateful place,
kono yado totemo	Perhaps even these lodgings
shinobare ya semu	Will stir nostalgic regret.

He was accompanied by several court dames and by just two men, Yukifusa and Tadaaki. No words could express the sorrow that each one felt as the moment of departure approached. The officers who were selected to escort him from Rokuhara, or who were engaged in other duties commensurate with their great fame, included ten of the most distinguished men of the realm. They were attired in magnificent brocade cloaks and robes of various hues, woven and dyed in contrasting patterns, and presented a rare and splendid sight even in these unhappy circumstances. From Rokuhara they proceeded westward along the Seventh Ward, and then turned southward at Omiya. The Imperial carriage halted in front of the Eastern Temple, apparently to permit the Emperor a brief moment of prayer. The carriages of spectators jammed the streets. Even ladies of quality, in wide-brimmed hats and turned-up robes, mingled with the pedestrians. Young and old, nuns, priests, and even wretched wood-cutters and hunters from the mountains thronged the place, as thick as bamboos in a forest. Just to see them all wiping their eyes and sniffling made one feel that no worse calamity could occur in this sorrowful world. It must have been thus when the Emperor Gotoba was exiled to Oki, but of that event I know only by report, not having witnessed it myself. It seemed to me then that so appalling a moment had never before been known. Even the insignificant or base people who normally could never have approached the Imperial presence were bewildered and dumbfounded by the pathos of today's leave-taking. The Emperor lifted the blinds of his carriage a little and gazed around him as though not to let a blade of grass or a tree escape his eyes. The soldiers of the escort, not being made of stone or wood, could be seen to wet the sleeves of their armor with their tears. The Emperor looked back until the treetops of the capital disappeared from sight. He still wondered if it might after all be just a dream.

When they arrived at the Toba Palace, His Majesty changed his apparel, and for appearance's sake partook of lunch, although he barely touched the food. From this place onward he was to travel by palanquin. The outriders and other courtiers wept as they returned to the capital with the empty carriage, and he was most touched by their distraction. In this manner the Emperor departed for his distant destination.

At the crossing of the Yodo River he recalled how when, long ago, he had paid a state visit to the Hachiman Shrine, his commissioner at the bridge-crossing had been Sasaki, the Lord of Sado, who had since entered the priesthood and was this day serving as one of his escorts. The recollection was difficult to bear.

shirube suru	Although this road
michi koso arazu	On which you are guiding me
narinu tomo	Is not the one of old,
Yodo no watari wa	At the Yodo crossing
wasureshi mo seji	I do not forget the past. . . .

The Emperor next crossed the Cape of Wada and the Karumo River, and was approaching the Barrier of Suma. The place "where the wind from the bay blows across the pass," of Yukihira's poem, must have been far inland from the bay which now the Emperor gazed on, lost in emotion. He felt as if even now the waves of which Genji had said, "they are lost in the sound of my weeping," were splashing on his sleeves, and they brought tears for many things. The Emperor next came to the province of Harima. Struck by the charm of the villages he saw, he asked what they were called, and they told him "Salt-House" and "Dripping Brine." "Just to ask the names makes the journey all the more bitter," he said. When he lifted the blinds of his palanquin and looked out, his face was young and handsome, so that all who were in attendance thought how splendid he looked. Just beyond the valley of Okura was the tomb of Hitomaro. And when he passed the bay of Akashi, how moving it was.[3]

mizu no awa no	I who must journey
kiete ukise wo	Across a world vanishing
wataru mi ni	Like foam on the waves,
urayamashiki wa	What I long for most of all
ama no tsuribune	Is a little fishing boat.

When he looked on the Springs of Nonaka, the Bay of Futami, and the Pine of Takasago, all celebrated in poetry, he thought how delighted he would be were it not this sort of journey, but in his present distraught frame of mind, which everything served only to deepen, he could only shut his eyes to them. "I must be in a terrible state," he thought. Clustered cherry trees were in blossom on a lofty peak, and he felt as though he were making his way through white clouds. But the very charm of the scene brought up memory on memory of the capital.

hana wa nao	The cherry blossoms
ukise mo wakazu	Unmindful of the sad world,
sakitekeri	Have burst into bloom.
miyako mo ima ya	And in the capital too
sakari naruramu	Now must be their glory.

On the twelfth, when he was stopping at a place on the Kako River, he was informed that his son, the Prince Sonchō, about to sail for exile in Sanuki, had arrived at Noguchi, east of the river, although the route he had taken differed somewhat from the Emperor's. Much moved by the news, the Emperor asked to meet his son, but his escorts refused permission, and the Prince passed on without a glimpse of him. What unbearable agitation must he have experienced then! It hardly need be stated here, but there is no man but would feel unspeakable bitterness and rancor toward a world where even so small a thing could not be granted.

On the seventeenth he reached the province of Mimasaka where

[3] This section has many references to the Suma and Akashi chapter of "The Tale of Genji," linking Godaigo's exile with Genji's.

he rested for two or three days on account of an indisposition. Since his lodgings here were only temporary, they were not very spacious, and the soldiers on duty were all able to see him from quite close up. His majestic appearance stirred them profoundly, and he looked at them filled with many thoughts.

aware to wa	My miserable state
nare mo miruramu	Is apparent even to you—
wa ga tami wo	Know that my concern
omou kokoro wa	For my beloved people
ima mo kawarazu	Even now remains unchanged.

At the sight of smoke rising from the eaves of the house adjoining his, the Emperor recited the verse, "Brushwood burning in a mountain hut" in a touching way.

yoso ni no mi	I had always thought it
omoi zo yarishi	Something quite remote from me.—
omoiki ya	Did ever I think
tami no kamado wo	Thus to see, so close at hand,
kakute mimu to wa	The kitchen fires of my people?

They continued on their journey. The Emperor, noticing that the direction from which they had come was now veiled over in mist, thought, "How great a distance I have come!" Each day that elapsed took him farther from the capital and increased his melancholy. Even the branches of cherry, which he had seen in their first faint bloom, with the passage of the days and the miles had lost their color more and more, and now lay scattered whitely on the twisting roads that led up and down through the mountains. He felt as though he were passing over patches of melting snow.

hana no haru wa	How hard it will be
mita mimu koto no	Once again to see the spring
kataki ka na	And cherry blossoms,
onaji michi wo ba	Even if perchance I travel
ikikaeru tomo	Back along this very road.

Yes, it would be extremely difficult but, he consoled himself, if he managed to keep alive he might yet be able to carry through his plans, though this was not to be depended on. . . .

At Nakayama of the Three-day Moon he recalled the poem that long ago the Emperor Gotoba had written about the place. How sad those times had been!

tsutaekiku	When I hear them tell
mukashigatari zo	Those stories of days gone by
ukarikeru	I am filled with grief.
sono na furinuru	O name that I long have known,
minazuki no mori	Forest of the Three-day Moon!

They were now half-way to their destination. The soldiers of the escort, high and low alike, changed to costumes of a style even gayer and more fashionable than those in which they had left the capital. Although in most respects it was paltry and strange for an Imperial procession, the evidence of the care which had been taken for their entertainment all along the way was such that the procession did not seem so wretched after all; the Emperor's reception was in fact most courteous. He was now an exile, but there seemed still to be a lingering respect for one who had been a sovereign and had ruled his country with majesty. He was treated everywhere with the greatest deference. Those who knew about ancient matters declared that on that procession to exile of former days no such courtesies had been shown.

About the first day of the fourth moon, recalling his life at the palace, the Emperor wrote:

samo koso wa	Indeed it is true
tsukihi mo shiranu	That I have quite forgotten
ware narame	The passage of time.
koromogae seshi	Is it not today that I was wont
kefu ni ya wa aranu	To change to summer clothes?

At the port of Yasuki in the province of Izumo he boarded ship. Twenty-four large and innumerable small vessels followed his. As the boats were rowed far out to sea and the way back was obscured by ever thickening mist, his spirits sank, and he felt that he understood for the first time what it meant to be "separated by two thousand leagues." [4] Thus he arrived in Oki.

Nothing remained in the way of relics of that former exile. There was a handful of houses and, in the distance, only a shed where the fishermen burnt salt. When he cast his eyes on this most miserable view, all thoughts of himself left his mind, and he recalled instead the events of the past. With sorrow and humility he tried to imagine what it must have been like for that other Emperor to have ended his days in such a place, and he realized that his present exile stemmed from his desire to fulfill the aspirations of his ancestor. Countless thoughts pursued him: he wondered whether the former Emperor in his grave was now taking pity on him.

The Emperor fixed upon a temple called Kokubunji, which was situated somewhat inland from the coast, as his residence, and had it renovated suitably. Now that he had definitely entered upon the life he was henceforth to lead, he felt calmed, but he still experienced an indescribable sensation of unreality. When all the soldiers who had escorted him to Oki withdrew, a terrible silence fell over the place, which made him feel all the more depressed. . . .

On the twenty-second day of the third moon the coronation procession took place in the capital, dazzling everyone by its splendor. The cloistered sovereigns, Gofushimi and Hanazono, who rode together, stopped their carriage by the eastern gate of the palace to watch the procession. Everything had been arranged with the greatest care and went off beautifully.

But, alas, the Emperor Godaigo's consort was wrapped in grief, as she had been since their parting, and never raised her head. Her sorrow was understandable: added to the unhappiness caused by a distant separation, there were the pangs in her heart that gave her no surcease. Without emotion, as if it were happening to someone quite remote, she received the news that her title of Empress had been taken from her, and a name as a nun bestowed. It was now for

[4] An allusion to a line by Po Chü-i: "I think of old friends separated from me now by two thousand leagues."

her a world bereft of joy. In days past she had grieved because she had been mocked at and made the object of universal gossip,[5] and the Emperor had shared her distress, but now she gave no thought at all to such matters. The various altars that had been erected for prayers for her safe delivery had been damaged beyond recognition and forgotten. Her days were now given over entirely to confused thoughts about the sadness of the world. As time went on without her even taking the necessary medicines, she fell insensibly into a decline, and it did not seem that she could long survive. From Oki there came only very infrequent messages, all of which contributed to her anxiety and depression. There was no certainty that they would meet again, and they were both exceedingly unhappy at the thought that, the uncertain world being what it is, they might soon end their lives still thus separated.

Naiji no Sammi, who accompanied the Emperor to Oki, had given birth to several of his children. Because of their tender years they were not sent to exile, but their guardian was changed, and they moved to a house in the northern hills. Although they were still small, they were aware of what had happened and often, when no one could see them, they would burst into tears of longing for their parents. The eldest of the children was seven years old. In his new surroundings the sky was dismal, and the fiercely blowing mountain winds made him sadder than before. He recited verses in Chinese and in Japanese:

> The garden pines are dark with age, the autumn wind is cold;
> The bamboo leaves grow thick, white snow now covers all.

tsukuzuku to	Having spent the day
nagamekurashite	In quiet meditation,
iriai no	Just to hear the sound
kane no oto ni mo	Of the evening temple bell
kimi zo koishiki	Makes me long for you, my lord.

It was most touching to see how, boy though he was, he kept a melancholy silence. Even though he spoke no word, everyone could

[5] There had been a scandal about a false pregnancy.

guess from his appearance how deeply he lamented the fates of both those in Kyoto and in Oki. . . .

This year there was an Imperial procession to the Kamo Festival, which was so unusual that people devoted the utmost care to the sightseeing carriages, and the stands along the way were built with greater splendor than ever before. The deputies of the reigning and cloistered sovereigns vied with one another as to who would present the most stunning appearance. The courtiers and the young men of noble families—all those who were privileged to wear the forbidden colors—attended in bright and elegant attire. Even their attendants created with their costumes the brilliant effect of a bouquet of flowers. From the carriages the court ladies' robes in every color—wistaria, azalea, verbena, carnation, and iris—overflowed in a most gay and charming manner.

When the festival was over and things had quieted down, all those nobles who had been seriously implicated as partisans of the Emperor Godaigo were sent to distant exile. The Major Counselor Kimitoshi had shaved his head and was spending his days in quiet retirement, but his crime was apparently unpardonable, and it was reported that he had been sent under escort to the distant north. About the same time also the Middle Counselor Tomoyuki was sent to the east. Among the many offenders his crimes were reported to be the most serious, and it seemed likely that a punishment even severer than exile would be his fate. His wife had served in the palace, and had formerly enjoyed the favors of the Emperor Godaigo and borne him a princess, but later he yielded her to Tomoyuki, although the latter was still of inferior rank at the time. During the years since then they had loved each other with a rare passion, and now that the world was proving so cruel to one after another of the great men, her worries could not but be extreme. As the days went by she grew increasingly unhappy, but as long as she knew that Tomoyuki still remained in Kyoto she could at least take comfort from asking the blowing winds about him. She realized, of course, that sooner or later he would share the same fate as the others, but when she heard that the moment had come, her feelings were quite indescribable. This spring, when the Emperor had left the capital, she thought that she had wept all the tears she possessed, but some indeed remained—she wept now more even than before, until it seemed she would weep her whole body away. Tomoyuki, torn by regret and an unbecoming weakness, wished that things could be again as they were, but suddenly reflecting that he must not let others see him in this womanish state he changed his expression and feigned indifference, as if he were completely undisturbed. Here are some of the many poems he composed during the winter of the previous year, after his arrest:

nagaraete	Though yet I survive
mi wa itazura ni	I shall meaninglessly die:
hatsu shimo no	Like the first frost
oku kata shiranu	Which cannot find a resting place,
yo ni mo furu ka na	I pass my days in the world.

ima wa haya	Now, already,
ika ni narinuru	Even while in the same world,
ukimi zo to	No one asks any more
onaji yo ni dani	What has happened to me
tou hito mo nashi	Who have thus been afflicted.

The lay priest Sasaki, the Lord of Sado, escorted him from the capital. At Ausaka Barrier Tomoyuki wrote:

kaeru beki	Since there will not be
toki shinakereba	A time when I may return,
kore ya kono	Mine is a journey
yuku wo kagiri no	But of going, once I pass
Ausaka no seki	Ausaka Barrier.

They stopped for a while at a place called Kashiwabara, where the priest was apparently waiting for a reply to the message he had sent to Kamakura about Tomoyuki's disposition. During this time the priest related to him various tales in which he showed his sympathy. "Everything that happens is the result of actions committed in a former existence. You are not the only one who has been implicated, and I couldn't very well help you if I didn't help the others.

It is hard for a man to be born as I was into a warlike family, and to have to spend all his time in service with his weapons." He did not say directly what he thought, but Tomoyuki understood what he was hinting at.

The priest had also served as escort on the Emperor's journey to Oki, and he began to relate what had happened on the way. "It was a most exalting and moving experience. I could easily imagine how you who had waited on him day and night must have felt about him. In every respect he equalled the grandeur of the sovereigns of old, and I was led to think that it was his very excess of ability in these degenerate and ill-starred times which caused things to happen as they did." Even when he discussed quite ordinary matters, he added telling observations, speaking always in a most gentle manner. The priest tried to make up for the unhappy situation by treating Tomoyuki most solicitously, offering him wines which were extravagant for one in his position, if a little rough owing to the remoteness of the place.

Although the messenger sent to Kamakura had apparently by this time already returned, the priest deliberately avoided mention of him. Tomoyuki was oppressed by the desire to find out his fate, and though he had resigned himself to death, his spirits were low. "What good would it do me to be sent off to some distant island?" he asked himself. "No one in this world lives to be a thousand years old, and indeed, the longer one lives, the greater the suffering. Sooner or later I must journey the road that none escape—it's all one. He whose mind is free of disturbance at the final hour will go to the Pure Land."

In spite of his resolve, however, his heart was still torn by longing for the capital, and many thoughts continued to unsettle him. He realized that in any case, at least to judge by appearances, his own end could not be far off. His escort had hinted to him of it, and since he had shown himself a man of kindness, Tomoyuki thought that he would not object if he became a priest. The following day Tomoyuki said, "I think I should like to shave my head." "That is most unfortunate. I wonder what they will think in Kamakura if they hear of it. However, I don't imagine it makes any difference."

He thus gave his consent. This happened on the nineteenth day of the sixth moon.

That day, as Tomoyuki could tell, was probably to be his last. It did not come as a surprise to him, but he could not help feeling how disgraceful it was that he, a prince, should meet with so unprecedented a fate.

kiekakaru	Now I can behold
tsuyu no inochi no	The moment of expiration
hate wa mitsu	Of my dew-like life.
sate mo Azuma no	What I most would like to see
sue zo yukashiki	Is the end of Azuma.[6]

It was evident from his words that he still harbored rebellious thoughts against Kamakura. Toward evening of the same day he was finally put to death. He did not behave in an unseemly manner during his last moments, even though his heart must have been filled with bitterness, but acted as though he considered his fate inevitable. It may be imagined how painfully his wife was afflicted by the news she so long had been dreading. Soon afterward she shaved her head and entered a convent where friends of former days were now living a life of holy devotions. . . .

In this manner one after another of the adherents of the Emperor Godaigo was executed or sent to distant exile, each meeting a lamentable fate, but to describe them all is beyond my powers. Only Prince Sonun escaped the tiger's mouth, wandering here and there with no safe refuge. It was wondered in pity how long he could survive.

On the little island of Oki the passing months and days brought with them only additional sorrows. The Emperor wondered, "Of what great crimes have I been guilty that I should be made to suffer so?" Even while he thus lamented his karma, he tried to think how he might atone for his sins. He gave himself to strict Buddhist discipline, and performed his devotions day and night. Perhaps he also thought that the power of the Law might help him to regain his

[6] Azuma ("the East") here stands for the military government in Kamakura which was responsible for Godaigo's exile.

throne. Whenever he himself lit the holy fire, many auspicious signs appeared, both in his dreams and in his waking hours.

At times when he was bored he used to pace the gallery-like part of the temple looking out at the bay in the distance. He could faintly see the little fishing boats, which reminded him of floating autumn leaves, and in his melancholy he would wonder, "Whither do they go?"

kokorozasu	I would ask of you
kata wo towaba ya	Whither is it that you head,
nami no ue ni	Little fishing boats,
ukite tadayou	Floating, drifting aimlessly
ama no tsuribune	On the waves of the sea.

He recited the verse "The boat rowed out to the bay now is rudderless; how sad it is to be alone, adrift."[7] He somehow managed to conceal the tears which fell, lending an indescribable nobility to his face. Although he was no longer young, he was still so graceful and handsome that it seemed almost sacrilegious even to himself that such majesty should be wasted in so dreary a place.

In the capital, now that the tenth moon had come, everyone was frantically busy with preparations for the Thanksgiving Service for the new reign. The Household Treasury, the Department of Works, and the guilds of seamstresses and dyers were all noisily engaged in their respective tasks. But for those loyal to the Emperor Godaigo, the occasion was a source only of tears.

Various people were commanded to compose poetry to be inscribed on the Heaven and Earth palace-screens, but as there was no one who could write them beautifully enough, it was debated whether to recall Yukifusa from exile. Word of this soon reached Oki. In the stillness of an evening, when no one else was in attendance, Yukifusa waited on the Emperor. In the course of one of his stories about things present and past, the Emperor remarked, "I wonder what they will decide to do about you in the capital. If they do recall you I shall certainly be most envious." The Emperor's eyes filled with tears in spite of himself, as he gazed at the lantern by his

[7] An allusion to a poem by Ono no Komachi in the "*Shokukokinshū.*"

side, and Yukifusa, who was watching him, quite lost heart. "If it were really some important business, I would go back, but to write poetry—how can I possibly return to the capital when I see him look that way?" Such were his thoughts, but he could not speak them.

It was just the time for the Emperor's midnight devotions. A wind from the sea was blowing fiercely, and there even came a harsh rattle of hail. The Emperor broke the ice that had formed during this terribly cold night to offer holy water to the Buddha, like some little priest in a mountain temple. Tadaaki and Yukifusa, who had come to worship with sprays of anise as offerings, were profoundly stirred, and wondered when the Emperor had learned the ceremony. The Emperor was beset by countless thoughts as he prayed that somehow once again he might rule the country, this time with a better understanding of the true natures of men.

TRANSLATED BY DONALD KEENE

SEAMI ON THE ART OF THE NŌ

The principal figure in the development of the Nō *was Seami (or Zeami) Motokiyo (1363-1443). He was the author of most of the* Nō *plays which are still performed, including three of the four given in this volume. In addition to the plays, he wrote a number of critical works on the* Nō *in which he described the aesthetic principles underlying his art. The language he used, perhaps necessarily so, is at times obscure, and offers special problems in translation. This was due in part to the influence of Zen Buddhism, with its emphasis on intuitive understanding: this Zen influence is particularly apparent in the first selection given here. The word* yūgen, *with which the second selection is concerned, had a primary meaning of "mystery" and, however used, generally retains something of the sense of a mysterious power. Seami gave to this word the meaning of the chief aesthetic principle of the* Nō.

•

THE ONE MIND LINKING ALL POWERS

Sometimes spectators of the *Nō* say that the moments of "no action" are the most enjoyable. This is one of the actor's secret arts. Dancing and singing, movements on the stage, and the different types of miming are all acts performed by the body. Moments of "no action" occur in between. When we examine why such moments without action are enjoyable, we find that it is due to the underlying spiritual strength of the actor which unremittingly holds the attention. He does not relax the tension when the dancing or singing comes to an end or at intervals between the dialogue and the different types of miming, but maintains an unwavering inner strength. This feeling of inner strength will faintly reveal itself and bring enjoyment. However, it is undesirable for the actor to permit this inner strength to become obvious to the audience. If it is obvious, it becomes an act, and is no longer "no action." The actions before and after an interval of "no action" must be linked by entering the state of mindlessness in which the actor conceals even from himself his own intent. The ability to move audiences depends, thus, on linking all the artistic powers with one mind.

> "Life and death, past and present—
> Marionettes on a toy stage.
> When the strings are broken,
> Behold the broken pieces!" [1]

This is a metaphor describing human life as it transmigrates between life and death. Marionettes on a stage appear to move in various ways, but in fact it is not they who really move—they are manipulated by strings. When these strings are broken, the marionettes fall and are dashed to pieces. In the art of the *Nō* too, the different types of miming are artificial things. What holds the parts together is the mind. This mind must not be disclosed to the audience. If it is seen, it is just as if a marionette's strings were visible. The mind must be made the strings which hold together all the powers of the art. If this is done the actor's talent will endure. This effort must not be confined to the times when the actor is appearing on the stage: day or night, wherever he may be, whatever he may be doing, he should not forget it, but should make it his constant guide, uniting all his powers. If he persistently strives to perfect this, his talent will steadily grow. This article is the most secret of the secret teachings.

[1] Poem by an unknown Zen master. The last two lines may mean, "When life comes to an end the illusions of this world also break into pieces."

ON ATTAINING THE STAGE OF YŪGEN

Yūgen is considered to be the mark of supreme attainment in all the arts and accomplishments. In the art of the *Nō* in particular, the manifestation of *yūgen* is of the first importance. When *yūgen* in the *Nō* is displayed, it is generally apparent to the eye, and it is the one thing which audiences most admire, but actors who possess *yūgen* are few and far between. This is because they do not know its true meaning and so do not reach that stage.

In what kind of place is the stage of *yūgen* to be found? Let us begin by examining the various classes of people on the basis of the appearance that they made in society. May we not say of the courtiers whose behavior is distinguished and whose appearance far surpasses that of other men, that they are at the stage of *yūgen*? From this we may see that the essence of *yūgen* is true beauty and gentleness. Tranquillity and elegance make for *yūgen* in personal appearance. In the same way, the *yūgen* of discourse lies in a grace of language and a complete mastery of the speech of the nobility and the gentry so that even the most casual utterance will be graceful. A musical performance may be said to possess *yūgen* when the melody flows beautifully and sounds smooth and sensitive. A dance will possess *yūgen* when the discipline has been thoroughly mastered and the audience is delighted by the performer's movements and by his serene appearance. Acting possesses *yūgen* when the performance of the Three Roles[2] is beautiful. If the characterization calls for a display of anger or for the representation of a devil, the actions may be somewhat forceful, but as long as the actor never loses sight of the beauty of the effect and bears in mind always the correct balance between his mental and physical actions and between the movements of his body and feet,[3] his appearance will be so beautiful that it may be called the "*yūgen* of a devil."

[2] Seami considered the Three Basic Roles to be those of the old person, the woman, and the warrior.

[3] Seami elsewhere discusses the relation between what the actor expresses with his body and what he knows but does not overtly express. At first an actor who has studied with

All these aspects of *yūgen* must be kept in mind and made a part of the actor's body, so that whatever part he may be playing *yūgen* will never be absent. Whether the character he portrays be of high or low birth, man or woman, priest, peasant, rustic, beggar, or outcast, he should think of each of them as crowned with a wreath of flowers. Although their positions in society differ, the fact that they can all appreciate the beauty of flowers makes flowers of all of them.[4] Their particular flower is shown by their outward appearance. An actor, through the use of his intelligence, makes his presentation seem beautiful. It is his intelligence which permits him to grasp the above principles; to learn poetry so as to impart *yūgen* to his discourse; and to study the most elegant costuming so as to give *yūgen* to his bearing. Though the characterization varies according to the different parts, the actor should realize that the ability to appear beautiful is the seed of *yūgen*. It is all too apt to happen that an actor, believing that once he has mastered the characterization of the different parts he has attained the highest stage of excellence, forgets his appearance and is therefore unable to enter the realm of *yūgen*. Unless, however, he enters that realm he will not attain to the highest achievements, and will therefore not become a great master. That is why there are so few masters. The actor must consider *yūgen* as the most important aspect of his art, and study to perfect his understanding of it.

The "highest achievements" of which I have spoken are beauty of form and manner. The most careful attention must be given to the appearance presented. When the form is beautiful, whether in dancing, singing, or in any type of characterization, it may be called a "highest achievement." When the form is ugly, the performance

---

a master does not know any more than what he has learned and what he expresses, but as he himself acquires mastery there are things which he comes to understand beyond what he has been taught, and which he suggests rather than expresses. The relation between the movements of the body and feet refers to a theory of Seami's that if the body and the feet move in the same manner the effect will be crude. Thus, in an agitated passage when the feet are stamping wildly, the movements of the body should be gentle or a disorderly effect will be produced which will mar the spectator's enjoyment.

[4] That is, their love of beauty makes them beautiful, irrespective of their station.

will be inferior. The actor should realize that *yūgen* is attained when all different forms of visual and aural expression are beautiful. It is when the actor himself has worked out these principles and made himself their master that he may be said to have entered the realm of *yūgen*. If he fails to work out these principles for himself, he will not master them, and however much he may aspire to attain *yūgen*, he will never in all his life do so.

TRANSLATED BY RYUSAKU TSUNODA AND DONALD KEENE

PLAN OF THE NO STAGE

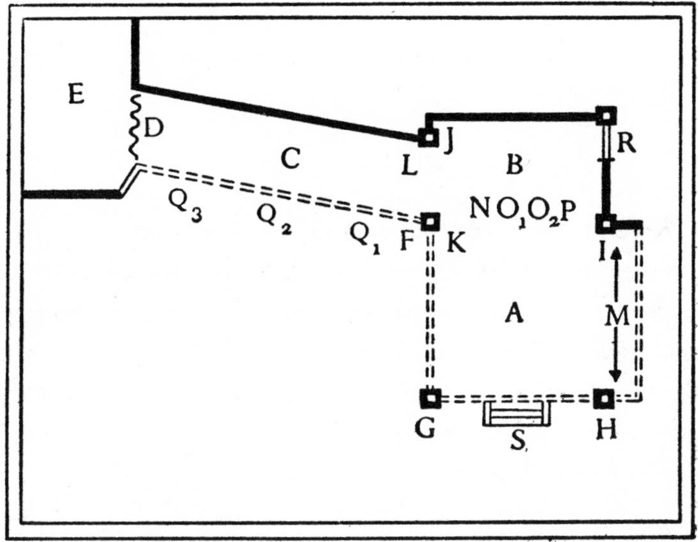

A Main Stage (*Butai*)
B Rear Stage (*Atoza*)
C Bridge (*Hashigakari*)
D Curtain (*Maku*)
E Mirror Room (*Kagami-no-ma*)
F Shite's Pillar (*Shite-bashira*)
G Facing Pillar (*Metsuke-bashira*)
H Waki's Pillar (*Waki-bashira*)
I Flute Pillar (*Fue-bashira*)
J Stage Attendant's Pillar (*Kōken-bashira*)
K Name-Saying Seat (*Nanoriza*)
L Kyōgen's Seat (*Kyōgen-za*)
M Chorus (*Ji-utai*)
N Drummer (*Taiko-kata*)
O Drummers (*Tsuzumi-kata*)
P Flute Player (*Fue-kata*)
Q Pine Trees (*Matsu-no-ki*)
R Hurry Door (*Kirido-guchi*)
S Steps to Audience (*Shirasu-bashigo*)

Shite: the protagonist, who usually makes two appearances, often the second time as a ghost.
Waki: the deuteragonist, often an itinerant monk.
Tsure: a companion of either the *shite* or *waki.*

SOTOBA KOMACHI

by Kan'ami Kiyotsugu

"Sotoba Komachi" concerns Ono no Komachi, a beautiful and heartless poetess of ancient Japan. One infatuated nobleman was refused a rendezvous until he should have come to her house in his chariot a hundred nights. He died just before completing his ordeal, but his unresolved love and passionate jealousy returned to possess Komachi when she was a wretched, withered old woman.

•

Persons
FIRST PRIEST
SECOND PRIEST
KOMACHI, as herself and as her former lover
CHORUS

BOTH PRIESTS: The mountains are not high on which we hide
The mountains are not high on which we hide
The lonely deepness of our hearts.
FIRST PRIEST: I am a priest from the Koya Hills
Coming down now to make my way to the city.
SECOND PRIEST: The Buddha that was is gone away.
The Buddha to be has not yet come to the world.
BOTH PRIESTS: At birth we woke to dream in this world between.
What then shall we say is real?
By chance we took the forms of men
From a thousand possibilities.
We stumbled on the treasure of the holy law
The seed of all salvation
And then with thoughtful hearts we put our bodies
In these thin and ink-black robes.
We knew of lives before this birth
We knew of lives before this birth

And knew we owed no love to those who to this life
Engendered us.
We recognized no parents.
No children cared for us.
We walked a thousand miles and the way seemed short.
In the fields we lay down
And slept the night in the hills
Which now became our proper dwelling place
Our proper home.

KOMACHI: "Like a root-cut reed
Should the tide entice
I would come
I would come I know but no wave asks
No stream invites this grief."
How sad that once I was proud
Long ago
Proud and graceful
Golden birds in my raven hair
When I walked like willows nodding, charming
As the breeze in spring.
The voice of the nightingale
The petals of the wood rose, wide stretched,
Holding dew
At the hour before their breathless fall:
I was lovelier than these.
Now
I am foul in the eyes of the humblest creatures
To whom my shame is shown.
Unwelcome months and days pile over me
The wreck of a hundred years
In the city to avoid the eyes of men
Lest they should say "Can it be she?"
In the evening
West with the moon I steal past the palace,
Past the towers
Where no guard will question in the mountains

In the shadows of the trees
None challenge so wretched a pilgrim as this
To Love's Tomb
The autumn hills
The River Katsura
Boats in the moonlight rowed by whom?
I cannot see. . . .
But rowed by whom!
Oh, too, too painful. . . .
Here on this withered stump of tree
Let me sit and collect my senses.

FIRST PRIEST: Come on. The sun is down. We must hurry on our way. But look! that old beggar woman sitting there on a sacred stupa. We should warn her to come away.

SECOND PRIEST: Yes, of course.

FIRST PRIEST: Excuse me, old lady, but don't you know that's a stupa there you're sitting on? the holy image of the Buddha's incarnation. You'd better come away and rest some other place.

KOMACHI: The holy image of the Buddha you say? But I saw no words or carvings on it. I took it for a tree stump only.

FIRST PRIEST: "Withered stumps
Are known as pine or cherry still
On the loneliest mountain."

KOMACHI: I, too, am a fallen tree.
But still the flowers of my heart
Might make some offering to the Buddha.
But this you call the Buddha's body. Why?

FIRST PRIEST: The stupa represents the body of Kongosatta Buddha, the Diamond Lord, when he assumed the temporary form of each of his manifestations.

KOMACHI: In what forms then is he manifested?

FIRST PRIEST: In Earth and Water and Wind and Fire and Space.

KOMACHI: The same five elements as man. What was the difference then?

FIRST PRIEST: The form was the same but not the power.

KOMACHI: And what is a stupa's power?

FIRST PRIEST: "He that has once looked upon a stupa shall for all eternity avoid the three worst catastrophes."

KOMACHI: "One sudden thought can strike illumination." Is that not just as good?

SECOND PRIEST: If you've had such an illumination, why are you lingering here in this world of illusion?

KOMACHI: Though my body lingers, my heart has left it long ago.

FIRST PRIEST: Unless you had no heart at all you wouldn't have failed to feel the presence of a stupa.

KOMACHI: It was because I felt it that I came perhaps.

SECOND PRIEST: In that case you shouldn't have spread yourself out on it without so much as a word of prayer.

KOMACHI: It was on the ground already. . . .

FIRST PRIEST: Just the same it was an act of discord.

KOMACHI: "Even from discord salvation springs."

SECOND PRIEST: From the evil of Daiba

KOMACHI: Or the love of Kannon.

FIRST PRIEST: From the folly of Handoku

KOMACHI: Or the wisdom of Monju.

FIRST PRIEST: What we call evil

KOMACHI: Is also good.

FIRST PRIEST: Illusion

KOMACHI: Is Salvation.

SECOND PRIEST: "Salvation

KOMACHI: Cannot be watered like trees."

FIRST PRIEST: "The brightest mirror

KOMACHI: Is not on the wall."

CHORUS: Nothing is separate.
Nothing persists.
Of Buddha and man there is no distinction,
At most a seeming difference planned
For the humble, ill-instructed men
He has vowed from the first to save.
"Even from discord salvation springs."
So said Komachi. And the priests:
"Surely this beggar is someone beyond us."

Then bending their heads to the ground
Three times did they do her homage
The difficult priests
The difficult priests
Who thought to correct her.

FIRST PRIEST: Who are you then? Give us your name; we will pray for your soul.

KOMACHI: For all my shame I will tell you. Pray for the wreck of Komachi, the daughter of Yoshizane of Ono, Lord of Dewa.

BOTH PRIESTS: How sad to think that you were she.
Exquisite Komachi
The brightest flower long ago
Her dark brows arched
Her face bright-powdered always
When cedar-scented halls could scarce contain
Her damask robes.

KOMACHI: I made verses in our speech
And in the speech of the foreign court.

CHORUS: When she passed the banquet cup
Reflected moonlight lay on her sleeve.
How was ever such loveliness lost?
When did she change?
Her hair a tangle of frosted grass
Where the black curls lay on her neck
And the color lost from the twin arched peaks
Of her brow.

KOMACHI: "Oh shameful in the dawning light
These silted seaweed locks that of a hundred years
Now lack but one."

CHORUS: What do you have in the bag at your waist?

KOMACHI: Death today or hunger tomorrow.
Only some beans I've put in my bag.

CHORUS: And in the bundle on your back?

KOMACHI: A soiled and dusty robe.

CHORUS: And in the basket on your arm?

KOMACHI: Sagittaries black and white.

CHORUS: Tattered coat

KOMACHI: Broken hat
CHORUS: Can scarcely hide her face.
KOMACHI: Think of the frost and the snow and the rain.
I've not even sleeves enough to dry my tears.
But I wander begging things from men
That come and go along the road.
When begging fails
An awful madness seizes me
And my voice is no longer the same. . . .
Hey! Give me something, you priests!
FIRST PRIEST: What do you want?
KOMACHI: To go to Komachi!
FIRST PRIEST: What are you saying? You *are* Komachi!
KOMACHI: No. Komachi was beautiful.
Many letters came, many messages
Thick as rain from a summer sky
But she made no answer, even once,
Even an empty word.
Age is her retribution now.
Oh, I love her!
I love her!
FIRST PRIEST: You love her! What spirit has possessed you to make you say such things?
KOMACHI: Many loved her
But among them all
It was Shosho who loved her deepest
Shii no Shosho, the Captain.
CHORUS: The wheel turns back.
I live again a cycle of unhappiness
Riding with the wheels
That came and went again each night.
The sun.
What time is it now?
Dusk.
The moon will be my friend on the road
And though the watchmen stand at the pass
They shall not bar my way.

KOMACHI (recostumed as her lover): My wide white skirts hitched up

CHORUS: My wide white skirts hitched up
My tall black hat pulled down
And my sleeves thrown over my head
Hidden from the eyes of men on the road
In the moonlight
In the darkness coming, coming
When the night rains fell
When the night winds blew the leaves like rain
When the snow lay deep

KOMACHI: And the melting drops fell
One by one from the rafters

CHORUS: I came and went, came and went
One night, two nights, three,
Ten (and this was the Harvest Night)
And did not see her.
Faithful as a cock that marks each dawn
I came and carved my mark upon the pillar.
I was to come a hundred nights,
I lacked but one. . . .

KOMACHI: Oh, dizziness . . . pain. . . .

CHORUS: He was grieved at the pain in his breast
When the last night came and he died
Shii no Shosho, the Captain.

KOMACHI: It was his unsatisfied love possessed me so
His anger that turned my wits.
In the face of this I will pray
For life in the worlds to come
The sands of goodness I will pile
Into a towering hill.
Before the golden, gentle Buddha I will lay
Poems as my flowers
Entering in the Way
Entering in the Way.

TRANSLATED BY SAM HOUSTON BROCK

BIRDS OF SORROW

[*Utō*] *by Seami Motokiyo*

The original title of the play, "Utō," is usually written in Japanese with three ideographs which may be loosely translated as "virtue-knowing bird." The utō *or* utōyasukata *of early legends is a species of sea bird found in northern Japan and widely hunted for the delectability of its flesh. According to tradition, the parent bird of the species hides its young so well in the sand that even it cannot find them and, when bringing them food, calls them with the cry "Utō," to which they reply with the cry "Yasukata." Hunters catch both parent birds and the young by imitating these cries. It is also said that the parent birds weep tears of blood upon seeing their young taken, and that hunters must wear large hats and raincloaks to protect themselves from the falling tears, the touch of which causes sickness and death. Because of its traits the bird becomes an apt symbol for the Buddhist tenet that the taking of life in any form whatsoever is a sin.*

•

Persons

A BUDDHIST MONK
THE GHOST OF A DEAD HUNTER
THE HUNTER'S WIFE
THE HUNTER'S CHILD
A VILLAGER
CHORUS

PART I

Place: Tateyama, a high mountain in Central Honshū, near the Sea of Japan.
Time: The month of April.

(The stage is completely bare. Two drummers and a flute player come through the curtain and, passing down the Bridge, take their usual seats at the rear of the stage. They are followed in silence by the Wife and Child. The Wife wears the mask and wig of a middle-aged woman; her inner kimono is the color of dried autumn leaves, over which is a kimono with a small pattern and a long outer kimono in somber colors which trails behind her on the floor. The Child, apparently six or eight years of age, wears a hakama and a brightly embroidered outer kimono over a scarlet inner kimono. They seat themselves near the Waki's Pillar. The Monk enters, accompanied by the introductory flute music. He is wearing a dark kimono and a peaked cowl of brocade which flows down over his shoulders, and carries a rosary. He passes down the Bridge onto the stage, where he stops at the Name-Saying Seat and, facing the audience, introduces himself.)

MONK: I am a wandering monk, making a pilgrimage throughout the provinces. I have never yet visited the village of Soto no Hama in Michinoku. Thinking on this, I was recently minded to go to Soto no Hama. And as the occasion is indeed favorable, I am planning to stop in passing and practice religious austerities upon Tateyama.

(Takes two steps forward, indicating he has arrived at the foot of the mountain.)

Coming swiftly along the road, already I have arrived here at Tateyama. With serene and reverent heart I now shall visit the mountain.

(Goes to center of stage, indicating he has climbed to the summit.)

But lo! upon arriving here on Tateyama, my eyes do indeed behold a living Hell. And the heart of even the boldest man must quail before this fell sight, more frightful even than demons and fiends. Here the countless mountain trails, grim and precipitous, split asunder as if to lead down into the Realm of Ravenous Ghosts, and down into the Realm of Bestiality.

(Describing his actions.) So saying, he is overcome with the memory of his past sins and for a time is unable to restrain the starting tears. Then, penitent, he descends to the foot of the mountain . . . to the foot of the mountain, penitent . . .

(The Monk goes toward the Chorus, indicating he has returned to the foot of the mountain. He turns and faces the Bridge. The curtain is swept back and a voice is heard from the blackness of the Mirror Room beyond the curtain. It is the Ghost of the Dead Hunter who speaks, calling out as though he has been running after the Monk.)

HUNTER: Hallo-o! Hallo-o! Wait, O worthy monk, for I must speak with you.

MONK: What is it you want with me?

(The Hunter enters. He is seen now in his mortal form, wearing the mask of a pleasant old man and a white wig. He wears a plain, tea-colored outer kimono of rough weave over garments of solid brown and light green. He moves slowly down the Bridge as he speaks.)

HUNTER: If you are going down to Michinoku, pray take a message there. I am one who was a hunter of Soto no Hama and who died in the past year's autumn. I beseech you to visit the home of my wife and child and to tell them to offer up for me the cloak of straw and the sedge-hat which are there.

MONK: This is a strange request that I hear. To carry the message is a simple thing, but if I address her thus without any proof, like the falling of sudden rain from an empty sky, is it likely that she will believe?

HUNTER: Indeed, you are right. Without some certain sign or token, it would surely be of no avail.

(The Hunter has been advancing along the Bridge; he pauses now at the First Pine and bows his head dejectedly. Then an idea comes to him and he raises his head.)

Ah! Now I remember—this was the kimono which I was wearing at the very hour of death.

(Describing his actions.) And thereupon he tears a sleeve from the kimono which he is wearing, a kimono made of hemp like that of Kiso long ago, and worn in the days of his life.

(The Hunter removes the left sleeve of his kimono, touches it to his forehead, and then holds it out in both hands toward the Monk.)

CHORUS: He says, "This give as a token." And so saying, gives it with tears to the wandering monk . . . with tears, to the wandering monk. . . .

(The Monk goes to the Hunter at the First Pine and takes the sleeve, then turns and comes onto the stage, while the Hunter starts along the Bridge toward the curtain.)

They bid farewell. The footsteps of the monk lead away toward Michinoku, down through the flaming, budding trees of spring, far and far away, amid the rising smoke and clouds of Tateyama, until his figure too becomes like a wisp of cloud.

(The Monk continues toward the front of the stage. The Hunter brings his hand to his forehead in a gesture of weeping. Then he turns around on the Bridge and looks long toward the stage, shading his eyes with his hand.)

The dead one weeps and weeps, watching the monk depart, and then vanishes, no one knows where . . . no one knows where. . . .

(The Hunter has turned and continued along the Bridge. Now the curtain is swept back and he moves into the blackness beyond the curtain.)

INTERLUDE

Place: Soto no Hama, a fishing village on the northernmost coast of Honshū several hundred miles from Tateyama.

(There has been a slight pause on the stage, during which time the Monk is understood to be traveling to Michinoku. Now he goes to the Name-Saying Seat, where he turns and addresses the actor who has been sitting motionless at the Kyōgen's Seat during Part I.)

MONK: Are you a native of Soto no Hama?

(The Villager rises and stands on the Bridge near the First Pine. He is wearing a simple plaid kimono and a kamishimo of brocade.)

VILLAGER: Yes, I am. May I help you?

MONK: Please show me the house here of the hunter who died last autumn.

VILLAGER: Why, of course. The dead hunter's house is that one you see there inside that high stockade made of crisscrossed bamboo. You can reach it in a moment if you please.

MONK: I understand. Thank you for your kindness. I shall go there at once and pay a visit.

VILLAGER: If there is anything else I can do for you, please say so.

MONK: Thank you very much.

VILLAGER: You are very welcome.

(The Villager resumes his seat. Later he makes an unobtrusive exit.)

PART II

Place: The home of the dead Hunter, both the interior and exterior being understood to be visible.

(The Monk has moved to the Stage Attendant's Pillar, where he pauses. The Wife speaks, as if to herself, from her seat at the Waki's Pillar.)

WIFE: Truly, long have I known this world to be a fleeting thing, becoming dreamlike even as it passes. But now more than ever before.

To what avail was my troth plighted? Now death has cut the ties which bound me to my husband. And this beloved child, left behind him like a footstep at the parting, only makes my grief more endless. . . . Oh, how can a mother's heart endure such sorrow?

(The Wife makes a gesture of weeping. The Monk has put the sleeve which he held into the breastfold of his kimono and has been advancing slowly toward the stage. Reaching the Shite's Pillar, he stops and turns toward the Wife, indicating he has reached the house.)

MONK: Pray let me in.
WIFE: Who is there?
MONK: I am a wandering monk, making a pilgrimage throughout the provinces. While I was practicing religious austerities upon Tateyama there came a weird old man and said, "If you are going down to Michinoku, please take a message. I am one who was a hunter of Soto no Hama and who died in the past year's autumn. Visit the home of my wife and child and tell them to offer up for me the cloak of straw and sedge-hat which are there." I replied, "If I address her thus without any proof, out of a clear sky, she surely will not believe." Thereupon he loosened and gave to me a sleeve of the hempen kimono he wore. I have journeyed and carried it with me until now. Perchance it is a token which will call memories to your heart.
WIFE: Surely this is a dream. Or else a piteous thing. Like unto the song of the cuckoo, heard at early morning, bringing back from Hell a last message from the dead, so now with these tidings that I hear from my departed one. And even as I listen, the tears are springing in my eyes.

(Making gesture of weeping.)

Nevertheless, it is too strange a thing, passing all belief. And therefore, crude though it be and lowly as cloth woven of wistaria bark, I will bring out his kimono. . . .

(A stage attendant comes to the Wife where she sits and gives her the folded kimono without a sleeve which the Hunter was wearing in Part I. She holds it up on her outstretched arms toward the Monk.)

MONK: That kimono long treasured as a memory of him . . . this sleeve long carried. . . .

(The Monk takes out the sleeve and holds it out toward the Wife.)

WIFE: Upon taking them out. . . .
MONK: . . . and comparing them well. . . .

(The Monk looks fixedly at the kimono which the Wife is holding.)

CHORUS: . . . there can be no doubt left.

(The Monk comes to the Wife and lays the sleeve in her arms upon the kimono. She bends her head over the articles, examining them closely, while the Chorus speaks for her.)

The cloth is the same—thin, crude stuff, for summer's wearing . . . thin, crude stuff for summer's wearing. And see! a sleeve is gone—this sleeve exactly fits. . . . It comes from him! O so dearly longed for. . . .

(The Wife bows low over the garments in a gesture of weeping. The Chorus now explains the actions of the Monk as he takes a large, black-lacquered hat from a stage attendant at the Flute Pillar, brings it to the very front of the stage and, placing it on the floor, kneels before it facing the audience.)

And forthwith does the Monk chant countless prayers of requiem. And especially, even as the dead one had entreated, does he offer up that very cloak of straw, offer up that very hat of sedge.

(The Monk rubs his rosary between his palms over the hat and intones a Buddhist Sutra.)

MONK: "Hail, O Spirit. May you be delivered from the endless round of incarnations. May you attain the instantaneous enlightenment of Buddhahood."

(Rising, the Monk goes and takes a seat near the Flute Pillar. There is an interval of music accompanied by cries of the drummers. The curtain is swept back and the Hunter appears, now in supernatural form. He wears a tragic mask of a gaunt old man, just human enough in appearance to be unearthly, and an unkempt black wig which flares wildly down over his shoulders. Over his outer kimono, dappled with white and gray, he wears a short apron made of white and brown feathers. He carries a long stick and a fan. He comes slowly down the Bridge, as though summoned by the Monk's prayers. Reaching the Shite's Pillar, he stops and chants an old poem.)

HUNTER: "At Soto no Hama of Michinoku there is the sound of birds, tenderly calling, tenderly cherishing—'*Utō*,' sing the parents in the sky, '*Yasukata*,' the young answer from the beaches."

(The Hunter makes a gesture indicating he is drawing near the house.)

Even as the Holy Sutra says, "Behold but once the *sotoba,* and be delivered for all time from the Three Evil Paths, beset by beasts and demons and hungry ghosts." Truly then a *sotoba* is a blessed thing, a memorial tablet carved fivefold, the five elements of the Buddha Body, the mere sight of which can save. But how much more if it be a *sotoba* raised expressly for my own sake, if a requiem be said in my own name.

For even in the icy Hell of the Scarlet Lotus the Fire of Holy Wisdom is not extinguished. For even in the Hell of Raging Fire the Waters of Dharma still quench.

And, nevertheless, still the burden of sin heaps high upon this flesh. . . . When may this soul find peace? . . . When can the birds find their stolen young? . . . O the killing!

(The Hunter turns and holds out his arms beseechingly toward the Monk.)

CHORUS: In the sunlight of Buddha, the All Compassionate, the sins of man become like dew upon the grass: make the blessing-bestowing Sun to shine on me, O monk.

(The Hunter drops his arms and turns back toward the audience. The Chorus now describes the locale, while the Hunter makes a slow tour round the stage, revisiting the scenes of his earthly life.)

The place is Michinoku. The place is Michinoku. And here, in a lonely fishing village, upon an inlet of the sea, fenced round as though on the Isle of Hedges—now by the interlacing lower branches of the pine trees which follow along the strand, now by the salt reeds which grow drooping and matted in the ebb and flow of the tide—here at Soto no Hama stands the rush-mat hut. A humble dwelling, its roof so sparsely thatched. But now when the moon shines through the thatch into the room—a home for one's heart. Oh! truly a home for one's heart.

(The Hunter returns now to the Name-Saying Seat, where he leans motionless on his stick, looking toward the Wife and Child, indicating he has reached the house. The Wife and Child raise their heads and look toward the Hunter.)

WIFE: Softly! the shape will vanish if you but say a single word.

(They rise and the Wife leads the Child a few steps toward the Hunter, describing her actions.)

The mother and child clasp hands . . . and there is nought but weeping.

(Leaving the Child standing, the Wife returns to her original position, kneels and weeps.)

HUNTER: Alas! in other days this was the wife of my bed, the child of my heart. But now we are estranged forever—like the parent bird I cry *"Utō"* and, waiting with beating heart, never hear the answering *"Yasukata."* Why? oh, why did I kill them? For even as my child is beloved, just so must the birds and beasts yearn for their young. And now when I long to stroke the hair of my son Chiyodō and say, "Oh, how I have missed thee!" . . .

(The Hunter extends his arms and suddenly rushes toward the Child. But at each step of the Hunter, the Child falls back a step, as though some unseen object were keeping a fixed distance between them. It is the legendary cloud-barrier of earthly lusts which obscures the Sun of Buddha and prevents sinful spirits from visiting the earth. The Child takes a seat beside the Wife, and the Hunter returns to the center of the stage and stands with his back to the Wife and Child, indicating he has been unable to enter the house and can no longer see inside.)

CHORUS: . . . the shadows of my earthly lusts do rush before my eyes—a cloud of grief now rolls between us, a grievous cloud now hangs about.

(The Hunter makes a gesture of weeping.)

I cannot see him! Just now he was standing there, my child, sturdy and strong as a young pine. . . .

Fugitive and fleeting . . . whither? . . . where? . . . I cannot find the hat—lost in the forests of the country of Tsu, in the shade of the spreading pine of Wada. I cannot reach the cloak—the flood tears, falling, drench my sleeves as might the spray from the waterfall at Minō. I cannot see the blessed *sotoba.*

(The Hunter makes slow circles round the stage, indicating his efforts to see through the cloud, and then stamps his foot in frustration.)

Who is this that stands outside, unable to enter his own home, barred from his wife and child, from cloak and hat, yes even from the *sotoba*? . . . "Having returned to Matsushima, to Ojima, I do not see the rush-mat huts on the islands—the villages are

desolate, by the waves laid waste." . . . The song is old, but now it is I, I who cannot find, cannot enter the rush-mat hut. . . .
The bird of Soto no Hama, unable to find its nest . . . raising its voice in grief . . . nought but weeping. . . .

(The Hunter circles slowly to the Shite's Pillar, where he kneels and makes a gesture of weeping.)

The vague and boundless past, dreamlike. . . . It was from the ruin of these past pleasures, from these evil days, that I descended to the Yellow Springs, to the bitter waters of Hell. . . .

(Still kneeling, the Hunter raises his head.)

HUNTER: My path of life led from birth far out beyond the four estates of man—I was neither scholar, farmer, artisan, nor merchant.

CHORUS: Nor did I delight in life's four pleasures—music nor chess, books nor paintings.

HUNTER: There was only the coming of day, the coming of night—and the killing!

CHORUS: Thoughtless, wasting the slow spring days in hunting—days meant for the leisurely enjoyment of living. But still the lust for killing was unappeased. And so when the nights of autumn became long and long, I kept them alight, sleepless, with my fishing flares.

HUNTER: Unheedful of the ninety days of summer's heat. . . .

CHORUS: . . . of the cold of winter's mornings. . . .

(The Chorus now begins a description of the Hunter's past life. The Hunter, still kneeling, gradually begins to look from side to side, slowly, as though seeing the scenes being described.)

"The hunter pursues the deer and does not see the mountains," says the proverb. And truly so it was with me—thinking only of bait and snares, I was like one drugged by the day lily, oblivious to every pain of the body, to every sorrow of the heart. Lashed by wind and wave, even as is the great sand dune of Sue-no-Matsu-yama . . . my garments wet and dripping as are the rocks which stand offshore, forever in the ebbing and flowing of the tide . . . coursing the beaches, crossing the sea even to the shores of the farther islands . . . my flesh burnt as though I had approached too near the salt-kilns of Chika. . . .

Still and always I pursued my evil ways, forgetful of the days of retribution, heedless of all regret.

(The Hunter touches his hands together in the conventional gesture which introduces a principal dance, bows his head and rises, grasping his stick. He begins gradually to keep rhythm with the music, but without yet moving from place.)

Now the ways of murdering birds are many, but this scheme by which these pitiful ones are taken. . . .

HUNTER: . . . can there be one more heartless than this?

(The Hunter now begins moving slowly about the stage, searching, keeping time with the music.)

CHORUS: You stupid, foolish bird! If only you had built your nest with feathers, high in the treetops of the forests, forests dense as that which lies about the Peak of Tsukuba . . . if only you had woven floating cradles upon the waves. . . . But no! here upon the beaches, as broad and sandy as those upon which wild geese settle for a moment's rest in their northward flight, you raise your young. And here, O bird of sorrow, you think to hide them. But then I, calling *"Utō,"* come . . . they answer *"Yasukata"* . . . and the nestlings are taken. It is as simple as this!

(Still searching, the Hunter has started toward the Bridge, but when the Chorus gives the cry of "Utō" *he pauses at the Name-Saying Seat and listens. And at the cry* "Yasukata" *he whirls back toward the stage, as though hearing the birds in the nest. He stamps his foot once and in the midst of a profound silence gives the bird call.)*

HUNTER: *Utō!*

(The Hunter strikes the stage with his stick and begins a pantomime of the hunt which preceded his death. The dance begins slowly with the discovery and pursuit of the birds and gradually mounts in ferocity to their capture and killing. At first the Hunter raises his stick in the direction of the Waki's Pillar, as though the imaginary birds are concealed in that vicinity, and brings it down to frighten them from the nest. The young birds are then understood to run toward the Bridge. He follows and, stopping near the Bridge, turns his body in an arc as though searching the horizon. Finally discovering the birds near the First Pine, he again flushes them with a wave of his stick. They run toward the front of the stage, with the Hunter in pursuit, wildly brandishing his stick. He catches up with them near the hat, which is still at the front of the stage, and brings his stick down with two sharp blows upon the stage, indicating the killing of the birds. Then he closes the movement with two stamps of the feet.)

CHORUS: From the sky the parent bird is weeping tears of blood.

(The emotion of the dance now suddenly changes. The Hunter falls back a few steps and looks up fearfully. Then, hurling away his stick, he runs and snatches up the hat.)

From the sky fall tears of blood. And I, covering myself with the sedge-hat, with the cloak of straw, try to escape the falling tears, dodging now this way, now that.

(Holding the hat in both hands above his head and moving it rapidly from side to side. Then sinking for a moment to his knees.)

But alas! these are not the enchanted cloak and hat which make invisible their wearer.

(Rising and moving toward the Waki's Pillar.)

Faster and faster fall the tears of blood, until my body cannot escape their mortal touch, until the world turns crimson before my eyes—crimson as the fabled Bridge of Maple Leaves, formed of magpie wings across the sky and at the dawn stained red by the tears of two parting lover-stars.

(Throws the hat violently aside and takes out fan. The Chorus now turns from a description of past events to a recital of the tortures which the Hunter is undergoing in Hell. The dance becomes quieter now, the Hunter using the fan to indicate the actions described. The fan is a large white one on which is painted a bird in flight.)

In the earthly world I thought it only an easy prey, this bird, only an easy prey. But now here in Hell it has become a gruesome phantom-bird, pursuing the sinner, honking from its beak of iron, beating its mighty wings, sharpening its claws of copper. It tears at my eyeballs, it rends my flesh. I would cry out, but choking amid the shrieking flames and smoke, can make no sound.

(The Hunter runs wildly about the stage, in agony.)

Is it not for the sin of killing the voiceless birds that I myself now have no voice? Is it not for slaughtering the moulting, earth-bound birds that I cannot now flee?

(The Hunter has started moving rapidly toward the Facing Pillar when suddenly he seems unable to move and sinks to his knees, cowering in the center of the stage.)

HUNTER: The gentle bird has become a falcon, a hawk!

CHORUS: And I!—I have become a pheasant, vainly seeking shelter, as though in a snowstorm on the hunting fields of Gatano, fleeing in vain over the earth, fearing also the sky, harassed by falcons above and tormented by dogs below.

(The Hunter rises and, looking up toward the sky and down to the earth, moves slowly, defeatedly, toward the Shite's Pillar.)

Ah! the killing of those birds! this heavy heart which never knows a moment's peace! this body endlessly in pain!

(The Hunter stops at the Shite's Pillar and, turning, points a finger at the Monk.)

Please help me, O worthy monk. Please help me. . . .

(The Hunter drops his arms, and the Chorus chants the conventional ending of a Nō *play.)*

And thereupon the spirit fades and is gone. . . .

(The Hunter stamps his feet, indicating he has disappeared, that the play is done. He walks slowly down the Bridge and through the curtain, followed in turn by the other actors and the musicians. The Chorus exits by the Hurry Door, and again the stage is left bare.)

TRANSLATED BY MEREDITH WEATHERBY AND BRUCE ROGERS

ATSUMORI

by Seami Motokiyo

This play is based on an episode in "The Tale of the Heike," which appears on page 179.

•

Persons
THE PRIEST RENSEI (formerly the warrior Kumagai)
A YOUNG REAPER, who turns out to be the ghost of Atsumori
HIS COMPANION
CHORUS

PRIEST: Life is a lying dream, he only wakes
Who casts the world aside.

I am Kumagai no Naozane, a man of the country of Musashi. I have left my home and call myself the priest Rensei; this I have done because of my grief at the death of Atsumori, who fell in battle by my hand. Hence it comes that I am dressed in priestly guise.

And now I am going down to Ichi no tani to pray for the salvation of Atsumori's soul.

(He walks slowly across the stage, singing a song descriptive of his journey.)

I have come so fast that here I am already at Ichi no tani, in the country of Tsu.

Truly the past returns to my mind as though it were a thing of today.

But listen! I hear the sound of a flute coming from a knoll of rising ground. I will wait here till the flute-player passes, and ask him to tell me the story of this place.

REAPERS *(together)*: To the music of the reaper's flute
No song is sung
But the sighing of wind in the fields.
YOUNG REAPER: They that were reaping,
Reaping on that hill,
Walk now through the fields
Homeward, for it is dusk.
REAPERS *(together)*: Short is the way that leads
From the sea of Suma back to my home.
This little journey, up to the hill
And down to the shore again, and up to the hill—
This is my life, and the sum of hateful tasks.
If one should ask me
I too would answer
That on the shore of Suma
I live in sadness.
Yet if any guessed my name,
Then might I too have friends.
But now from my deep misery
Even those that were dearest
Are grown estranged. Here must I dwell abandoned
To one thought's anguish:
That I must dwell here.

PRIEST: Hey, you reapers! I have a question to ask you.

YOUNG REAPER: Is it to us you are speaking? What do you wish to know?

PRIEST: Was it one of you who was playing on the flute just now?

YOUNG REAPER: Yes, it was we who were playing.

PRIEST: It was a pleasant sound, and all the pleasanter because one does not look for such music from men of your condition.

YOUNG REAPER: Unlooked for from men of our condition, you say!
Have you not read:
"Do not envy what is above you
Nor despise what is below you"?
Moreover the songs of woodmen and the flute-playing of herdsmen,

Flute-playing even of reapers and songs of wood-fellers
Through poets' verses are known to all the world.
Wonder not to hear among us
The sound of a bamboo flute.

PRIEST: You are right. Indeed it is as you have told me.
Songs of woodmen and flute-playing of herdsmen . . .

REAPER: Flute-playing of reapers . . .

PRIEST: Songs of wood-fellers . . .

REAPERS: Guide us on our passage through this sad world.

PRIEST: Song . . .

REAPER: And dance . . .

PRIEST: And the flute . . .

REAPER: And music of many instruments . . .

CHORUS: These are the pastimes that each chooses to his taste.
Of floating bamboo wood
Many are the famous flutes that have been made;
Little Branch and Cicada Cage,
And as for the reaper's flute,
Its name is Green Leaf;
On the shore of Sumiyoshi
The Korean flute they play.
And here on the shore of Suma
On Stick of the Salt-kilns
The fishers blow their tune.

PRIEST: How strange it is! The other reapers have all gone home, but you alone stay loitering here. How is that?

REAPER: How is it, you ask? I am seeking for a prayer in the voice of the evening waves. Perhaps *you* will pray the Ten Prayers for me?

PRIEST: I can easily pray the Ten Prayers for you, if you will tell me who you are.

REAPER: To tell you the truth—I am one of the family of Lord Atsumori.

PRIEST: One of Atsumori's family? How glad I am!

Then the priest joined his hands *(he kneels down)* and prayed:

Namu Amidabu.

Praise to Amida Buddha!
"If I attain to Buddhahood,
In the whole world and its ten spheres
Of all that dwell here none shall call on my name
And be rejected or cast aside."

CHORUS: "Oh, reject me not!
One cry suffices for salvation,
Yet day and night
Your prayers will rise for me.
Happy am I, for though you know not my name,
Yet for my soul's deliverance
At dawn and dusk henceforward I know that you will pray."
So he spoke. Then vanished and was seen no more.

(Here follows the Interlude between the two Acts, in which a recitation concerning Atsumori's death takes place. These interludes are subject to variation and are not considered part of the literary text of the play.)

PRIEST: Since this is so, I will perform all night the rites of prayer for the dead, and calling upon Amida's name will pray again for the salvation of Atsumori.

(The ghost of Atsumori appears, dressed as a young warrior.)

ATSUMORI: Would you know who I am
That like the watchmen at Suma Pass
Have wakened at the cry of sea birds roaming
Upon Awaji shore?
Listen, Rensei. I am Atsumori.

PRIEST: How strange! All this while I have never stopped beating my gong and performing the rites of the Law. I cannot for a moment have dozed, yet I thought that Atsumori was standing before me. Surely it was a dream.

ATSUMORI: Why need it be a dream? It is to clear the karma of my waking life that I am come here in visible form before you.

PRIEST: Is it not written that one prayer will wipe away ten thousand sins? Ceaselessly I have performed the ritual of the Holy Name that clears all sin away. After such prayers, what evil can be left? Though you should be sunk in sin as deep . . .

ATSUMORI: As the sea by a rocky shore,
Yet should I be saved by prayer.

PRIEST: And that my prayers should save you . . .

ATSUMORI: This too must spring
From kindness of a former life.[1]

PRIEST: Once enemies . . .

ATSUMORI: But now . . .

PRIEST: In truth may we be named . . .

ATSUMORI: Friends in Buddha's Law.

CHORUS: There is a saying, "Put away from you a wicked friend; summon to your side a virtuous enemy." For you it was said, and you have proven it true.

And now come tell with us the tale of your confession, while the night is still dark.

CHORUS: He[2] bids the flowers of spring
Mount the treetop that men may raise their eyes
And walk on upward paths;
He bids the moon in autumn waves be drowned
In token that he visits laggard men
And leads them out from valleys of despair.

ATSUMORI: Now the clan of Taira, building wall to wall,
Spread over the earth like the leafy branches of a great tree:

CHORUS: Yet their prosperity lasted but for a day;
It was like the flower of the convolvulus.
There was none to tell them[3]
That glory flashes like sparks from flint-stone,
And after—darkness.
Oh wretched, the life of men!

ATSUMORI: When they were on high they afflicted the humble;
When they were rich they were reckless in pride.

1 "Atsumori must have done Kumagai some kindness in a former incarnation." This would account for Kumagai's remorse.

2 Buddha.

3 I have omitted a line the force of which depends upon a play on words.

And so for twenty years and more
They ruled this land.
But truly a generation passes like the space of a dream.
The leaves of the autumn of Juyei [4]
Were tossed by the four winds;
Scattered, scattered (like leaves too) floated their ships.
And they, asleep on the heaving sea, not even in dreams
Went back to home.
Caged birds longing for the clouds—
Wild geese were they rather, whose ranks are broken
As they fly to southward on their doubtful journey.
So days and months went by; spring came again
And for a little while
Here dwelt they on the shore of Suma
At the first valley.[5]
From the mountain behind us the winds blew down
Till the fields grew wintry again.
Our ships lay by the shore, where night and day
The sea gulls cried and salt waves washed on our sleeves.
We slept with fishers in their huts
On pillows of sand.
We knew none but the people of Suma.
And when among the pine trees
The evening smoke was rising,
Brushwood, as they called it,[6]
Brushwood we gathered
And spread for carpet.
Sorrowful we lived
On the wild shore of Suma,
Till the clan Taira and all its princes
Were but villagers of Suma.

ATSUMORI: But on the night of the sixth day of the second month
My father Tsunemori gathered us together.

[4] The Taira evacuated the capital in the second year of Juyei, 1188.

[5] Ichi no tani means "First Valley."

[6] The name of so humble a thing was unfamiliar to the Taira lords.

"Tomorrow," he said, "we shall fight our last fight.
Tonight is all that is left us."
We sang songs together, and danced.

PRIEST: Yes, I remember; we in our siege-camp
Heard the sound of music
Echoing from your tents that night;
There was the music of a flute . . .

ATSUMORI: The bamboo flute! I wore it when I died.

PRIEST: We heard the singing . . .

ATSUMORI: Songs and ballads . . .

PRIEST: Many voices

ATSUMORI: Singing to one measure.

(Atsumori dances.)

First comes the royal boat.

CHORUS: The whole clan has put its boats to sea.
He[7] will not be left behind;
He runs to the shore.
But the royal boat and the soldiers' boats
Have sailed far away.

ATSUMORI: What can he do?
He spurs his horse into the waves.
He is full of perplexity.
And then

CHORUS: He looks behind him and sees
That Kumagai pursues him;
He cannot escape.
Then Atsumori turns his horse
Knee-deep in the lashing waves,
And draws his sword.
Twice, three times he strikes; then, still saddled,
In close fight they twine; roll headlong together
Among the surf of the shore.
So Atsumori fell and was slain, but now the Wheel of Fate
Has turned and brought him back.

[7] Atsumori. This passage is mimed throughout.

(Atsumori rises from the ground and advances toward the Priest with uplifted sword.)

"There is my enemy," he cries, and would strike,
But the other is grown gentle
And calling on Buddha's name
Has obtained salvation for his foe;
So that they shall be reborn together
On one lotus seat.
"No, Rensei is not my enemy.
Pray for me again, oh pray for me again."

TRANSLATED BY ARTHUR WALEY

THE DAMASK DRUM

[*Aya no Tsuzumi*] *by Seami Motokiyo*

•

Persons

A COURTIER
AN OLD GARDENER
THE PRINCESS

COURTIER: I am a courtier at the Palace of Kinomaru in the country of Chikuzen. You must know that in this place there is a famous pond called the Laurel Pond, where the royal ones often take their walks; so it happened that one day the old man who sweeps the garden here caught sight of the Princess. And from that time he has loved her with a love that gives his heart no rest.

Some one told her of this, and she said, "Love's equal realm knows no divisions," [1] and in her pity she said, "By that pond there stands a laurel tree, and on its branches there hangs a drum. Let him beat the drum, and if the sound is heard in the palace, he shall see my face again."

I must tell him of this.

Listen, old Gardener! The worshipful lady has heard of your love and sends you this message: "Go and beat the drum that hangs on the tree by the pond, and if the sound is heard in the palace, you shall see my face again." Go quickly now and beat the drum!

GARDENER: With trembling I receive her words. I will go and beat the drum.

COURTIER: Look, here is the drum she spoke of. Make haste and beat it!

(He leaves the Gardener standing by the tree and seats himself at the foot of the Waki's Pillar.)

[1] A twelfth-century folk song speaks of "The Way of Love which knows no castes of 'high' and 'low'."

GARDENER: They talk of the moon tree, the laurel that grows in the Garden of the Moon. . . . But for me there is but one true tree, this laurel by the lake. Oh, may the drum that hangs on its branches give forth a mighty note, a music to bind up my bursting heart.

Listen! the evening bell to help me chimes;
But then tolls in
A heavy tale of day linked on to day,

CHORUS: *(speaking for the Gardener):* And hope stretched out from dusk to dusk.

But now, a watchman of the hours, I beat
The longed-for stroke.

GARDENER: I was old, I shunned the daylight,
I was gaunt as an aged crane;
And upon all that misery
Suddenly a sorrow was heaped,
The new sorrow of love.
The days had left their marks,
Coming and coming, like waves that beat on a sandy shore . . .

CHORUS: Oh, with a thunder of white waves
The echo of the drum shall roll.

GARDENER: The afterworld draws near me,
Yet even now I wake not
From this autumn of love that closes
In sadness the sequence of my years.

CHORUS: And slow as the autumn dew
Tears gather in my eyes, to fall
Scattered like dewdrops from a shaken flower
On my coarse-woven dress.
See here the marks, imprint of tangled love,
That all the world will read.

GARDENER: I said "I will forget,"

CHORUS: And got worse torment so
Than by remembrance. But all in this world

Is as the horse of the aged man of the land of Sai;
And as a white colt flashes
Past a gap in the hedge, even so our days pass.[3]
And though the time be come,
Yet can none know the road that he at last must tread,
Goal of his dewdrop-life.
All this I knew; yet knowing,
Was blind with folly.

GARDENER: "Wake, wake," he cries—

CHORUS: The watchman of the hours—
"Wake from the sleep of dawn!"
And batters on the drum.
For if its sound be heard, soon shall he see
Her face, the damask of her dress . . .
Aye, damask! He does not know
That on a damask drum he beats,
Beats with all the strength of his hands, his aged hands,
But hears no sound.
"Am I grown deaf?" he cries, and listens, listens:
Rain on the windows, lapping of waves on the pool—
Both these he hears, and silent only
The drum, strange damask drum.
Oh, will it never sound?
I thought to beat the sorrow from my heart,
Wake music in a damask drum; an echo of love
From the voiceless fabric of pride!

GARDENER: Longed for as the moon that hides
In the obstinate clouds of a rainy night
Is the sound of the watchman's drum,
To roll the darkness from my heart.

[2] A story from *"Huai-nan Tzŭ."* What looks like disaster turns out to be good fortune and *vice versa*. The horse broke away and was lost. A revolution occurred during which the government seized all horses. When the revolution was over the man of Sai's horse was rediscovered. If he had not lost it the government would have taken it.

[3] This simile, which passed into a proverb in China and Japan, occurs first in *"Chuang Tzŭ,"* chap. xxii.

CHORUS: I beat the drum. The days pass and the hours.
It was yesterday, and it is today.
GARDENER: But she for whom I wait
CHORUS: Comes not even in dream. At dawn and dusk
GARDENER: No drum sounds.
CHORUS: She has not come. Is it not sung that those
Whom love has joined
Not even the God of Thunder can divide?
Of lovers, I alone
Am guideless, comfortless.
Then weary of himself and calling her to witness of his woe,
"Why should I endure," he cried,
"Such life as this?" and in the waters of the pond
He cast himself and died.

(Gardener leaves the stage.)

Enter the Princess.

COURTIER: I would speak with you, madam.
The drum made no sound, and the aged Gardener in despair has flung himself into the pond by the laurel tree, and died. The soul of such a one may cling to you and do you injury. Go out and look upon him.

PRINCESS *(speaking wildly, already possessed by the Gardener's angry ghost, which speaks through her.)*[4]
Listen, people, listen!
In the noise of the beating waves
I hear the rolling of a drum.
Oh, joyful sound, oh joyful!
The music of a drum.
COURTIER: Strange, strange!
This lady speaks as one
By phantasy possessed.
What is amiss, what ails her?
PRINCESS: Truly, by phantasy I am possessed.
Can a damask drum give sound?

[4] Compare the "possession" in *"Sotoba Komachi."*

When I bade him beat what could not ring,
Then tottered first my wits.

COURTIER: She spoke, and on the face of the evening pool
A wave stirred.

PRINCESS: And out of the wave

COURTIER: A voice spoke.

(The voice of the Gardener is heard; as he gradually advances along the Bridge it is seen that he wears a "demon mask," leans on a staff, and carries the "demon mallet" at his girdle.)

GARDENER'S GHOST: I was driftwood in the pool, but the waves of bitterness

CHORUS: Have washed me back to the shore.

GHOST: Anger clings to my heart,
Clings even now when neither wrath nor weeping
Are aught but folly.

CHORUS: One thought consumes me,
The anger of lust denied
Covers me like darkness.
I am become a demon dwelling
In the hell of my dark thoughts,
Stormcloud of my desires.

GHOST: "Though the waters parch in the fields
Though the brooks run dry,
Never shall the place be shown
Of the spring that feeds my heart." [5]
So I had resolved. Oh, why so cruelly
Set they me to win
Voice from a voiceless drum,
Spending my heart in vain?
And I spent my heart on the glimpse of a moon that slipped
Through the boughs of an autumn tree.[6]

CHORUS: This damask drum that hangs on the laurel tree

GHOST: Will it sound, will it sound?

[5] Adapted from a poem in the "*Gosenshū.*"
[6] Adapted from a poem in the "*Kokinshū.*"

(He seizes the Princess and drags her toward the drum.)
Try! Strike it!
CHORUS: "Strike!" he cries;
"The quick beat, the battle-charge!
Loud, loud! Strike, strike," he rails,
And brandishing his demon stick
Gives her no rest.
"Oh woe!" the lady weeps,
"No sound, no sound. Oh misery!" she wails.
And he, at the mallet stroke, "Repent, repent!"
Such torments in the world of night
Abōrasetsu, chief of demons, wields,
Who on the Wheel of Fire
Sears sinful flesh and shatters bones to dust.
Not less her torture now!
"Oh, agony!" she cries, "What have I done,
By what dire seed this harvest sown?"
GHOST: Clear stands the cause before you.
CHORUS: Clear stands the cause before my eyes;
I know it now.
By the pool's white waters, upon the laurel's bough
The drum was hung.
He did not know his hour, but struck and struck
Till all the will had ebbed from his heart's core;
Then leapt into the lake and died.
And while his body rocked
Like driftwood on the waves,
His soul, an angry ghost,
Possessed the lady's wits, haunted her heart with woe.
The mallet lashed, as these waves lash the shore,
Lash on the ice of the eastern shore.
The wind passes; the rain falls
On the Red Lotus, the Lesser and the Greater.[7]
The hair stands up on my head.
"The fish that leaps the falls

[7] The names of two of the Cold Hells in the Buddhist Inferno.

To a fell snake is turned," [8]
I have learned to know them;
Such, such are the demons of the World of Night.
"O hateful lady, hateful!" he cried, and sank again
Into the whirlpool of desire.

TRANSLATED BY ARTHUR WALEY

[8] There is a legend that the fish who succeed in leaping a certain waterfall turn into dragons. So the Gardener's attempt to raise himself to the level of the Princess has changed him into an evil demon.

THE BIRD-CATCHER IN HADES

[*Esashi Jūō*]

"The Bird-Catcher in Hades" in theme rather resembles "Birds of Sorrow," and is thus a good example of how the methods of kyōgen *differ from those of* Nō. *Nothing is known of the authorship of this or the following* kyōgen, *and we cannot say much more about the date than that in their present form they are probably of the sixteenth century. It should be noted that "The Bird-Catcher in Hades" is a text of the now defunct Sagi school of* kyōgen, *and is no longer performed.*

•

Persons
EMMA, the King of Hades
KIYOYORI, a bird-catcher
DEMONS
CHORUS

(The stage is completely bare. Two drummers and a flute-player, passing down the Bridge, take their usual seats at the rear of the stage. They are followed by Emma. He wears a devil's mask and a red wig. On his head there is a gold crown. His kimono is bright and large-patterned, and is resplendently decorated with gold thread. His hakama and outer kimono are of a similarly elaborate material, and he wears a brocade sash. His followers also wear devils' masks and red wigs, and their clothing is similar to his, though less elaborate. They carry bamboo poles. They come from the Bridge and immediately take their places on the stage in two rows facing one another, with Emma standing closest to the Waki's Pillar.)

DEMONS *(singing):* Emma, the King of Hades,
Emma, the King of Hades,
Comes to the Meeting of the Six Ways.

EMMA: Yai, yai! Are my satellites around?

DEMONS: Ha! Here we are.

EMMA: If any sinners come along, drive them into Hell.

DEMONS: We certainly will.

(Emma moves around the stage by the Chorus, finally taking his place at the end of the other row of Demons. The Demons all sit. Kiyoyori enters from the Bridge. He wears a plain kimono and a white cloak. He does not wear a mask, but he has a band tied around his forehead. He carries a long pole in his hand. He stops at the First Pine.)

KIYOYORI: All men are sinners, and I am no more a sinner than the rest of them.

My name is Kiyoyori, a bird-catcher, who was well known in the terrestrial plane. But my life span, like all things in the vale of tears, came to its end, and I was caught by the wind of impermanence. Now I am on the way to the world of darkness.

(He moves along the Bridge onto the stage, singing.)

Without a pang of parting,
Without a tinge of remorse,
I forsake the world of impermanence,
And as I wander about with no guide,
I have already come to the Meeting of the Six Ways.

Indeed, this is already the Meeting of the Six Ways of Existence. After due consideration, I wish to go to Heaven.

ONE OF THE DEMONS: Ha! Ho! I smell a man. Why, no wonder! Here comes a sinner. I will report to Emma.

(He stands and faces Emma.)

Oh, please, Sir! Here comes the first sinner.

EMMA: Make haste and drive him into Hell.

DEMON: Very well, Sir.

Come, you sinner! Hell is ever at hand, but one cannot say that about Heaven. Make haste.

(He and the other Demons attempt to beat Kiyoyori, who defends himself skilfully with his pole. He then sits in the center of the stage.)

Yai, yai! You are different from most of the sinners of the earth. What was your profession on the terrestrial plane?

KIYOYORI: I was Kiyoyori, the famous bird-catcher.

DEMON: Bird-catcher? Taking life from morning till night! Your sins are unfathomably great. I must send you to Hell at once.

KIYOYORI: Oh, no! I am not such a bad sinner as you make me out to be. Please let me go to Heaven.

DEMON: No, that cannot be! But first I shall ask the King about your case.

Pardon, Sir!

EMMA: Well, what is it?

DEMON: The sinner who has just arrived says that he was a very famous bird-catcher on the terrestrial plane. So I told him that, having taken life day and night, he committed deep sin and certainly is doomed to Hell. But he protests and says that we misjudge him thoroughly. What shall we do about him?

EMMA: Call the sinner to me.

DEMON: Very well, Sir.

Come along this way. King Emma wishes to see you.

KIYOYORI: I am coming.

DEMON: Here is that sinner you sent for.

EMMA: Come, you sinner! You have been sinning all through your life snaring birds, and you are indeed a very wicked man. I am going to send you to Hell at once.

KIYOYORI: What you say about me is very true, but the birds I caught were used to feed the falcons. There was really no serious harm in that.

EMMA: A falcon is another kind of bird, isn't it?

KIYOYORI: Yes, indeed.

EMMA: Well, then! That puts the case on a slightly different basis. I do not consider that a serious offense.

KIYOYORI: I am glad you don't. It really was more the falcon's fault than mine. That being the case, I hope you will send me straight to Heaven.

EMMA: Since I, the mighty King of Hades, have not yet tasted a bird, catch one with your pole, and let me taste it. Then I will grant your wish without further ado.

KIYOYORI: Nothing could be simpler. I shall catch a few birds and present them to you.

CHORUS: To the bird-hunt, bird-hunt!
All at once from the southern paths of the mountain of death,
Many birds come flocking.
Swifter than a flash
The bird-catcher darts and
Snares many with his pole.

(While the Chorus is singing, Kiyoyori darts about the stage waving his pole. He makes his way to the back of the stage, where he spreads open his fan and pretends to put the birds on it.)

KIYOYORI: I will roast them for you. Here, they are ready. Please try one.

(He goes to Emma and offers him the fan.)

EMMA: Well, well! I will have a taste.
Munch-munch! Crunch-crunch!
Oh, this is uncommonly delicious.

KIYOYORI *(to the Demons):* You would like to try them, too?

(He goes to each Demon in turn.)

DEMONS: Indeed, we shall!
Munch-munch! Crunch-crunch!
What marvelous flavor!

EMMA: I have never tasted anything so wonderful. Since you have given us such a treat, I am going to send you back to the terrestrial plane. There you may catch birds for another three years.

KIYOYORI: I am greatly obliged to you, I am sure.

(During the following song of the Chorus, Kiyoyori dances joyfully with open fan.)

CHORUS: For another three years, you shall snare birds!
Pheasant, goose, peacock, stork, and many others.

Thus commanded, Kiyoyori has turned his steps once more to the world beneath. But Emma, loath to see him depart, bestows on Kiyoyori his jeweled crown. Our bird-catcher marches lightly to the world below, there to begin his second span of life.

(Kiyoyori dances with crown, then leaves by Bridge, followed by Emma and the Demons.)

TRANSLATED BY SHIO SAKANISHI

BUSU

Persons

MASTER

TARŌ KAJA

JIRŌ KAJA

(The Master, Tarō kaja, and Jirō kaja enter the stage along the Bridge. Tarō kaja and Jirō kaja seat themselves by the Name-Saying Seat. The Master as he introduces himself goes to the Waki's Pillar.)

MASTER: I am a gentleman of this vicinity. I plan to go away to the mountains for a few days, and now I shall summon my servants to give them instructions about what to do during my absence. Tarō kaja, where are you?

TARŌ: Here, Master.

(He gets up and goes toward the Master, then bows.)

MASTER: Call Jirō kaja too.

TARŌ: Yes, Master. Jirō kaja, the master wants you.

JIRŌ: I obey.

(He also comes forward and bows.)

TOGETHER: We are before you, Master.

MASTER: I have called you because I am going to the mountains for a few days, and I want you both to take good care of the house while I am away.

TARŌ: Your orders will be obeyed, Master, but you have always taken one of us with you on your journeys, and today too

TOGETHER: One of us would like to accompany you.

MASTER: No, that is out of the question. Today I have something important to leave in your care, and both of you must guard it. Wait here.

TOGETHER: Very good, Master.

(The Master goes to the Flute Pillar where he picks up a round lacquered cask about two feet high. He deposits it in the center of the stage, and returns to his former position.)

MASTER: This is what is known as *busu,* a deadly poison. If even a wind blowing from its direction should strike you, it will mean instant death. Be on your guard.

TARŌ: Yes, Master.

JIRŌ: Excuse me, Master, but I would like to ask you something.

MASTER: What is it?

JIRŌ: Why do you keep such a dreadful poison in the house?

MASTER: The *busu* loves its master, and as long as it is the master who handles it, there is not the slightest danger. But if either of you so much as approach it, you will suffer instant death. Beware even of being touched by the wind from its direction.

JIRŌ: Yes, Master.

MASTER: Now I shall be leaving.

TARŌ: May you have a pleasant journey,

TOGETHER: And come back soon.

MASTER: Thank you.

(The Master goes to the Bridge, where he seats himself at the First Pine, indicating that he has disappeared. Tarō and Jirō see him off, then seat themselves at the back of the stage.)

TARŌ: He always takes one of us with him. I wonder why today he left both of us to look after the house.

JIRŌ: I wonder why.

TARŌ: At any rate, it's always lonesome being left here by oneself, but since we are both here today, we can have a pleasant talk.—Oh!

JIRŌ: What is the matter?

TARŌ: There was a gust of wind from the *busu*!

JIRŌ: How frightening!

TARŌ: Let's move a little farther away.

JIRŌ: A good idea.

(They hastily move toward Bridge, then sit.)

TARŌ: Just as you said before, why should the master keep in the house a thing so deadly that even a breath of wind from it will cause instant death?

JIRŌ: However much it may love its master, I still don't understand why he keeps it.

TARŌ: You know, I'd like to have a look at the *busu.* What do you think it can be?

JIRŌ: Have you gone mad? Don't you know that even the wind from its way means certain death?

TARŌ: Let's go up to it fanning from this side. In that way we won't get any wind from it.

JIRŌ: That's a good idea.

(The two men stand, and fanning vigorously approach the cask.)

TARŌ: Fan, fan hard.

JIRŌ: I am fanning.

TARŌ: I'm going to untie the cord around it now, so fan hard.

JIRŌ: Right!

TARŌ: I've unfastened it. Now, I'll take off the cover.

JIRŌ: Do it quickly!

TARŌ: Keep fanning!

JIRŌ: I am fanning.

TARŌ: It's off! *(They flee to the Bridge.)* Oh, that's a relief!

JIRŌ: What's a relief?

TARŌ: That thing—it's not an animal or it would jump out.

JIRŌ: Perhaps it is only playing dead.

TARŌ: I'll have a look.

JIRŌ: That's a good idea.

(They approach the cask as before.)

TARŌ: Fan, fan hard!

JIRŌ: I am fanning!

TARŌ: Now I'm going to have a look, so fan hard!

JIRŌ: Right!

TARŌ: I've seen it! I've seen it! *(They flee as before to the Bridge.)*

JIRŌ: What did you see?

TARŌ: Something dark gray that looked good to eat. You know, I think I'd like a taste of that *busu.*

JIRŌ: How can you think of eating something which will kill you even if you only catch a whiff of it?

TARŌ: I must be bewitched by the *busu.* I can't think of anything but eating it. I will have a taste.

JIRŌ: You mustn't.

(He takes Tarō's sleeve, and they struggle.)

TARŌ: Let me go!

JIRŌ: I won't let you go!

TARŌ: I tell you, let me go!

JIRŌ: I tell you, I won't let you go!

(Tarō frees himself and approaches the cask. He uses his fan to scoop out the contents.)

TARŌ *(singing):* Shaking off with sorrow the sleeves of parting,
I come up to the side of the *busu.*

JIRŌ: Alas! Now he will meet his death.

TARŌ: Oh, I am dying. I am dying. *(He falls over.)*

JIRŌ: I knew it would happen. Tarō kaja! What is it? *(He rushes to him.)*

TARŌ: It's so delicious, I'm dying. *(He gets up.)*

JIRŌ: What can it be?

TARŌ: It's sugar!

JIRŌ: Let me have a taste.

TARŌ: Go ahead.

JIRŌ: Thank you. It really is sugar!

(The two of them eat, using their fans to scoop out the busu. Tarō, seeing that Jirō is too busy eating to notice, carries off the cask to the Waki's Pillar. While he is eating, Jirō comes up and takes the cask to the Facing Pillar.)

TARŌ: You mustn't eat it all by yourself. Let me have it!

JIRŌ: No, you were eating before I did. Give me some more.

TARŌ: Let's both eat it.

JIRŌ: A good idea.

(They put the cask between them.)

TARŌ: Delicious, isn't it?

JIRŌ: Really delicious.

TARŌ: The master told us that it was *busu,* thinking we wouldn't eat it then. That was really most disagreeable of him. Eat up! Eat up!

JIRŌ: It was disagreeable of him to have told us that we would die instantly if we got so much as a whiff of it. Eat up! Eat up!

TARŌ: I can't stop eating.

JIRŌ: It feels as if our chins are sagging, doesn't it?

TARŌ: Eat up! Oh, it's all gone!

JIRŌ: Yes, all gone.

TARŌ: Well, you can be proud of yourself.

JIRŌ: *I* can be proud of myself? It was *you* who first looked at the *busu* and first ate it. I'll tell the master as soon as he gets back.

TARŌ: I was only joking. Now, tear up this *kakemono.*[1]

JIRŌ: Very well.

(He goes to the Waki's Pillar and makes motions of tearing a kakemono.)

Sarari. Sarari. Pattari.

TARŌ: Bravo! First you looked at the *busu,* then you ate it, and now you've torn up the master's *kakemono.* I'll inform him of that as soon as he returns.

JIRŌ: I only did it because you told me. And I shall inform the master of that.

TARŌ: I was joking again. Now smash this bowl.

JIRŌ: No, I've had enough.

TARŌ: Then let's smash it together.

JIRŌ: All right.

(They go to the Facing Pillar and make motions of picking up a large bowl and dashing it to the ground.)

TOGETHER: *Garari chin.*

TARŌ: Ah—it's in bits.

JIRŌ: Now what excuse will we make?

TARŌ: When the master returns, the first thing to do is to burst into tears.

JIRŌ: Will tears do any good?

TARŌ: They will indeed. He'll be coming back soon. Come over here.

JIRŌ: Very well.

(They go to the back of the stage and sit there. The Master stands up and speaks at the First Pine.)

MASTER: I have completed my business now. I imagine that my servants must be waiting for my return. I shall hasten home. Ah, here I am already. Tarō kaja, Jirō kaja, I've returned!

[1] A picture or writing on silk or paper.

(He goes to the Waki's Pillar.)

TARŌ: He's back! Now start weeping! *(They weep.)*

MASTER: Tarō kaja, Jirō kaja! Where are you? What is the matter here? Instead of being glad that I have returned they are both weeping. If something has happened, let me know at once.

TARŌ: Jirō kaja, you tell the master.

JIRŌ: Tarō kaja, you tell the master.

MASTER: Whichever of you it is, tell me quickly.

TARŌ: Well, then, this is what happened. I thought that it wouldn't do for me to sleep while on such important duty, but I got sleepier and sleepier. To keep me awake I had a wrestling match with Jirō kaja. He is so strong that he knocked me over, and to keep from falling, I clutched at that *kakemono,* and ripped it as you can see.

MASTER: What a dreadful thing to happen! *(He looks at the Waki's Pillar in amazement.)* How could you tear up a precious *kakemono* that way?

TARŌ: Then he threw me back and spun me over the stand with the bowl on it, and the bowl was smashed to bits.

MASTER: What a dreadful thing! *(He looks at the Facing Pillar in amazement.)* You even smashed my precious bowl. What I am going to do?

TARŌ: Knowing that you would soon return, we thought that we could not go on living, so we ate up the *busu,* hoping thus to die. Isn't that so, Jirō kaja?

JIRŌ: Exactly.

TARŌ *(singing):* One mouthful and still death did not come.

JIRŌ *(singing):* Two mouthfuls and still death did not come.

TARŌ *(singing):* Three mouthfuls, four mouthfuls

JIRŌ *(singing):* Five mouthfuls

TARŌ *(singing):* More than ten mouthfuls

(They get up and begin to dance.)

TOGETHER: *(singing):* We ate until there wasn't any left,
But still death came not, strange to tell,
Ah, what a clever head!

(They approach the Master while fanning, then suddenly strike him on the head with their fans. They run off laughing.)

MASTER: What do you mean "clever head"? You brazen things! Where are you going? Catch them! You won't get away with it! *(He runs after them to Bridge.)*

TOGETHER: Forgive us! Forgive us!

TRANSLATED BY DONALD KEENE

POEMS IN CHINESE

BY BUDDHIST MONKS

When the Japanese Zen priest Mugaku Sogen (1226-1286) was in China and threatened by invading Mongol troops, he composed a four-line poem. Years later another Zen priest, Sesson Yūbai (1290-1347), when he was in prison and threatened with death, took Mugaku's poem and, using each line as the opening verse of a new poem, composed the following:

Through all Heaven and Earth, no ground to plant my single staff;
Yet is there a place to hide this body where no trace may be found.
At midnight will the wooden man mount his steed of stone
To crash down ten thousand walls of encircling iron.

In the nothingness of man I delight, and of all being,
A thousand worlds complete in my little cage.
I forget sin, demolish my heart, and in enlightenment rejoice;
Who tells me that the fallen suffer in Hell's bonds?

Awful is the three-foot sword of the Great Yüan,[1]
Sparkling with cold frost over ten thousand miles.
Though the skull be dry, these eyes shall see again.
Flawless is my white gem, priceless as a kingdom.

Like lightning it flashes through the shadows, severing the spring wind;
The God of Nothingness bleeds crimson, streaming.
I tremble at the soaring heights of Mount Sumera;[2]
I will dive, I will leap into the stem of the lotus.

Sesson Yūbai

[1] Yüan was the name taken by the Mongols for their dynasty.

[2] The central mountain of the Buddhist universe.

Song of idleness

I lay sick by the low window, propped on a crooked bed,
And thought how orderly the universe is.
A white bird flew across the dark sky;
And my mind rolled forth ten thousand feet.

Kokan (1278-1346)

To a monk departing on a trading mission to China

Judge for yourself if the weather be hot or cold;
A fellow must not be cheated by others.
And see that you take not Japan's good gold
And barter it off for Chinese brass!

Daichi (1290-1366)

To a Korean friend

The old man of the village suddenly called us back
To drink three cups beneath the crooked mulberry.
Mankind is small but this drunkenness wide and great—
Where now is Japan, where your Korea?

Mugan (died 1374)

Mountain temple

I have locked the gate on a thousand peaks
To live here with clouds and birds.
All day I watch the hills
As clear winds fill the bamboo door.
A supper of pine flowers,
Monk's robes of chestnut dye—
What dream does the world hold
To lure me from these dark slopes?

Zekkai (1336-1405)

TRANSLATED BY BURTON WATSON

THREE POETS AT MINASE

[*Minase Sangin*]

In the first moon of 1488 three of the greatest masters of linked-verse, Sōgi (1421-1502), Shōhaku (1443-1527), and Sōchō (1448-1532) met at Minase, a village between Kyoto and Osaka. As part of an observance at the shrine, which stood on the site of the Minase Palace of the Emperor Gotoba, they composed one hundred verses, of which fifty are here translated.

The art of linked-verse was an extremely demanding one. Generally three or more poets took part, composing alternate verses of 5, 7, 5, syllables and 7, 7 syllables. Many rules had to be observed exactly: for example, if spring or autumn were mentioned in one verse, the following two to four verses also had to mention it. However, it was not necessary that the actual words "spring" or "autumn" be used; many natural phenomena, such as mist, blossoms, or singing birds, stood for spring, while others, such as fog, the moon, or chirping crickets, stood for autumn.

Beyond the technical difficulties imposed by the rules of linked-verse were the major consideration of keeping the level so high that it would not run the risk of resembling a mere game, and the problem of making each "link" fit smoothly into the chain. Any three links taken from a sequence should produce two complete poems. Thus:

Except for you
Whom could I ever love,
Never surfeiting?

Nothing remotely suggests
The charms of her appearance.

Except for you
Whom could I ever love
Never surfeiting?
Nothing remotely suggests
The charms of her appearance.

	Nothing remotely suggests
Even plants and trees	*The charms of its appearance.*
Share in the bitter grief of	*Even plants and trees*
The ancient capital.	*Share in the bitter grief of*
	The ancient capital.

Here we have two poems of entirely different meaning linked together: the first concerns a lover's delight in his mistress, the second the grief of the poet over the destruction of the capital. This kind of multiple stream of consciousness is a uniquely Japanese literary development, and was fostered in part by the ambiguity of the Japanese language, which permits many varieties of word play and is extremely free in the use of pronouns.

•

TEXT	COMMENTARY
Snow yet remaining The mountain slopes are misty— An evening in spring. *Sōgi*	Early spring (mist). Allusion: "When I look far out, the mountain slopes are misty. Minase River—why did I think that only in autumn the nights could be lovely?" *(by Emperor Gotoba).*
Far away the water flows Past the plum-scented village. *Shōhaku*	Spring (plum blossoms). Description continued. Water.
In the river breeze The willow trees are clustered. Spring is appearing. *Sōchō*	Spring. Description continued, far scenery. Water.
The sound of a boat being poled Clear in the clear morning light. *Sōgi*	Water. Dawn. Near scenery.

The moon! does it still Over fog-enshrouded fields Linger in the sky? *Shōhaku*	Autumn (moon). Dawn.
Meadows carpeted in frost— Autumn has drawn to a close. *Sōchō*	Autumn.
Heedless of the wishes Of piping insects, The grasses wither. *Sōgi*	Late autumn. The insects wish that the winter would not come.
When I visited my friend, How bare the path to his gate! *Shōhaku*	Late autumn. The grasses have withered, exposing the path.
Remote villages— Have the storms still to reach you Deep in the mountains? *Sōchō*	Late autumn. Villages so remote that winter has yet to reach them.
In unfamiliar dwellings Is loneliness and sorrow *Sōgi*	Emotional verse leading from loneliness of remote villages.
Now is not the time To be thinking of yourself As one all alone. *Shōhaku*	Buddhist rebuke (or consolation?) for emotion expressed.
Did you not know beforehand That all things must fade away? *Sōchō*	Impermanence. Buddhist sentiment continued.
The dew grieves for its Early passing and grieves for The flower that stays. *Sōgi*	Impermanence. The dew is shorter-lived even than the flower it clings to. Parable for man and the things of beauty in the world. Spring.

During the misted darkness
Of the last rays of the sun.
Shōhaku

Spring (mist). Evening.

The day has ended.
Joyously singing, the birds
Return to their nest.
Sōchō

Spring (birds). Evening.

I walk deep in dark mountains,
Not even the sky my guide.
Sōgi

Evening. Travel.

Although it has cleared
My sleeves are soaked with showers—
This traveling cloak.
Shōhaku

Travel. The sleeves are wet not only with rain but with tears caused by his lonely journey.

The light of the moon reveals
My wretched pillow of grass.
Sōchō

Travel. "Pillow of grass" denotes a journey. The traveler with tear-wet sleeves is disclosed by the moon. Night. Autumn (moon).

Many are the vain
Nights unvisited by sleep
As autumn deepens.
Sōgi

Night. Autumn. Love (lying awake at night).

In dreams I quarreled with her;
A wind was stirring the reeds.
Shōhaku

Night. Autumn (reeds). In his dream he quarrels with his beloved, and wakens to hear the wind. Love.

I looked—all were gone,
The friends I loved at home,
Vanished without a trace
Sōchō

Dream. When he awakens (like Rip van Winkle) his friends are all dead. May also refer to women he loved. Love. Old age.

Years of old age before me, What is there on which to lean? *Sōgi*	Old age—friends are gone.
Faded though they are, At least I still have my songs— Take pity on them! *Shōhaku*	The poems of an old man.
They too make good companions When the sky is at twilight. *Sōgi*	Loneliness relieved by poetry.
Today in clouds I crossed the peak and found The blossoms scattered. *Sōchō*	Spring (blossoms). What he thought were "clouds of cherry blossoms" were only clouds. Link: sky-clouds. Clouds may be companions.
Listen! did you hear the cries Of the wild geese of spring? *Shōhaku*	Spring. Link: geese flying over peak.
How bright the moon is Without the haze—drowsy one, Wait, just a little. *Sōgi*	Spring (hazy moon). Link: Geese flying under moon, familiar subject of painting. Enjoins him not to fall asleep when the moon is so lovely (not the usual hazy spring moon).
Lying in dew, on my way, I see an autumn daybreak. *Sōchō*	Autumn (moon of previous verse taken in different sense). Link: moon-daybreak.
Over the villages, Far off, beyond the last field, The fog is settling. *Shōhaku*	Autumn (fog). Description continued.

There comes with the blowing wind
The sound of cloth-beaters' mallets.
Sōgi

Autumn (cloth-beating). The sound emerges from the fog.

Even freezing days
In the evening find me
In thinnest garments.
Sōchō

A lonely, poverty-stricken scene. Link: cloth-garments.

How forlorn a way to live—
The mountains where I gather brush.
Shōhaku

Poverty. A humble wood-cutter.

"Yet there may be hope,"
I thought, but this way of life
Has come to an end.
Sōgi

Poverty. Despair.

Ah, the misery of it!
Whither now shall I turn?
Sōchō

Poverty. Despair.

Parting after bliss,
Resolved to wait as long
As life is left me.
Shōhaku

The misery of poverty shifts to the misery of separation after making love. Love.

Still it lasts—what does it mean?
This longing I feel for her.
Sōgi

Love. Separation.

Except for you
Whom could I ever love,
Never surfeiting?
Sōchō

Love.

Nothing remotely suggests
The charms of her appearance.
Shōhaku

Love.

Even plants and trees Share in the bitter grief Of the ancient capital. *Sōgi*	Link: the beloved's appearance shifts to the appearance of Kyoto before the disastrous Ōnin Rebellion which devastated the city (1467-1477).
The sad house where once I lived Is now but a remembrance. *Sōchō*	Destruction caused by the rebellion.
Let this keepsake Of a mother not long dead Bring consolation. *Shōhaku*	Death brought about by rebellion.
In the months and days to come I'll see her perhaps in dreams. *Sōgi*	In time to come he will only be able to see his mother in dreams.
Sailing for China, I will take a final leave— Farewell to these shores. *Sōchō*	Even if he goes to China he will see her in his dreams.
Let us hearken to the Law We come not to this world again. *Shōhaku*	"These shores" interpreted as the mortal world, as opposed to the "other shores" of Paradise. The Buddhist Law.
Till we two could meet How frequently did love's tears Fall and melt away. *Sōgi*	Meeting with Buddha in Paradise shifts to meeting a woman. Love. Autumn (tears, literally "dew").
Ah, it was the autumn wind, Not she I was waiting for. *Sōchō*	Autumn. There is a pun imbedded meaning "weary of myself"

A pine-cricket
All in vain is chirping now,
In my weed-grown house.
Shōhaku

Autumn (pine-cricket). It chirps in vain because she does not hear it. The house is deserted.

On the mountain I staked out
Now lodges only the moon.
Sōgi

Autumn (moon). Links to loneliness of preceding verse. Pun: "shines clear" for "lodges."

I awake from sleep
To the tolling of the bell,
My dreams unfinished.
Sōchō

His plans for the future are interrupted.

I have piled upon my brow
The frosts of night after night.
Shōhaku

With age his hair turns white, as he remembers as he lies awake at night.

TRANSLATED BY DONALD KEENE

THE THREE PRIESTS

[*Sannin Hōshi*]

Among the characteristic literary products of the Muromachi Period were the Otogi sōshi *(or nursery tales). These were for the most part children's stories of didactic intent, but sometimes they rose above the rather elementary level of the medium and became genuine literature. The finest of these stories is generally considered to be "The Three Priests." It is of the "confessional" variety of* Otogi sōshi. *In this translation only the stories of the first two priests are given; the third priest's story is in no way connected with the other two. The authorship is unknown, and the date can only be surmised as probably early sixteenth century.*

•

Mount Kōya lies far from the capital. It is a remote place, where no human voices are heard, where many lofty peaks tower, and such profound silence fills the valleys that ever since Kōbō Daishi [1] here entered the Realm of Meditation it has been counted a holy site to await the coming of the Buddha of the Future. There are platforms for those who wish to sit in contemplation, and halls where salvation may be gained by invoking the name of Amida. At this mountain, where one may live in retreat from the world in whatever manner one chooses, there met three priests, come together by chance from the different places where they had their abodes. In the course of a conversation one of them said, "We are all three priests. Let us each confess to the others why he has abandoned the world. This can surely do no harm, for they say that confession reduces the sins."

[1] Also called Kūkai (see page 63). Kōbō Daishi founded a monastery on Mount Kōya and died there.

Another of them, a priest of perhaps forty-two years, was a man whom long and bitter penances had emaciated and weakened, but there remained about him an aristocratic air, and his teeth were deeply blackened.[2] Above his torn robes he wore a priest's stole. He had seemed to be immersed in thought, but he looked up and said, "I should like to be the first to speak.

"Since what I have to relate occurred in the capital, it may well be that you have already heard of it. Formerly I was called Kasuya no Shirōzaemon, and I was in the personal service of the Shogun Takauji. From the age of thirteen I was in attendance at his palace, and I used to accompany him on pilgrimages to temples and shrines and on excursions to view the moon and the cherry blossoms, never failing to be present.

"It happened once, when the Shogun was visiting the Nijō Palace, that the other young men in his service were having a party, and messages came from them two or three times, urging me to hurry back and join them. It was less the desire to be with them than impatience over the slowness of the Shogun to leave which led me to look into his private room to see how much longer he was likely to remain. The second or third round of the drink offerings[3] was being passed to him. Just then a court lady entered the room bearing what appeared to be a gift, a silken garment on a stand. She was not yet twenty. Her long hair was swept up, revealing a face of indescribable beauty. Not even Yang Kuei-fei or (in our own country) Ono no Komachi could possibly have surpassed her. Ah, what man but would desire to converse with such a woman, to lay his pillow beside hers! I prayed that she might appear again so that I could have another glimpse of her. From that moment on my mind was in turmoil, my heart was turned to smoke. However much I tried to forget my yearning for her, I could not. The love in which I was plunged grew more and more hallucinatory.

"When the Shogun left the palace that night I returned to my lodgings. The lady's face would not leave my mind. I could not eat and, taking to my bed, failed to appear at court for four or five days.

[2] Members of the aristocracy blackened their teeth.
[3] Three cups were offered after feasts of the aristocracy.

The Shogun asked why I was not present, and when it was reported to him that I was ill, he immediately summoned his personal physician and bade him cure me. When the doctor came to my house I arose from bed and put on a court hat and robes to converse with him. After he had felt my pulse for a while he said, 'This is most unusual. I cannot discover any specific malady, and I wonder if your illness arises because you harbor resentment toward someone? Or perhaps you are worried over an important lawsuit?'

"I pretended that my indisposition was nothing. 'Ever since childhood I have been subject to this illness, but if I rest for a fortnight or so I shall certainly recover. Please wait until then. I do not imagine that it is anything serious.' The doctor then reported to the Shogun, 'This is no normal illness. Either some grave worry is weighing on him, or he is suffering from the malady which in former times might have been called "love".'

"The Shogun said, 'Even nowadays love is not an unknown complaint. I should like to discover what is actually on Kasuya's mind.' On being informed that Sasaki Saburōzaemon was my closest friend, he summoned Sasaki and ordered him to visit my house, look after me, and find out what the trouble was.

"Sasaki accordingly visited me. First of all, he asked in a hurt tone, 'You and I are the closest friends among all the Shogun's attendants, as close as brothers. Why have you failed to let me know of your illness?' After he had continued in this vein for a while, I said, 'It is not that serious an illness. I have not even told my mother about it. I can see why you should be indignant, but I promise you that if anything more consequential develops, I shall inform you of it. But it embarrasses me to have you treat this illness with such undue concern. Please go now. Don't you think that it will appear rather odd if you neglect your court duties just to watch over me?'

"I several times repeated words to this effect, but he insisted on looking after me. For several days he remained with me, constantly questioning me about my thoughts. I concealed them as long as I could, but, deciding that I was being excessively cautious, I finally revealed to him what had happened. When Sasaki heard the cause of my illness he exclaimed, 'If all that is ailing you is love, you will soon be cured!' He stole out of the room before I knew it, and went at once to the palace.

"When the Shogun heard his report, he declared that meeting the lady would be an easy matter to arrange, and himself deigned to write a letter on my behalf to the Nijō Palace, which he sent with Sasaki. The reply stated that since the lady in question was the Court Dame Onoe, it would not be proper for her to visit a commoner, and that I should therefore go to her. The Shogun was kind enough to have this reply forwarded to my lodgings. I shall never be able to repay my indebtedness to him for his great kindnesses.

"Even then I could not help but feel what a wretched world it was. It was clear that even if I were able to meet the Lady Onoe, it could only be for one night. I thought that now was a fitting time for me to abandon the world, but on further reflection it occurred to me how extraordinary it was that I, one Kasuya, should have had the intercession of the Shogun in my love with a great lady from the Nijō Palace. I would be shamed for the rest of my life if it were said that it was out of cowardice that I had abandoned the world. I decided that I would go to her even if it were but for one night, and then let the future take care of itself.

"One night, having at last made up my mind, I set out late in the evening for the Nijō Palace with three young companions and a guide. I did not take any special pains to create a splendid appearance, but dressed in a dignified manner. I was guided into a beautiful room, decorated with screens and Chinese paintings, in which there were four or five gaily attired court ladies of about the same age.

"After they had each offered the formal three cups of saké, there was a tea ceremony and perfume-blending. I could not be sure which of the ladies was Onoe, only having seen her that once. They were all so lovely that I was quite at a loss to decide, but when one of them came quite close to me with a wine cup from which she had drunk, and offered it to me,[4] I realized that she was the Lady Onoe, and I accepted the cup.

"The crowing of the cocks announced the approach of dawn, and

[4] It is a mark of intimacy to offer one's own cup to another person.

the tolling of the temple bells proclaimed the moment of lovers' farewell. We vowed that our love would last into the distant future. She left the chamber while it was still dark and stepped out onto the veranda. She was truly exquisite at that moment, with her dark eyebrows and crimson lips just visible, and a captivating perfume clinging to her sleep-tangled hair. She composed the verse, 'Strange it is —this morning, because of someone I have met but once, see how the dew has fallen on my sleeve!'

"I answered, 'Because of love I shall wrap up the dew that fell on your sleeve the night we met, and make it my keepsake.'

"From then on I frequently visited the palace, and sometimes she even secretly came to my lodgings. 'People will surely get word of this,' the Shogun said, and he granted the lady a large estate outside the city where we might more easily meet.

"At the time I was a devout believer in the Tenjin of Kitano,[5] and it had been my practice to spend the night of the twenty-fourth of each month in prayers at his shrine. I had been neglecting my devotions because of this lady, but now that it was the twenty-fourth of the twelfth month, the last Tenjin day of the year, I paid a visit to confess my remissness of the previous months. While I was praying late at night, I heard someone near me say, 'Oh, how dreadful! Who could it be?' I felt somehow uneasy and asked what had happened. They told me that at a certain place near the capital a court lady of seventeen or eighteen had been killed and her clothes torn from her. The more I heard, the more agitated I became, and unable to stand the strain, I rushed off.

"I found that my worst fears had been realized—it was she. Even her hair had been sheared off by the robber. I stood there, dumbfounded, uncertain whether it was a nightmare or reality. For what sin was this the punishment? Oh, the bitter grief that I then experienced! I had always been overjoyed to be with her, but now I regretted every moment. Why had my heart been thus consumed for love of her, only to have her die and leave me behind? And was it

[5] Sugawara no Michizane (see page 166) has been enshrined as a god under the name of Tenjin. The chief Tenjin shrine is in the northwest part of Kyoto. On the night of the twenty-fourth and the following day of each month there is a special observance.

not entirely on account of me that she, a court lady, had been put to a pitiless sword before she was twenty? Imagine if you can what feelings tormented me! If I had known of the danger to her, no demons could have frightened me. I would have charged alone into three hundred, five hundred, enemy, so little did I value my life. But the deed had occurred without my knowing of it, and I had been powerless. That very night I shaved my head and became a priest. It is now some twenty years that I have lived on this mountain, praying for the repose of her soul."

When he had finished speaking the other two priests wetted with tears the sleeves of their dark robes.

• •

The next priest to speak was a man about fifty. He stood six feet tall, had a jutting collarbone, angular chin, high cheekbones, thick lips, and a prominent nose. He was dark of complexion and very powerfully built. Above his tattered robes he also wore a stole thrust in at the breast. As he spoke he fingered a large rosary. "I should like to be the next to tell my story," he said. The others urged him to do so. He began, "Strange to relate, it was I who killed the lady!" Kasuya started up at the words; his color changed, and an attitude of determination came over him.

The second priest said, "Please remain calm for a little while, and I shall tell you in detail what happened." Kasuya composed his feelings and asked him to begin at once. The second priest said, "Since you gentlemen are from Kyoto, I believe that you may have heard of me. My name is Aragorō of the Third Ward. I began my career of robbery at the age of eight, and first killed a man at twelve. That lady was about the three hundred eightieth person I had killed. I always prided myself on my skill at burglary with violence, but, perhaps because of accumulated sins, from the tenth month of that year I had not been able to carry off a single successful robbery. I tried my hand at mountain banditry, but failed at that too. Every time I thought that I had at last found a way to make a living, it would suddenly come to nothing. I fell on difficult times, and there was often nothing in the house to eat. My wife and children were so wretched a sight that I could not bear to look at them, and from the eleventh month, as I recall, I began living away from home, passing my nights and days in the shelter of some old temple building or hidden in the sacred hall of a shrine. After having spent many days wandering about, I thought that I should like to see what was happening at home. But no sooner did I set foot inside the house than my wife seized me and began to weep bitterly.

"'How hateful of you! Why have you acted in such an inhuman way? It happens commonly enough that relations between a husband and wife become unbearable, and I have no intention of wasting my breath in useless lamenting over it. Now that your heart has changed and our ties have come to an end there is no point in my trying to cling to you. Please divorce me at once. Have you any conception of what it has been like for me, a lone woman trying to maintain a family? It is almost New Year now, but I shall have to find work so that I can support the little ones. You have no property, you don't know anything about trade or farming. All you can do is to steal things from people, and now you can't even manage to do that. You don't think about what will happen to the children—you've even left your own house to live elsewhere. I see that it has all been because of me. But no matter how much this house bores you, how can you not care whether your children are starving to death? These past two or three days I have had no money. There has been nothing to cook, and the children are weeping with hunger. You can imagine how unhappy it makes me to look at them.'

"When she finished speaking, I said, 'It must be an accumulation of karma from the previous world. Everything I have tried has failed. I have been living elsewhere, it is true, but I have come back now because of my love for the children. Please calm yourself and wait a bit longer. Something will turn up today or tomorrow.'

"I thought in my heart that I should certainly get something that night. I could scarcely wait for it to grow dark. When twilight came with the echo of the temple bells, I went out with my usual sword. I stood in the shadows of a wall and waited impatiently for someone to pass. I felt sure that, no matter who came along, even if he were the most formidable soldier, I should finish him off with one blow of my sword. I waited with my fists tensely clenched. Just then an open sedan chair went by, borne by some young men who were noisily chatting. I realized that I could not do very much with them, and let the chair pass. Then from a distance of a hundred yards or so up the road, I detected the scent of some unusual perfume. I said to myself, now someone of importance is coming. I was overjoyed at the thought that my luck had after all not quite run out.

"When I looked I could see a radiantly beautiful court lady approaching, rustling her silken robes as she walked. She was accompanied by two maids, one of whom walked ahead of her and the other followed with an embroidered case in her arms. They went by my hiding place, apparently without noticing me. I let them pass, then ran after them. The maid walking in front let out a scream and disappeared. The other maid dropped her bundle and ran off, crying for help. The lady, however, seemed unperturbed, and remained where she was without uttering a sound. I rushed up to her with my sword drawn, and cold-bloodedly began to tear off her clothes. 'Give me your underrobe too!' I ordered her. She answered, 'Please spare me that. It is to the everlasting shame of a woman if her underrobe is removed.' She unfastened the amulet bag from her neck and threw it at me. 'Take this instead of my underrobe.' Her perfume was so rich that I was almost overcome. But, in my depravity, I would not grant her even this. I insisted that she give me her underrobe too. 'If my underrobe is removed I have no desire to live any longer. Please take my life,' she said. 'Gladly,' I answered, and stabbed her to death with one thrust of my sword. I hastily stripped off her underrobe before the blood could reach it. Then I picked up the bag that the maid had dropped and hurried home, saying to myself, 'How happy this will make my wife and children.'

"When I knocked at the door, my wife was surprised at how soon I had returned, and asked through the door if I had been unsuccessful again.

" 'Open the door quickly!' I said, and threw the bag inside. 'You certainly got it in a hurry,' she cried, and, too impatient to open the mouth of the bag, she cut the drawstrings. There were twelve unlined costumes, each impregnated with the same fragrance. The scent was so strong that people passing in the alley in front of my house stopped in surprise, and it reached even the houses of our neighbors.

"My wife and children were enraptured. My wife, shameful to say, went so far as to put on the underrobe. 'This is the first time in my life that I have worn such a robe. The lady you took it from must have been quite young. About how old was she?'

"I thought that she was asking out of pity, and answered, 'It was dark and I could not see very well, but she was certainly not as much as twenty-one. I imagine she was about eighteen.'

" 'I thought as much,' said my wife, and without a word of explanation rushed outside. I wondered what business could have taken her out in such a frantic manner. After a while she returned, saying, 'You are really much too magnanimous a robber. As long as you are committing a crime you should try to get the most out of it. I just went to cut off her hair. My own is rather thin, but if I twist hers into plaits it will really look beautiful. I wouldn't change it, not even for the robes.' She poured some hot water in a bowl and sprinkled it on the hair, which she hung up to dry. She was so elated that she was dancing about for joy. 'I have all a woman could ask for. Oh, how happy I am!'

"I stared at her. She filled me with disgust and revulsion. It was because of actions in a previous existence that I had been born a human being and, having had the rare fortune to receive a human body, I should at least have been acquainted with human feelings, even if I was not to become a truly virtuous man. I had instead become a man of great wickedness. All I had thought of night and day was killing people. Not a single moment had gone by but was devoted to plans for robbery. I could not escape Fate. In the end, I knew, I should suffer the torments of hell. To go on thus committing grievous sins, dragging out a meaningless existence, not realizing the hollowness and futility of my life, seemed revolting even to me. And now the monstrous behavior of my wife had struck me dumb with horror. I repented bitterly that I had slept with such a woman, that our lives had been joined. Now that I understood the baseness of her nature, I wondered for what purpose I had killed that lady. I could think of nothing but the misery of my deed. I felt as though my entrails were dissolving, but I could not content myself merely with weeping. I decided that I would shave my hair, making what had happened my guide in the way of salvation. That very night I went to see a Buddhist monk, whose disciple I became. Shortly afterward I climbed this mountain.

"I realize how much you must hate me. Kill me in any way you choose. Even though you cut me into a thousand slices, I shall not complain. I should mention, however, that if you kill me it may harm the lady in whatever life she is living now. The Three Treasures are my witness that I do not say this because of any attachment to this life. Now I have said all that I have to say. I leave the rest to you."

The priest Kasuya said, "Even if you had been led to abandon the world by some perfectly commonplace thing, how could I ever hate a fellow priest? But I know now that you abandoned the world because of the same lady, and I feel all the more closely tied to you. It must be that the lady was a manifestation of a bodhisattva who took the form of a woman to save us, who otherwise would have missed the Way. When I realize what compassion she showed in guiding us, I find it all the harder to forget the things of the past. If they had not happened, how would we ever have become priests and forsaken the transient world? To have received this absolute happiness must be our joy within sorrow. From today forward I shall be grateful for that event which led me to seek the Way." So speaking he wetted with tears the sleeve of his dark robes.

TRANSLATED BY DONALD KEENE

TOKUGAWA PERIOD

1600–1868

WHAT THE SEASONS BROUGHT TO THE ALMANAC-MAKER

[*Kōshoku Gonin Onna, Book III*] *by Ihara Saikaku*

Saikaku's "Five Women Who Loved Love" (1686) is one of the masterpieces of Tokugawa literature. It consists of five independent stories, of which the third is here given. These stories are in turn divided into five chapters, each with a title of its own. The incidents described were based on actual events which took place shortly before Saikaku's novel, and were already familiar to many people in the form of ballads and recitations by professional storytellers.

•

THE BEAUTY CONTEST

According to the almanac for 1682, New Year's Day was to be devoted to the practice of calligraphy. Then, having started the year auspiciously, men could start making love on January 2.[1] In the Age of the Gods this art was taught by the wagtail bird [2] and ever since those days it has brought endless mischief between the sexes.

In Kyoto there lived a lady known as the Almanac-maker s Beautiful Spouse, who stirred up a mountain of passion in the capital and figured again and again in notorious romances. Her moon-shaped eyebrows rivaled in beauty the crescent borne aloft in the Gion Festival parade; her figure suggested the cherry buds, not yet blossoms, of Kiyomizu; her lovely lips looked like the topmost leaves of Takao in full autumnal glory. She lived in Muromachi-dori, the

[1] The tradition of practicing penmanship on New Year's Day is roughly equivalent to the Western custom of making New Year's resolutions. On that day continence was to be observed.

[2] Literally, the "love-knowing" bird, which taught the ways of love to Izanagi and Izanami, the first man and woman.

style center for women of discriminating taste in clothes, the most fashionable district in all Kyoto.

It was late spring; men felt gay and the wistaria hung like a cloud of purple over Yasui, robbing the pines of their color. People thronged up Higashiyama and turned it into a living mountain of figures.

There was in the capital a band of four inseparable young men who were known for their handsome appearance and riotous living. Thanks to large inheritances they could spend every day in the year seeking their own pleasure. One night, till dawn, they might amuse themselves in Shimabara with China-girl, Fragrance, Flora-point, and Highbridge. Next day they would make love to Takenaka Kichisaburō, Karamatsu Kasen, Fujita Kichisaburō, and Mitsuse Sakon in the Shijō-gawara section.[3] Night or day, girls or boys, it made no difference to their pleasure.

After the theatre one evening they were lounging around a tea shop called Matsuya and one of them remarked, "I have never seen so many good-looking local girls as I did today. Do you suppose we could find others who would seem just as beautiful now?" They thought they might, and decided to watch for pretty girls among the people who had gone to see the wistaria blossoms and were now returning to their homes. After a worldly actor in the group had been chosen as chief judge, a "beauty contest" was conducted until the twilight hours, providing a new source of amusement for the jaded gentlemen.

At first they were disappointed to see some maids riding in a carriage which hid them from sight. Then a group of girls strolled by in a rollicking mood—"not bad, not bad at all"—but none of the girls quite satisfied their exacting standards. Paper and ink had been brought to record the entries, and it was agreed that only the best should be put on their list.

Next they spied a lady of thirty-four or thirty-five with a graceful

[3] Theatre section where the *kabuki* drama originated; built on land reclaimed from the bed of the Kamo River in Kyoto. The names Takenaka, etc., are the assumed names of actors.

long neck and intelligent-looking eyes, above which could be seen a natural hairline of rare beauty. Her nose, it was true, stood a little high, but that could easily be tolerated. Underneath she wore white satin, over that light blue satin, and outside—reddish-yellow satin. Each of these garments was luxuriously lined with the same material. On her left sleeve was a hand-painted likeness of the Yoshida monk, along with his passage, "To sit alone under a lamp, and read old books. . . ."[4] Assuredly, this was a woman of exquisite taste.

Her sash was of folded taffeta bearing a tile design. Around her head she had draped a veil like that worn by court ladies; she wore stockings of pale silk and sandals with triple-braided straps. She walked noiselessly and gracefully, moving her hips with a natural rhythm. "What a prize for some lucky fellow!" a young buck exclaimed. But these words were hardly uttered when the lady, speaking to an attendant, opened her mouth and disclosed that one of her lower teeth was missing, to the complete disillusionment of her admirers.

A little behind her followed a maiden not more than sixteen or seventeen years old. On the girl's left was a woman who appeared to be her mother, on her right a black-robed nun. There were also several women and a footman as escorts, all taking the greatest care of their charge. It seemed at first as if the girl were engaged to be married, but at second glance she proved to be married already, for her teeth were blackened and her eyebrows removed. She was quite pretty with her round face, intelligent eyes, ears delicately draped at the side of her head, and plump fingers, thin-skinned and white. She wore her clothes with matchless elegance; underneath were purple-spotted fawns on a field of pure yellow, outside, the design of a hundred sparrows upon gray satin. Over her rainbow-colored sash she wore a breast-belt which enhanced the charm of her carriage. The tiestrings of her richly lined rainhat were made from a thousand braids of twisted paper. They could easily see under the hat—a delight for the eyes, or so they thought until someone noticed a wide scar, three inches or more, on the side of her face. She could

[4] See page 234.

hardly have been born with such a deformity, and they all laughed when one of the playboys remarked, "She must really hate the nurse who is responsible for that!"

Then another girl, perhaps twenty-one or twenty-two, came along wearing a garment of cotton homespun, even the lining of which was so tattered and patched that the wind, blowing it about, exposed her poverty to all. The material of her sash came from an old coat and was pitifully thin. She wore socks of purple leather, apparently the only kind she could afford, and tough, rough Nara sandals. An old cloth headpiece was stuck on the top of her head. It was anybody's guess how long ago the teeth of a comb had run through her hair, which fell in sloppy disarray, relieved hardly at all by her haphazard attempts to tuck it up.

But while she made no pretensions to style or fashion, the girl, walking alone, seemed to be enjoying herself. As far as her facial features were concerned, she certainly left nothing to be desired; indeed, the men were captivated by the sight of her.

"Have you ever seen anyone with so much natural beauty?"

"If she had some fine clothes to wear, that girl would steal men's hearts away. Too bad that she had to be born poor."

They pitied her deeply, and one fellow, seeing that she was on her way home, followed hopefully to learn who she was. "She is the wife of a tobacco-cutter down at the end of Seiganji-dori," someone told him. It was disappointing—another straw of hope gone up in smoke!

Later a woman of twenty-seven or twenty-eight passed that way. Her arms were covered by three layers of sleeves, all of black silk and lined in red. Her crest was done in gold, but discreetly on the inner lining, so as to be faintly visible through the sleeve. She had a broad sash which tied in front and was made from dark striped cloth woven in China. Her hair was rolled up in a bun, set further back on the head than the type worn by unmarried ladies, and done up with a thick hair ribbon and two combs. Covering it was a hand-painted scarf and a rainhat in the style of Kichiya,[5] also set jauntily

[5] Kyoto actor famous for his impersonation of women, who set many styles in ladies' apparel, particularly from 1673 to 1681.

back on her head so as not to hide the good looks in which she obviously took pride. Her figure twisted sinuously as she stepped lightly along.

"That's the one, that's the one!"

"Quiet down! Let's get a better look at her."

Sure enough, on closer inspection they found that the lady was accompanied by three servants, each carrying a baby.

"Must have had three kids in three years."

Behind her the babies kept calling out "Mama, mama" while the lady walked on, pretending not to hear them. "They may be her children, but she would just as soon not be seen with them. 'Charm fades with childbirth!' people say." Thus the men shouted and laughed and ridiculed her until she almost died of chagrin.

Next, with a litter borne luxuriously beside her, came a thirteen- or fourteen-year-old girl whose hair was combed out smooth, curled a bit at the ends, and tied down with a red ribbon. In front her hair was parted like a young boy's and held in place by five immaculate combs and a gold hair-clasp. Her face was perfectly beautiful, and I shall not tire you with needless details. A black inkslab pattern adorned her white satin chemise; a peacock design could be perceived in the iridescent satin of her outer garment. Over this hung lace made from Chinese thread and sleeves which were beautifully designed. A folded sash of twelve colors completed her ensemble. Her bare feet nestled in paper-strap clogs, and one of the litter-bearers carried a stylish rainhat for her.

The girl was holding a bunch of wistaria blossoms over her head, as if to attract the attention of someone who could not find her. Observed in this pose, she was clearly the most beautiful girl of all they had seen that day. "What is the name of this fine lady?" they asked politely of an attendant. "A girl from Muromachi," was the reply. "She is called the Modern Komachi."[6]

Yes, she had all the beauty of a flower. Only later did they learn how much deviltry was hid beneath it.

[6] See page 264.

THE SLEEPER WHO SLIPPED UP

The life of a bachelor has its attractions, but nights get rather lonely for a man without a wife. So it seemed to a certain maker of almanacs who had lived alone for many years. There were many elegant ladies in the capital, but his heart was set on finding a woman of exceptional beauty and distinction, and such a desire was not easily satisfied. Finally in despair because of his solitary existence, he asked some relatives to find him a suitable mate, and it was arranged for him to meet the girl known as the Modern Komachi, that delicate beauty whom our playboys had seen in the theatre section last spring holding wistaria blossoms over her head.

The almanac-maker was completely charmed with her. "She's the one," he told himself, and without more ado rushed out, ludicrously enough, to arrange an immediate marriage. He found an old woman, a professional go-between, who was widely known as a very fast talker, and thanks to her the negotiations were conducted successfully. A keg of saké was sent to confirm the contract, and on the appointed day Osan was welcomed into her new home.

Deeply attached to his wife and absorbed in the intimacies of their life together, the almanac-maker was blind to everything else—to the flower-fragrant nights of spring and to the rising of the autumn moon. Night and day for three years his wife diligently performed the many tasks which married life required of her, carefully spinning pongee thread by hand, supervising the weaving of cloth by her servant women, looking after her husband's personal appearance, burning as little fuel as possible for economy's sake, and keeping her expense accounts accurate and up to date. In fact she was just the sort of woman any townsman would want in his home.

Their house was prospering and their companionship seemed to hold a store of endless bliss, when it became necessary for the almanac-maker to travel to Edo for business reasons. The parting was sad, but there was nothing to be gained by grieving over it. When he was ready to leave, he paid a visit to Osan's father in Muromachi to tell him about the trip, and the old man was quite concerned about his daughter's welfare during the period of her husband's absence, when she would be left to manage all of his affairs. He wondered if there were not some capable person who could take over the master's business and also assist Osan in running the household. Deciding on a young man named Mōemon, who had served him faithfully for many years, he sent the fellow to his son-in-law's place.

This Mōemon was honest and extremely frugal, so much so that he completely neglected his personal appearance, even economizing on his coat-sleeves, which measured only two and one half inches at the wrist. His forehead was narrow, and when his hair grew out after he reached manhood, Mōemon never bothered to buy a hat to cover it. Moreover, he went about without the protection of a short sword, and slept with his abacus under his head, the better perhaps to reckon how great a fortune he could amass in a night spent dreaming of money-making.

It was fall, and a bitter storm one night set Mōemon to thinking how he might fortify himself against the rigors of winter. He decided on a treatment of moxa cauterizing. A maidservant named Rin, who was adept at administering the burning pills, was asked to do the job for him. She twisted several wads of cottony herb, and spread a striped bedcover over her dressing table for Mōemon to lie on. The first couple of applications were almost more than he could bear. The pain-wracked expression on his face gave great amusement to the governess, the housemistress, and all the lowly maids around him. When further doses had been applied, he could hardly wait for the final salting down which would finish the treatment. Then, accidentally, some of the burning fibers broke off and dropped down along his spine, causing his flesh to tighten and shrink a little. But out of consideration for the girl who attended him, Mōemon closed his eyes, clenched his teeth, and mustered up all his patience to endure the pain. Rin, full of sympathy for him, extinguished the vagrant embers and began to massage his skin. How could she have known that this intimate contact with his body would arouse in her a passionate desire for Mōemon, which at first she managed to conceal from others but eventually was to be whispered about and even reach her mistress's ears?

Unable to suppress her desire for Mōemon, Rin hoped that somehow she might communicate with him, but as her education had only been of the most humble sort, she could not write anything, not even the crude-looking characters which Kyūshichi, a fellow servant, used to scribble out as personal reminders. She asked Kyūshichi if he would write a letter for her, but the knave only took advantage of her confidence by trying to make this love his own.

So, slowly, the days passed without relief, and fall came with its long twilight of drizzling rains, the spawning season for intrigue and deception. One day, having just finished a letter to her husband in Edo, Osan playfully offered to write a love letter for Rin. With her brush she dashed off a few sweet lines of love and then, addressing the wrapper "To Mr. Mō—, from someone who loves him," Osan gaily turned the note over to Rin. Overjoyed, the girl kept looking for a suitable opportunity to deliver it, when all at once Mōemon was heard calling from the shop for some fire with which to light his tobacco. Fortunately there was no one else in the courtyard at that time, so Rin seized the occasion to deliver the letter in person.

Considering the nature of the thing, Mōemon failed to notice his mistress's handwriting and simply took Rin for a very forward girl, certainly an easy conquest. Roguishly he wrote out a reply and handed it to Rin, who was unable to read it of course, and had to catch Osan in a good mood before she could learn its contents.

"In response to the unexpected note which your feelings toward me prompted you to write, I confess that, young as I am, your advances are not wholly distasteful to me. I must remind you that such trysts as you propose may produce complications involving a midwife, but if you are ready to meet all of the expenses incidental to the affair—clothes, coats, bath money, and personal toiletries—I shall be glad to oblige to the best of my ability."

"Such impudence!" Osan exclaimed when she finished reading the blunt message to Rin. "There is no dearth of men in this world, and Rin is hardly the worst-looking of all women. She can have a man like Mōemon any time she wants."

Thus aroused, Osan decided to write further importunate messages for Rin and make Mōemon her loving slave. So she sent several heartbreaking appeals to him, moving Mōemon to pity and then to passion. At last, to make up for his earlier impertinence he finally wrote Rin an earnest note in reply. It contained a promise that on the night of May 14, when it was customary to stay up and watch the full moon, he would definitely come to see her. Mistress Osan laughed aloud when she saw this, and told the assembled maids, "We shall turn his big night into a night of fun for all!"

Her plan was to take the place of Rin that night, disguise herself in cotton summer clothes, and sleep in Rin's bed. It was also arranged for the various women servants to come running with sticks and staves and lanterns when Osan called out. Thus all were ready and in their places when the time came, but before she knew it Osan herself fell blissfully asleep, and the women servants too, exhausted by all the excitement that evening, dozed off and started to snore.

Later, during the early morning hours, Mōemon stole through the darkness with his underclothes hanging half-loose around him. Impatiently he slipped naked between the bedcovers; his heart throbbed, but his lips were silent. And when his pleasure was had, Mōemon sensed the faint, appealing fragrance which arose from the lady's garments. He lifted up the covers and started to tiptoe away. "Indeed, she must know more of life than I suspected. I thought she was innocent, that she had loved no man before, that now—but someone has been here ahead of me," he concluded apprehensively. "I must pursue this no further."

When he had gone Osan awoke of her own accord. To her surprise the pillows were out of place and everything was in disorder. Her sash, missing from her waist, was nowhere at hand; her bed tissues were a mess. Overcome with shame at the realization of her undoing, Osan considered. "There is no way to keep this from others. From now on I may as well abandon myself to this affair, risk my life, ruin my reputation, and take Mōemon as my companion on a journey to death."

She confided this resolution to Mōemon, and though it was contrary to his previous decision, nevertheless, being halfway in and feeling the call to love, Mōemon gave himself over to visiting her each night without a care for the reproofs of others, and spent himself in this new service as thoroughly as he had in his work. Thus, together the lovers played with life and death, the most dangerous game of all.

THE LAKE WHICH TOOK PEOPLE IN

It is written in "The Tale of Genji," "There is no logic in love." When the image of Kwannon was put on display at Ishiyama Temple, the people of Kyoto left the cherry blossoms of Higashiyama and flocked to see it. Travelers, on their way to and from the capital, stopped for a visit when they crossed Ausaka Pass. Many among them were fashionably dressed ladies; not one of whom seemed to be making the pilgrimage with any thought of the Hereafter. Each showed off her clothes and took such pride in her appearance that even Kwannon must have been amused at the sight.

It happened that Osan and Mōemon also made the pilgrimage together. They and the flowers they saw seemed to share a common fate; no one could tell when they might fall. Nor could anyone tell whether the lovers again might see this bay and the hills around Lake Biwa, so Mōemon and Osan wanted to make it a day to remember. They rented a small boat in Seta, and wished their love would last as long as the Long Bridge of that town,[7] though their pleasure might still be short-lived. Floating along, the lovers made waves serve them as pillow and bed, and the disorder of Osan's hairdress testified to the nature of their delight. But there were mo-

[7] The Long Bridge (*Seta no Nagahashi*) opens a passage studded with references to places around Lake Biwa, east of Kyoto, in which the characters' moods are described in terms of the names of the places they pass. (This passage is called a *michiyuki,* as in a play.)

ments, too, when the beclouded Mirror Mountain seemed to reflect a more somber mood in Osan. Love for these two was as dangerous a passage as Crocodile Strait, and their hearts sank when at Katada someone called the boat from shore; for a minute they feared that a courier had come after them from Kyoto.

Even though they survived this, it seemed as if their end might be told by the snows of Mt. Hiei, for they were twenty years old and it is said that the snow on this Fuji of the capital always melts before twenty days have passed. So they wept and wetted their sleeves, and at the ancient capital of Shiga,[8] which is now just a memory of past glory, they felt sadder still, thinking of their own inevitable end. When the dragon lanterns were lit, they went to Shirahige Shrine and prayed to the gods, now even more aware of the precariousness of their fate.

"After all, we may find that longer life only brings greater grief." Osan told him. "Let us throw ourselves into the lake and consecrate our lives to Buddha in the Eternal Land." But Mōemon, though he valued his life hardly at all, was not so certain as to what would follow after death. "I think I have hit upon a way out," he said. "Let us each send letters to the capital, saying that we shall drown ourselves in the lake. We can then steal away from here to anywhere you please and pass the rest of our years together."

Osan was delighted. "When I left home, it was with that idea in mind. So I brought along five hundred pieces of gold in my suitcase."

That, indeed, was something with which to start life anew. "We must be careful how we do this," Mōemon cautioned, as they set about writing notes to various people: "Driven by evil desires, we have joined in a sinful love which cannot escape Heaven's decree. Life has no place for us now; therefore today we depart forever from the Fleeting World." Osan then removed a small image of the Buddha Sakyamuni which she had worn as a charm for bodily protection, and trimmed the edges of her black hair. Mōemon took off the dirk which he wore at his side, made by Seki Izumi no Kami with an iron guard embellished by twisting copper dragons. These things would be left behind so that people could identify them as belonging

[8] Capital of the Emperor Tenchi (666-682) on the southwestern shore of Lake Biwa.

to Mōemon and Osan. Then, as a final precaution, they even left their coats and sandals at the foot of a willow by the shore. And since there lived at the lakeside men with a long tradition as experts in fishing, who could leap from the rocks into the water, Mōemon secretly hired two of them and explained his plan. They readily agreed to keep a rendezvous with the couple that evening.

When Mōemon and Osan had prepared themselves properly, they opened the bamboo door of the inn and roused everyone by shouting, "For reasons best known to ourselves we are about to end our lives!" They then rushed away, and presently from the height of the craggy rock faint voices were heard saying the *nembutsu,*[9] followed by the sound of two bodies striking the water. Everyone wept and raised a great commotion over it. Meanwhile Mōemon, carrying Osan on his shoulder, made his way to the foot of the mountains and plunged into the dense growth of fir trees, and the two fishermen, who had dived under the waves, surfaced on the beach at a place where no one would expect them.

All the people were beating their hands and lamenting the tragedy. With help from men living along the shore they made a search but found nothing. Then, as dawn broke, more tears fell upon the discovery of the lovers' personal effects. These were quickly wrapped up and sent back to Kyoto.

Out of concern for what people would think, the families involved privately agreed to keep the matter to themselves. But in a world full of busy ears the news was bound to leak out, and all spring long it gave people something to gossip about. There was indeed no end to the mischief these two souls created.

THE TEAHOUSE WHICH HAD NOT HEARD OF GOLD PIECES

Hand in hand, Mōemon and Osan trekked across the wilderness of Tamba. They had to make their own road through the stubborn

[9] An invocation meaning "Homage to Amida Buddha," by which believers in Amida expect to achieve salvation.

underbrush. At last they climbed a high peak, and looking back whence they had come, reflected on the terrors of their journey. It was, to be sure, the lot they had chosen; still, there was little pleasure in living on in the role of the dead. They were lost souls, miserably lost, on a route that was not even marked by a woodsman's footprints. Osan stumbled feebly along, so wretched that she seemed to be gasping for what might be her last breath, and her face lost all its color. Mōemon tried every means to revive and sustain his beloved, even catching spring water in a leaf as it dripped from the rocks. But Osan had little strength left to draw on. Her pulse beat more and more faintly; any minute might be her last.

Mōemon could offer nothing at all in the way of medicine. He stood by helplessly to wait for Osan's end, then suddenly bent near and whispered in her ear, "Just a little farther on we shall come to the village of some people I know. There we can forget all our misery, indulge our hearts' desire with pillows side by side, and talk again of love!"

When she heard this, Osan felt better right away. "How good that sounds! Oh, you are worth paying with one's life for!"

A pitiful woman indeed, whom lust alone could arouse, Osan was carried by Mōemon pickaback into the fenced enclosure of a tiny village. Here was the highway to the capital, and a road running along the mountainside wide enough for two horses to pass each other. Here, too, was a teahouse thatched with straw built up of cryptomeria branches woven together. A sign said "Finest Home Brew Here," but the rice cakes were many days old and dust had deprived them of their whiteness. On a side counter were tea-brushes, clay dolls, and dancing-drummer dolls—all reminiscent of Kyoto and therefore a tonic to the weary travelers, who rested there a while. Mōemon and Osan enjoyed it so much that upon leaving they offered the old innkeeper a gold piece. But he scowled unappreciatively, like a cat that is shown an umbrella.[10] "Please pay me for the tea," he demanded, and they were amused to think that less than fifteen miles from the capital there should be a village which had not yet heard of gold pieces.

[10] Roughly equivalent to "casting pearls before swine."

Thence the lovers went to a place called Kayabara, where lived an aunt of Mōemon's whom he had not heard from for many years—who might be dead for all he knew. Calling on her, Mōemon spoke of their family past, and she welcomed him as one of her own. The rest of the evening, with chin in hand and tears in her eyes, the old woman talked of nothing but his father Mosuke; but when day broke she became suddenly aware of Osan, whose beauty and refinement aroused her suspicions. "Who is that?" the aunt asked. Mōemon had not prepared himself for all the questions she might ask, and found himself in an awkward spot. "My younger sister," he replied. "For many years she has served in the home of a court official, but it was a strict family and she disliked the fretful life of the capital. She thought there might be an opportunity to join a quiet, leisurely household—something like this—in the mountains. So she terminated her service and came along with me in hopes of finding housework and gardening to do in the village. Her expenses need be no concern; she has about two hundred pieces of gold in savings."

Thus he blithely concocted a story to satisfy the old woman. But it is a greedy world wherever one goes, and Mōemon's aunt thought there might be something in this for her. "Now," she exclaimed, "that is really most fortunate. My son has no wife yet and your sister is a relative, so why not have her marry him?" [11]

It was a distressing proposal. Osan sobbed quietly, cursing the fate which had led her to such a dismal prospect. Then as evening fell the son came home. He was frightful to behold, taller than anyone she had ever seen, and with his head set like a Chinese lion gargoyle on his squat neck. A fierce light gleamed in his big, bloodshot eyes. His beard was like a bear's, his arms and legs were as thick as pine trees, and a wistaria vine held together the rag-woven clothes he wore. In one hand he carried an old matchlock, in the other a tinder-rope. His hunting basket was full of rabbits and badgers, as much as to say: "This is how I make a living." He was called Zetarō the Rock-jumper.

In the village it was no secret that he was a mean man. But when

[11] Marriage between relations once removed was not at this time taboo. On the contrary, a match between cousins was thought highly desirable.

his mother explained to him her proposal for a marriage with the lady from Kyoto, Zetarō was pleased. "Good, let's waste no time. To-night will do." And he reached for a hand mirror to look at his face. "Nice looking fellow," he said.

His mother prepared the wedding cup, offered them salted fish and passed around a wine bottle which had its neck broken off. She used floormats as screens to enclose the room which would serve as a nuptial chamber. Two wooden pillows were also provided, two thin sleeping mattresses, and one striped bedcover. Split pine logs burned in a brazier. It would be a gay evening.

But Osan was as sad as could be, and Mōemon terribly depressed. "This is the price I must pay for having spoken so impulsively. We are living on when we should have died in the waters of Lake Biwa. Heaven will not spare us now!" He drew his sword and would have killed himself had not Osan stopped and quieted him. "Why, you are much too short-tempered. There are still ways to get out of this. At dawn we shall depart from here—leave everything to me."

That night while she was drinking the wedding cup with good grace and affability, Osan remarked to Zetarō, "Most people shun me. I was born in the year of the Fiery Horse." [12]

"I wouldn't care if you were a Fiery Cat or a Fiery Wolf. I even like blue lizards—eat 'em in fact. And you see I'm not dead yet. Twenty-eight years old, and I haven't had one case of worms. Mister Mōemon should take after me! As for you: a soft creature brought up in the capital isn't what I'd like for a wife, but I'll tolerate you, since you're my relative." In this generous mood he lay down and snuggled his head comfortably in her lap.

Amidst all their unhappiness Osan and Mōemon found the brute somewhat amusing. Nevertheless, they could hardly wait until he went to bed, at last giving them a chance to slip away. Again they hid themselves in the depths of Tamba; then after many days had passed came out upon the road to Tango. One night they slept in a

[12] This year marked the coincidence of Fire with Fire on the old lunar calendar, the horse itself representing Fire. It was considered a dangerous year to be born in, and women born then were said to bully and frequently kill their husbands. Zetarō's reply is in the nature of a crude joke, for there is no year of the Fiery Wolf.

chapel of the god Monju, who appeared to Osan in a dream midway through the night. "You have committed the worst of sins. Wherever you go, you cannot escape its consequences. But that is all part of the unredeemable past; henceforth you must forsake your vain ways, shave off the hair you take such delight in, and become a nun. Once separated, the two of you can abandon your evil passion and enter upon the Way of Enlightenment. Then perhaps your lives may be saved!"

It was a worthy vision, but Osan said to herself, "What becomes of me now does not matter. I left my husband at the risk of my life because this love appealed to me. Monju may understand the love of men for men,[13] but he knows nothing about the love of women."

That instant she awoke from her dream, just as the morning breeze blew in through Hashidate's seaside pines, bearing with it the dust of the world. "Everything is dust and defilement," Osan told herself, and all hope was lost of ever saving her.

THE EAVESDROPPER WHOSE EARS WERE BURNED

Men take their misfortunes to heart, and keep them there. A gambler does not talk about his losses; the frequenter of brothels, who finds his favorite engaged by another, pretends to be just as well off without her; the professional street-brawler is quiet about the fights he has lost; and a merchant who speculates in goods will conceal the losses he may suffer. All act as one who steps on dog dung in the dark.

But of them all the man who has a wanton, mischievous wife will feel his misfortune most, convinced that there is no more heartless creature in the world than she. To the outer world Osan's husband treated her as a closed issue: she was dead, and nothing more could be said or done about her. There were times when he was reminded of their years together and would feel the greatest bitterness toward

[13] According to a vulgar belief, Manjusri (Monju in Japanese) was the lover of Sakyamuni. He was therefore taken as the patron god of homosexuality.

Osan, yet he would still call in a priest to hold services in her memory. Ironically enough, he offered one of her choice silk garments as an altar cloth for the local temple, where, fluttering in the fickle wind of Life and Death, it became a further source of lamentation.

Even so, there is no one bolder than a man deeply attached to the things of this world, and Mōemon, who before was so prudent that he never went outdoors at night, soon lost himself in a nostalgic desire to see the capital again. Dressing in the most humble attire and pulling his hat down over his eyes, he left Osan in the care of some villagers and made a senseless trip to Kyoto, all the while fearing more for his own safety than a man who is about to deliver himself into the hands of an enemy.

It began to get dark when he reached the neighborhood of Hirozawa, and the sight of the moon, reflected in the double pond, made him think again of Osan, so that his sleeve became soaked with idle tears. Presently he put behind him the rapid Narutaki, with its myriad bubbles, dancing over the rocks, and hurried on toward Omuro and Kitano, for he knew that way well. When he entered the city his fears were multiplied. "What's that!" he would ask himself, when he saw his own silhouette under the waning moon, and his heart would freeze with terror.

In the quarter with which he was so familiar, because his former master lived there, he took up eavesdropping to learn the state of things. He heard about the inquiry which was to be made into the overdue payment from Edo, and about the latest style in hairdress, as discussed by a gathering of young men, who were also commenting on the style and fit of each other's clothes—the sort of silly chatter that love and lust inspire in men. When these topics of conversation were exhausted, sure enough they fell to talking about Mōemon. "That rascal Mōemon, stealing a woman more beautiful than all others! Even though he paid with his worthless life for it, he certainly got the best of the bargain; a memory worth dying with!" But a man of more discernment upheld morality against Mōemon. "He's nobody to raise up in public. He'd stink in the breeze. I can't imagine anyone worse than a man who'd cheat both his master and a husband at once."

Overhearing this, Mōemon swore to himself, "That's the voice of the scoundrel Kisuke, of the Daimonjiya. What a heartless, faithless fellow to be so outspoken against me. Why, I lent him eighty ounces of silver on an I.O.U.! But I'll get even for what he just said: I'll get that money back if I have to wring his neck." Mōemon gnashed his teeth and stood up in a rage. Still there was nothing a man hiding from the world could do about the insults offered him, and while he suppressed his outraged feelings another man started to speak. "Mōemon's not dead. He's living with Mistress Osan somewhere around Ise, they say, having a wonderful time."

This shook Mōemon and sent chills through his body. He left in all haste, took a room in a lodging house along Third Street, and went to bed without even taking a bath. Since it was the night of the seventeenth,[14] he wrapped up twelve copper coins in a piece of paper and handed it to a beggar who would buy some candles and keep the vigil for him that night. Then he prayed that people would not discover who he was. But could he expect that even Atago-sama, the patron of lovers, would help him in his wickedness?

In the morning, as a last memory of the capital before leaving it, he stole down Higashiyama to the theatre section at Shijō-gawara. Someone told him that it was the opening day of a three-act play by Fujita. "I must see what it is like and tell Osan when I return." He rented a cushion and sat far back to watch from a distance, uneasy at heart lest someone recognize him. The play was about a man whose daughter was stolen away. It made Mōemon's conscience hurt. Then he looked down to the front rows. There was Osan's husband himself; at the sight Mōemon's spirit almost left him. He felt like a man with one foot dangling over Hell, and the sweat stood like pearls on his forehead. Out he rushed through an exit to return to the village in Tango, which he did not think of leaving again for Kyoto.

At that time, when the Chrysanthemum Festival was almost at hand, a chestnut peddler made his annual trip to the capital. While speaking of one thing and another at the house of the almanac-

[14] The moon of the seventeenth night was known as the "stand-and-wait moon," and people would keep all-night vigils.

maker, he asked where the mistress was, but as this was an awkward subject in the household none of the servants ventured to answer. Frowning, Osan's husband told him, "She's dead."

"That's strange," the peddler went on, "I've seen someone who looks very much like her, in fact, someone who doesn't differ from her one particle. And with her is the living image of your young man. They are near Kirito in Tango."

When the peddler had departed, Osan's husband sent someone to check up on what he had heard. Learning that Osan and Mōemon were indeed alive, he gathered together a good number of his own people, who went and arrested them. There was no room for mercy in view of their crime. When the judicial inquiry was duly concluded, the lovers, together with a maidservant named Tama who had earlier been their go-between, were paraded as an example before the crowds along the way to Awataguchi, where they died like dewdrops falling from a blade of grass. Thus they met their end on the morning of September 22, with, it should be remarked, a touching acquiescence in their fate. Their story spread everywhere, and today the name of Osan still brings to mind her beautiful figure, clothed in the pale orange slip which she wore to her execution.[15]

TRANSLATED BY W. THEODORE DE BARY

15 Those condemned to death were allowed to wear only an undergarment to the execution.

THE UMBRELLA ORACLE

[*Saikaku Shokoku-banashi, I, iv*] *by Ihara Saikaku*

Saikaku wrote his famous "Tales from the Provinces," the collection from which this story is taken, in 1685. From his early youth he had been fond of travel and now, at the age of forty-three, he attempted to record the most interesting of the stories, tales, legends, and incidents that he had heard or witnessed in his travels throughout Japan.

•

Commendable indeed is the spirit of philanthropy in this world of ours!

To the famous "Hanging Temple of Kwannon" in the Province of Kii, someone had once presented twenty oil-paper umbrellas which, repaired every year, were hung beside the temple for the use of any and all who might be caught in the rain or snow. They were always conscientiously returned when the weather improved—not a single one had ever been lost.

One day in the spring of 1649, however, a certain villager borrowed one of the umbrellas and, while he was returning home, had it blown out of his hands by a violent "divine wind" that blew up suddenly from the direction of the shrine on Tamazu Isle. The umbrella was blown completely out of sight, and though the villager bemoaned its loss there was not a thing he could do.

Borne aloft by the wind, the umbrella landed finally in the little hamlet of Anazato, far in the mountains of the island of Kyushu. The people of this village had from ancient times been completely cut off from the world and—uncultured folk that they were—had never even seen an umbrella! All of the learned men and elders of the village gathered around to discuss the curious object before them

—reaching agreement, however, only upon the fact that none of them had ever before seen anything like it.

Finally one local wise man stepped forth and proclaimed, "Upon counting the radiating bamboo ribs, there are exactly forty. The paper too is round and luminous, and not of the ordinary kind. Though I hesitate to utter that August Name, this is without a doubt the God of the Sun,[1] whose name we have so often heard, and is assuredly his divine attribute from the Inner Sanctuary of the Great Shrine of Ise, which has deigned to fly to us here!"

All present were filled with awe. Hurriedly the salt water of purification was scattered about the ground and the divinity installed upon a clean reed mat; and the whole population of the village went up into the mountains and, gathering wood and rushes, built a shrine that the deity's spirit might be transferred hence from Ise. When they had paid reverence to it, the divine spirit did indeed enter the umbrella.

At the time of the summer rains the site upon which the shrine was situated became greatly agitated, and the commotion did not cease. When the umbrella was consulted, the following oracle was delivered: "All this summer the sacred hearth has been simply filthy, with cockroaches boiled in the holy vessels and the contamination reaching even to my Inner Shrine! Henceforth, in this entire province, let there not be a single cockroach left alive! I also have one other request. I desire you to select a beautiful young maiden as a consolation offering for me. If this is not done within seven days, without fail, I will cause the rain to fall in great torrents; I will rain you all to death, so that the seed of man remains no more upon the earth!"

Thus spake the oracle.

The villagers were frightened out of their wits. They held a meeting, and summoned all the maidens of the village to decide which one should serve the deity. But the young maidens, weeping and wailing, strongly protested the umbrella-god's cruel demand. When asked the reason for their excess of grief, they cried, "How could we

[1] The deity of the sun was normally a goddess, but about this time popular belief had him a god.

survive even one night with such a god?"—for they had come to attach a peculiar significance to the odd shape which the deity had assumed.

At this juncture a young and beautiful widow from the village stepped forward, saying, "Since it is for the god, I will offer myself in place of the young maidens."

All night long the beautiful widow waited in the shrine, but she did not get a bit of affection. Enraged, she charged into the inner sanctum, grasped the divine umbrella firmly in her hands and screaming, "Worthless deceiver!" she tore it apart, and threw the pieces as far as she could!

TRANSLATED BY RICHARD LANE

THE ETERNAL STOREHOUSE OF JAPAN

[*Nippon Eitaigura*] *by Ihara Saikaku*

This collection of brief tales dealing with how to make or lose a fortune was first published in 1688. It is not only of high literary value, but gives us invaluable descriptions of the life of the townsmen in the late seventeenth century. It bears the subtitle, "The Millionaire's Gospel, Revised Version."

THE TYCOON OF ALL TENANTS

"This is to certify that the person named Fuji-ichi, tenant in a house belonging to Hishiya Chozaemon, is to my certain knowledge the possessor of one thousand *kamme* in silver. . . ."

Such would be the form of testimonial when Fuji-ichi sought new lodgings. It was his proud claim that in the whole wide world there was no millionaire quite like himself. For although he was worth a thousand *kamme,* he lived in a rented house no more than four yards wide. In this way he became the talk of Kyoto. However, one day he accepted a house as surety for a loan of thirty-eight *kamme;* in the course of time, as the interest mounted, the surety itself became forfeit; and for the first time Fuji-ichi became a property owner. He was much vexed at this. Up to now he had achieved distinction as "the millionaire in lodgings," but now that he had a house of his own he was commonplace—his money in itself was mere dust by comparison with what lay in the strong rooms of the foremost merchants of Kyoto.

Fuji-ichi was a clever man, and his substantial fortune was amassed in his own lifetime. But first and foremost he was a man who knew his own mind, and this was the basis of his success. In addition to carrying on his regular business, he kept a separate ledger, bound from odd scraps of paper, in which, as he sat all day in his shop, pen in hand, he entered a variety of chance information. As the clerks from the money exchanges passed by he noted down the market ratio of copper and gold; he inquired about the current quotations of the rice brokers; he sought information from druggists' and haberdashers' assistants on the state of the market at Nagasaki; for the latest news on the prices of ginned cotton, salt, and saké, he noted the various days on which the Kyoto dealers received dispatches from the Edo branch shops. Every day a thousand things were entered in his book, and people came to Fuji-ichi if they were ever in doubt. He became a valuable asset to the citizens of Kyoto.

Invariably his dress consisted of an unlined vest next to his skin, and on top of that a cotton kimono, stuffed on occasion with three times the usual amount of padding. He never put on more than one layer of kimono. It was he who first started the wearing of detachable cuffs on the sleeves—a device which was both fashionable and economical. His socks were of deerskin and his clogs were fitted with high leather soles, but even so he was careful not to walk too quickly along the hard main roads. Throughout life his only silk garments were of pongee, dyed plain dark blue. There was one, it is true, which he had dyed a persistently undisguisable seaweed brown, but this was a youthful error of judgment, and he was to regret it for the next twenty years. For his ceremonial dress he had no settled crests, being content with a three-barred circle or a small conventional whirl, but even during the summer airing time he was careful to keep them from direct contact with the floor. His pantaloons were of hemp, and his starched jacket of an even tougher variety of the same cloth, so that they remained correctly creased no matter how many times he wore them.

When there was a funeral procession which his whole ward was obliged to join, he followed it perforce to the cemetery, but coming back he hung behind the others and, on the path across the moor at Rokuhara, he and his apprentices pulled up sour herbs by the roots.

"Dried in the shade," he explained, "they make excellent stomach medicine."

He never passed by anything which might be of use. Even if he stumbled he used the opportunity to pick up stones for fire-lighters, and tucked them in his sleeve. The head of a household, if he is to keep the smoke rising steadily from his kitchen, must pay attention to a thousand things like this.

Fuji-ichi was not a miser by nature. It was merely his ambition to serve as a model for others in the management of everyday affairs. Even in the days before he made his money he never had the New Year rice cakes prepared in his own lodgings. He considered that to bother over the various utensils, and to hire a man to pound the rice, was too much trouble at such a busy time of the year; so he placed an order with the rice-cake dealer in front of the Great Buddha. However, with his intuitive grasp of good business, he insisted on paying by weight—so much per pound. Early one morning, two days before the New Year, a porter from the cake-maker, hurrying about his rounds, arrived before Fuji-ichi's shop and, setting down his load, shouted for someone to receive the order. The newly pounded cakes, invitingly arrayed, were as fresh and warm as spring itself. The master, pretending not to hear, continued his calculations on the abacus, and the cake-man, who begrudged every moment at this busy time of the year, shouted again and again. At length a young clerk, anxious to demonstrate his businesslike approach, checked the weight of the cakes on the large scales with a show of great precision, and sent the man away.

About two hours later Fuji-ichi said: "Has anyone taken in the cakes which arrived just now?"

"The man gave them to me and left long ago," said the clerk.

"Useless fellow!" cried Fuji-ichi. "I expect people in my service to have more sense! Don't you realize that you took them in before they had cooled off?"

He weighed them again, and to everyone's astonishment their weight had decreased. Not one of the cakes had been eaten, and the clerk stood gazing at them in open-mouthed amazement.

It was the early summer of the following year. The local people from the neighborhood of the Eastern Temple had gathered the first crop of eggplants in wicker baskets and brought them to town for sale. "Eat young eggplants and live seventy-five days longer" goes the saying, and they are very popular. The price was fixed at two coppers for one eggplant, or three coppers for two, which meant that everybody bought two.

But Fuji-ichi bought only one, at two coppers, because—as he said—"With the one copper I now have in pocket I can buy any number of larger ones when the crop is fully grown."

That was the way he kept his wits about him, and he seldom made a mistake.

In an empty space in his grounds he planted an assortment of useful trees and flowers such as willow, holly, laurel, peach, iris, and bead-beans. This he did as an education for his only daughter. Morning-glory started to grow of its own accord along the reed fence, but Fuji-ichi said that if it was a question of beauty such short-lived things were a loss, and in their place he planted runner-beans, whose flowers he thought an equally fine sight. Nothing delighted him more than watching over his daughter. When the young girl grew into womanhood he had a marriage screen constructed for her, and since he considered that one decorated with views of Kyoto would make her restless to visit the places she had not yet seen, and that illustrations of "The Tale of Genji" or "The Tales of Ise" might engender frivolous thoughts, he had the screen painted with busy scenes of the silver and copper mines at Tada. He composed Instructional Verses on the subject of economy and made his daughter recite them aloud. Instead of sending her to a girls' temple school, he taught her how to write himself, and by the time he had reached the end of his syllabus, he had made her the most finished and accomplished girl in Kyoto. Imitating her father in his thrifty ways, after the age of eight she spilt no more ink on her sleeves, played no longer with dolls at the Doll Festival, nor joined in the dancing at Bon.[1] Every day she combed her own hair and bound it in a simple bun. She never sought others' help in her private affairs. She mastered the art of stretching silk padding and learned

[1] A summer festival.

to fit it perfectly to the length and breadth of each garment. Since young girls can do all this if properly disciplined, it is a mistake to leave them to do as they please.

Once, on the evening of the seventh day of the New Year, some neighbors asked leave to send their sons to Fuji-ichi's house to seek advice on how to become millionaires. Lighting the lamp in the sitting room, Fuji-ichi set his daughter to wait, bidding her let him know when she heard a noise at the private door from the street. The young girl, doing as she was told with charming grace, first carefully lowered the wick in the lamp. Then, when she heard the voices of the visitors, she raised the wick again and retired to the scullery. By the time the three guests had seated themselves the grinding of an earthenware mortar could be heard from the kitchen, and the sound fell with pleasant promise on their ears. They speculated on what was in store for them.

"Pickled whaleskin soup?" hazarded the first.

"No. As this is our first visit of the year, it ought to be rice-cake gruel," said the second.

The third listened carefully for some time, and then confidently announced that it was noodle soup. Visitors always go through this amusing performance. Fuji-ichi then entered and talked to the three of them on the requisites for success.

"Why is it that today is called the Day of the Seven Herbs?" one asked him.

"That was the beginning of economy in the Age of the Gods: it was to teach us the ingredients of a cheap stew."

"Why do we leave a salted bream hanging before the God of the Kitchen Range until the sixth moon?" asked another.

"That is so that when you look at it at meal times you may get the feeling of having eaten fish without actually doing so."

Finally he was asked the reason for using thick chopsticks at the New Year.

"That is so that when they become soiled they can be scraped white again, and in this way one pair will last the whole year.

"As a general rule," concluded Fuji-ichi, "give the closest attention to even the smallest details. Well now, you have kindly talked with me from early evening, and it is high time that refreshments were served. But not to provide refreshments is one way of becoming a millionaire. The noise of the mortar which you heard when you first arrived was the pounding of starch for the covers of the Account Book."

TRANSLATED BY G. W. SARGENT

THE NARROW ROAD OF OKU

[*Oku no Hosomichi*] *by Matsuo Bashō (1644-1694)*

•

The months and days are the travelers of eternity. The years that come and go are also voyagers. Those who float away their lives on boats or who grow old leading horses are forever journeying, and their homes are wherever their travels take them. Many of the men of old died on the road, and I too for years past have been stirred by the sight of a solitary cloud drifting with the wind, to ceaseless thoughts of roaming.

Last year I spent wandering along the seacoast. In autumn I returned to my cottage on the river and swept away the cobwebs. Gradually the year drew to its close. When spring came and there was mist in the air, I thought of crossing the Barrier of Shirakawa into Oku. Everything about me was bewitched by the travel-gods, and my thoughts were no longer mine to control. The spirits of the road beckoned, and I could do no work at all.

I patched up my torn trousers and changed the cords on my bamboo hat. To strengthen my legs for the journey I had moxa burned on my shins. Then the thought of the moon at Matsushima began to occupy my thoughts. When I sold my cottage and moved to Sampū's villa, to stay until I started on my journey, I hung this poem on a post in my hut:

Kusa no to mo	Even a thatched hut
Sumikawaru yo zo	In this changing world may turn
Hina no ie	Into a doll's house.

When I set out on the twenty-seventh of March, the dawn sky was misty. Though the pale morning moon had lost its light, Fuji could still be seen faintly. The cherry blossoms on the boughs at Ueno and Yanaka stirred sad thoughts within me, as I wondered when again I should see them. My dearest friends had all come to Sampū's house the night before so that they might accompany me on the boat part of the way. When we disembarked at a place called Senju, the thought of parting to go on so long a journey filled me with sadness. As I stood on the road that was perhaps to separate us forever in this dreamlike existence, I wept tears of farewell.

Yuku haru ya	Spring soon ends—
Tori naki uo no	Birds will weep while in
Me wa namida	The eyes of fish are tears.

I set out after composing this poem, the first of my journey, but I could barely go ahead, for when I looked back I saw my friends standing in a row, to watch me perhaps till I should be lost to sight.

This year, 1689, the thought came to me of going on a walking trip to the distant provinces of Oku. It did not matter if I should have the misfortune to grow gray on my travels, for I wanted to see places I had heard so much about but never visited. On the contrary, it seemed to me that I should be fortunate if I managed to come home alive. Leaving the future to decide this uncertainty, I pursued my journey to a town called Sōka, which we were barely able to reach the day of our departure . . .

On the thirtieth of March we stopped at the foot of Nikkō Mountain. The innkeeper told us, "My name is Buddha Gozaemon. People call me Buddha because I am so honest in everything I do, so even if you are staying just for the night, please make yourselves completely at home." Wondering what kind of Buddha had appeared in this world of sin and dust to protect such poor pilgrims as ourselves, I watched our host's actions, and saw that he was ignorant and crude, but of an open and resolute disposition. He was one of those Confucius describes as, "Strong, resolute, simple, and slow to speak—such a one is near to Goodness." His purity of heart was indeed most admirable . . .

When we crossed the Natori River and entered Sendai, it was the day that they celebrate by covering their roofs with irises. We found an inn and stayed four or five days. A painter named Kaemon lives here. I heard he was a person of taste and got to know him. He told me that for years he has been tracing places mentioned in poetry whose whereabouts are now unknown, and spent a whole day showing some to me. The fields of Miyagi were "thick with clover," and I could imagine how lovely they would look in autumn. Now was the time when rhododendrons were blooming in Tamada, in Yokono, and on Azalea Hill. We went into a pine forest which grew so thickly that sunlight could not penetrate the branches. This they call Under-the-Trees. It is because the dew fell thickly in former times too that the poet wrote, "Samurai, tell your lord to take his umbrella!"

We spent one day visiting the Hall of the Healing Buddha, the Amatsu Shrine, and other holy places. Kaemon presented me with sketches of Matsushima, Shiogama and other celebrated spots along our route, and also the parting gift of a pair of straw sandals with dark blue cords. Such attentions showed him to be a person of true refinement.

Ayame kusa	I will bind iris
Ashi ni musuban	Blossoms around my feet—
Waraji no o	Cords for my sandals!

We continued on our way, following a map that Kaemon had drawn for us. At the foot of the mountains which border the narrow road of Oku, the famous To sedge was growing. They say that even now the people of the district present the governor every year with mats made of it. . . .

The urn-shaped monument stands at Taga Castle in the village of Ichimura. It is over six feet high and about three feet wide, I should imagine. An inscription can faintly be seen underneath the moss incrustation. It records the distance to various far-off parts of the country and then adds, "This castle was built in 724 by Ono-Asomi Azumabito, Inspector and Governor General, and repaired in 762 by Emi no Asomi Asakari, Councilor, Commanding General of the Eastern Sea and Eastern Mountain districts, and Governor General. First day of the twelfth moon."

Many are the names that have been preserved for us in poetry from ancient times, but mountains crumble and rivers disappear, new roads replace the old, stones are buried and vanish in the earth, trees grow old and give way to saplings. Time passes and the world changes. The remains of the past are shrouded in uncertainty. And yet, here before my eyes was a monument which none would deny had lasted a thousand years. I felt as if I were looking into the minds of the men of old. "This," I thought, "is one of the pleasures of travel and living to be old." I forgot the weariness of my journey, and was moved to tears for my joy.

We next visited the Tama River of Noda, and Rock-off-the-Shore, places celebrated in poetry. There is a temple on a mountain called Pine-till-the-End. When I saw that the ground between the pines was filled with graves, I was overcome by sadness at the thought that even the most enduring pledge of devotion between husband and wife must come to this. Then, as I reached the Bay of Shiogama, I heard the evening bell toll its message of evanescence.

The sky had cleared a little after a steady rain. Under the faintly shining evening moon the island of Magaki across the water seemed close enough to touch. Little fishing boats were rowing towards the shore, and I could hear the voices of the fishermen as they divided up the catch. I thought to myself with pleasure, "Now at last I understand the poem

Michinoku wa	In Michinoku
Izuku wa aredo	Every place has its charm
Shiogama no	But Shiogama
Ura kogu fune no	When the boats are rowed to shore
Tsunade kanashimo	Is most wonderful of all."

That night I listened to a blind musician play the lute and chant north-country ballads which were quite unlike the usual war tales or dance-songs. The sound of his high-pitched countrified voice close to my pillow was distressing, but it gave me a special satisfaction to think that the traditional way of reciting the old ballads had not been forgotten in this remote place.

Early the next morning we visited the Myōjin Shrine in Shiogama. As rebuilt by the governor of the province, the shrine has imposing pillars, brightly painted rafters, and flight upon flight of stone steps. The morning sun was shining brilliantly on the vermilion lacquered fence around the shrine. I was profoundly impressed by the fact that it was the custom of our country to have shrines which contain the miraculous manifestations of the gods in such remote places, at the very end of the world.

In front of the shrine there is an old iron lantern. A metal door bears the inscription, "Presented by Izumi Saburō in 1187." It was strange how these words evoked for me scenes of five hundred years ago. Izumi was a brave and loyal warrior whose fame has lasted down to our time, and he is held in universal esteem. As it has been truly said, "A man should follow the ways of virtue and be faithful to his duties. Fame will then follow of itself."

It was already about noon. We hired a boat and crossed to Matsushima. After another five miles on the water we arrived at the beach of the island of Ojima.

No matter how often it has been said, it is none the less true that Matsushima is the most beautiful place in Japan, in no way inferior to T'ung-t'ing or the Western Lake in China. The sea curves in from the southeast forming a bay three miles across. The tides flow in with great beauty. There are countless islands. Some rise up and point to the sky; the low-lying ones crawl into the waves. There are islands piled on one another or even stacked three high. To the left the islands stand apart, and to the right rise linked together. Some look like mothers with babes on their backs, and some as if the babes were at their breasts, suggesting all the affection of maternal love. The green of the pines is of a wonderful darkness, and their branches are constantly bent by winds from the sea, so that their crookedness seems to belong to the nature of the trees. The scene suggests all the mysterious charm of a beautiful face. Matsushima must have been made by the God of the Mountains when the world was created. What man could capture with his brush the wonder of this masterpiece of nature?

On Ojima, an island which thrusts out into the sea, are found the remains of the Zen master Ungo's hut, and the rock upon which he used to meditate. Even now I could see under the pine trees a few priests who had abandoned the world. They live in peace in the little thatched huts from which the smoke of fallen leaves and pine cones was rising. I did not know who they were, but I felt drawn to them. As I walked in their direction I could see the moon shining on the sea, and Matsushima bathed in a beauty unlike that of the day. I returned to the beach and took a room in an inn. My room was on the second floor, with an open window looking out on the bay. When I lay down to sleep in the breeze and the clouds, I experienced a feeling of strange pleasure.

I lay down without composing any poem, but could not sleep. I remembered that when I left my old cottage I was presented with a poem in Chinese about Matsushima, and with a Japanese one on Matsugaura Island. I opened my knapsack and made the poems my companions for the night.

On the eleventh we visited the Zuigan Temple. This temple was founded many years ago by the thirty-second Zen abbot, when he returned to Japan after study in China. The seven halls of the temple now shine in gold and blue splendor worthy of Buddha's own dwelling in Paradise.

On the twelfth we set out for Hiraizumi by way of the pine of Anewa and the bridge of Odae, names familiar to me from poetry. The countryside was deserted, and the road no better than a trail that hunters or woodsmen might follow. We lost our way, and finally took entirely the wrong road, to emerge at a harbor called Ishinomaki. Far out across the water we could see Kinka Mountain "where bloom the golden flowers." Hundreds of merchant ships were gathered in the bay. In the town the houses fought for space, and smoke rose continuously from the salt-kilns.

I thought to myself, "I never intended to come anywhere like this . . ." We looked for lodgings for the night, but were refused by everyone. Finally we found a miserable little hut where we passed the night. Early the next morning we set out uncertainly on another unfamiliar road. As we traveled over a long embankment we could see in the distance Sleeve-Crossing, the Colt Pastures, the Vine Fields of Mano, and other places famous in poetry. We skirted the Long Marsh, a depressing place. We stopped for the night at a town called Toima, and then went on to Hiraizumi. We had covered over forty miles, I believe.

The three generations of glory of the Fujiwara of Hiraizumi vanished in the space of a dream. The ruins of their Great Gate are two miles this side of the castle; where once Hidehira's mansion stood are now fields, and only the Golden Cockerel Mountain remains as in former days.

We first climbed up to Castle-on-the-Heights, from where we could see the Kitagami, a large river that flows down from the north. Here Yoshitsune once fortified himself with some picked retainers, but his great glory turned in a moment into this wilderness of grass. "Countries may fall, but their rivers and mountains remain. When spring comes to the ruined castle, the grass is green again."[1] These lines went through my head as I sat on the ground, my bamboo hat spread under me. There I sat weeping, unaware of the passage of time.

Natsugusa ya	The summer grasses—
Tsuwamono domo ga	Of brave soldiers' dreams
Yume no ato	The aftermath.

The holy images were on display in the two halls of the Chūson Temple, known to me already by tales of its wonders. The Sutra Hall contains statues of the three generals of Hiraizumi; in the Golden Hall are their coffins and an enshrined Buddhist trinity. The "seven precious things" had been scattered and lost, the pearl-inlaid doors were broken by the wind, and the pillars fretted with gold were flaked by the frost and snow. Just as I was thinking that soon the temple would crumble and dissolve into grass, I noticed that it had recently been enclosed, and the roof tiled to withstand the wind and rain. A monument of a thousand years will be preserved a while longer.

Samidare no	Have the rains of spring
Furinokoshite ya	Spared you from their onslaught
Hikari-dō	Bright hall of gold?

We lingered to look at the road stretching far off to the north, then stopped at the village of Iwate. We intended to cross into Dewa

[1] From a famous poem by Tu Fu (712-770).

Province through the Barrier of Shitomae. Few travelers journey this road, and we were looked upon with suspicion by the guards at the border. Only with much trouble did we manage to get through.

By the time we had climbed the big mountain there, the sun had already set. Discovering a guard's house, we asked for a place to sleep. For three days a terrible storm raged, and we had no choice but to remain in the mountains.

Nomi shirami	Plagued by fleas and lice
Uma no shito suru	I hear the horses staling—
Makura moto	What a place to sleep!

Our host told us, "The road to Dewa lies through the mountains, and is so badly marked that you had best get a guide to show the way." "Very well," I said, and hired one, a strong young fellow who wore a scimitar at his side and carried an oak stick. He walked ahead and, thinking uneasily that today we were certain to meet with danger, we followed him. The journey was just as our host had described it—high mountains densely overgrown in which not a single bird-cry was heard. It was dark under the trees, so dark that it was like walking at midnight. Feeling as though dust were raining from the edges of the clouds, we pushed our way through clumps of bamboo, crossed streams, and stumbled over rocks, until we finally reached the town of Mogami, our bodies bathed in a cold sweat.

When our guide left us he said with a smile, "Something unpleasant always happens on this road. I was lucky to have been able to lead you here safely." To hear such words, even after our safe arrival, made our hearts pound.

At Obanasawa I called on Seifū, a man of noble aspiration, rich though he is. Since he often visits Kyoto, he knew how it feels to be a traveler, and detained us for several days, showering every attention on us, out of sympathy for our long journey.

Suzushisa wo	Making the coolness
Wa ga yado ni shite	My own dwelling, I lie
Nemaru nari	Completely at ease.

In the domain of Yamagata is a mountain temple called the Ryūshaku, a place noted for its tranquillity. People had urged us "just to take a look," and we had turned back at Obanasawa to make the journey, a distance of about fifteen miles. It was still daylight when we arrived. After asking a priest at the foot of the mountain for permission to spend the night, we climbed to the temple at the summit. Boulders piled on rocks had made this mountain, and old pines and cedars grew on its slopes. The earth and stones were worn and slippery with moss. At the summit the doors of the hall were all shut, and not a sound could be heard. Circling around the cliffs and crawling among the rocks we reached the main temple. In the splendor of the scene and the silence I felt a wonderful peace penetrate my heart.

Shizukasa ya	Such stillness—
Iwa ni shimiiru	The cries of the cicadas
Semi no koe	Sink into the rocks.

After having seen so many splendid views of both land and sea, my heart was stirred by the thought of Kisagata. From the port of Sakata we journeyed to the northeast, climbing over hills, following along the shore, and plodding through the sand, a distance of about twenty miles in all. As the sun was sinking in the sky, a breeze from the sea stirred up the sand, and a misty rain started to fall, hiding Chōkai Mountain. We groped ahead in the darkness. I felt sure that if Kisagata were exquisite in the rain, it would prove no less wonderful when it cleared. We squeezed into a fisherman's thatch-covered hut, and waited for the rain to stop.

The next morning the weather cleared beautifully. When the morning sun rose in all its splendor, we took a boat on the lagoon of Kisagata. We put in first at Nōin Island, where we visited the remains of the hut where Nōin lived in seclusion for three years. On the opposite shore, when we landed from our boat, we saw an old cherry tree, which stands as a memento of Saigyō, who wrote of it:[2]

[2] See page [illegible]

Kisagata no	At Kisagata
Sakura wa nami ni	A cherry tree is covered
Uzumorete	At times by the waves:
Hana no ue kogu	Fishermen must row their boats
Ama no tsuribune	Above the cherry blossoms.

Near the water is a tomb they say is the Empress Jingū's, and the temple standing near it is called the Ebb-and-Flow-Pearl Temple. I had never before heard that the Empress had come to this region. I wonder if it can be true.

Seated within a little room of the temple, I rolled up the bamboo blinds and took in all at once the whole spectacle of Kisagata. To the south loomed Mount Chōkai, supporting the heavens; its image was reflected in the water. I could see the road to the west as far as Muyamuya Barrier, and to the east an embankment along the water, over which the road leads to Akita far in the distance. The sea is to the north. The place where the waves of the sea break into the lagoon is called Tide-crossing. Kisagata is about two miles in either direction.

In appearance Kisagata is much like Matsushima, but there is a difference. Matsushima seems to be smiling, while Kisagata wears a look of sorrow. There is a sadness mingled with the silent calm of Kisagata as though of a troubled soul.

Kisagata ya	Kisagata—
Ame ni Seishi ga	Seishi [3] sleeping in the rain,
Nebu no hana	Wet mimosa blooms. . . .

Today we passed through the most dangerous places in the north country, known as "Parents Forget their Children," "Children Forget their Parents," "Dogs Go Back," and "Colts Return." I was so exhausted that I drew my pillow to me and lay down as soon as we reached an inn. I could hear the voices of young women, probably two of them, talking in a room one removed from ours at the western end of the house. The voice of an old man also joined in the conversation, and I gathered from their words that the women

[3] A famous Chinese beauty (Hsi-shih) known for her mournful expression.

were prostitutes from Niigata. They were on their way to visit the shrine at Ise, and the man had escorted them here, as far as the Barrier of Ichifuri. He was to return the next day, and the women were writing letters and giving him little messages to take back.

"We are wandering by the shores that the white waves wash. Daughters of fishermen, we have fallen to this miserable state. What retribution awaits us for our inconstant vows, the sins we daily commit? We are wretched indeed. . . ." These were the words I heard as I fell asleep.

The next morning, when we were about to start on our journey, the two women approached us in tears, saying, "The sadness of a journey to an uncertain destination leaves us very uneasy and depressed—may we follow behind you, even if out of sight? Grant us this great favor, you who wear priest's garments, and help us to attain the way of the Buddha."

I answered, "I am very sorry, but we have a great many places to visit. You would do much better to go along with some ordinary travelers. You are under the protection of the gods, and I am sure that no harm will come to you." With these words we left, but I could not help feeling sorry for them.

Hitotsu ya ni Under the same roof
Yūjo mo netari Prostitutes too were sleeping—
Hagi to tsuki The moon and clover.

TRANSLATED BY DONALD KEENE

PROSE POEM ON THE UNREAL DWELLING

[*Genjūan no Fu*] *by Matsuo Bashō*

•

My body, now close to fifty years of age, has become an old tree that bears bitter peaches, a snail which has lost its shell, a bagworm separated from its bag; it drifts with the winds and clouds that know no destination. Morning and night I have eaten traveler's fare, and have held out for alms a pilgrim's wallet. On my last journey my face was burnt by the sun of Matsushima, and I wetted my sleeve at the holy mountain. I longed to go as far as that shore where the puffins cry and the Thousand Islands of the Ainu can be seen in the distance, but my companion drew me back, telling how dangerous so long a journey would be with my sickness. I yielded. Then I bruised my heels along the rough coast of the northern sea, where each step in the sand dunes is painful. This year I roamed by the shores of the lake in quest of a place to stay, a single stalk of reed where the floating nest of the grebe might be borne to rest by the current. This is my Unreal Dwelling, and it stands by the mountain called Kokubu. An ancient shrine is near, which so purifies my senses that I feel cleansed of the dust of the world. This abandoned thatched hut was where the uncle of the warrior Suganuma retreated from the world. He went away some eight years ago; his dwelling remains behind at these crossroads of unreality. Indeed it is true that all the delusions of the senses are summed up in the one word *unreality,* and there is no way to forget even for a moment change and its swiftness.

The mountains do not extend to any great depth, but the houses are spaced well apart. Stone Mountain is before my hut, and behind stands Gorge Mountain. From the lofty peaks descends a fragrant wind from the south, and the northern wind steeped in the distant sea is cool. It was the beginning of the fourth moon when I arrived, and the azaleas were still blossoming. Mountain wistaria hung on the pines. Cuckoos frequently flew past, and there were visits from the swallows. Not a peck from a woodpecker disturbed me, and in my joy I called to the wood dove, "Come, bird of solitude, and make me melancholy!" I could not but be happy—the view would not have blushed before the loveliest scenes of China.

Between Hieda Mountain and the peak of Hira, I can see the pine of Karasaki engulfed in mist, and at times a castle glittering in the trees; when the rain clears by the bridge of Seta, sunset lingers in the pine groves. Mikami Mountain looks like Fuji, and reminds me of my old cottage at its foot. Nearby on Tanagami Mountain I have sought the traces of the men of old. Sometimes, wishing to enjoy an uninterrupted view, I climb the peak behind my hut. On the summit I have built a shelf of pine boughs, on which I spread a round straw mat: this I call the "monkey's perch." I am no follower of that eccentric who built a nest in a crab-apple tree where he drank with his friends, for that was in the city and noisy; nor would I give up my perch for the hut which Wang the Sage once tied together. On the lofty summit I sit, picking lice.

Once in a while, when I feel energetic, I gather firewood and dip spring water. I love the drops which fall tok-tok along the green of a single spray of fern, and nothing is so light as my stove.

The man who used to live here had most refined tastes, and did not clutter up the hut even with objects of art. Apart from the household shrine there is just the little alcove for hanging nightclothes. Once, when he heard that the High Priest of Mount Kora was in the capital, he asked him for a plaque to decorate the alcove. The priest nonchalantly took his brush in hand and wrote the words "Unreal Dwelling." On the back he inscribed his name to serve as a memento to later people who might see it.

In this hut where I live as a hermit, as a passing traveler, there is no need to accumulate household possessions. All I have is a broad-brimmed hat of nettle wood and a rush raincoat, which I hang on a post above my pillow. During the day the old gentleman who looks after the shrine or villagers from the foot of the mountain come here and pass the day in stories of a kind to which I am unaccustomed, how boars are grubbing up the rice seedlings, or about rabbits infesting the bean fields. Or when, as very rarely happens, visitors come from afar, we sit calmly at night, the moonlight our companion, arguing with our shadows.

But I should not have it thought from what I have said that I am devoted to solitude and seek only to hide my traces in the wilderness. Rather, I am like a sick man weary of people, or someone who is tired of the world. What is there to say? I have not led a clerical life, nor have I served in normal pursuits. Ever since I was very young I have been fond of my eccentric ways, and once I had come to make them the source of a livelihood, temporarily I thought, I discovered myself bound for life to the one line of my art, incapable and talentless as I am. I labor without results, am worn of spirit and wrinkled of brow. Now, when autumn is half over, and every morning and each evening brings changes to the scene, I wonder if that is not what is meant by dwelling in unreality. And here too I end my words.

TRANSLATED BY DONALD KEENE

CONVERSATIONS WITH KYORAI

[*Kyoraishō*] *by Mukai Kyorai*

The brevity and apparent simplicity of the seventeen-syllabled haiku *led to its wide popularity in Japan, where only a very inarticulate person remained incapable of an extemporary verse. However, in the hands of its masters, the* haiku, *far from representing an impromptu reaction to the sights of nature, was usually a highly conscious form of verse, demanding compliance with exacting aesthetic principles. Bashō (1644-94) was famous not only as the supreme* haiku *poet, but as the foremost interpreter of its theories. His conversations with his pupil Kyorai (1651-1704) contain a fair sample of his views. Some of them are translated below.*

The method employed by Kyorai in demonstrating various facets of "the Master's" opinions was to give a verse, either a haiku *or a fourteen-syllabled "second verse"* (waki), *and then report what the Master said about it. The notes in brackets are intended to help elucidate special points.*

•

[*One of the ideals of the* haiku *was to have each word indispensable and inalterable, no doubt a product of the brevity of the form. In the following conversation a critic suggests that the wording of a poem by Bashō might have been changed.*]

Yuku haru wo	The departing spring
Ōmi no hito to	With the men of Ōmi
Oshimikeru	Have I lamented.

Bashō

The Master said, "Shōhaku criticized this poem on the grounds that I might just as well have said "Tamba" instead of "Ōmi," or "departing year" instead of "departing spring." How does this criticism strike you?" Kyorai replied, "Shōhaku's criticism completely misses the mark. What could be more natural than to regret the passing of the spring, when the waters of the Lake of Ōmi are veiled so enchantingly in mist? Besides, it is especially fitting in a poem written by one like yourself who is living by the lake." The Master said, "Yes, the poets of old loved spring in this province almost as much as in Kyoto." Kyorai, deeply struck by these words, continued, "If you were in Ōmi at the close of the year, why should you regret its passing? Or, if you were in Tamba at the end of spring, you would not be likely to have such feelings. What truth there is in the poetry of a man who has been genuinely stirred by some sight of nature!" The Master said, "Kyorai, you are a person with whom I can talk about poetry." He was very pleased.

• •

Kiyotaki ya	Clear cascades!
Nami ni chiri naki	In the waves immaculate,
Natsu no tsuki	The summer moon.

Bashō

One day when the Master was lying on his sickbed in Osaka, he called me to him and said, "This verse resembles one I composed not long ago at Sonome's house:

Shiragiku no	The white chrysanthemum
Me ni tatete miru	Even when lifted to the eye
Chiri mo nashi	Remains immaculate.

I have therefore changed the 'Clear cascades' verse to:

Kiyotaki ya	Clear cascades!
Nami ni chirikomu	Into the waves scatter
Aomatsuba	Blue pine needles.

The rough draft of the original version must be in Yamei's house. Please destroy it." But it was too late—the poem had already appeared in several collections.

. .

[*"The Monkey's Cloak"* (Sarumino) *was a collection of verse by Bashō and members of his school, published in 1691. In the following, Bashō is struck by the words "skylark of Akashi" because of the graceful allusion to another poem.*]

Omokaji ya	Port the helm!
Akashi no tomari	There, by Akashi harbor,
Hototogisu	A skylark!

Kakei

This poem was being considered for inclusion in "The Monkey's Cloak." Kyorai said, "It's just like the Master's

No wo yoko ni	Across the fields
Uma hikimuke yo	Turn the horse's head—
Hototogisu	A skylark!

It should not be included." The Master said, "The 'skylark of Akashi' is not a bad image." Kyorai replied, "I don't know about the 'skylark of Akashi,' but the poem merely substitutes a boat for a horse. It shows no originality." The Master commented, "He hasn't made any advance in the conception of the verse, but you may include it or not as you please on the basis of the Akashi skylark." We finally did not include it.

. .

[*The art of making a* haiku *from a trifling incident.*]

Kiraretaru	Stabbed to death!
Yume wa makoto ka	Was my dream true?
Nomi no ato	The marks of a flea.

Kikaku

Kyorai said, "Kikaku is really a clever writer. Who else would ever have thought of writing a poem merely about being bitten by a flea?" The Master said, "You're quite right. He deals with trifling matters in a most eloquent way." This criticism seemed to me to describe Kikaku's art completely.

• •

[*Bashō likens himself to a wild duck stricken while in flight; a fisherman's hearth has not only crickets but shrimps.*]

Yamu kari no	A sick wild duck
Yosamu ni ochite	Falling in the evening cold—
Tabine ka na	These traveler's lodgings!

Bashō

Ama no ya wa	The fisherman's hut—
Koebi ni majiru	Mixed with little shrimps
Itodo ka na	Some crickets!

Bashō

When we were compiling "The Monkey's Cloak" we were asked to choose one of these two poems for inclusion. Bonchō said, "The verse about the sick wild duck is good, but the other about the crickets mixing with the little shrimps has a freshness which makes it truly outstanding." Kyorai answered, "The verse about the shrimps is unusual, but had I noticed the scene in the fisherman's hut I could have written it myself. The one about the wild duck, on the other hand, is so noble in tone, so subtly perceptive, that I wonder how anyone could have conceived it." After some discussion we finally asked permission to include both verses. The Master later said, laughing, "You seem to have argued yourselves into thinking that a sick duck and a little shrimp have about equal value."

• •

[*In the attempt to make the* haiku *as suggestive as possible, deliberately ambiguous language was often used. Here, however, Bashō discovers a meaning in Kyorai's poem which the author did not think of.*]

Iwahana ya	The tips of the crags—
Koko ni mo hitori	Here too is someone,
Tsuki no kyaku	Guest of the moon.

Kyorai

Kyorai said, "Shadō thinks that the last line should be 'monkey of the moon,' but I think that 'guest' is better." The Master said, "How can he suggest such a word as 'monkey'? What had you in mind when you wrote the poem?" Kyorai answered, "One night, when I was walking in the mountains by the light of the harvest moon, composing poetry as I went along, I noticed another poet standing by the crags." The Master said, "How much more interesting a poem it would be if by the lines 'Here too is someone, guest of the moon' you meant yourself. You must be the subject of the verse."

• •

[*Shimokyō was a very quiet district of Kyoto.*]

Shimokyō ya	Shimokyō!
Yuki tsumu ue no	On the piled-up snow
Yo no ame	The night rain.

Bonchō

This verse at first lacked an opening line, and everyone from the Master downward tried to think of one. At length the Master settled on the above line. Bonchō said "yes" to it, but still didn't seem satisfied. The Master said, "Bonchō, why don't you think of a better opening line? If you do, I'll never write another *haiku.*" Kyorai said, "Anyone can see how good a line it is, but it's not so easy to appreciate that no other line would do. If members of some other school heard what you said, they would think that you were ridiculously pleased with yourself, and they would make up any number of opening lines. But the ones which they considered to be good would seem laughably bad to us."

• •

[*The difference in subjects suited to the classical* waka *and the* haiku.]

Inoshishi no	Is that the path
Ne ni yuku kata ya	The wild boar travels to his lair?
Ake no tsuki	The moon at dawning.

Kyorai

When I asked the Master what he thought of this verse, he pondered for a long time without saying whether it was good or bad. I mistakenly thought that, master though he was, he didn't know how hunters wait at night for a boar to return to his lair at dawn, and I explained it all to him in great detail. Then he remarked, "The interest of that sight was familiar even to the poets of former times. That is why we have the *waka:*

Akenu to te	Now that it has dawned
Nobe yori yama ni	A wind from the clover
Iru shika no	Wafts away the spoor
Ato fukiokuru	Of the deer returning
Hagi no uwakaze	From the fields to their mountains.

When a subject can be treated even within the elegant framework of the *waka,* there does not seem to be much point in giving so prosy a description within the freer compass of the *haiku*. The reason why I stopped to think for a while was that the verse seemed somehow interesting, and I was wondering if something couldn't be done with it. But I fear it's hopeless."

. .

[*Kyorai takes Bashō too literally.*]

Yūsuzumi	The evening cool—
Senki okoshite	I got lumbago,
Kaerikeri	And went back home.

Kyorai

When I was first studying *haiku* I asked the Master how to write an opening verse. He replied, "It must be written firmly and clearly." As a test of my abilities I composed the above verse. When I asked his opinion of it, he gave a great laugh and said, "You still haven't got the idea!"

• •

[*Bashō's technique in linked-verse demonstrated: by evoking the excitement caused by the blossoming of the cherry tree he gives a most dramatic picture of the arrival of spring in a dark wood.*]

Kuromite takaki	Somber and tall
Kashi no ki no mori	The forest of oaks
Saku hana ni	In and out
Chiisaki mon wo	Through the little gate
Detsu iritsu	To the cherry blossoms.

Bashō

When the former verse was given, I thought how difficult it would be to add a verse about cherry blossoms without destroying the image of the forest of oaks. When I asked the Master to add such a verse, this was how he did it.

TRANSLATED BY DONALD KEENE

HAIKU BY BASHŌ AND HIS SCHOOL

Haranaka ya
mono ni mo tsukazu
naku hibari

On the moor: from things
detached completely—
how the skylark sings!

Kane tsukanu
mura wa nani wo ka
haru no kure

A village where they ring
no bells!—oh, what *do* they do
at dusk in spring?

Chō tori no
shiranu hana ari
aki no sora

To bird and butterfly
it is unknown, this flower here:
the autumn sky.

Ara umi ya
Sado ni yokotau
ama-no-gawa

How rough a sea!
and, stretching over Sado Isle,
the Galaxy. . . .

Yagate shinu
keshiki wa miezu
semi no koe

Very soon they die—
but of that there is no sign
in the locust-cry.

Hiya-hiya to
kabe wo fumaete
hirune kana

How very cool it feels:
taking a noonday nap, to have
this wall against my heels.

Invitation to Etsujin

Futari mishi
yuki wa kotoshi mo
furikeru ka

Snow that we two
saw together—this year
is it fallen anew?

Inazuma ya
yami no kata yuku
goi no koe

A sudden lightning gleam:
off into the darkness goes
the night heron's scream.

Tabi ni yande
yume wa kareno wo
kakemeguru

On a journey, ill—
and my dreams, on withered fields
are wandering still.

Matsuo Bashō (1644-1694)

• •

Yado no haru
nanimo naki koso
nanimo are

My hut, in spring:
true, there is nothing in it—
there is Everything!

Yamaguchi Sodō (1642-1716)

• •

Kojiki kana
Tenchi wo kitaru
natsugoromo

There a beggar goes!
Heaven and Earth he's wearing
for his summer clothes!

Neko ni kuwareshi wo
semi no tsuma wa
sudakuran

Eaten by the cat!
Perhaps the cricket's widow
is bewailing that.

Meigetsu ya
tatami no ue ni
matsu no kage

Bright the full moon shines:
here upon the matted floor,
shadows of the pines.

Enomoto Kikaku (1661-1707)

• •

No mo yama mo
yuki ni torareta
nani mo nashi

Mountains and plains,
all are taken by the snow—
nothing remains.

Naitō Jōsō (1661-1704)

TRANSLATED BY HAROLD G. HENDERSON

CHIKAMATSU ON THE ART OF THE PUPPET STAGE

[*from Naniwa Miyage*] *by Hozumi Ikan*

The art of the puppet stage has probably reached greater heights in Japan than elsewhere in the world, and it was the medium for which Chikamatsu Monzaemon (1653-1725), the greatest Japanese dramatist, wrote his masterpieces. The following account of Chikamatsu's views on the jōruri, *or puppet stage, was written after his death, in 1738, by a friend. It is one of the most important examples of dramatic criticism in the literature.*

•

This is what Chikamatsu told me when I visited him many years ago:

Jōruri differs from other forms of fiction in that, since it is primarily concerned with puppets, the words must all be living and full of action. Because *jōruri* is performed in theatres that operate in close competition with those of the *kabuki,* which is the art of living actors, the author must impart to lifeless wooden puppets a variety of emotions, and attempt in this way to capture the interest of the audience. It is thus generally very difficult to write a work of great distinction.

Once when I was young and reading a story about the court,[1] I came across a passage which told how, on the occasion of a festival, the snow had fallen heavily and piled up. An order was given to a guard to clear away the snow from an orange tree. When this happened, the pine next to it, apparently resentful that its boughs were still bent with snow, recoiled its branches. This was a stroke of the pen which gave life to the inanimate tree. It did so because

1 "The Tale of Genji." The particular reference is to a passage in the chapter translated by Waley as "The Village of Falling Flowers."

the spectacle of the pine, resentful that the snow had been cleared from the orange tree, recoiling its branches and shaking off the snow that bends it down, is one which creates the feeling of a living, moving thing. Is that not so?

From this model I learned how to put life into my *jōruri*. Thus, even descriptive passages like the *michiyuki*,[2] to say nothing of the narrative phrases and dialogue, must be charged with feeling or they will be greeted with scant applause. This is the same thing as what is called evocative power in poetry. For example, if a poet should fail to bring emotion to his praise of even the superb scenery of Matsushima or Miyajima in his poem, it would be like looking at the carelessly drawn portrait of a beautiful woman. For this reason, it should be borne in mind that feeling is the basis of writing.

When a composition is filled with particles, its literary quality is somehow lowered. Authors of no merit inevitably try to cast their writings exactly in the form of *waka* or linked-verse, stringing together alternating lines of five and seven syllables. This naturally results in the use of many unnecessary particles. For example, when one should say *"Toshi mo yukanu musume wo,"* they say such things as *"Toshiha mo yukanu, musume wo ba."* This comes from concerning one's self with the syllable count, and naturally causes the language to sound vulgar. Thus, while verse is generally written by arranging long and short lines in order, the *jōruri* is basically a musical form, and the length of the lines recited is therefore determined by the melody. If an author adheres implicitly to the rules of metrics, his lines may prove awkward to recite. For this reason I am not concerned with metrics in my writings and I use few particles.

The old *jōruri* was just like our modern street storytelling,[3] and was without either flower or fruit. From the time I first began to write *jōruri*, I have used care in my works, which was not true of the old *jōruri*. As a result, the medium was raised considerably. For

[2] The journey, such as that of the lovers in "The Love Suicides at Sonezaki." See page 404.

[3] These were popular recitations of ballads, gossip, etc., which flourished particularly about this time.

example, inasmuch as the nobility, the samurai, and the lower classes all have different social stations, it is essential that they be distinguished in their representation from their appearance down to their speech. Similarly, even within the same samurai class, there are both daimyō and retainers, as well as others of lower rank, each rank possessed of its distinct qualities; such differences must be established. This is because it is essential that they be well pictured in the emotions of the reader.

In writing *jōruri,* one attempts first to describe facts as they really are, but in so doing one writes things which are not true, in the interest of art. In recent plays many things have been said by female characters which real women could not utter. Such things fall under the heading of art; it is because they say what could not come from a real woman's lips that their true emotions are disclosed. If in such cases the author were to model his character on the ways of a real woman and conceal her feelings, such realism, far from being admired, would permit no pleasure in the work. Thus, if one examines a play without paying attention to the question of art, one will certainly criticize it for containing many unpleasant words which are not suitable for women. But such things should be considered art. In addition, there are numerous instances in the portrayal of a villain as excessively cowardly, or of a clown as funny, which are outside the truth and which must be regarded as art. The spectator must bear this consideration in mind.

There are some who, thinking that pathos is essential to a *jōruri,* make frequent use of such expressions as "It was touching" in their writing, or who when chanting do so in voices thick with tears. This is foreign to my style. I take pathos to be entirely a matter of restraint. It is moving when the whole of a play is controlled by the dramatic situation, and the stronger and firmer the melody and words, the sadder will be the impression created. For this reason, when one says of something which is sad that it is sad, one loses the implications, and in the end, even the impression of sadness is slight. It is essential that one not say of a thing that "it is sad," but that it be sad of itself. For example, when one praises a place renowned for its scenery such as Matsushima by saying, "Ah, what a fine view!" one has said in one phrase all that one can about the sight, but without effect. If one wishes to praise the view, and one says numerous things indirectly about its appearance, the quality of the view may be known of itself, without one's having to say, "It is a fine view." This is true of everything of its kind.

Someone said, "People nowadays will not accept plays unless they are realistic and well reasoned out. There are many things in the old stories which people will not now tolerate. It is thus that such people as *kabuki* actors are considered skilful to the degree that their acting resembles reality. The first consideration is to have the retainer in the play resemble a real retainer, and to have the daimyō look like a real daimyō. People will not stand for childish nonsense as they did in the past." I answered, "Your view seems plausible, but it is a theory which does not take into account the real methods of art. Art is something which lies in the slender margin between the real and the unreal. Of course it seems desirable, in view of the current taste for realism, to have the retainer in the play copy the gestures and speech of a real retainer, but in that case should a real retainer put rouge and powder on his face like an actor? Or, would it prove entertaining if an actor, on the grounds that real retainers do not make up their faces, were to appear on the stage and perform with his beard growing wild and his head shaven? This is what I mean by the slender margin between the real and the unreal. It is unreal, and yet it is not unreal; it is real, and yet it is not real. Entertainment lies between the two."

In this connection, there is the story of a certain court lady who had a lover. The two loved each other very passionately, but the lady lived far deep in the women's palace, and the man could not visit her quarters. She could see him therefore only very rarely, from between the cracks of her screen of state at the court. She longed for him so desperately that she had a wooden image carved of the man. Its appearance was not like that of an ordinary doll, but did not differ in any particle from the man. It goes without saying that the color of his complexion was perfectly rendered; even the pores of his skin were delineated. The openings in his ears and nostrils were fashioned, and there was no discrepancy even in the number of teeth in the mouth. Since it was made with the man posing beside it, the only difference between the man and this doll was the presence in one, and the absence in the other, of a soul. However, when the lady drew the doll close to her and looked at it, the exactness of the reproduction of the living man chilled her, and she felt unpleasant and rather frightened. Court lady that she was, her love was also chilled, and as she found it distressing to have the doll by her side, she soon threw it away.

In view of this we can see that if one makes an exact copy of a living being, even if it happened to be Yang Kuei-fei, one will become disgusted with it. If when one paints an image or carves it of wood there are, in the name of artistic license, some stylized parts in a work otherwise resembling the real form; this is, after all, what people love in art. The same is true of literary composition. While bearing resemblance to the original, it should have stylization; this makes it art, and is what delights men's minds. Theatrical dialogue written with this in mind is apt to be worth while.

TRANSLATED BY DONALD KEENE

THE LOVE SUICIDES AT SONEZAKI

[*Sonezaki Shinju*] *by Chikamatsu Monzaemon*

During the fourth moon of 1703 an assistant in the Osaka firm of Hirano committed suicide with a prostitute named Ohatsu within the grounds of the Sonezaki Shrine. Within a fortnight Chikamatsu's play based on this incident was being performed by puppets at the Takemoto Theatre. This is the first of his plays about love suicides, and one of his greatest works. The poetry of the journey of the two lovers is particularly famous, and is in fact one of the most beautiful passages in all of Japanese literature. In this translation the parts sung by the chanter are rendered in verse with a few minor exceptions, while the parts spoken by him for the puppets are in prose.

•

Scene I: The Ikutama Shrine

NARRATOR: A graceful young man who had served his term
As an apprentice in the firm of Hirano,
His breast burning with passion concealed
Lest billowing scandal should spread,
Given sometimes to one cup of wine,
And known for his elegant locks,
Renowned as expert in matters of love,
But now like fragrant wood buried,
A mere clerk selling sauces and oil,
And making the round of his clients
Followed by a boy who bears a dripping cask,
Now comes he to Ikutama Shrine.
From inside a teahouse, a woman's voice
Cries, "Tokubei, Tokubei, is it not you?"
She claps her hands; he nods in recognition.

TOKUBEI (*to the boy*): Chōzō, I'll be following presently, but I want you now to call on the temples in Tera Street, make the round of the uptown mansions, and then go back to the shop. Tell them that I'll be back soon. Don't fail to call at the dyer's in Azuchi Street and collect the money he owes us. And stay away from Dōtombori.[1]

NARRATOR: He watches as long as the boy remains in sight
Then lifts up the bamboo blinds.

TOKUBEI: Ohatsu, did you call me? What's the matter?

NARRATOR: He starts to remove his bamboo hat.

OHATSU: Please don't take off your hat. I have a customer today from the country, who's making the round of the Thirty-three Temples of Kwannon. He's been telling everyone that he won't stop drinking before night. At the moment he's off at the theatre, but if he should return and find you here, he might cause trouble. Even the chair-bearers all recognize you, so please keep your face covered.

I've been so worried of late, not having had a single word from you. I couldn't very well go to your shop to ask what had happened to you, but I must have called a hundred times at the other teahouses. They didn't have any news of you either, but one of the musicians asked his friends about you, and they told him you had gone back to the country. I couldn't believe it was true. It has really been a terrible experience. Didn't you even wish to learn what had happened to me? Was that the way you wanted things to end between us? I've been sick with worry. If you think I'm making it up, just feel this swelling!

NARRATOR: His hand she takes and clasps against her breast,
And weeps reproachful and entreating tears
Exactly like a proper wedded wife:
Man though he is, he also weeps aloud.

TOKUBEI: All that you say is true, perfectly true, but what good would it have done to tell you and make you unhappy? The misery I've suffered since we met last is such that even if New Year and every other holiday in the calendar came all at once they

[1] A street in Osaka famed for its theatres and houses of pleasure.

couldn't cause more commotion. My mind has been in a turmoil; my finances are in complete chaos. That is why I went to Kyoto and couldn't get in touch with you. By some miracle my life has been prolonged, but in such a way that if they put it on the stage the audiences would weep.

NARRATOR: His words run out, and he can only sigh.

OHATSU: Are you joking? Why have you kept so trivial a thing from me? You must have had some more serious reason for hiding. Why don't you tell me?

NARRATOR: She clings to his knees and bitter tears
Soak her dainty handkerchief.

TOKUBEI: Stop your weeping. It wasn't that I was hiding anything. Even if I had told you, it wouldn't have served any useful purpose. At any rate, my worries have now largely been settled, and I can tell you about them.

My master has always treated me with particular kindness because I'm his nephew, and for my part I've served him with absolute honesty. There's never been a penny's discrepancy in the accounts. It's true that recently when I bought on credit a couple of yards of silk, I used his name, but that's the one and only time I've done so, and even if I have to return the money at once, I can sell the clothes back without a loss. My master, noticing how honest I am, proposed that I marry his wife's niece. He said he would give me a dowry of two *kamme* of silver, which would permit me to set up in business for myself. But how could I shift my affections to somebody else when I have you? While things were still undecided, my mother—she's really my stepmother—talked things over with my uncle without my knowing about it, and then went back to the country with the money in her clutches. Innocent fool that I am, I hadn't the slightest suspicion of this.

The trouble began last month when they tried to force me to marry. I got angry and said, "Master, I don't understand you. In spite of my unwillingness to get married, you've bribed my old mother into giving her consent. You've gone too far, Master. I can't understand the mistress's attitude either. Just imagine if I were to accept this young lady, whom I've always treated with the utmost deference, as my wife, with dowry and all—I should spend my whole life fawning on her. How could I possibly assert myself? It goes against me so much that even were my dead father to rise from his grave and command me to marry, I should still be unwilling."

The master was furious at my long argument and angrily said, "I know your real reasons. You're involved with Ohatsu, or whatever her name is, from the Temma Teahouse, and that's why you are so averse to marrying my wife's niece. Very well—after what's been said, I'm no longer willing to give you the girl, and since there's to be no marriage, return the money. Settle the account by the seventh of April at the latest. Now get out of here and never set foot in Osaka again."

I too felt my manhood rise. "Right you are!" I cried and left at once for my village. But when I got there I found that my so-called mother wouldn't release the money from her grasp, not even if this world turned into the next. I went to Kyoto to borrow from the wholesale sauce and oil merchants in the Fifth Ward, who are friends of mine and would normally be glad to lend me money, but as ill luck would have it, they didn't have any to spare. I went back again to the country, and finally, by getting the whole village to plead on my behalf, I managed to extract the money from my mother. Now I intend to pay back the dowry and settle things once and for all. But if I can't stay here in Osaka, how shall I be able to meet you?

Though my bones be crushed to powder, though my flesh be torn away, and like an empty shell I sink in the slime of Shijimi River,[2] if I am parted from you, what shall I do?

NARRATOR: Thus suffocated by his grief he weeps.

Ohatsu seeks to hold the tears that well,
Imparting to him all the strength she has.

OHATSU: How you've suffered! And when I think that it's all been on account of me, I'm happy, sad, and most grateful all at once. But you must be more courageous. Even if your uncle has forbidden you to set foot in Osaka, you haven't committed robbery or

[2] The word *shijimi* means a kind of small shellfish, and the name of the river should be understood in that sense here and at the beginning of Scene II.

arson—there must be some way for you to stay here, and I shall discover it. And if a time should come when we can no longer meet, did our promises of love hold only for this world? There have been those before us who have chosen death. At the Mountain of Death, by the River of Three Ways,[3] none will hinder and none will be hindered in love.

NARRATOR: Amidst these words of strong encouragement
She falters, choked by tears, and then resumes

OHATSU: The seventh is tomorrow. Return the money quickly, since you must hand it over in any case. In that way you may get into your uncle's good graces again.

TOKUBEI: I agree with you, and I'm impatient to give it back. But on the twenty-eighth of last month Kuheiji the oil merchant, whom you know, implored me to lend him the money. He said he needed it just for one day, and promised to return it on the morning of the third. I decided to lend the money to him since I didn't need it until the seventh, and it was for a friend as close to me as a brother. He didn't get in touch with me on the third or the fourth, and yesterday he was out and I couldn't get to see him. I intended to call on him this morning, but I've spent the whole time making the rounds of my customers in order to wind up all my business by tomorrow. I'll go see him tonight and settle things. He's a decent fellow and he knows the predicament I'm in. I can't imagine that anything will go wrong. Don't worry, Ohatsu!

NARRATOR: "Hatsuse is far away,
So is Naniwa-dera;
The sounds of the temple bells
At many famous places
Are voices of the Eternal Law.
If, on an evening in spring
One visits a mountain shrine
One sees . . ." but who comes now singing?[4]

[3] A mountain and a river in the Japanese afterworld.

[4] A passage from the *Nō* play *"Miidera,"* here quoted mainly because the first word, *"Hatsuse,"* echoes the name Ohatsu in the preceding line. Most of this passage would be sung not by one chanter but by a chorus, as in the *Nō* play.

TOKUBEI: Oh, Kuheiji! You certainly are a bold rascal! What business have you running off on pleasure excursions when you still haven't got in touch with me? Today we settle accounts.

NARRATOR: He takes Kuheiji's arm and holds him back.

Kuheiji's face betrays his irritation.

KUHEIJI: What are you talking about, Tokubei? These people with me are all residents of the ward, and we've just been to a meeting to raise funds for pilgrimages to Ise. We had a bit to drink, but now we're on the way home. What do you mean by grabbing my arm? Don't be rowdy.

TOKUBEI: I'm not being rowdy. All I want is for you to return the two *kamme* of silver you borrowed from me on the twenty-eighth of last month, which you were supposed to repay on the third.

NARRATOR: Before he can even finish his words

Kuheiji bursts into a roar of laughter.

KUHEIJI: Have you gone crazy, Tokubei? In all the years I've known you I can't remember having borrowed a penny from you. Don't accuse me of anything or you'll regret it.

NARRATOR: He shakes himself loose, then he and his friends

Whip off their bamboo hats.

Tokubei changes color in amazement.

TOKUBEI: None of that, Kuheiji! You came weeping to me, saying that if you couldn't borrow the money to tide you over the end of the month you would go bankrupt, and so, even though the money is indispensable to me in my present predicament, I lent it to you to prove my friendship. I thought that it was one of those occasions we always used to talk about. I told you that I wouldn't even need a receipt, but you insisted on putting your seal to one, just to keep things straight. Don't deny it, Kuheiji!

NARRATOR: Tokubei with bloodshot eyes upbraids him.

KUHEIJI: What's that? I'd like to see just which seal it is.

TOKUBEI: Do you think I'm afraid to show you?

NARRATOR: He draws it forth from his inside pocket.

TOKUBEI: If these gentlemen are from the ward, I am sure that they will recognize your seal. Will you still dispute it?

NARRATOR: When he unfolds the paper and displays it
Kuheiji claps his hands in recollection.

KUHEIJI: Yes, it's my seal all right. Oh, Tokubei, I never thought that you would do such a thing, not even if you were starving and forced to eat dirt. Know then, that on the twenty-fifth of last month I lost a wallet containing my seal. I put up notices everywhere advertising for it, but without any success, so as of this month—as I've already informed these gentlemen—I changed my seal. Could I possibly have affixed my seal to a paper on the twenty-eighth when I lost it on the twenty-fifth? No—what happened was that you picked it up, wrote a promissory note, and then put my seal to it. And now you are trying to extort money from me. That makes you a worse criminal than a forger. You would do better, Tokubei, to commit out-and-out robbery. You deserve to have your head cut off, but for old times' sake, I'll forgive you. Now see if you can get any money out of this.

NARRATOR: He throws the note in Tokubei's face
And glares at him in feigned innocence.
Tokubei is filled with rage and cries aloud.

TOKUBEI: You've been damned clever. You've put one over on me. Oh, what mortification! What am I to do? Am I supposed to let you get away shamelessly with my money? You've planned everything so cleverly that even if I go to court I'm sure to lose. I'll take it back with my fists!

Look here! You're dealing with Tokubei of the firm of Hirano, a man with a sense of honor. Do you get me? I'm not someone to cheat a friend out of his money. Come on, let's have it out!

NARRATOR: He seizes hold of Kuheiji.

KUHEIJI: You insolent little apprentice! I'll knock that out of you.

NARRATOR: Kuheiji grabs him by the front of his kimono,
And they exchange some hard and heavy blows.
Ohatsu, barefoot, rushes up to them.

OHATSU: I beg you everybody, help stop them! I think I know the men who are fighting. Where are my chair-bearers? Why doesn't somebody stop them? Oh—it's Tokubei!

NARRATOR: She writhes in anguish but is powerless.
Her customer, country bumpkin that he is,
Bundles her into a palanquin and says,
"There's no point in your getting hurt."

OHATSU: No, please, just wait a moment! Oh, I'm so unhappy.

NARRATOR: Leaving only her tearful voice behind,
The palanquin is rushed back to her house.
Tokubei is all alone;
Kuheiji has his five companions.
The teahouse owners, anxious for their trade,
Drive them with sticks as far as Lotus Pond.
Who tramples him? Who beats him? One cannot tell.
His hair is disheveled, his sash undone,
Again and again he stumbles and falls.

TOKUBEI: Kuheiji, you swine! Do you think you're going to escape alive?

NARRATOR: He staggers about searching for him,
But Kuheiji has fled and vanished.
Tokubei falls heavily in his tracks,
And weeping bitter tears, he cries aloud.

TOKUBEI (*to the bystanders*): I no longer have the face to appear before you. I'm ashamed of myself. I didn't say a word about Kuheiji but was the truth. I've always thought of him as a brother, and when he came weeping to me, saying he would never forget my kindness as long as he lived, I gave him the money so that it would help both of us, even though I knew that if I didn't have it tomorrow, the seventh, I would have no choice but death. He made me write the note in my own hand and put his seal to it, but it was a seal which he had already reported as lost. Now he has turned the tables on me. Oh, it's humiliating and mortifying to be thus kicked and beaten, unable to assert my manhood or to redeem my debt. I wouldn't have regretted it if I had died after tearing and biting him to death.

NARRATOR: He strikes the ground and gnashes his teeth,
Clenches his fists and laments aloud,
And all who watch are struck with sympathy.

TOKUBEI: There is no sense in my going on talking like this. Before three days have passed I, Tokubei, will make amends and show to all of Osaka the purity of my heart.

NARRATOR: The meaning of these words is later known.

TOKUBEI: I have bothered you all a great deal. Please forgive me.

NARRATOR: He speaks these words apologetically,
Picks up his battered hat and puts it on,
His face downcast in the sinking rays of the sun
Clouded by the tears in which he is plunged,
Dejectedly he makes his way back home,
A sight so sad that all avert their eyes.

Scene II: Inside the Temma Teahouse

NARRATOR: The breezes of love are clamorous
Where Shijimi River flows, and the denizens
Like empty shells, bereft of their senses,
Wander the dark ways of love lit each night
By burning lanterns, fireflies that glow
The four seasons, stars that shine every night,
By Plum Bridge, which blossoms even in summer,[5]
Rustics on a visit, city connoisseurs
All following the twisting roads of love,
Where wise men may get lost and fools get by;
Behold the new gay quarter's liveliness!

But pitiful indeed is Ohatsu
Of Temma Teahouse, after she returns,
Nought can she think of but the day's events,
She cannot drink her saké, her spirits are low,
And as she sits weeping, some courtesans
And others of the quarter come up to her.

FIRST COURTESAN: Ohatsu, have you heard about it? They say that Tokubei was given a thrashing for something bad he did. Is it true?

[5] Umeda Bridge, the name of which means "plum field."

SECOND COURTESAN: No, I had it from a customer that he was trampled to death.

NARRATOR: They say Tokubei was fettered for fraud,
Or trussed for counterfeiting someone's seal,
Not one decent thing have they to report:
Every question of condolence brings her grief.

OHATSU: Oh, please don't say any more. The more I hear the worse my breast pains me. I think that I'll be the first to die. I wish that I were dead already.

NARRATOR: She gives herself to tears, then with one hand
She brushes them away and looks outside—
There in the dark, with covered face, is Tokubei.
At just a glimpse of his anxious, furtive form
Her heart leaps and she wants to rush to him,
But in the back room are the master and his wife,
And by the front gate stands the cook,
While in the garden sharp-eyed waits the maid.

OHATSU: I'm feeling so oppressed. I think I'll step out for a breath of air.

NARRATOR: She steals out softly.

OHATSU: What has happened to you? I've heard all kinds of rumors and I've been so worried I've almost gone crazy.

NARRATOR: She lifts his hat and gazes at his face,
And weeps without a sound, in silent grief,
Sad and painful tears—he too is lost in tears.

TOKUBEI: I've been the victim of a clever plot, as no doubt you've heard, and the more I resist it the worse off I am. Everything has turned against me now. I can't survive this night. I've made up my mind to it.

NARRATOR: As he whispers voices come from inside.

VOICES: Come on in, Ohatsu. You don't want people to start gossiping about you.

OHATSU: We can't talk here any longer. Do as I show you.

NARRATOR: She hides him in the skirts of her great-robe:
He crawls behind her to the central door
Then slips beneath the porch next to the step.

Ohatsu sits inside next to the door,
And nonchalantly lights her tobacco.

Just at this juncture Kuheiji bursts in,
With two or three of his foulmouthed friends
And a couple of blind musicians.

KUHEIJI: Hello, girls. You're looking lonesome. How about it if I become a customer? Hello, boss. I haven't seen you in a long time.

NARRATOR: He strides arrogantly into the room.

HOST: Bring the tobacco tray and some saké cups.

KUHEIJI: No, don't bother with the saké. I've had all I want to drink. There's something I've got to discuss with you. You know Tokubei, the number one customer of your Ohatsu? Well, he found a seal I lost, and tried to cheat me with a forged note for two *kamme* of silver. The facts were too much for him, and he was lucky to get out of it alive. Now he's completely discredited. Everybody will tell you that what I say is the truth, so even if Tokubei says the exact opposite, don't you believe him for a minute. You'd best not let him in at all. Sooner or later he's going to wind up on the scaffold.

NARRATOR: He volleys forth his words convincingly.
Beneath the porch Tokubei gnashes his teeth,
And trembles all over in helpless rage.
Ohatsu, afraid he might reveal himself,
With her foot calms him, calms him splendidly.
The host is loath to answer yes or no,
For Tokubei's a customer from old.
Instead he asks, "How about some soup?"
And covering his confusion leaves the room.
Ohatsu lost in tears exclaims.

OHATSU: You're very clever, but I can't let you get away with it. I know everything about Tokubei. We've told each other all our inmost secrets ever since we became lovers years ago. He doesn't have the least particle of deceit in him—unfortunately for him. His generosity has been his undoing. He's been tricked by you, but he doesn't have the evidence to prove it. Now Tokubei has no choice but to die. I wish I could hear him say that he is resolved to die.

NARRATOR: She says these words as if but to herself,
Then questions with her foot: he nods his head,
And taking her ankle strokes his throat
To let her know that he is willed to die.

OHATSU: I knew it. I knew it. No matter how long one lives it comes to the same thing. Only death can wipe out the disgrace.

KUHEIJI: What's Ohatsu talking about? What's all this about Tokubei dying? Well, if he does die, I'll take good care of you after he's gone. I think you're really soft on me too!

OHATSU: You're most solicitous, I'm sure. If you bestow your favors on me, I'll kill you for your pains. Is that agreeable? Do you imagine that I could go on living even for a moment if I were separated from Tokubei? Kuheiji, you dirty thief! Nobody could hear your nonsense without being amazed. No matter what happens, I'm going to die with Tokubei. I shall die with him.

NARRATOR: She taps him with her foot; beneath the porch
He reverently takes it in his hands,
Then embracing her knees he weeps for love.
She too can scarcely keep her features calm,
And though no word is spoken, heart to heart
Answering each other they softly weep.
That no one knows makes it sadder still.

KUHEIJI: This place gives me the creeps. Let's get out of here. It's a funny thing how the whores here seem to dislike customers like us with lots of money to spend. Let's head for the Azaya and have a drink there. By the time we've tossed around a couple of gold pieces we'll be ready to go home to bed. Oh, my wallet is so heavy I can hardly walk!

NARRATOR: Thus spewing forth all manner of abuse
They noisily depart.

HOST *(to the servants):* It's time already to put out the lights. Lay out beds for the guests who are spending the night. Ohatsu, you sleep upstairs. Get to bed early.

OHATSU: Master, Mistress. I shall probably never see you again. Farewell to you both. And farewell to you too, all of you who work here.

NARRATOR: Thus lightly taking leave she goes to bed.
They fail to mark her words and only later know
That this was her farewell to them for life.
The foolishness of men is sad indeed.

HOST: Look after the fire under the kettle. Don't let the mice get at the relishes.

NARRATOR: They shut the place for the night and bar the gate,
Then soon asleep are snoring merrily.
So short the night, before they'd time to dream
The second hour of the morning comes.
Ohatsu dressed for death in robes of spotless white
And black kimono dark as are the ways of love,
Tiptoes to the staircase and looks below.
Tokubei appears from underneath the house,
Beckons, nods, and points, speaking with his heart.
Below the stairs a servant girl is sleeping;
A hanging lantern brightly lights the room.
Ohatsu, wondering how to escape,
Attaches to a palm-leaf broom her fan,
And from the second step of the staircase
Attempts in vain to blow away the flame.
At last by stretching every inch she puts it out,
But tumbles from the stairs with a crash.
The lamp is out and in the darkness
The servant girl turns over in her sleep.
Trembling, they grope for each other.
The host awakens in his private chamber.

HOST: What was that noise just now? Servants! The night lamp has gone out. Get up and light it!

NARRATOR: The servant sleepily rubbing her eyes
Gets up from bed stark naked.

SERVANT: I can't find the flint box.

NARRATOR: While she wanders about searching for it,
Ohatsu dodges back and forth avoiding her,

And in the nightmare darkness gropes for Tokubei.
At last they catch each other's hands
And softly creep out to the entranceway.
The latch is open, but the hinges creek,
And frightened by the noise they hesitate.
Just then the maid begins to strike the flints;
They time their actions to the rasping sound,
And with each rasp the door is opened more,
Until, sleeves twisted round them through they push,
And one after the other pass outside,
As though they tread upon a tiger's tail.
Exchanging glances then, they cry for joy,
Rejoicing that they are to go to death.
The life left to them now is just as brief
As sparks that fly from blocks of flint.

Scene III: The Journey

NARRATOR: Farewell to the world, and to the night farewell.
We who walk the road to death, to what should we be likened?
To the frost by the road that leads to the graveyard,
Vanishing with each step ahead:
This dream of a dream is sorrowful.
Ah, did you count the bell? Of the seven strokes
That mark the dawn six have sounded.
The remaining one will be the last echo
We shall hear in this life. It will echo
The bliss of annihilation.
Farewell, and not to the bell alone,
We look a last time on the grass, the trees, the sky,
The clouds go by unmindful of us,
The bright Dipper is reflected in the water,
The Wife and Husband Stars inside the Milky Way.[6]

[6] A Chinese legend, widespread also in Japan, tells how these two stars (also called the Herd Boy and the Weaver Girl) meet once a year on a bridge built by magpies in the sky.

TOKUBEI: Let's think the Bridge of Umeda
The bridge the magpies built and make a vow
That we will always be Wife and Husband Stars.
NARRATOR: "With all my heart," she says and clings to him:
So many are the tears that fall between the two,
The waters of the river must have risen.
On a teahouse balcony across the way
A party in the lamplight loudly discuss
Before they go to bed the latest gossip,
With many words about the good and bad
Of this year's crop of lovers' suicides.
TOKUBEI: How strange! but yesterday, even today,
We spoke as if such things didn't concern us.
Tomorrow we shall figure in their gossip—
Well, if they wish to sing about us, let them.
NARRATOR: This is the song that now we hear:
"Why can't you take me for your wife?
Although you think you don't want me . . ."[7]
However we think, however lament,
Both our fate and the world go against us.
Never before today was there a day
Of relaxation, and untroubled night,
Instead, the tortures of an ill-starred love.
"What did I do to deserve it?
I never can forget you.
You want to shake me off and go?
I'll never let you.
Take me with your hands and kill me
Or I'll never let you go,"
Said the girl in tears.
TOKUBEI: Of all the many songs, that it should be that one,
This very evening, but who is it that sings?
We are those who listen; others like us
Who've gone this way have had the same ordeal.
NARRATOR: They cling to one another, weeping bitterly,

[7] This is a popular ballad of the time describing a love suicide.

And wish, as many a lover has wished,
The night would last even a little longer.
The heartless summer night is short as ever,
And soon the cockcrows chase away their lives.

TOKUBEI: Let us die in the wood before the dawn.

NARRATOR: He takes her hands.
At Umeda Embankment, the night ravens.

TOKUBEI: Tomorrow our bodies may be their meal.

OHATSU: It's strange this year is your unlucky year [8]
Of twenty-five, and mine of nineteen too.
That we who love should both be cursed this way
Is proof how close the ties that join us.
All the prayers that I have made for this world
To the gods and to the Buddha, I here and now
Direct to the future, and in the world to come,
May we remain together on one lotus.[9]

NARRATOR: One hundred eight the beads her fingers tell
On her rosary; her tears increase the sum.
No end to her grief, but the road has an end.
Their heart and the sky are dark, the wind intense:
They have reached the wood of Sonezaki.

Shall it be there, shall it be here?
And when they brush the grass the dew which falls
Vanishes even quicker than their lives,
In this uncertain world a lightning flash—
A lightning flash or was it something else?

OHATSU: Oh, I'm afraid. What was that just now?

TOKUBEI: Those were human spirits. I thought that we'd be the only ones to die tonight, but others have gone ahead of us. Whoever they may be, we'll journey together to the Mountain of Death. *Namu Amida Butsu. Namu Amida Butsu.*[10]

[8] In the *yin-yang* system a man's twenty-fifth, forty-second, and sixtieth years were dangerous; for a woman her nineteenth and thirty-third years.

[9] In the Buddhist paradise people are born again on lotuses.

[10] An invocation to Amida Buddha used in Jōdo and Shin Buddhism.

OHATSU: How sad it is! Other souls have left the world. *Namu Amida Butsu.*

NARRATOR: The woman melts in helpless tears of grief.

OHATSU: To think that other people are dying tonight too! That makes me feel wretched.

NARRATOR: Man that he is, his tears are falling freely.

TOKUBEI: Those two spirits flying together over there—they can't be anyone else's! They must be ours, yours and mine!

OHATSU: Those two spirits? Are we already dead then?

TOKUBEI: Ordinarily, if we were to see a spirit we'd knot our clothes and howl to save our lives,[11] but now instead we are hurrying toward our last moments, and soon are to live in the same place with them. You mustn't lose the way or mistake the road of death!

NARRATOR: They cling to each other, flesh against flesh,
Then fall with a cry to the ground and weep.
Their strings of tears unite like grafted branches,
Or a pine and palm that grow from a single trunk.
And now, where will they end their dew-like lives?

TOKUBEI: This place will do.

NARRATOR: The sash of his jacket he undoes;
Ohatsu removes her tear-stained outer robe,
And throws it on the palm tree with whose fronds
She now might sweep away the sad world's dust.
Ohatsu takes a razor from her sleeve.

OHATSU: I had this razor ready just in case we were overtaken on the way or got separated. I made up my mind that whatever might happen I would not give up our plan. Oh, how happy I am that we are to die together as we had hoped!

TOKUBEI: You make me feel so confident in our love that I am not worried even by the thought of death. And yet it would be a pity if because of the pain that we are to suffer, people said that we looked ugly in death. Wouldn't it be a good idea if we fastened our bodies to this twin-trunked tree and died immaculately? Let us become an unparalleled example of a beautiful way of dying.

OHATSU: Yes, as you say.

11 A type of exorcism practiced against spirits.

NARRATOR: Alas! she little thought she thus would use
Her sash of powder blue. She draws it taut,
And with her razor slashes it in two.

OHATSU: My sash is divided, but you and I will never part.

NARRATOR: Face to face they sit, then twice or thrice
He ties her firmly so she will not move.

TOKUBEI: Is it tight?

OHATSU: Yes, it's very tight.

NARRATOR: She looks at him, he looks at her, they burst into tears.

BOTH: This is the end of our unfortunate lives!

TOKUBEI: No, I mustn't weep.

NARRATOR: He raises his head and joins his hands.

TOKUBEI: When I was a small child my parents died, and it was my uncle who brought me up. I'm ashamed of myself that I am dying this way without repaying my indebtedness to him, and that I am causing him trouble that will last after my death. Please forgive me my sins.

Now soon I shall be seeing my parents in the other world. Father, Mother, come welcome me there!

NARRATOR: Ohatsu also joins her hands in prayer.

OHATSU: I envy you that you will be meeting your parents in the world of the dead. My father and mother are still alive. I wonder when I shall meet them again. I had a letter from them this spring, but the last time I saw them was at the beginning of autumn last year. When they get word tomorrow in the village of my suicide, how unhappy they will be. Mother, Father, brothers and sisters, I now say good-bye to the world. If only my thoughts can reach you, I pray that I may be able to appear in your dreams. Dearest Mother, beloved Father!

NARRATOR: She weeps convulsively and wails aloud.
Her lover also sheds incessant tears,
And cries out in despair, as is most natural.

OHATSU: There's no use in talking any longer. Kill me, kill me quickly!

NARRATOR: She hastens the moment of death.

TOKUBEI: I'm ready.

NARRATOR: He swiftly draws out his dagger.
TOKUBEI: The moment has come. *Namu Amida. Namu Amida.*
NARRATOR: But when he tries to bring the blade against the skin
Of the woman he's loved, and held, and slept with
So many months and years, his hands begin to shake,
His eyes cloud over. He attempts to stay
His weakening resolve, but still he trembles,
And when he makes a thrust the point goes off,
Deflecting twice or thrice with flashing blade,
Until a cry tells it has reached her throat.
TOKUBEI: *Namu Amida. Namu Amida. Namu Amida Butsu.*
NARRATOR: He presses the blade ever deeper
And when he sees her weaken he falters too.
He stretches forth his arms—of all the pains
That life affords, none is as great as this.
TOKUBEI: Am I going to lag on after you? Let's draw our last breaths together.
NARRATOR: He thrusts and twists the razor in his throat
Until it seems the handle or the blade must snap.
His eyes grow dim, and his last painful breath
With the dawn's receding tide is drawn away.[12]
But the wind that blows through Sonezaki Wood
Transmits it, and high and low alike,
Gather to pray for them who beyond a doubt
Will in the future attain to Buddhahood.
They thus become a model of true love.

TRANSLATED BY DONALD KEENE

[12] It was believed that the spirit left the body as the tide went out.

A WAYWARD WIFE

[Seken Musume Kataki, 1, 2] *by Ejima Kiseki*

Ejima Kiseki (1667-1736) as a novelist was clearly in the tradition of Saikaku, and numerous echoes if not actual imitations of the earlier writer may be found in Kiseki's works. However, his "character-books" (katakimono) *have a charm and humor of their own, and have enjoyed deserved popularity. The following tale is from his "Characters of Worldly Young Women" (1716), one of Kiseki's most famous works.*

•

"Obviously morning-glories are best at morning," declares the mistress, "not to say how much cooler it is." And so that night she leaves orders to fill tiers of lacquer boxes with savory rice and a variety of tidbits, prepared exactly to her taste, to arrange several chairs at a back hedge as far as possible from the house, and to lay a floral carpet. "Cedar picks for the food, a gold lacquer tray . . . be sure to use that exquisite tea from Toganoo! Have the bath ready before six. As to my hair, you may do it in three folds, and please take out a sheer gown with wide sleeves and a pink lining—the sash ought to be dark gray satin, the undersash pale but speckled with huge dots. It must all seem quite perfect: you know how the neighbors stare. So put the maids in fresh summer kimonos, won't you? And do send a sedan chair to Kama no za for my sister, at the usual time." After issuing a bewildering set of instructions to her housekeeper, who has long had charge of kitchen affairs, she retires to lie at ease in the shelter of an ample mosquito net; and tiny bells tinkle at its corners as the servants fan her, by turns, till she drops off to sleep.

Such are her airs merely to look at flowers in her own garden.

And modern matrons have their other caprices too. They reserve three boxes for the latest play, but then, stopping at Chōraku Temple to hear ballads chanted when an image is on view. become so absorbed that they omit to go to the theatre. Yet their boredom is not easily dispelled by the suitable feminine pleasures of incense-guessing, poem cards, playing the koto or the samisen, painting, and flower-arranging. "There's wrestling at Makuzugahara, and Shichigorō takes on the Thunderbolt!" they cry. "We can't miss it!" Off they dash, in sedan chairs decorated by autumn landscapes or sprinkled gold.

Did anyone hear of women at wrestling matches in former times? But since men now dote on their wives, and meet each request with a nod and a smile of fatuous tolerance, these ladies do not hesitate to display their morbid zest for outings—with picnic lunch—to watch the beheading of criminals at Awataguchi. It recalls how Chieh-chi, consort of King Chou of the Yin Dynasty, having exhausted her notable repertoire of diversions, found a superior pastime in seeing executions by the "wrapping and roasting" process; or how King Yu of Chou, infatuated with Pao-ssu, had the signal rockets fired to amuse her. Indeed, these are only classic examples of the familiar petticoat tyranny. The grocer need simply say, "Madam's orders," to be paid off in large coins for a watermelon costing 365 *momme;* and no sooner has he gone than two stout bearers are dispatched to Yakichi's, on Fourth Avenue, to settle a 27,206-coppers account for vegetable jelly. You may imagine the other luxuries. Smoking, for instance, used to be unknown as a feminine practice, except among courtesans; yet today women who abstain are as few as monks who fast.

Now there was a certain man who, though of merchant lineage, was highly esteemed, being known throughout the capital for his wealth. Generations ago his family had withdrawn from all but the infrequent business of handing down superb heirlooms. When snow fell he performed the tea ceremony; at blossom time he wrote poems in a traditional vein. He was careful to ignore whatever might be considered practical.

As a husband, he behaved with impeccable lordliness, never

glancing into the kitchen. His wife, a radiant beauty, was the irregular offspring of a person of rank. Not only was she adept in the poetics of the ancient school, she had a rare gift for music, and particularly for the reed pipes: frost gathered in midsummer when she blew winter melodies; with longevity tunes she made her husband utterly feeble. She was addicted to the pursuit of elegance, whether in arts or manners. For summer nights she had her room screened from mosquitoes by panels of silk gauze: inside were placed a five-foot-square tray-garden and a floating lamp, as well as fireflies specially procured from Uji and Seta. Thus she relieved the discomforts of hot weather. In winter she warmed herself at a covered brazier large enough for eight people, and had little girls with bobbed hair chafe the soles of her feet. Husband and wife slept in the perfume of precious incense, while its smoke, wreathing up in as many shapes as from Fuji, Asama, and Muro no yashima,[1] curled through their clothing. Devotees of the cult of fragrance, they lived in a style of unfailing splendor. Where the father had strewn the seeds of riches the son now possessed mountains wooded in silver-bearing trees; but the clatter of interest money in his scales only annoyed him, just as the subtle rhythms of the hand drum irritate the vulgar. No one carrying an account book visited his mansion on the last day of the year: all bills were paid early in November, as if the New Year (not greeted by the customary gate-pines) had arrived too soon.

Yet his wife was unhappy. Though she lived in luxurious fashion, and though her husband was handsome and sophisticated, a man who, far from counting among the Twenty-four Paragons of Filial Piety, was more devoted to wife than mother—despite all this good fortune, which would seem to have left no desire unfulfilled, she perversely disliked being a woman.

One thought obsessed her: "Why was I cursed with this sex? Tied down to a skinny devil, and no chance to enjoy myself as I please!"

Boldly she extracted her husband's consent to have her hair trimmed in masculine style, the rich pinned coiffure replaced by a

[1] Famous active volcanoes.

boyish arrangement in two folds, with the back hair drawn up. In dress too she flouted convention: a short skirt (exposing the under-garment), a coat of "eight-roll" cloth, a gold-mounted sword, medium long, and a wide rush hat of the "Mist-on-Fuji" kind. Thus attired, and accompanied by her husband, she set out each day on another, more distant excursion. "Let's climb Mount Kōya," she would say, "Those monks are so terribly woman-shy they'll be fun to tease." Or: "Now let's go to the whale-spearing at Kumano Bay." Her demands were endless. Surely if men yielded to all such whims, these hussies would insist on crossing the ocean—"to see the castle of that fellow Coxinga[2] one hears so much about."

But since the poor husband had a genius for being hoodwinked, he delighted in her singular conduct ("How original to dress up like a man!"), and even took her along to Shimabara.[3] When they were shown into a reception room at Hanabishiya, he said, "See what a dashing wife I have! You won't find such a curiosity-seeker in all China; and as for looks—well, I'm afraid your famous beauties are a little outclassed. Smart, isn't she?" And he engaged the most celebrated courtesans, for his wife as well as himself. They gave pleasure their undivided attention: doubtless the voluptuous joys of Paradise were exceeded.

One day this couple went to a fashionable teahouse in Gion; and there, with the aid of professional jesters, they held a lavish and rather noisy party. The husband began to boast of his wife's accomplishments. "You girls should hear her play the reed pipe," he said. "I suppose you're on good terms with men of discrimination, and you've heard all kinds of music; but it may be that a really expert artist on this instrument has not yet performed in Gion."

At this the proprietor and his wife bowed low, pressing their foreheads tightly to the matting. "Never," they assured him, "not once

[2] Coxinga was the hero of Chikamatsu's play, "The Battles of Coxinga," which had scored a tremendous success in the preceding year. His castle would presumably be one in China.

[3] The licensed quarter of Kyoto; Hanabishiya was the name of one of the houses.

in all the years since the God of Gion descended from the heavens. But if Destiny now grants us the privilege of hearing your lady on the flute, clearly we were born at an auspicious hour."

Elated by these words, he exclaimed, "Come, Madam! You must outdo yourself for this audience." And he settled comfortably against the pillar of the alcove, his nose tilted as triumphantly as if he were the Emperor Hsüan Tsung.[4]

His wife, who was of course a virtuoso, chose the song that Chang Liang played on Chou-li Mountain during the battle between Han and Ch'u, the song beginning, "When the autumn wind drives the leaves, and the traveler thinks of his far-off home . . ." And she poured out all her skill.

In the next room, strange to say, an uproarious party lapsed into melancholy. Hitherto lively guests reflected on the evil of squandering money that had been earned by the sweat of their parents; they felt inclined to go home without waiting for the supper already ordered. The charming boys called in to add to the gaiety remembered their native villages, and how their true fathers had toiled under cruel burdens, barely able to get along from one day to the next. Samisen in hand, they sat with tears shining in their eyes. No one asked the company of the house courtesans, who for that matter (though it was time to settle monthly accounts) were reviving nostalgic memories, and feeling they had landed in a somewhat thorny bed of roses. "The other girls [5] have the knack of it," remarked their mistress obliquely, "but our kites are too tail-heavy to get off the ground." Even this seemed to pass unheard, and their sorrowful expression did not alter. Squirming with reluctance, they withdrew to a dark room ("Oil lamps are expensive . . ."); they wanted tea, but shrank from troubling anyone; and as they talked of their holidays, now regretted, they wept freely.

But the girls who were on their own had begun to choke and sniff a bit, too. Oblivious of the guests, they told each other their grievances. "No matter if we work so hard we have to strip down like

[4] Chinese emperor of the T'ang Dynasty, who had as his mistress the peerless beauty Yang Kuei-fei.

[5] That is, the ones brought in from outside the teahouse.

wrestlers, meals and clothes cost a lot, and it's a struggle to make ends meet. But how else can we earn a living?"

The jesters worried about the annual reckoning, which was not yet near, and thought, "Better to run away from all this, or hang yourself and be done with it." They dropped their game of capping humorous verses. "It's a miserable life," they sighed. "We jesters have to drink when we'd rather not; we have to praise the tiresome little songs of our patrons, hear ourselves called fools by real blockheads, force a smile if we're offended, and tell a roomful of people what even a woman would keep secret. No, there's nothing so bitter as to entertain for a living. If you happen to please, you may be hired five times and get only one piece of silver, or two at most. In this wide world, is there no country where it rains hard cash?" Enlacing their fingers, they contemplated the vanity of things.

Even the staunchly avaricious proprietor and his wife were somehow or other seized by an extraordinary fit of conscience. "If only we could do business without lying!" A single note had scattered their wits and they shed unexpected tears.

Just then several guests appeared at a doorway leading from an inner room. "I've always found it gay here," one of them commented, "but today is very odd—you might as well be marooned on Demon Island." He exchanged a few inappropriate family inquiries with a courtesan (hired out of his own pocket), compassionately handed her an extra coin, wiped his eyes, and left the teahouse at once.

TRANSLATED BY HOWARD HIBBETT

HIZAKURIGE

by Jippensha Ikku

Hizakurige *is a humorous Japanese word meaning "a journey on foot." It is an apt title for this book telling of the adventures of two happy-go-lucky travelers along the road between Edo and Osaka. The book, issued serially beginning in 1802, was an immense success in its day, and the author, Jippensha Ikku (1766-1831), wrote numerous sequels. The two heroes, Yajirobei, or Yaji, and Kitahachi, or Kita, have been taken into the hearts of the Japanese, and their irrepressible earthy humor is considered typical of the real Edoite.*

The following section occurs fairly early in their journey.

•

They went down the hill till they reached Nissaka, the rain coming down harder and harder till it was impossible to go on, as everything was blotted out. Finally they took refuge under the eaves of an inn.

"How annoying!" said Yaji. "Such terrible rain!"

"Well, we're not willow trees, to be planted by the roadside," said Kita. "We can't stand under the eaves of people's houses forever. What do you think, Yaji? We've crossed the River Ōi. Don't you think we might stop here for the night?"

"What?" said Yaji. "Don't talk nonsense! It can't be two o'clock yet. It would be absurd to stop now."

Then the old landlady came out of the inn.

"You can't go on in this rain," she said. "Please stop here."

"I think we ought to," said Kita. "I say, Yaji, look! There are some women stopping in the back room there."

"Eh?" said Yaji. "Where? That's interesting."

"Won't your honors stop here?" repeated the old woman.

"Well, suppose we do," said Yaji.

They went in and washed their feet, and were soon conducted to a room at the back next to the one where they had seen the women. . . .

Then the supper trays were brought in and they set to work to eat, uttering all sorts of jokes.

"By the way," said Yaji to the maid, "the guests in the back room are women, aren't they? Who are they?"

"They're witches," said the maid.

"What, witches?" said Kita. "That's interesting. Let's call up somebody."

"It's too late, isn't it?" said Yaji. "They won't come after four o'clock."

"It's only a little past two," said the maid.

"Well, just ask them," said Yaji. "I'd like to have a talk with my dead wife."

"Fancy wanting to do that!" said Kita.

"I'll ask them afterward," said the maid.

So when the meal was finished she went into the next room to ask the witches. They agreed, and Yaji and Kita were conducted into their room. There the witches produced the usual box and arranged it, while the maid, who knew what was wanted, drew some water and brought it.

Yaji, with his mind fixed on his departed wife, poured some water over the anise leaves and the younger witch began to invoke the gods.

"First of all," she chanted, "I reverently call upon Bonten and Taishaku and the four gods of Heaven, and in the underworld the great Emma and the five attendants who wait on him. Of our country's gods I invoke the seven gods of Heaven and the five gods of Earth, and of the gods of Ise, Amaterasu Ōmikami, and the forty descendants of the Outer Shrine and the eight descendants of the Inner Shrine. I invoke the God of Rain, the God of Wind, the God of the Moon and the God of the Sun, the God of the North Shrine of the Benku Mirror, and the spirit of the great Sun Goddess of Ama no iwato, and Kokuzō, the God of Ten Thousand Good Fortunes of Asama ga dake, and the others in the sixty provinces of Japan, and also in the country of the gods, at the Great Shrine of Izumo. By the ninety-eight thousand gods of the country and the thirteen thousand Buddhas of the holy places, through the fearful road of the underworld I come. Ah, horror! The spirits of his ancestors crowd upon me, each couple as inseparable as the bow and the arrow. The skies may change and the waters may change, but the bow is unchangeable. One shot from it sends an echo through all the holy places of the temples. Ah! Ah! Oh, joyful sight! Well have you summoned me. I had for a bedfellow a warrior famous with the bow, but alas! averse to a pure diet, in life he devoured fish even to the bones, and now, in punishment, is changed into a devil in the shape of an ox, his duty being to keep the gates of Hell, from which he has no release. Thus have I come alone."

"Who are you?" asked Yaji. "I don't understand what it's all about!"

"I have come for the sake of him who offered me water, the mirror of my body, my child-treasure."

"Mirror of the body?" said Kita. "I'll tell you what, Yaji, it's your mother."

"My mother, eh?" said Yaji. "I don't have anything to say to her."

"Has the mirror of my body nothing to say to me?" continued the witch. "To me, your bedfellow, whom you have thus without shame summoned from the depths? Ah, what agony I went through when I was married to you—time and again suffering the pangs of hunger and shivering with cold in the winter. Ah, hateful! Hateful!"

"Forgive me," said Yaji. "At that time my fortunes were low. How pitiful your lot that you should have been brought to the grave with care and hardships."

"Halloa, Yaji," said Kita. "Are you crying? Ha, ha, ha! Even devils have tears."

"I shall never forget it," the witch went on. "When you were ill you gave your sickness to me. Our only child, who had to carry on our name, grew weak and thin because there was no rice to fill his empty stomach. Every day the bill collectors were knocking at the door and the rent remained unpaid. Yet I did not complain—not even when I slipped in the dogs' dirt in the lane."

"Don't talk of it," said Yaji. "You'll break my heart."

"And then, when through my labors I had saved enough money to buy a kimono, I had to pawn it for your sake and never saw it again. Never again did it come back to me from the pawnbroker's."

"At the same time you must remember what a pleasant place you are in now," said Yaji, "while I have to worry along down here."

"What? What is there pleasant about it? It is true that by the help of your friends you erected a stone over my grave, but you never go near it, and you never contribute to the temple to get the priests to say prayers for my soul. I am nothing to you. The stone over my grave has been taken away and put into the wall, where all the dogs come and make water against it. Not a drop of water is ever placed on my grave. Truly in death we suffer all sorts of troubles."

"True, true," said Yaji.

"But while you thus treat me with neglect," the witch went on, "lying in my grave I think of nobody but you and long for the time when you will join me in the underworld. Shall I come to meet you?"

"No, no, don't do that," said Yaji. "It's really too far for you."

"Well then, I have one request to make."

"Yes, yes. What is it?"

"Give this witch plenty of money."

"Of course, of course."

"How sad the parting!" cried the witch. "I have yet much to tell you, countless questions to ask you, but the messenger of Hell recalls me!"

Then, recovering from her trance, the witch twanged her bow.

"Thank you very much," said Yaji. He took out some money and wrapped it in paper and gave it to her.

"Ha, ha!" laughed Kita. "Now all your hidden shames are revealed to the world. Ha, ha, ha! But I say, Yaji, you look very downcast. What do you say to a drink?"

Yaji agreed and clapping his hands ordered the maid to bring some saké.

"How far have you come today?" asked the witch.

"We came from Okabe," answered Yaji.

"How quick you are," said the witch.

"Oh, that's nothing," said Yaji. "We can walk as fast as Idaten.[1] If we're put to it we can walk thirty-five miles a day."

"But then we shouldn't be fit for anything for ten days after," put in Kita.

While they were talking the saké was brought in.

"Won't you have a little?" said Yaji to the young witch.

"I never touch a drop," she answered.

"Will your companion have any?" asked Yaji.

"Mother, Mother! Come here," called the young witch.

"Oh, it's your mother, is it?" said Kita. "I must take care what I say in front of her. But come, do have some."

Soon they began to drink and enjoy themselves, the cup passing from hand to hand very quickly. Yet strangely enough, the witches, however much they drank, never seemed to be any the worse for it, while Yaji and Kita got so drunk they could not speak plainly. After making all sorts of jokes which it would be too tedious to repeat, Kita at last in a drunken voice said, "I say, Mother, won't you lend me your daughter for the night?"

"No, no, she's going to lend her to me," said Yaji.

"What an idea!" cried Kita. "You'd better try and be good tonight. Haven't you any pity for your dead wife who spends her time in thinking of you and hoping you will join her quickly? Didn't she say she'd come and meet you after a bit?"

"Here, don't talk about that," said Yaji. "What should I do if she did come to meet me?"

"Then you had better be good," said Kita. "Now, old lady, what do you think?"

Kita here gave the young witch a loving caress, but she pushed him off and ran away, saying "Be quiet."

"If my daughter doesn't want to," said the mother, "what about me?"

"Well, if it comes to that I don't care who it is," said Kita, who was lost in a drunken dream.

[1] A Buddhist protecting god, known for his swiftness.

While they were talking the supper was brought in and there was a good deal of joking too tedious to repeat, and finally Yaji and Kita, the effects of the saké having already passed off, went back into their own room where, as soon as it was dark, they went to bed. In the next room also the witches were apparently going to bed, worn out by their travels.

"That young witch is sleeping on this side, I know," said Kita in a low voice. "I'll creep in to her after a bit. Yaji, you'd better go to sleep."

"Get out," said Yaji. "I'm going to be the one to get her."

"Isn't he bold?" said Kita. "It would make a cat laugh."

Thus talking they crept into bed and fell asleep. It was already about nine o'clock, and the night watchman's rattle, as he went round the inn, echoed through the pillows of the travelers. In the kitchen the sound of the preparations for the next morning's meal had died away, and all that could be heard was the barking of the dogs. It was just when night was at its darkest and eeriest that Kitahachi decided the time was right to creep out of bed and peep into the next room. The night light had gone out, and he felt his way in very softly and crept into the bed where he thought the young witch was sleeping. To his surprise the witch, without saying anything, caught hold of his hand and pulled him in. Delighted with his reception, Kitahachi sank down under the coverlet with her arm for a pillow and soon realized his desire, after which they both fell asleep quite unconscious of their surroundings.

Yajirobei, who was thus left sleeping alone, soon opened his eyes. "I wonder what time it is," he muttered. "I must go to the toilet. It's so dark I can't see the way."

Thus pretending that he was going to the toilet he crept into the next room, quite unaware of the fact that Kitahachi was already in there. Feeling about, he came to the side of the bed where Kita was lying, and thinking in the darkness that it was the young witch's lips from which moans were coming, he put his lips to those of Kitahachi and took a bite.

"Oh! Oh!" yelled Kitahachi.

"Halloa! Is that you, Kitahachi?" said Yaji.

"Oh, it's Yaji, is it?" said Kita. "Ugh! Ugh! How beastly!" and he began spitting.

At the sound of their voices the witch into whose bed Kita had crept woke up.

"What are you doing?" she said. "Don't make such a noise. You'll wake my daughter up."

This was another surprise for Kita, for it was the old witch's voice. Cursing himself for his stupidity he got out of the bed and crept away softly into the next room. Yaji was going to do the same when the old witch caught hold of him.

"You mustn't make a fool of an old woman by running away," she said.

"No, no," stuttered Yaji. "You've made a mistake. It wasn't me."

"You mustn't try to deceive me," said the old woman. "I don't make a regular business of this, but when I meet a traveler on the road and sleep with him I like to get a little just to help me along. It's a shame to make a fool of me by running away. There, just go to sleep in my bosom till dawn."

"What a nuisance you are," said Yaji. "Here, Kitahachi, Kitahachi."

"Take care," said the old woman. "You mustn't call so loud."

"But I don't know anything about it," said Yaji. "It's that Kitahachi that's got me into all this mess."

Thus saying Yaji struggled out of her grasp, only to be caught again and thrown down. But at last, after a good deal of kicking, he managed to get away into the next room, where he repeated to himself

> "By stealth I entered, witch's love to earn,
> But which was witch I could not well discern."

TRANSLATED BY THOMAS SATCHELL

SHINO AND HAMAJI

[*Hakkenden, xxv*] *by Takizawa Bakin*

The commanding literary figure in Japan during the first half of the nineteenth century was Bakin (1767-1848). His novels were widely read and extravagantly admired. He wrote in several distinct genres; of these his didactic works (yomihon), *in which he sought to "encourage virtue and chastise vice," were the most important if not the most popular. His greatest work, "The Biographies of Eight Dogs" (Satomi Hakkenden, 1814-1841) is an immensely long novel telling of the exploits of eight heroes who have the same noble dog as their spiritual ancestor. Each of them symbolizes a virtue: the first, Shino, stands for "filial piety."*

The number of readers of the "Eight Dogs" is dwindling, but those who peruse its pages will probably be held by the story, however fantastic it may be, and will be rewarded by episodes such as the one given here. Shino is being sent away from home by his wicked aunt and uncle (the foster parents of Hamaji) so that they can find a more desirable son-in-law. Shino suspects this, but his desire to restore his family fortunes (impelled by filial piety) causes him to leave the woman to whom he is engaged.

•

Shino had gone to bed, but could not sleep in his impatience for the dawn. His head was filled with thoughts about the future. He realized that he was alone, that there was no one to stop him from leaving, but he could not help feeling unhappy that he was now to go far from the graves of his parents and the place where he was born. Hamaji, who regretted his departure no less than he, slipped out of bed and, taking care lest her parents now snoring in the back room should waken, those parents toward whom she felt a resentment she could not voice, she soundlessly stepped over the threshold of the barrier of her maiden reserve, which had hitherto kept her from going to Shino. Her knees trembled, and she could scarcely walk. How dreary, sad, bitter, and hateful the inconstant world now seemed.

When Hamaji came close to Shino's pillow, he saw that someone had entered his room. He drew his sword to him and sprang to his feet. "Who is it?" he cried, but no sound answered him. He wondered uneasily whether some enemy had come to observe whether he was asleep, with the intent of stabbing him to death. He grew more and more tense. He flashed the light of the lamp and peered into the darkness. Then he saw that it was Hamaji. Without warning she had appeared, and now lay motionless on the other side of the mosquito netting, seemingly shaken by grief but unwilling to reveal it by her tears.

Shino was a brave soldier who would not flinch before the fiercest enemy, but now he was disturbed. Controlling his emotions, he left the mosquito netting and, unfastening the cords by which the netting hung, drew his pallet to where she lay. "Hamaji, what has brought you here in the middle of the night, when you should be sleeping? Have you never heard the proverb, 'Don't arouse suspicion by tying your shoes in a melon field or by lifting your arms to straighten your hat under a plum tree'?"[1] When he had thus admonished her, Hamaji, brushing away her tears, lifted her head in indignation. "How cruel of you to ask me in that impersonal way why I have come! If we were joined but casually, and husband and wife only in name, you might well speak in that way, but were we not wedded with my parents' consent? Whatever might be the proper behavior under normal circumstances, it is heartless of you tonight, our last night for farewells, to order me out with a careless word. You are pretending not to know what I feel because you are afraid that it might bring discredit to you. How hardhearted of you!"

[1] That is, the mere fact that Hamaji is in his room will make people think that they have been making love, just as if a man stoops in a melon field it is assumed that he is stealing a melon.

Shino sighed in spite of himself. "I am not made of wood or stone, and whether I wish it or not, I know what tender emotions are. But it can serve no purpose for me to voice my feelings—it will only arouse the antipathy of your parents. I know that you will be true to me, and you must know what lies within my heart. Koga is a bare forty miles from here—it takes no more than three or four days to make the journey there and back. Please wait till I return."

He tried to persuade her, but Hamaji, wiping her eyes, exclaimed, "What you say is false. Once you leave here, what will ever make you return? The bird in the cage longs for the sky because it misses its friends; when a man leaves his home it must be because he is thinking of his advancement. You cannot depend on the likes and dislikes of my parents. They are sending you off now because you are in the way, and they have no desire for your return. Once you leave here, when will you come back? Tonight is the last we have of parting. . . .[2]

"Ever since the seventh moon of last year the little stream of our love has been dammed and its passage cut, but one thing remains unchanged, like the downward flow of water, the sincerity of my heart. Not a day has passed but that I have prayed morning and night for your safety, success, and prosperity, but you remain extremely hard of heart. Is it because of duty to your aunt that you are deserting your wife? If you had in you one-hundredth of the depth of feeling that I have, you would say to me, 'For one reason or another the day of my return may be doubtful. Let us steal off secretly, together.' We are man and wife—who would slander you as being my paramour? But however cruel I think you are, I cannot, with my woman's heart, bear separation from you. Rather than that I be deserted and left to die of longing for you, kill me with your sword. I shall wait for you in the world to come, a hundred years if need be." To these she added many words of persuasion, relating one after another the painful griefs she bore, and though she kept herself from weeping aloud, a thousand tears coursed down to soak her sleeves.

Shino could not very well say that it would bring embarrassment

[2] A long passage is omitted here in which Hamaji describes her real family.

if her voice were heard outside the room, and since there was no way now to undo the ties that bound them, he could only sigh sadly. He said, with his hands folded on his knees, "Every one of your reproaches is justified, but what can I do, Hamaji? My departure is by command of my uncle and aunt. I know that they are really sending me to a distant place so as to get a new husband for you. The problem is that I am, and yet I am not, your husband.[3] Your parents probably suspect our true feelings. However, if now I let myself be guided by my emotions and take you off with me, what man will not say that it was a deed of lust? It will be painful for you to remain behind, but it will be for my sake. And if I go, though it is difficult for me to do so, will that not also be for your sake? Even if we are parted for a brief while, as long as our hearts remain constant a time will surely come when we can be fully married. Please go back to bed before your parents awaken. Please go quickly."

His words were in vain; she remained as she was and merely shook her head. "Having gone this far, it doesn't matter any longer.[4] If my parents waken to find me here and reprove me for it, I too shall have something to say. I will not move from here unless I hear you say that you want me to go with you. Otherwise, kill me." Weak as is a woman's will, hers was firmly set and would not alter.

Shino was quite at a loss. A note of irritation came into his voice, although he still kept it low. "You still do not understand. As long as we remain alive a time will surely come when we can meet. How can death be the proper state for man? If you interfere with me, now that I have this rare chance of winning success granted to me by my aunt and uncle, you are not my wife. Perhaps you are an enemy from a previous existence."

Hamaji sank deeper in tears. "There is nothing I can do when you make me feel that if I obtain my heart's desire I shall become your enemy. If my thoughts are really selfish, I shall put them aside

[3] They have been engaged with the consent of her foster parents, but a wedding ceremony has not actually taken place.

[4] Hamaji considers that she has already destroyed her reputation.

and remain here. May your journey be a safe one. Be careful lest, these terribly hot days, you get sunstroke on the way. In the winter months when the wind blows down the northern mountains, send me messages about yourself with the wind. I shall think only of the fact that you are alive and safe. If the weakening thread of my life should break, now will be our parting for this existence, and all I shall have to depend upon is the yet unseen world to come. Our ties are certain to endure through both worlds. Please never change your heart." Thus she spoke of uncertainties; however wise her prayers may have seemed, the heart of this innocent maiden was pitiful.

Shino in spite of himself also felt downcast, and unable to comfort her could only nod. There was nothing else for him to say. Just then the first cock-crow announced the dawn, and Shino, pulling himself together, said, "In a few moments your parents will waken. Hurry! Hurry!"

Hamaji at last got up, and recited the poem,

"Yo mo akeba	Now that dawn has come
Kitsu ni hamenan	Perhaps the foxes will eat
Kudakake no	Those cursed roosters,
Madaki ni nakite	Crowing in the early morn,
Sena wo yaritsutsu	Chasing you away from me.[5]

That poem was inspired by the casual love of a traveler, but now is the moment of separation with a departing husband. If the cocks do not crow the sky will not grow light; if the dawn does not come, no one will waken. Oh, hateful crowing of the cock! For us only are there no nights of meeting—between us stands an unyielding barrier. Even the moon at dawn brings only sorrow."

As she murmured these words, about to leave, there was a cough outside the door and a faint rapping on the door. "The cocks have crowed, are you not awake yet?" It was his servant who called. Shino hastily answered and the man withdrew to the kitchen. "Quickly, before he returns!" Shino said, pushing her out. Hamaji, her eyelids swollen from weeping, looked back from the darkness

[5] Quoted from "The Tales of Ise," 13. This tale is of a traveler in the north of Japan who spends one night with a country girl and then leaves her.

where she stood, but her eyes were too misted with tears for her to see him. She leant against the wall a moment, and then went to weep in her room.

Sadder even than parting at death is parting in life, than which is nothing sadder. Ah, rare indeed is this maiden! Yet has she to share a bedquilt with her husband, yet to range her pillow by his and sleep with entwined arms. Their love was more admirable than that of a century of ordinary husbands and wives. Shino, though drawn by love, does not waver in his heart, but by being faithful to his love, maintains the proper separation between men and women. Those who wander in the maze of the passions show insufficient wisdom and a lack of discrimination. Few of all the many young people who have once approached the brink have escaped being drowned. But here we have a case of a righteous husband and a chaste wife. Hamaji's love was not one of pleasures and lust. Shino's sighs were of sorrow, and not of weakness. Hamaji's love is still to be sought; men like Shino are rarer than ever.

TRANSLATED BY DONALD KEENE

HAIKU OF THE MIDDLE AND LATE TOKUGAWA PERIOD

Nashi no hana
tsuki ni fumi yomu
onna ari

Blossoms on the pear;
and a woman in the moonlight
reads a letter there . . .

Sakura chiru
nawashiro-mizu ya
hoshi-zukiyo

Scattered petals lie
on the rice-seedling waters:
stars in the moonlit sky.

Harusame ni
nuretsutsu yane no
temari kana

As the spring rains fall,
soaking in them, on the roof,
is a child's rag ball.

Harusame ya
dōsha no kimi no
sasamegoto

Ah, the rains of spring!
Dear lady driving with me here.
your whispering!

Harusame ya
kawazu no hara no
mada nurezu

Spring rain: and as yet
the little froglets' bellies
haven't got wet.

Mijika yo ya
asase ni nokoru
tsuki ippen

Night that ends so soon:
in the shallows still remains
one sliver of the moon.

Mi ni shimu ya
bōsai no kushi
neya ni fumu

What piercing cold I feel:
my dead wife's comb, in our bedroom,
under my heel. . . .

Medieval scene

Toba dono e
go-rokki isogu
nowaki kana

To great Toba's Hall
five or six horsemen hasten:
a storm wind of the fall.

Yosa Buson (1716-1784)

• •

Samidare ya	All the rains of June:
aru yo hisoka ni	and then one evening, secretly,
matsu no tsuki	through the pines, the moon!

Ōshima Ryōta (1718-1787)

• •

Haru no mori	The grove in spring:
tori toru tori mo	the birds that catch the birds—they too
neburi kana	are slumbering.

Takakuwa Rankō (1726-1798)

• •

Soko noite	Get out of my road
take uesase yo	and allow me to plant these
hikigaeru	bamboos, Mr. Toad.

Miura Chora (1729-1780)

• •

Mezurashi to	"Marvelous!" I say,
miru mono goto ni	and with each single thing I see
haru ya yuku	springtime fades away.

Takai Kitō (1741-1789)

• •

Yo ga yokuba	If the times were good,
mo hitotsu tomare	I'd say, "Sit down!—one more of you!"
meshi no hae	flies around my food.

• •

Isshaku no	A one-foot waterfall
taki mo oto shite	it too makes noises, and at night
yūsuzumi	the coolness of it all!

• •

Uguisu ya *doroashi nuguu* *ume no hana*	A bush warbler comes— and starts to wipe his muddy feet among the blossoming plums.

• •

Tōyama no *medama ni utsuru* *tombo kana*	In its eye the far-off hills are mirrored— dragonfly!
Asagao no *hana de fuitaru* *iori kana*	A morning-glory vine in its full bloom, has thatched this hut of mine.
Utsukushi ya *shōji no ana no* *ama-no-gawa*	A lovely thing to see: through the paper window's holes the Galaxy.
Ware to kite *asobe yo oya no* *nai suzume*	Come to me—with each other let's play—little sparrow without any mother.
Furusato ya *yoru mo sawaru mo* *ibara no hana*	The place where I was born: all I come to—all I touch— blossoms of the thorn!
Toshikasa wo *urayamaretaru* *samusa kana*	When one is old one is envied by people— oh, but it's cold!

Kobayashi Issa (1763-1828)

TRANSLATED BY HAROLD G. HENDERSON

WAKA OF THE TOKUGAWA PERIOD

Hiku koto ni	I played the koto—
Koe mo oshimanu	Unbegrudging of its voice
Hototogisu	A nightingale sang;
Kan ni taekane	I could not check my feelings,
Ware mo oto ni naku	I too cried with the music.

Toda Mosui (1629-1706)

. .

Ura ura to	From the deep heart's core
Nodokeki haru no	Of the spring serenity,
Kokoro yori	Splendid, resplendent,
Nioi idetaru	A perfume has arisen—
Yamazakura hana	The mountain cherry blossoms!

Kamo no Mabuchi (1697-1769)

. .

Hito mina wa	Everybody hates
Aki wo oshimeri	To see the autumn go by.
Sono kokoro	This feeling would seem
Sora ni kayoite	To be shared by the heavens—
Shigurekemu kamo	See how it is drizzling now!

Kaku kite wa	I, as a stranger,
Mezurashimi kikedo	Listen in wonderment, but
Kono nami no	What of fishermen
Yo na yo na hibiku	By whose huts night after night
Ama no fuseya wa	Echoes the sound of the waves?

Tayasu Munetake (1715-1771)

. .

Hachi no ko ni	In my begging bowl
Sumire tampopo	Violets and dandelions
Kokimazete	Are mixed together:
Sanze no hotoke ni	These will be my offering
Tatematsuriten	To the Buddhas of Three Worlds.
Kaze wa kiyoshi	The wind is fresh,
Tsuki wa sayakeshi	The moon pellucidly bright.
Iza tomo ni	Come, then, together
Odoriakasan	We'll spend the night in dancing,
Oi no nagori ni	A final fling of old age!

Ryōkan (1757-1831)

TRANSLATED BY DONALD KEENE

Mountain Home

Wa ga yado wo	Oh to have a home
Koko ni mo ga na to	In such a quiet leafy spot,
Miyakobito	Yearns the city man;
Ii no mi iite	Yet he never builds a hut
Sumanu yamazato	In mountain country.

Book

Itsu yori ka	Open and forgotten
Hirakenagara no	Several hours by the window,
Mado no fumi	The book was fingered
Kaze bakari koso	Only by capricious winds.
Moteasobikere	

Plum wind

Ka bakari to	Fragrance alone, I thought,
Omoishi kaze ni	Was the wind's burden,
Kesa yori wa	But petals too
Hana mo majirite	Are circling the plum garden.
Okuru umezono	

Visitor on a late spring day

Kurehatsuru	It were better not to call
Haru no yūbe no	Than to leave me in the loneliness
Sabishiki ni	Of the late spring afternoon.
Kaeraba towanu	
Hito ya masaramu	

Ōkuma Kotomichi (1798-1868)

TRANSLATED BY YUKUO UYEHARA AND MARJORIE SINCLAIR

The silver mine

Akahada no	Stark naked, the men
Danshi mureite	Stand together in clusters;
Aragane no	Swinging great hammers
Marogari kudaku	They smash into fragments
Tsuchi uchifurite	The lumps of unwrought metal.

Solitary pleasures

Tanoshimi wa	It is a pleasure
Kami wo hirogete	When, spreading out some paper,
Toru fude no	I take brush in hand
Omoi no hoka ni	And write far more skilfully
Yoku kakeshi toki	Than I could have expected.

Tanoshimi wa	It is a pleasure
Momohi hineredo	When, after a hundred days
Naranu uta no	Of twisting my words
Futo omoshiroku	Without success, suddenly
Idekinuru toki	A poem turns out nicely.

Tanoshimi wa	It is a pleasure
Asa okiidete	When, rising in the morning
Kinō made	I go outside and
Nakarishi hana no	Find that a flower has bloomed
Sakeru miru toki	That was not there yesterday.

Tanoshimi wa	It is a pleasure
Mare ni uo nite	When, a most infrequent treat,
Kora mina ga	We've fish for dinner
Umashi umashi to	And my children cry with joy
Iite kuu toki	"Yum-yum!" and gobble it down.
Tanoshimi wa	It is a pleasure
Sozoro yomiyuku	When, in a book which by chance
Fumi no naka ni	I am perusing,
Ware to hitoshiki	I come on a character
Hito wo mishi toki	Who is exactly like me.
Tanoshimi wa	It is a pleasure
Yo ni tokigataku	When, without receiving help,
Suru fumi no	I can understand
Kokoro wo hitori	The meaning of a volume
Satorieshi toki	Reputed most difficult.
Tanoshimi wa	It is a pleasure
Ebisu yorokobu	When, in these days of delight
Yo no naka ni	In all things foreign,
Mikuni wasurenu	I come across a man who
Hito wo miru toki	Does not forget our Empire.

Tachibana Akemi (1812-1868)

TRANSLATED BY DONALD KEENE

Longing to attack the southern barbarians
[Directed against the Spanish and Portuguese soldiers and missionaries, who had arrived in Japan from the south.]

False religions delude the land with a ceaseless clamor.
I would strike the barbarian tribes, but the time comes not.
When will the great roc rise and southward soar?
Long have I waited the wind of his ten-thousand-mile wings.

Date Masamune (1567-1636)

The rainy season

How many days of spring rain since I have seen the sun?
Yet I delight in the new pools that shine before my porch.
Last year the burning drought continued through the fall.
Even in river towns I heard the water-seller's cry.

Kan Sazan (1748-1827)

Dutch ships (1818)

In Nagasaki Bay, where sky and sea meet to the west,
At heaven's edge a little dot appears.
The cannon of the lookout tower sounds once;
In twenty-five watch stations, bows are bared.
Through the streets on all sides the cry breaks forth:
"The redhaired Westerners are coming!"

Launches set out to meet their ship, we hear the drums echo;
In the distance signal flags are raised to stay alarm.
The ship enters the harbor, a ponderous turtle,
So huge that in the shallows it seems sure to ground.
Our little launches, like strung pearls,
Tow it forward amid a clamorous din.
The barbarian hull rises a hundred feet above the sea,
The sighing wind flapping its banners of felt.
Three sails fly amid a thousand lines,
Fixed to engines moving up and down like well-sweeps.
Blackskinned slaves,[1] nimbler than monkeys,
Scale the masts and haul on the lines.
The anchor drops with shouts from the crew;
Huge cannon bellow forth again and again their roar.
The barbarian heart is hard to fathom; the Throne ponders
And dares not relax its armed defense.
Alas, wretches, why come they to vex our anxious eyes,
Pursuing countless miles in their greed what gain?
Their ships pitiful leaves upon the monstrous waves,
Crawling like gigantic ants after rancid meat.
Do we not bear ox-knives to kill but a chicken,
Trade our most lovely jewels for thorns? [2]

Rai Sanyō (1780-1832)

Weeping for Tatsuzō: today spring ended
[*On the death of his small son.*]

Spring is gone, the boy is gone;
Two griefs this day.
Spring returns.
And this dead child?

[1] Javanese servants of the Dutch.

[2] I.e., are not all the alarms and defense measures of the government unnecessary, and are we not losing by trading with the foreigners?

Flowers of illusion one moment bewitch the eye—
How toys the crafty Creator with men!
Next year in the eastern fields when I search the paths of spring,
Who will carry the wine gourd and follow the old man?

Rai Sanyō

Hearing of the earthquake in Kyoto (1830)

By post news from the capital, terrible beyond recall:
"This month, the second day, earthquakes from dusk to dawn.
Seven days and nights the tremors, until the earth must sunder.
We beseech in tears the sky.
Of ten houses nine destroyed;
Families cower in the streets as roof tiles shower down. . . ."
Of my home no word.
Dumbly I scratch my head and gaze
East toward my home on the Kamo banks:
The youngest clinging to my frail wife,
They flee to the river sands,
Fearful for the abandoned house,
While stone embankments topple,
Laying the willow roots bare.
Through deep tides to distant flats
Which way escape?
The eldest boy wades the stream,
The youngest on his nurse's back.
From the nest upturned though the eggs be spared,
The mother sickens with care, bearing alone a family's burden
How can I face you again?
I speed this letter back,
And wait an answer that may never come.
Your death or life unknown,
In this chaos whom shall I entreat?
When dread fate crushes the multitudes,
How can I ask of him or her? . . .

I watch the clouds hurrying north.
Dragons of the sea-rain howl as,
Trembling in dark fear,
I beat out the bars of this long dirge.

Rai Sanyō

No title
[*An attack on the Shogunate*]

You, whose ancestors in the mighty days
Roared at the skies and swept across the earth,
Stand now helpless to drive off wrangling foreigners—
How empty your title, "Queller of Barbarians"!

Yanagawa Seigan (1789-1858)

A song of history: Peter the Great

He pushed back the eastern borders three thousand miles,
Learned the Dutch science and taught it to his people.
Idly we sit talking of our long dead heroes—
In a hundred years have we bred such a man?

Sakuma Shōzan (1811-1864)

On hearing that the port of Shimoda has been opened to the foreigners

For seven miles by the river hills the dogs and sheep forage.[3]
The hues of spring visit the wastes of quake-ridden earth.
Only the cherry blossoms take not on the rank barbarian stench,
But breathe to the morning sun the fragrance of a nation's soul.

Gesshō (1817-1858)

[3] To many Japanese of this period the meat-eating Westerners were no more than reeking animals. The author was a Buddhist priest.

In prison

I sought to drive back the clouds, with these hands sweep clear the
evil stars,
But the ground beneath me faltered, I plunged to Edo Prison.
Idiot frogs fret at the bottom of their well;
The brilliance of the great moon falters on the horizon.[4]
I await the death sentence; from home no news.
In my dreams, the ring of swords; I slash at sea monsters.
When the wind and rain of many years have cloaked my stone in
moss,
Who will remember this mad man of Japan?

Rai Mikisaburō (1825-1859)

TRANSLATED BY BURTON WATSON

THE BIOGRAPHY OF SNOWFLAKE

Rai Sanyō wrote this biography of Snowflake (Oyuki), *a character famed in Osaka song and story, at the request of a friend who had come into the possession of a collection of her poems. Snowflake died about 1803.*

Snowflake was a lady swashbuckler of Osaka. It was in Osaka that General Hideyoshi built his fortress, and it remains a city of spirited and prodigal people who love to affect a rough and ready manner. Many citizens of Osaka have made names for themselves as cavaliers, but Snowflake was the only woman among them. She was the daughter of the mistress of a wealthy merchant, but from an early age was brought up by the Miyoshi family, who were also rich tradesmen. The Miyoshi family adopted a son whom they wished to marry to Snowflake, but she despised the boy as a puny weakling, and would have none of it. At this time she took a vow never to marry. When her foster father died, she inherited the estate.

[4] The frogs refer to the shortsighted statesmen of the Shogunate; the moon to the powerless Emperor in Kyoto.

By nature Snowflake was of a high-spirited, gallant disposition. She devoted little attention to business affairs, but studied instead calligraphy and painting with the Master of the Willow Stream Garden, and took lessons in swordsmanship and judo. She was pale, large, and portly, with great strength in her limbs. Two women attendants named Tortoise (Okame) and Mountain Peak (Oiwa)—both of whom were very strong and brave—constantly followed Snowflake about. At this time she had just turned sixteen, and her two companions were likewise in the bloom of their beauty. Young idlers and ruffians meeting them on the street would often tease the girls and challenge them to a battle. At such times Snowflake would glance meaningfully at her attendants, and they would thereupon knock the boys to the ground, often so hard that they could not get up again.

The place called Snake Hill in the southern suburbs was at this time very wild and deserted, and even in the daytime no one dared walk there. Snowflake once took a short cut through the spot when two robbers came upon her and tried to seize her sash, but she knocked them flat. In no time the story got around, and everyone stayed out of her way.

Snowflake, not having a husband, was ambitious to become a lady-in-waiting and to be admitted to the inner palace. Her excellent calligraphy won her a post as clerk in the palace for five years, where she was engaged in recording past events of the court. When she gave up this post, she shaved her head and became a nun, living in the Moon River Temple next door to the Temple of the Heavenly Kings. Snowflake always wore white clerical robes, but continued as before to go wandering about with her female companions.

Once when the temple was having an unveiling of the inner shrine and a great crowd of men and women had come to worship, it suddenly began to rain. Snowflake immediately bought over a thousand umbrellas which she distributed, one to a person. On the occasion of another great ceremony at the temple, she bade the priest in charge of music to have the ceremony performed with the utmost splendor. When someone asked her the reason, she replied, "Today is the two hundredth anniversary of the death of my ancestor, Prime Minister

Hidetsugu!" She also presented secretly a sum of money to the Hōkō Temple, asking that it be used as a personal offering to the spirit of General Hideyoshi. She was always giving herself such absurd airs.

Her fortune eventually ran out, and she built a little house in the village of Namba where she lived out the rest of her days. She bought a coffin and hung it up by the gate, and spent all day drinking with her friends nearby. One day she went out in the hot sun and dropped dead in the street. The villagers, recognizing her, carried her body into the shop where she had always bought her wine, and rushed off to inform her household. Her corpse was prepared and then laid away in the coffin. They buried her at the Temple of the Secret Spring in Namba. She was seventy-five when she died. A marker carved like snowflakes was set up for her, along with stones in the shape of a tortoise and a mountain peak, which are still there. For this reason people say that her two companions were buried with her.

The story of Snowflake cannot, of course, be taken as a model of conduct. But in her time there were women who conducted themselves like men, while today we see only men who behave as women. I have hoped herein to divine the rise and fall of Fortune and to elicit, perhaps, a sigh.

TRANSLATED BY BURTON WATSON

SHORT BIBLIOGRAPHY

GENERAL WORKS

Aston, W. G. *A History of Japanese Literature*. London, 1899.
Benl, Oscar. *Die Entwicklung der japanischen Poetik*. Hamburg, 1951
Bonneau, Georges. *Anthologie de la poésie japonaise*. Paris, 1935.
———. *L'expression poétique dans le folk-lore japonais*. Paris, 1933.
Bowers, Faubion. *Japanese theatre*. New York, 1952.
Florenz, Karl. *Geschichte der japanischen Litteratur*. Leipzig, 1905.
Keene, Donald. *Japanese Literature*. New York, 1955.
Miyamori, Asatarō. *Masterpieces of Japanese Poetry*. Tokyo, 1936.
Piper, Maria. *Die japanische Theater*. Frankfurt a. Main, 1937.
Revon, Michel. *Anthologie de la littérature japonaise*. Paris, 1910.
Sansom, George. *Japan; a short cultural history*. London, 1931.
Waley, Arthur. *Japanese poetry*. Oxford, 1919.

ANCIENT AND HEIAN PERIODS

Beaujard, André (tr.). *Les notes de chevet de Séi Shōnagon*. Paris, 1934.
Bonneau, Georges. *Le monument poétique de Heian*. Paris, 1933–4.
Man'yōshū. Published for Nippon gakujutsu shinkōkai. Tokyo, 1940.
Omori, Annie S. and Doi, Kochi (trs.). *Diaries of Court Ladies of Old Japan*. Tokyo, 1935.
Porter, William N. (tr.). *The Tosa Diary*. London, 1912.
Reischauer, Edwin O. and Yamagiwa, Joseph K. (trs.). *Translations from Early Japanese Literature*. Cambridge (Mass.), 1951.
Seidensticker, E. G. (tr.). "Kagerō Nikki," *Transactions, Asiatic Society of Japan*, Third Series, 4, 1955.
Waley, Arthur (tr.). *The lady who loved insects*. London, 1929.
———. *The pillow-book of Sei Shōnagon. London*, 1928.
———. *The tale of Genji*. 1 vol. London, 1935.
———. "Some Poems from the Man'yōshū and Ryōjin-hishō," *Journal of the Royal Asiatic Society*, 1921.
Whitehouse, Wilfrid (tr.). *Ochikubo Monogatari*. Kobe, 1934.

KAMAKURA AND MUROMACHI PERIODS

Peri, Noël. *Le nô.* Tokyo, 1944.

Pound, Ezra. *The Translations of Ezra Pound.* New York, 1953.

Sadler, A. L. (tr.). "Heike Monogatari," *Transactions, Asiatic Society of Japan,* 46, 2 (1918) and 49, 1 (1921).

Sakanishi, Shio (tr.). *Kyôgen, comic interludes of Japan.* Boston, 1938.

Sansom, George (tr.). "The Tzuredzure gusa of Yoshida no Kaneyoshi," *Transactions, Asiatic Society of Japan,* 39 (1911).

Shidehara, Michitarō and Whitehouse, Wilfrid (trs.). "Seami's Sixteen Treatises," *Monumenta Nipponica,* 4, 2 (1941) and 5, 2 (1942).

Suzuki, Beatrice Lane (tr.). *Nōgaku, Japanese nō plays.* New York, 1932.

Waley, Arthur (tr.). *The Nō Plays of Japan.* London, 1921.

TOKUGAWA PERIOD

Blyth, R. H. *Haiku.* 4 vols. Tokyo, 1949–52.

———. *Senryū, Japanese satirical verses.* Tokyo, 1950.

Bonneau, Georges. *Le Haiku.* Paris, 1935.

Henderson, Harold Gould. *The Bamboo Broom.* Boston, 1934.

Iacovleff, Alexander and Elisséeff, Serge. *Le théâtre japonais.* Paris, 1933.

Keene, Donald (tr.). *The Battles of Coxinga.* London, 1951.

Miyamori, Asatarō (tr.). *An anthology of haiku.* Tokyo, 1932.

———. *Masterpieces of Chikamatsu.* Kobe, 1926.

Satchell, Thomas (tr.). *Hizakurige.* Kobe, 1929.

Shively, Donald H. (tr.). *The love suicide at Amijima.* Cambridge (Mass.), 1953.

Uyehara, Yukuo and Sinclair, Marjorie (trs.). *The Poems of Kotomichi Ōkuma.* Honolulu, 1955.

Whitehouse, Wilfrid (tr.) "Ugetsu Monogatari" (by Ueda Akinari), *Monumenta Nipponica,* 1, 2 (1938) and 4, 1 (1941).

NOTE: A much more extensive bibliography may be found in Borton, Hugh, et al., *A Selected List of Books and Articles on Japan in English, French and German,* Revised Edition, Cambridge (Mass.)., 1954.